COMPETITOR INTELLIGENCE

A WORD OF CAUTION

This book describes and encourages honest, ethical means of gathering competitor information. Should any of the techniques or sources in this book be used illegally, the author and publisher do not claim responsibility for such misuse. The author and publisher recommend that any reader in doubt about the use of a source or technique in a particular industry consult with an attorney before beginning research.

COMPETITOR INTELLIGENCE

How to Get It; How to Use It

LEONARD M. FULD

President and Founder, Information Data Search, Inc.

JOHN WILEY & SONS

New York   Chichester   Brisbane   Toronto   Singapore

85465

Library of Congress Cataloging in Publication Data:

Fuld, Leonard M.
  Competitor intelligence.

  Includes index.
  1. Business intelligence.   I. Title.

HD38.7.F85   1985   658.4'7   84-19539
ISBN 0-471-80967-5

Printed in the United States of America

10 9 8 7 6 5 4 3 2 1

To Suzi and Elan,
with all my love and intelligence.

ACKNOWLEDGMENTS

This book is based on years of research assignments carried out for scores of clients in industries as wide and diverse as there are pages in the telephone book. But this book, like most others, has greatly benefited from the generous time and patience of those people that surround the author.

First, I would like to thank Jennifer Swanson for helping me compile a number of the lists that fill the book. I would also like to thank the rest of my staff for uncovering new ideas and sources in intelligence-gathering. Many of these sources and techniques have never been written about before and could only have been discovered by these front-line researchers.

Then there are those executives who have attended the Competitor Intelligence Seminars sponsored by my firm, Information Data Search. They clued me in on special sources of information that they had used successfully, and gave me leads on other potential sources. Their own intelligence war stories inspired me, and taught me that there is always another creative way to tackle a research problem. I owe them many thanks for their advice and constructive criticism.

I would also like to thank those who have spent the time to review preliminary drafts of this book and offered their thoughts and suggestions.

John Mahaney, my editor, deserves my warm thoughts and thanks for his quick wits, good humor, and sound editorial advice.

Then there are those people who never receive acknowledgments because for one reason or another they did not contribute directly to a particular chapter or paragraph. These are my parents and my in-laws, who managed to have a great deal of patience, allowing me to ramble, taking their time and leaning on their shoulders. To them, thank you. They can tell you that entrepreneurs are not always easy to have as relatives.

Finally, I would like to thank my wife, Suzi, for her devotion, good spirits and common sense. During the long and lonely hours of writing, she tempered my worrying and heard my ideas on intelligence-gathering when she would have much preferred my opinion on more important household or family matters. To my wife, my love and devotion and many thanks.

L.M.F.

WAR STORIES

CONTENTS

PART 2. THE BASIC SOURCES OF INTELLIGENCE

PART 3.   CREATIVE SOURCES AND TECHNIQUES

PART 4. ADDRESSES AND PHONE NUMBERS OF PUBLISHERS AND SOURCES

COMPETITOR INTELLIGENCE

INTRODUCTION

How to Use This Book and Where It Will Help You Most

There are many books that will teach a reader how to conduct a survey, sample a population, do basic library research, or write a research paper. Yet there are few sources a researcher can turn to when having to scrutinize a competitor's income statement, distribution channels, or marketing strategy. Somehow these other sources fail to impart the nitty-gritty information that will allow you to track your competition. The present book attempts to accomplish this with a down-to-earth series of lists and lessons.

The entire field of competitive strategy—a popular subject in today's business press—assumes you already have all the facts about your competitor in hand. Unfortunately, this assumption is way off the mark. Sometimes the most difficult part of competitor analysis is collecting accurate and reliable intelligence in the first place.

Too often, obtaining even the most basic pieces of information, such as plant location or number of employees, becomes an enormous obstacle, which in turn can hold up an entire assignment. After all, how can you proceed to collect information on a plant or a service office if you can't find it?

This book deals with the mundane: with the specific tools and techniques you can use to get that microscopic, "insider" corporate information.

It may be a wonderful experience to be able to project a competitor's growth rate, using your favorite spreadsheet package. But where are you going to find the facts you need to construct that forecast?

This text answers the most fundamental questions about intelligence-gathering:

1. How do you do it? What is the technique?
2. Where do you find the intelligence? What and where are the sources?

1

This book will help you determine your competitor's:

Income statement and balance sheet.
Marketing strategy.
Service plans.
Salesforce deployment.
Production.
Sources of supply.
Product features.
Impending product announcements.
Plant capacity.
Number of employees.

A STEP-BY-STEP GUIDE TO INTELLIGENCE-GATHERING

This book offers you a "soup-to-nuts" approach to intelligence-gathering. Simply listing sources is not enough; that would provide no guidance as to which source is best or which to use first. Instead, this book gives you the basic understanding of how and why intelligence-gathering works, as well as an explanation of the techniques that will allow you to put theory into practice. Then the many sources of intelligence information are listed, first the basic and then the more creative sources. By the time you reach the creative sources, you should be able to understand and, more important, use intelligence-gathering techniques and sources to your competitive advantage.

Every profession has a certain amount of lore. I find intelligence-gathering exciting and full of adventure. To help you feel and understand the full import of certain sources and techniques, I have introduced what I call "War Stories" into the text. These stories recount actual research assignments tackled and solved, illustrating certain techniques and sources.

Part 1 of this book ("Competitor Intelligence: What It Is, Where to Find It, How to Use the Sources") explains to the researcher who is making the first stabs at corporate intelligence research why it is possible to collect a great amount of detail on competitors. It presents the basic interview and questionnaire-design techniques. Also, this section presents the first-time researcher with valuable checklists, as well as tips for obtaining the most intelligence out of distributors, suppliers, retailers, consultants, and editors.

In Part 2 ("The Basic Sources of Intelligence") I take what are normally considered traditional sources and bring them into the realm of company intelligence-gathering. I cite scores of industries in this section, demonstrating, for example, how industry directories are an excellent investigative tool. Among other things Part 2 lists dozens of data bases that contain vital corporate information, and offers tips on how the corporate researcher can best employ these data bases.

Part 3 ("Creative Sources and Techniques") instructs the reader how to locate creative intelligence sources that will reveal vital facts. This section brings together the experience of researchers in many industries and shows how corrugated boxes, box cars, technical manuals, help-wanted ads, and even the Yellow Pages can reveal a great deal about your competitor. Most important, it demonstrates how to locate new intelligence sources to meet different needs. Since no book can provide all of the possible sources and techniques to meet every contingency, Part 3 is designed to give the researcher intelligence independence.

INDUSTRIES COVERED

This book is chock full of sources that apply to scores of industries. Specialized techniques are offered for gathering intelligence in telecommunications, electronics, commercial banking, insurance, software, pharmaceuticals, and chemical processing.

In addition, this book reveals the company-specific information available in thousands of other books, magazines, and reference works for the following industries:

Advertising
Aerospace
Agriculture
Air travel
Apparel
Appliances
Automobiles
Banking
Beverages
Broadcasting
Building materials

Chemicals
Drugs and cosmetics
Electrical equipment and power
Electronics
Engineering
Food and grocery
Food processing
Gas (natural)
Health and medical
Hotel and lodging
Household and institutional furniture
Incentives and premium products
Industrial arts
Insurance
Investment banking
Iron and steel
Laboratory diagnostic supplies
Lumber
Machinery
Meat processing
Medical and dental supplies
Nonferrous metals
Packaging and containers
Paper
Petroleum
Photography
Plastics
Publishing
Railroads
Retailing
Rubber
Savings and loan banking
Soft drinks
Steel
Telephones

Textiles
Tobacco
Transportation
Wood and lumber

FOREIGN INTELLIGENCE SOURCES

Corporate intelligence is not limited to the United States. For that reason, I have included hundreds of foreign sources along with the best techniques to gain access to them. Obscure foreign business magazines are cited, as well as libraries in the United States that subscribe to them. You will find special approaches to foreign sources discussed in detail.

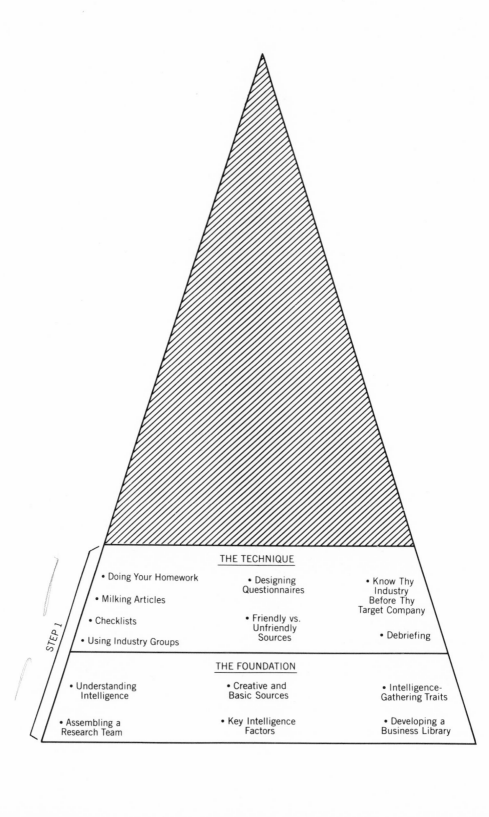

STEP 1

THE TECHNIQUE

• Doing Your Homework

• Milking Articles

• Checklists

• Using Industry Groups

• Designing Questionnaires

• Friendly vs. Unfriendly Sources

• Know Thy Industry Before Thy Target Company

• Debriefing

THE FOUNDATION

• Understanding Intelligence

• Assembling a Research Team

• Creative and Basic Sources

• Key Intelligence Factors

• Intelligence-Gathering Traits

• Developing a Business Library

PART 1

COMPETITOR INTELLIGENCE

What It Is,
Where to Find It,
How to Use the Sources

When they first receive an assignment, most researchers are anxious to roll up their sleeves, dig into the sources, and get to work. Unfortunately, by charging into the research thicket without much forethought or planning, most of these Light Brigade intelligence-gatherers encounter a lot of frustration and no intelligence.

This section is designed to alert the researcher to the special ways corporate intelligence behaves and how best to find it. Insights are offered and tips given on how to approach the experts—the distributors, press, suppliers, and so on. The purpose of the questionnaire in the intelligence-gathering process is explained. Above all, this section gives the researcher an overview of exactly what competitor intelligence is and how to use it to advantage.

CHAPTER 1

LAYING THE FOUNDATION

WHAT IS COMPETITOR INTELLIGENCE?

For the purposes of this book, "competitor intellience" is defined as "highly specific and timely information about a corporation."

Information that is out-of-date or too general is not competitor intelligence. Instead, it represents history and background data. Rapidly changing and detailed information on your competitor is a highly perishable commodity. Much like a container of milk, it has a short shelf-life. Once the information is allowed to sit around and not be used, its value declines rapidly.

CORPORATE INTELLIGENCE-GATHERING: A BRIEF OVERVIEW

The word "intelligence" conjures up images of sleuths with magnifying glasses in hand, or a meeting of two furtive individuals in the back corner of a bar to exchange thousands of dollars for some valuable inside information.

As you will see in the following pages, information on your competitors can be collected efficiently and accurately through totally honest and ethical methods. Admiral Ellis Zacharias, Deputy Chief of Naval Intelligence during World War II, agreed. In his book, *Secret Missions: The Story of an Intelligence Officer* (Putnam, 1946, pp. 117–18), he said that 95 percent of all necessary intelligence, corporate or military, can be found in the public arena.

In the world of commerce, this intelligence-gathering goes on every day, without necessarily being called by its rightful name. An article that appeared in *Barron's* (March 19, 1979, p. 4) clearly pointed out that gathering corporate intelligence is everyone's job and that virtually everyone collects it—knowingly and unknowingly:

Agents for Hire

Directly or indirectly, corporations deploy hundreds (thousands, by some estimates) of agents with widely divergent backgrounds and contrasting methods of operation. Here will be a Ph.D. preparing a scholarly analysis of long-range policy trends, based on private talks with government specialists. There will be a young free-lance lawyer with a phone-answering machine for an office, hustling to make it, not so much as a lawyer but as a Washington operator. Here a former newspaper reporter worming advance information or an unreleased document out of a carefully cultivated source—but for a private client now, not the reading public. And, of course, the high-prestige types—large law firms, well-established information-gathering companies and the official Washington representatives (often bearing a vice president's title) of the nation's major corporations.

In effect, the sources you need to uncover competitor information may already be there, ready for the picking . . . if you know where to look. That is where understanding the intelligence jigsaw puzzle will make a big difference.

INTELLIGENCE-GATHERING: THE JIGSAW PUZZLE

Corporate intelligence-gathering has its roots in a number of very different, yet complementary disciplines. These include sales prospecting, library science, statistics, accounting, detective sleuthing, military intelligence, and jigsaw puzzles. The application of many of these disciplines to corporate intelligence-gathering is easily understood. But a few may seem out of place.

Sales prospecting includes tracking down your competitor's customers. Detective sleuthing describes the common-sense approach to gathering company information. Never overlook the obvious; by counting the parking spaces or spotting a building's structure you can learn a great deal about your competitor's size and operations.

Military intelligence implies a down-to-earth dogged pursuit of your competitor's activities. It does not imply any illegal or covert activities on your part.

The strangest of the disciplines mentioned, jigsaw puzzles, simply implies an ability to take what on the surface appear to be unrelated pieces of information and fit them together to form a complete picture. For instance, the discipline of the jigsaw puzzle might enable you to fit together the following:

1. You may come across a competitor's help-wanted ad that says it is hiring a host of programmers to produce a new software product.
2. In addition, you discover through your sales force that this same competitor is opening a sales office in a different region.
3. You have also heard through the grapevine that certain prospective clients whom you've been wooing for months have suddenly been approached by this competitor for possible test marketing of a new product.
4. A credit report states that this same competitor has just filed four new UCC filings for major pieces of equipment.

The above might be just a few random pieces of the jigsaw puzzle that you have come across in your daily business routine. This book suggests you take these seemingly random pieces of information and assemble a corporate intelligence picture of the firm. What does the information in the example suggest?

1. The competitor is planning to hire or has already hired a considerable number of new programmers for a soon-to-be released product.
2. The product may be further along than the help-wanted ad suggests, since the company is already opening new sales offices. You should track where these new offices are located, since they may form a pattern that will tell you which states or regions the competitor is concentrating sales in.
3. The clients the competitor approached may become valuable sources of information on the new product.
4. The UCC filings usually make clear what the equipment was that the competitor purchased. You should find out what the equipment is being used for; it very likely could be for the marketing or production of the new product.

This is the jigsaw puzzle discipline. If you can master the knack for spotting bits and pieces of the puzzle, then you are well on your way to assembling a much more complete picture of your competitors and their activities.

HOW INTELLIGENCE TRAVELS IN THE REAL WORLD

Once you accept the fact that business information is transmitted whenever there is a buyer and a seller, you begin to see how easily even the most guarded information becomes public. Let's look at the example below.

Action	Actors	Public source	Intelligence revealed
Purchase of property for building a new plant	Company management	Filing with town assessor	Details on capacity
	Seller	Bank filing (UCC)	Expansion plans
	Lawyers		
	Industrial realtors		
	Notary public		

Here we have a company buying a piece of property for a new plant. Look at how the intelligence flows. Not only are there a seller and a buyer (company management), but there are also lawyers, realtors, and a notary public involved in the sale. Next, see what happens to this information. The information does not remain bottled up. It moves on. Aside from all the parties involved in talking about it, there are public filings that announce the sale—the assessor's filing and the UCC.

Even the casual observer will be quick to spot all kinds of information that has leaked out about the purchase. Such information may concern the company's capacity or its overall expansion plans.

Let's examine another business event. In this case, a government agency was going to step in to regulate the chemical processes taking place in a manufacturing plant.

Action	Actors	Public source	Intelligence revealed
Environmental regulation	Company	State notification	Plant process
	Community action groups	Federal environmental impact statement	Plant operations
	Local newspaper	News reports	Capacity
	State environmental agency	Community gossip	Product type
	Federal Environmental Protection Agency	Reporters	
	Realtors		
	Neighboring plants		

The above example demonstrates that even one event causes a wave of information to cascade down to the surrounding community and into the public domain.

The two examples given were in the manufacturing or production area. Now let's explore the banking industry to see if company intelligence leaks out in the same manner. The next example traces a bank's newly announced cash-management service.

Action	Actors	Public source	Intelligence revealed
Announcement of new cash-management product	Bank	Trade news	Features
	Corporate end-users	Conferences	Pricing
	Financial reporters	Written proposals	

The world of banking is actually a very small one. The announcement of a new financial product is watched closely by the competitors and the activity is reported in the trade press. Competitors send out proposals, which in turn reveal much about the bank's marketing strategy and target market. Since these proposals in many cases are custom-designed, a competitor with a keen sense of organization can learn a good deal about that bank's strategy.

The idea that information leaks out is not a new one. Sometimes, though, it is a difficult one for the beginning researcher to grasp, especially when the closer that researcher gets to the work, the more difficult it is to see alternate sources—or any sources at all.

The lesson to learn from the examples above, and one to keep in mind throughout the book, is this:

> Each business transaction reveals data. By understanding the transaction, you can locate the intelligence source.

ARE THERE TRULY ANY BUSINESS SECRETS?

The answer is yes. Within the bounds of ethical and legal research techniques and methods, there are definite secrets. The Coca-Cola formula or the source codes for a computer program are trade secrets, and the only way to obtain them is through theft or subterfuge.

But take heart. For most (95% or more) of your intelligence needs, all of the information you will need to make a crucial business decision is available and readily accessible . . . provided you know where to look. And that is what this book aims to do: to show you where to look and save you time in the process.

HOW INTELLIGENCE BEHAVES

Another, more appropriate name for this section might be "How Intelligence Misbehaves." Company information has a strange way of secreting itself in dark corners and popping up at odd and potentially embarrassing moments. It is the job of the researcher to understand the intelligence flow and catch the information before it strays out of reach.

For instance, if you suspect even for a moment that someone within your company is leaking vital data to a competitor, you are probably right. Often, this employee may be totally unaware of his or her infraction. How does this leakage occur, and how can you, the researcher, capitalize on it?

Have you ever attended night school? If you have, you may find this scenario familiar. The teacher has asked the class to hand in term papers, let's say for a marketing exercise. Frequently the papers students submit are nothing more than thinly disguised versions of their own company's marketing strategy or corporate plan. Employees may mean no harm to their companies—after all, how can a little, insignificant term paper upset anybody?

This question was thrown out to marketing executives attending Information Data Search intelligence seminars, and they confirmed the above with other stories, nodding of heads, and a great many familiar chuckles. At least half of each seminar group acknowledged that they had experienced just such term paper leakage.

On the other hand, companies themselves are usually guilty of the same violations. In an informal survey, Information Data Search polled a number of major pharmaceutical houses and high technology companies—mostly Fortune 500s—asking them if they knew where and when their employees had published papers or given talks. Nine out of ten of the companies interviewed said they had no idea. When asked where the papers were appearing, we received answers such as "all over the ballpark."

HOW DOES INTELLIGENCE FLOW?

Once the information about a particular company is released, it takes an erratic path until it reaches the public forum—if it ever reaches the public at all. Here is the usual sequence of events:

1. Rumor stirs of an impending announcement from within the company.
2. The event becomes known somewhat before the fact to knowledgeable sources—for example, to brokers, suppliers, and dealers.
3. The event occurs.
4. The event reaches the industry through trade shows, the trade press, and salespeople.
5. The general press picks up the news.
6. Information may be entered into a data bank.
7. Finally, the articles are printed on microfilm and are cataloged in indexes to be filed away on a library shelf.

FIVE KEY INTELLIGENCE FACTORS

Often the ease or difficulty one has in locating information on a competitor will depend on environmental factors or the way the industry operates. There are five key factors—almost barometers—that can tell you your ability to gain "intelligence access" to a company. As strange as it may sound, the way an industry works very much determines how accessible company information is to the researcher. The five key factors are:

1. *Regionality.* The more local or regional a company's sales and operating territory is, the easier one can find data about that company. What does this imply?

In industries where companies sell and operate nationally, where sources of supply, distribution, and sales are country-wide, one will find it extremely difficult to locate knowledgeable sources—sources who know much about one particular plant.

On the other hand, where a company or plant operates almost totally on a local level, one can expect to find out a good deal about that plant or service division. For example, one can go to the town newspaper, the county employment office, or a local trucking or shipping company for intelligence. The general rule that the regionality factor teaches is the more local you go, the more likely you are to tap into knowledgeable sources of valuable intelligence.

2. *Dynamism.* Here is an informative but somewhat perplexing factor. This factor states that the more dynamic and actively growing an industry, the easier it is to get the intelligence you are looking for. Yet you will also find that along with the information you receive, you also encounter accuracy problems.

Take the personal computer industry as an example. There's an awful lot of gossip and news about all the latest personal computers. The question, though, is whether the information you have received is accurate. Often in a dynamic industry it is not. In personal computers, one may get five estimates of market share for a company, and all five can be dramatically different.

3. *Regulation.* The more regulated the industry, the higher the intelligence access for any one company. Translated into more basic terms: The more companies have to account for their actions to a governmental authority, the more information they will disclose about their activities. Banks and airlines are examples of regulated industries.

4. *Concentration.* In industries where a few companies control a large market share, these companies will also know a lot about competitors, and

vice versa. The more concentrated the industry, the greater the intelligence access to an individual corporation.

5. *Integration.* In industries where the companies operating within them control all their sources of supply and distribution—in other words, where the companies are highly integrated—one has a poor chance of finding much out about a competitor. Why? Because one's competitor controls all the possible contacts and sources of information.

In reality, few companies are totally integrated. Most firms have to go outside for some supplies, or may have to contract for independent representatives to sell their wares. But in general, high integration means low access.

ETHICS AND LEGALITIES

Because the legal issues may vary from industry to industry with regard to intelligence-gathering, I will deal with the legal and ethical concepts in a general sense. I strongly encourage any reader (as mentioned at the beginning of the book) to consult with an attorney should you have even the slightest doubt about your methods.

Here are some of the legal and ethical dos and don'ts I observe when gathering competitor information.

Dos	Don'ts
Corroborate findings.	Do not deliberately mislead to get an answer.
Identify yourself and your company by name when interviewing over the telephone or in person.	
Cite all quoted sources in your report.	Do not overstate your report to stretch a point.

Antitrust: Another Issue

When obtaining competitive information, you should be aware of possible legal barriers. In certain instances, your exchanging of price or market share information with other competitors may result in a violation of the Sherman Act, more commonly known as the Sherman Antitrust Act.

The Sherman Act, an antitrust bill sponsored by Senator John Sherman in 1890, and subsequent court tests of the Act, have defined what is meant by creating a trust or destroying competition.

In today's corporate world the Sherman Act attempts to prevent price fixing among the market's major competitors, while at the same time trying to avoid restraint of trade.

Here is where you, the researcher, must be careful. If you are operating in a market with few competitors and if you talk prices with those competitors, you could be accused of swapping price information. In turn, the courts could cite you for price-fixing.

Again, this brief section should serve only to warn you of potential legal pitfalls that you may encounter. To be safe, before beginning any questionable research, contact your attorney.

Why Honest and Ethical Intelligence-Gathering Works

If you need to resort to bribery, electronic bugging, or subterfuge to find competitor information, then you don't need this book. Another title for this text might be *How to Find out About Your Competitors and Sleep Well, Too.*

In nine out of ten cases, you can find the vital details about your competitor if you know where to look. All it takes is an understanding of the most productive sources and the ability to construct an effective research strategy. The following chapters are designed to do just that: give you an understanding, and impart to you years of intelligence-gathering experience to save you weeks of wasted research.

But the question remains: Why does honest and ethical intelligence-gathering work?

It works because of intelligence-gathering's most fundamental rule:

Whenever money is exchanged, so is information.

In other words, when someone buys or sells a piece of merchandise, or when a company buys property to build a new plant, information is exchanged along with the money. No one buys or sells anything in a vacuum, without conversation or documents stating the reason and scope of the sale.

Look at yourself and your daily business transactions. What happens when you go out to buy a new car? Do you simply walk into the dealership and plunk down the sticker price for the car? No, you will probably ask dozens of questions about the automobile and bicker with the salesperson until you both come to an agreed-upon price. If this one dealership does not satisfy you, you will move on to another. During this entire process, you are learning a good deal about the car, the dealerships, and other models that vie for your consumer dollar.

By definition, every time someone buys or sells an item, information is also passed along about his or her operation. That is why no corporation, no matter how small or how large, can truly hide its activities from businesses around it. And that is why, with the sources and techniques suggested in this book, you should be well on your way toward answering many of your competitive questions.

CREATIVE VERSUS BASIC INTELLIGENCE SOURCES

What Is an Intelligence Source?

An intelligence source is anything that can supply timely and highly specific information on a company. This definition may seem meaningless and general, sort of a corporate cop-out. But in truth it defines a wide variety of traditional and creative sources, both of which are very often needed to locate the necessary intelligence on your target company.

If you were to examine all the possible sources you may need to find the data on a corporation, you would look at a universe of basic and creative sources. Each half of that universe would contain both primary and secondary sources (see Figure 1.1).

Before I go any further, let me explain what I mean by a basic source and a creative source. As the name implies, a basic source is the source you would ordinarily think of when looking for information on a corporation. When hunting for a financial statement, you may search for an annual report or a state filing. If you want background on a company's management, you can look for relevant articles in a library index, and then actually copy the articles from microfilm.

Now, what if the search were not that simple? Let's say there is no annual report or state filing available. To compound the problem, the company was just started two years ago and there has been very little printed about it. Going to a library index, in this case, will not work. What do you do then? This is when you turn to a creative source.

You may not have an entire income statement, but you can locate the elements to create an estimated income statement. Town records or a quick

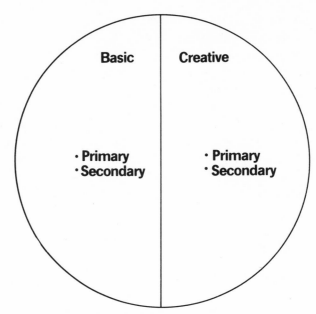

Figure 1.1.   Intelligence sources.

count of the number of parking spaces in the plant can give you the number of employees. Local interviewing with state and town experts will give labor rates. The area commercial realtor may tell you the value of the property and whether or not the company is leasing or is the owner. A check with a box supplier can tell you the plant's production or sales output. The city chamber of commerce or a university's alumni records may have details on some of the company's managers.

Using these creative or unusual sources you will see an income statement taking shape.

A primary source is the original source of the information. The secondary source is a source that has recorded or interpreted the information found in the primary source. An annual report or a news article is a secondary source. An interview with an expert, or an aerial photograph, is a primary source of intelligence. Yet, as I mentioned before, both basic and creative sources come in primary and secondary forms.

You will need both basic and creative sources to solve most difficult intelligence cases (see "Doing Your Homework" in Chapter 2 for further details). The following example illustrates the distinction between creative and basic intelligence sources.

The intelligence question is:

I need to locate financial statements and marketing strategies on my competitor. The company is privately held and maintains a low profile. I believe, though, that I have seen some articles about it. Where do I look for details?

The question could be answered with these basic and creative sources:

	Basic Source	Creative Source
Primary	Retrieve a state filing	Check the Yellow Pages for marketing information available in the display ads
Secondary	Search for articles in a library magazine index	Call the local newspaper for unindexed articles about the company

Why Basic Sources Don't Always Work

Usually any question you may have about a competitor has two overriding requirements:

1. *Currency.* The information you collect must be up to date; otherwise, it is useless to you.
2. *Narrow focus.* Your questions are specific. You are looking for a highly detailed answer to a single part of a competitor's activities (for example, you need to know how one out of a competitor's 20 warehouses operates).

These two requirements will often disqualify any basic source. Why? State filings, for instance, are at least six months to one year behind their publication date. Magazine articles may be three to six months old before they hit the newsstands.

Also, publishers have to meet the needs of their readership. They cannot afford to concentrate on articles of limited interest. You, for example, may be the only reader who would be interested in a story on your competitor's warehousing operation.

So keep this in mind next time you are using a basic source to solve your intelligence problem. Remember, such sources can be useful, but they have well-defined limits.

What Is a Creative Source?

The word "creativity" immediately conjures up the artist's canvas or the composer's scoresheet. Here the artist takes a blank surface and brings out of that space a new image or theme. It is this same kind of creativity that allows the corporate researcher to locate a piece of information that at first glance did not seem to be there.

True, most of the time you will use the same sources—directories, articles, credit reports. And for most projects all of these more basic, common sources will suffice. But what happens when you enter a new industry or encounter a company whose inner workings you cannot even begin to imagine? What do you do then?

For instance, what do you do when someone asks you to find the original manufacturer of a mouthwash that has not been sold for ten years? What do you do when your supervisor asks you to find the number of retail outlets for a small regional retail chain, and you discover that none of the standard directories contains a listing? How do you find the number of employees in a particular plant, when Standard & Poor's directory only lists the parent company's figures? Where do you go to look for plant-by-plant hiring patterns? How do you go about locating details on a competitor's pension trust management program, its fee structure and services?

All of the above questions could be relatively easy to solve, provided you take off your research blinders and try alternate sources.

For example, a simple call to a merchandising manager of a large supermarket chain could answer the mouthwash question. Finding a knowledgeable and helpful manager might take as little as 15 minutes.

Finding the number of retail outlets could lead to a stroll through the local Yellow Pages, where all the stores are listed for the metropolitan area in question.

When needing to know the number of employees in a plant, why not go to a state filing or an aerial photograph or a town assessor's office?

Plant-by-plant hiring patterns may appear in help-wanted display ads in the local newspaper. Track those ads and you can discover much more than just hiring patterns.

Should you need to understand a competitor's pension fund program, take the back-door approach. Locate the clients and interview them. Client lists in this industry happen to be readily available, and those interviewed will likely be more than willing to talk.

These are a few of the creative sources and methods that a researcher must employ to tackle difficult projects. You will find that each assignment, no matter how simple or familiar, will have some new twist or esoteric question.

The key to creativity is persistence. Don't give up when an obstacle appears. Take a step back and examine it. Ask yourself:

Where might the information be recorded?

Who ordinarily tracks such information (the government, an association, a newsletter)?

What are alternate indicators and where can you find them?

Remember, take those blinders off! (For more information see Part 3 of this book.)

PUBLIC DOES NOT ALWAYS MEAN PUBLISHED

Many times in this book, I refer to publicly available information. To clarify a point, public data does not necessarily mean published data.

Books and articles, as we have already discussed, are only one source of intelligence about your competitors. There are other sources that are also publicly available, yet are not found in published form. They include telephone interviews, counting the number of parking spaces in a parking lot, and attending a trade show. All the intelligence you discover about your competitor through these nonpublished sources is still valid intelligence and is very much in the public arena.

We are all taught an underlying notion from grade school on up that what you see in print is not only the truth, but is the best way to find information.

In the task of gathering intelligence, though, just the opposite axiom is the case, because what you will find in print about your competitor may be old and inaccurate. For up-to-date information, for intelligence that gives a true reading of the market and its competitors, you need to go after the experts through interviews as well as by attending trade shows.

THE BUSINESS LIBRARY: YOUR FIRST INTELLIGENCE SOURCE

Know your library. Remember, never overlook the straightforward solution to an intelligence problem. The library is one of those solutions. While it may serve to answer only 10 percent or less of your truly difficult intelligence problems, it is also your insurance against missing a simple article or directory listing that will get you off to a fast start in your research. When doing your homework for an intelligence-gathering assignment, the library should be your first stop.

Since competitor intelligence, by definition, must be current, how can a library help? What are its resources?

It may offer a collection of specialty trade directories that you cannot find anywhere else. These names are leads—entries into an industry. Some of the types of directories and other sources of information you will find in a business library are listed below:

Industry dictionaries.   These will quickly bring you up to speed on the insider's lingo and terminology.

Trade magazines.   Obscure periodicals that no one else may stock can often be found in a specialty business library.

Case studies and theses.   Business schools generate reams of these industry cases and student theses each year. They contain a wealth of information—and perhaps some insight into your target company.

Statistical collections.   A good business library will house a combination of government statistical publications, such as those of the U.S. Department of Labor and Department of Commerce. Almost every sizable trade association produces an annual industry statistics volume. You will find many of these at your local business library.

Literature indexes.   For almost every body of industry literature there is a corresponding index that some enterprising publisher has seen fit to print. Examples include F&S, PAIS, Business Periodicals Index, and Engineering Index.

Computer search service.   There is hardly a business library today that does not have a computer search service available to its patrons. Although we will discuss data bases in another chapter, know now that a data base search—with all its problems—is still the quickest and most effective way to scan the literature.

Union catalog. Each library has a union catalog listing the library holdings by subject, title, and author. The more progressive libraries have placed their catalogs on microforms, or online.

Special bibliographies. Librarians have compiled special bibliographies as a beginning researcher's shopping list to the best sources to look for in a particular industry.

The reference librarian. Never forget the best resource any business library has. The reference librarian works with the library's collection every day and becomes familiar with materials you have no idea even exist. If you are stumped, or need to bounce some of your research thoughts off someone, try the reference desk librarian.

Corporate report collections. Some libraries may only stock the Fortune 500 annual reports; others may offer SEC filings for all publicly traded companies going back 20 years. In addition, a number of the better-endowed libraries subscribe to the often expensive Wall Street Investment services, which issue reports on publicly held companies.

Tips to Finding a Business Library

There are general business libraries and specialty business libraries. Some libraries serve a broad community, and others operate within the confines of a corporation.

There are literally thousands of these business libraries throughout the country, most of them small and many dedicated to a special industry segment. Yet, finding these libraries is relatively easy, provided you know where to look:

Business schools. Almost every business school will have some sort of library or literature collection. Just locate the major business schools in your area and find out what the admissions policy is. A number of university business libraries have begun to restrict outside public use of their collections. You may need a special pass or have to pay a sometimes-steep fee to use the library.

Corporate libraries. Companies large and small have established literature collections. And they can be found in all stages of organization—from those containing a card catalog to those that operate haphazardly out of someone's back office. Some corporate libraries, like GTE's, may have satellite libraries at various locations with the network linked through a computerized index.

WAR STORY 1

The Case of the Obscure Magazine

Information Data Search was once asked to determine the release date of a new high-technology consumer product. Let's call the product, for argument's sake, Tech-Widgit. Our client told us that Tech-Widgit was expected to be released some time in the spring of the coming year, and he had asked us to better identify the exact release date.

A search through the standard library indexes proved fruitless. After calling a few magazines in the field, we finally found one editor who had heard of a periodical that might be useful. This magazine was a rather expensive, glossy newsletter, whose subscribers were not likely to include a typical public or university library.

We made a few telephone calls to some of the city's major libraries without luck. No one had the publication. We then flipped open our Boston area Special Library Association membership directory and looked for a library that carried this type of magazine collection. By the second call, we located a corporate library that subscribed to the magazine. The librarian was happy to allow us to come down and review her recent issues. Not only did we find the article that gave a speculative release date for Tech-Widgit, but we also located other information we did not expect to find.

You can find the library you are looking for by just calling a company whose industry you are examining, or by contacting your local chapter of the Special Libraries Association.

Special Libraries Association (SLA).   This is networking at its very best. Most SLA chapters have published their own directories, with indexed listings of member libraries (many of them corporate and university). The New York chapter reflects the largest assembly of business libraries in the United States.

The national headquarters of SLA is in New York City. There are local SLA chapters throughout the country. To locate an SLA chapter, contact your local library (corporate or public), and the reference librarian there should be able to answer your questions.

Directories of business libraries.   There are a number of these. One of the more popular is the Directory of Special Libraries and Information Centers published by Gale Research in Detroit.

Public business libraries.   Fear not. Your local public library has not deserted you. In fact, a number of municipal libraries have excellent business collections. In Boston, there is the Boston Public Library's Kirstein Business Branch. In Brooklyn, there is the downtown branch of the Brooklyn Public Library, which is considered one of the best business libraries in the country.

Major Business Libraries: Use Them!

By definition, universities with prestigious business schools will also have excellent business libraries. These repositories contain unusual magazines and trade news that you would be hard pressed to find elsewhere.

In addition to the magazine collections, business libraries are also likely to house an extensive file of annual reports. Because many of these libraries were originally funded by wealthy families with interests in particular industries, certain libraries will specialize in collecting business information from industries represented by these families.

These libraries should be the starting point for any corporate research you may begin. If you are not located near one of the libraries, in many instances they will respond to a telephoned or a written request for information, often charging only for photocopying and postage costs.

THE RIGHT RESEARCH STUFF: THE FOUR INTELLIGENCE-GATHERING TRAITS

Expert corporate researchers are not made of sugar and spice, nor are they made of microchips. They are often hard-nosed perfectionists. They can smell out a source. Most of all, good researchers are not born, they are molded and shaped. A good researcher learns his or her sources and then pursues the corporate target.

If I were to name the four traits or aspects of a good intelligence-gatherer, they would be as follows:

1. *Insight.* Know your sources before beginning the assignment. Understand which sources might help or speed up the research process. Know where, for instance, you can go to find financials or lists of experts. This insight allows you to save time and begin probing into the target company almost immediately, without wasting time. Here is where this book will come in handy.

2. *Creativity.* When the basic sources fail, the trained researcher will uncover new sources to address the problem.

3. *Strategy.*   In order to save precious time—especially with an eleventh-hour deadline—the astute researcher will devise a plan of attack, a means to efficiently find the vital intelligence. Random research means wasted time, lost dollars, and failure to meet deadlines.

4. *Persistence.*   Where all else fails, keep trying. All too often someone will tell you that no one has that information; and just as often, you can bet that someone surely does. Countless projects were solved because the researcher tried just one more contact, made just one additional phone call.

ASSEMBLING YOUR RESEARCH TEAM OR CLUSTER

We have already discussed what characteristics make a good researcher. Taking that thought a step further, you also have to ask yourself, "What, or who, makes a good research team? What are the ingredients for team intelligence-gathering?"

There are no definitive answers to this question. When examining the issue a bit closer, however, you will see that the answers you want will often dictate the talent you need.

Let's look at a typical corporate intelligence case. Here someone in your organization has requested that you find everything you can on Company X. Someone has given you the mandate to dig up company financials, recent articles, managerial profiles, marketing strategies, and a basic overview of their plant operations.

What does this shopping list tell you? First, you need to conduct a computerized literature search, followed by a manual search in your library. To assemble managerial profiles—assuming the information is not found in the press—you will need extensive interviewing. The financial analysis will require someone with a business or accounting background. That same person can also take care of the marketing strategies and plant overview.

By going down your shopping list and looking at the requirements, you have pinpointed a classic research cluster. This cluster consists of these three people:

1. *Library data base researcher.*   This person will perform all data base searching and library research.

2. *Business interviewer.*   This person has the business savvy and interviewing talent needed to retrieve the nonpublished information.

3. *Analyst/coordinator.* Here you want someone who can offer the financial analysis as well as the ability to coordinate the research team you have assembled.

For small, fairly short projects, you will find that you often will not need all three persons. In many instances, one individual will fill all three slots. Conversely, where your assignment is large and you may be under a tight deadline, your research cluster may consist of many more than just three individuals.

HOW TO STOCK YOUR OWN INTELLIGENCE LIBRARY

Keep this goal in mind: An effective intelligence library should provide you with contacts, not necessarily with the information itself.

Because of the expense of maintaining a large corporate library, executives and librarians find it hard to select which publications to place on their shelves. This should not be your concern. As a collector of corporate intelligence, let the public and university libraries stock the magazines and newspapers. Besides, you can now electronically order the articles you absolutely need through any number of the data base suppliers and timesharing systems mentioned in the data base section.

You should only concern yourself with building a powerful intelligence library. This library, as mentioned, will lead you to valuable sources rather than be a repository of information itself.

In short, a corporate intelligence library should be lean and mean. The following sources are the ones that I would recommend you stock.

General

Data bases	See chapter 7.
Thomas Register	See chapter 4.
Yellow Pages	See chapter 12.
Standard & Poor's (or Dun & Bradstreet Million Dollar Directory)	See chapter 4.
Texts on financial and operating ratios	See chapter 11.
World Almanac	

General

| U.S. Industrial Out-
look Handbook | See chapter 2. |

Specific

Annual Reports or SEC 10-K statements for targeted industries and companies	See chapter 3.
Buyer's guides	See chapter 14.
Trade show directories	See chapter 14.
Industry directories	See chapter 5.
Key industry magazines and special issues	See chapter 6.
Target companies' product catalogs and buyer's guides	See chapter 14.

GETTING STARTED

The Basic Techniques for Collecting Competitor Intelligence

DOING YOUR HOMEWORK

This book advocates the use of creative sources, such as aerial photographs, the Yellow Pages, or corrugated boxes. But do not mistake its underlying rule: Always do your homework first.

That means, never overlook a simple article or an entry in a trade directory. Sometimes the most basic source will answer your questions. While you may use the corrugated box technique in one out of ten cases, you should search the literature in every case, not just in one out of ten.

Remember Murphy's law of intelligence-gathering: "The corporate information you have been seeking is probably located in the very source you decided to overlook . . . because that source was too obvious."

Of course, this is not usually the case. In reality, news articles and trade directories in most instances only serve as leads to guide you to your answer. They usually do not provide you with the actual answers.

One way to make sure you have done your homework is to use a checklist of intelligence sources you should use in any project.

Here is an example of a basic list of research tools you should have available or at least have access to.

Research Checklist

1. Company Financials	2. Market Share
Dun & Bradstreet report	Literature search
10-K	Simmons Market Research
Annual report	Bureau
State filing	A. C. Nielsen Company
Published article	Market studies
Moody's	EIS
Wall Street Transcript	F&S Predicasts

3. Company Background	4. Industry Background
F&S indexes	Published articles
Standard & Poor's	Trade magazines
Dun & Bradstreet report	U.S. Industrial Outlook
Newspaper index	Investment reports
Published articles	Value Line
Wall Street Transcript	Special annual issues of industry handbooks

5. Competitors	6. Industry Experts
Standard & Poor's	Articles
Thomas Register	Key magazines
Industry buyer's guides	Directory of Directories
Yellow Pages	Associations
City directories	Competitors
Key magazines	Stockbrokers
Associations	Consultants
	Government experts
	University professors

7. Management Personnel	8. Foreign Information
Who's Who (General Industry)	Consulates
Local newspapers	Embassies
PR departments	American–(foreign) Chamber of Commerce
College alumni associations	

7. Management Personnel	8. Foreign Information
Wall Street Journal New York Times Chamber of Commerce	International Trade Commission Special libraries International D&B

9. Advertising Information	10. Government Experts
Advertising Age ADTRACK Local newspapers LNA Advertising agencies	Washington researchers' guides FCC Department of Commerce, Bureau of Labor Statistics Environmental Protection Agency Federal Trade Commission

You can be certain that as your intelligence-gathering expertise improves and you gain more insight into your particular industry, you will develop your own checklist of sources. This list is simply a place to start. It combines the ba ic sources with a number of creative sources and techniques. The sources themselves are discussed in greater detail throughout the book.

Project Checklist

The first part of this book explains what to do with the sources you will find in the second half of the book. The first portion deals with technique.

The technique section takes the reader through the intelligence-gathering process step-by-step. Below is a quick reference list of project steps one should take when researching a company. These steps assume you know nothing about the industry or about the company before the assignment is given to you.

1. *Define the question.*   Make sure you know what you are specifically looking for. Is it an income statement, knowledge of the competitor's distribution channels, management profile?

2. *Learn the industry structure.*   Assuming you know nothing or very little of the target company's industry, learn the industry's structure before you plunge into your company-specific research.

3. *Know your sources (basic and creative).*   Before grabbing at the sources you always use (library indexes, Thomas Register), stop. Ask yourself what

other sources there might be that would be more efficient to use and possibly more productive.

4.   *Conduct a literature search.*   No literature search today would be complete without using a data base index. When used correctly, a data base sweep can search the literature at lightning speed, much faster than one could pore manually over the Readers' Guide to Periodical Literature or the Funk & Scott Index.

5.   *Retrieve the articles/explore the library.*   Your library can get you off to a running start with names of experts to call and references to your target company.

6.   *Milk those articles.*   Examine the articles you retrieved in your search for names of individuals who may know far more about your target company than the article in which they were mentioned had revealed.

7.   *Prepare strategy.*   Once you have located the potential sources and have developed a tentative experts list, you must begin pairing off the sources. You will begin to discriminate between the better and the best sources available, which will yield the most accurate intelligence in the most efficient fashion.

8.   *Begin interview process.*   Don't wait for all your library research to be completed. Begin the interviewing as soon as you can. Through the interview process you will begin to revise your intelligence-gathering strategy as the project proceeds.

9.   *Debriefing and recording of results.*   When the project is over, it's not officially over. In order to learn from past experience, you should debrief each other on lessons you have learned and new creative sources you may have stumbled upon. In addition, record your new expert names in an index for future reference.

RESEARCH CHECKLISTS FOR THE BEGINNER

Intelligence-gathering can be frustrating, especially for the beginner who does not know enough to distinguish among the many types of sources.

The following sets of lists should help that person select the people to call and the reference books to pull off the shelf. These lists are a purely subjective ranking of the secondary and primary sources I have found most useful when conducting a search. The category labelled "first choice" does not necessarily mean the best choice. It implies only that this list is more likely to offer the answers than are the second and third choices.

These lists will suggest both specific sources to use (e.g., Nielsen, Moody's Investors Manuals), as well as general categories, such as trade magazines and the U.S. Department of Commerce. Both basic and creative sources are mentioned.

Each of the lists is arranged by objective. There is a list for those looking for general market data on an industry, and there is a list for the researcher trying to assemble an income statement on a corporation. In addition, there are lists for those who need to gather background information on a company as well as on its management.

Not all sources will apply in every circumstance. There will also certainly be other sources you may use often that are not even hinted at in these pages. That is because it is virtually impossible to account for every intelligence-gathering situation or case.

Use these sources simply as a guide. They may save you a great deal of work and wasted time, and they may lead you to other sources that will deal directly with your specific case.

Research Priority List Number 1: Market Overviews

LIST OBJECTIVE.   To enable the researcher to locate general market data on the industry and the companies he or she is researching. These sources will yield information on market shares, industry size, and trends.

FIRST CHOICE

Trade magazine annual issues.   Almost every trade magazine published has at least one annual issue where it reviews its industry. These issues often discuss the major players in the industry, also offering statistics on sales volume and market data contained nowhere else. Examples of these magazines are *Iron Age, American Metal Market*, and *Advertising Age.*

U.S. Department of Commerce.   This branch of the government tracks industry shipments and trends. The two major works published annually by this group are the *U.S. Industrial Outlook Handbook* and the *Current Industrial Reports.*

Market studies.   This category applies to the thousands of privately published reports produced by stock analysts, publishing houses, and market research firms. These reports may be given away for the asking, or can cost thousands of dollars. The data in these reports may not contain much detail on the competition, but may prove valuable for overall market data.

Wall Street Transcript.   This is a useful source for both specific company information as well as for reviews of an entire industry. This newspaper's

Roundtable discussions offer excellent reviews of an industry's key issues and trends.

Commercial data bases.   Data bases, such as Predicasts' Promt file, collect market information from a wide variety of sources and display the information in either statistical or textual form.

Competitors, suppliers.   If you can catch someone who has been in the business for a number of years and is willing to talk, you can learn about some of the subtler aspects of the market. In addition, these participants will be able to give you a regional feel for the market.

SECOND CHOICE

Purchasing agents.   They know about what is selling and about the pricing of products. They are also hard to catch for an interview. Whatever your questions are, be specific and to the point. These folks have little time for chitchat and don't care much about the weather, unless it affects their product line's price.

Retailers.   Although retailers do not know much about the supply and manufacturing side of the business, they can tell you what sells and what doesn't, and what product lines they are phasing out.

SAMI/Nielsen.   These are two leading market survey firms. Each polls a population to determine what goods and services they are buying. Many of their studies concern consumer product purchases. Unless you are a subscriber, it may be difficult or expensive to buy one of their reports. There are scores of other—many highly specialized—survey firms that operate in narrower markets. Nielsen's and SAMI's data have become benchmarks for many industries.

Stock analysts.   Like purchasing agents, stock analysts are not open to much idle conversation. It is their job to watch a market and the companies within that market. Analysts publish reports on their industries. Since brokers and analysts have begun cutting back on free distribution of their reports, request a copy through your broker.

Office of Technology Assessment.   This government group tracks the latest technology to come out of American industry. It issues reports and data on these technologies.

Labor unions.   Although offered from a narrow perspective, labor unions monitor the employment climate for an industry. A union information office may give you an idea of market performance in light of industry hirings and layoffs.

THIRD CHOICE

Local newspapers.   Especially in a highly regionalized industry, town newspapers will report on major corporations within an area.

Annual reports.   A company's annual report will frequently compare its performance to that of the industry. In the course of making this comparison, it will describe the industry in some detail.

Research Priority List Number 2: Company Financials

LIST OBJECTIVE.   To help the researcher assemble a financial statement. This list includes both those sources that directly contain company financials and those that can supply a portion of a financial statement (e.g., labor costs, plant assets) where no complete statement exists in the public domain.

FIRST CHOICE

SEC documents.   Discussed later on in the text, the 10-K, 10-Q, proxy, and prospectus statements are filed by all publicly traded corporations. The agency responsible for recording and storing these filings is the Securities and Exchange Commission. One can obtain these reports by writing the SEC in Washington, or by contacting Disclosure, Inc. of Bethesda, Maryland, an SEC vendor.

If you can obtain a public filing with financials, you are way ahead of the game. The only items you may find hard to break out from these filings are divisional or product line sales.

Annual report.   Most public and some private corporations will publish their own version of the SEC-required 10-K annual report. This is usually a slick version of the 10-K, designed to impress current and prospective stockholders. Yet, these annuals frequently contain the same income statement and balance sheet information as one would find in the 10-K. Just write the company you are studying and it will be more than happy to place you on their mailing list for an annual.

Credit report.   This source will be discussed in a later section. But keep in mind that credit reports, while short on financials, can sometimes pull together all the publicly filed financial information. Occasionally, a credit report will also reveal an income statement for a privately held corporation. These sales figures are, many times, estimates or unverified information given by the company itself. So beware. When you begin a major company analysis where financials are a crucial part of the study, always order a credit report on the company.

Trade news articles.   A lengthy feature piece in a trade magazine will likely disclose some financial information about a company. It may discuss plant size, number of employees, or even sales. Take these reports with a grain of salt. For although these articles look authoritative, they are occasionally nothing more than articles written by the company's public relations agency with some editing on the part of the magazine.

Wall Street Transcript.   This is a source cited often in this book. It regularly publishes quarterly and annual statements released by publicly held companies. These statements are reduced to the bare bones, with little text accompanying them. See "What Did the CEO Say? Ask the Transcript" at the start of Chapter 9 for more information on the Transcript.

Moody's Investors Manuals.   A rather expensive source to subscribe to, but one that manages to index news summaries and financials for most publicly held companies, as well as for public utilities, municipalities, banks, and insurance companies.

Standard & Poor's Daily News Data Base.   This date base essentially contains the same information as the Moody's manuals, except that in this instance the information is available online.

Second Choice

Competitors.   You will find that competitors are not only knowledgeable about their competition, but may also give you a good deal of information for the price of an information swap.

UCC filings.   Most researchers find this source more of a tease than a helpful piece of intelligence. But UCC's can be useful in disclosing a new plant asset on which your target may have taken out a loan. See the UCC section for further details.

EIS Data Bases.   EIS (Economic Information Systems) publishes two data bases, the EIS Manufacturing and Nonmanufacturing data bases. Each record offers an estimated number of employees and sales volume as well as market share. EIS's market share and sales estimates are just that. While the data bases are often accurate, occasionally they are far off the mark. I would recommend using them to start off your study, wherever a credit report or public filing is not available.

State filings.   As each year passes, state governments require less information from privately held corporations located in their states than they did the year before. So, in many states, companies do not have to do more than give their name, address, and stockholders or owners. Nevertheless, the same rule applies—where you have no other source, it is worth asking for a filing. (See the "State Your Case" section in Chapter 3 for more information.)

General press.   Where a company has received a lot of press, you are bound to find some financial details mentioned. A business reporter would be derelict if he or she neglected to get at least a sales or growth rate figure for an article. You will probably have more luck with newspapers located near the plant or company you are studying than you would with a major regional paper.

Town assessor's office.   The town assessor's office can supply you with tax, ownership, and zoning information that the company may have filed. Or the assessor can put you in touch with a local town realtor who may know more. Often these filings are skimpy, but may still contain more data than are found in a state filing.

Real estate agents.   Here you should be looking for a commercial real estate agent, who can give you square footage costs of a company's plant and, perhaps, specifications on the plant and equipment.

Courts.   Court filings may reveal details on a company's indebtedness or problems it may be having involving trademark infringement. Bankruptcy or Chapter 11 filings contain a good amount of detail on the filing companies.

THIRD CHOICE

Industry financial ratios.   If all you have are a few data items, such as sales and current assets, you can construct a more complex income statement or balance sheet using industry financial ratios. A tricky tool, they can nevertheless give you a good sense of a company's proportions. Be careful in their use. See the "Financial Ratios" section in Chapter 11 for further discussion.

Interviews.   Although not a scientific approach, interviews can occasionally reveal good guesstimates of a company's sales and assets. Sometimes this may be the only way you will get a set of financials on a small, privately held company.

Visual sightings.   Counting the number of parking spaces and applying a rough formula for number of riders per car will give you an approximate employment figure for the plant or office. Eyeballing a plant can tell you something about its operating machinery and, perhaps, asset value. This is a highly creative, and not always accurate, tool for gauging competitor assets and employment information. See Chapter 13 for more details.

Research Priority List Number 3: Management Profiles

LIST OBJECTIVE. To supply the sources most used for assembling management profiles.

FIRST CHOICE

Local newspapers. Very often a national press release on an executive's promotion will only be carried in his or her hometown newspaper or in the newspaper where the plant or office is located. Local newspapers may have also done a feature story on the executive, especially if the executive or the company he or she works for contributes to the economic health of the community.

Who's Who directories. There are many varieties of biographical directories. Some, like Marquis' *Who's Who in Finance and Industry*, cover all industries and the major executives in each. Other directories are geared toward one industry, such as *Who's Who in Electronics.* You will find, overall, that a Who's Who will list only five percent or fewer of those you might consider important executives. So don't be surprised if you do not find your candidate.

Dun & Bradstreet Credit Reports. D&B reports, and others like them, are designed to analyze a company, not its officers, although frequently they do have some form of biographical sketch. It is a good place to start when assembling a biography. For example, it may tell you where an executive attended school and where he or she lives. These are both leads to follow through on: contact the alma mater and the local newspaper or Rotary Club.

Annual report and proxy. Annual reports will sometimes contain brief rundowns on the senior executives. Proxies, on the other hand, list the company's officers in some detail. Again, these sources only apply to publicly held companies.

SECOND CHOICE

Voter registry and assessor's offices. A local town hall will record the number of occupants in a house, and who owns the house, as well as the home owner's age and the number of members in his or her family. Usually, clerks in these offices are very helpful.

Colleague interviews. A touch-and-go source. Sometimes a colleague may be very helpful, especially where he or she has only good things to say about the individual.

THIRD CHOICE

Trade journals.   Trade magazines will often cover many of the industry's key promotions. Occasionally they will write up a complete profile on one of its professionals who achieved industry greatness. Instead of focusing on family life and hobbies, these types of articles reveal much about an executive's management style and financial wizardry.

Trade associations.   Associations are very protective of their membership—and rightfully so. But again, when they have nothing but good to say about one of their members they will be happy to talk. When a trade association is unusually reticent, don't worry. They just may not know anything about an executive. One tip: smaller associations are far more helpful and knowledgeable than are larger ones in this regard. They know their members, who may number only in the hundreds, whereas an association with thousands of members is not likely to recall a particular name or face.

Research Priority List Number 4: Company History

LIST OBJECTIVE.   To be able to piece together company activities (e.g., acquisitions, name changes, major changes in management).

FIRST CHOICE

SEC filings.   The Securities and Exchange Commission's 10-Ks offer company history and management analysis sections. Again, this only applies to publicly traded companies. Another filing, the initial prospectus, discusses a new corporation and its brief history.

Annual reports.   Many private as well as public companies publish a fairly complete company history in their annual reports.

Moody's Investors Manual.   The Moody's service provides capsule histories of all companies listed in its manuals. The companies included are either publicly held or are banks or financial institutions. It is one of the best summaries of a company's past activities.

Trade news/special reports.   Trade magazines will feature at least one company per issue, profiling the company. These articles are rich with company stories and activities. If there is no library index that covers the trade press in your industry, then select the most likely magazines and call up their editors or library. They will know whether or not they have recently published an article on your target company. If they have not, the editor can steer you to a competing publication that probably has. (In most industries, one trade magazine will follow its competing magazines very closely. The competing editors may even know each other socially.)

Case studies. These are summaries of a company's operations, written and compiled by various university business schools throughout the country. Case studies can vary in length, some amounting to as many as 30 or 40 pages, single spaced. They will study a particular company's operations, financials, marketing strategy, or organizational structure. Much of the information contained in a case study will come from the subject company itself. Case studies may prove a valuable way to understand an industry and its structure, as well as a single company's operations. Note, however, that the data is often dummied up, meaning that for reasons of confidentiality financials may have been altered.

The Case Clearing House at Harvard's Business School is the best known source for case studies. Stanford University also supplies case studies.

Local reporters. Regional and town newspapers will frequently cover a new company from its inception. Even if the newspapers have not written full stories about the firm, they know a great deal of hearsay about it.

SECOND CHOICE

Industry interviews. Competitors, suppliers, and those who come into contact with a company on a daily basis will have a fairly good idea of the company's background.

Stock trading statistics. Standard & Poor's daily stock reports, for instance, will allow the researcher to track the progress of a company's stock, how it was traded, and if there were any splits.

Market studies. Capsule reports describing a company may be contained within a larger market research report. These company summaries are usually very general. The information is considerably dated. It is usually not worth your while to purchase an entire research study to obtain a one or two paragraph write-up of the company.

State corporate filings. Most states require a company to file initial articles of incorporation and amendments to describe the nature of the business and how it was capitalized.

Commercial data bases. You can find publicly traded companies described in Disclosure's data base, available on the Dialog system. These data bases, discussed at length in Chapter 7, can also lead you to articles on the target company.

THIRD CHOICE

Textbooks.   Occasionally a textbook will cover the history of a company. The chance of finding the right book that is properly indexed, though, is slim.

Local business schools.   University business schools conduct their own reviews of various companies. Most likely, a professor will select a company that is close to the school so that he or she can conduct interviews and on-site visits. Therefore, you can locate a study on a local company by looking for the nearby business school.

KNOW THY INDUSTRY BEFORE THY TARGET COMPANY

You have to know something about your target company's industry before you can begin to research the target. Otherwise you may waste a lot of time and energy speaking to the wrong contacts and asking the wrong questions. Understanding your target's industry is the first step in creating a strategy for researching a company.

By the way, when I talk about an "industry," I mean any industry, including service, health care, banking, insurance, as well as manufacturing. The rules and concepts that apply to the personal computer case soon to be discussed apply to any industry. In banking, for instance, substitute "licensee bank" for "distributor." In other words, different industries call the same positions by different names, but their functions may be identical.

By just leafing through the scores of intelligence sources in this book, even the beginning researcher will soon realize the plethora of sources available on any one company. You can use general checklists and educated guesses as to the best person to speak to, but the question remains: Who are the best contacts and who knows the most about an industry and about your target company in particular?

The answer is a simple one: The best sources of information are those already involved in the industry—on almost any level. They can be manufacturers, suppliers, distributors, trade magazines, or consumer groups.

Using this concept as a premise, this section has a twofold purpose: (1) to show you the books and directories that list these industry mavens, and (2) to explain what kinds of expertise each industry group has and how each can help you in tracking down details on the target company.

Questions these mavens must answer before you can begin locating data on a particular corporation are:

1. How many importers, suppliers, manufacturers, distributors, consumer groups, trade organizations, and news media are there in the industry?
2. Of these groups, which ones control the largest share of the market?

This second question is crucial. If you can answer it, you are almost certain to locate the intelligence on your target. (See "Five Key Intelligence Factors", Chapter 1.)

Why is this second question so crucial? Because if you can determine that, let's say, there are hundreds of manufacturers in an industry, but that this same industry has only two trade magazines, which control 80 percent of the readership for that industry, you now have some key information in your hands.

The chances that one of these hundreds of manufacturers knows anything about your target company are small. But the chances of an editor of a trade magazine knowing about a company in this industry are far greater, since he or she has probably spoken to the company president at some time in the past.

In other words, the group with the largest market share also knows a lot about that market.

Caveat—Do Your Homework First!

Don't forget to do your homework. Search the business literature. You may still be able to answer your intelligence questions from a straightforward press announcement or news article.

This section is only here to provide you with alternate sources to interview. This section assumes you have done your homework and that the articles yielded zero or poor intelligence.

HOW TO USE INDUSTRY GROUPS TO YOUR BEST ADVANTAGE

Just knowing that an industry group exists does not mean that you can successfully get the information you need from it. This section, therefore, has two aims:

WAR STORY 2

Are Keyboards the Key to Computers?

Over the past few years (and it may come as no surprise) we have had to conduct a great many intelligence-gathering assignments in personal computers and personal electronics.

What we learned about the industry certainly paid off in less research time spent and in more accurate answers. In the story explained here, we had to understand how a particular home computer manufacturer operated; but first we examined the industry it operated in. The following are the important industry factors (keep the Concentration Factor from Chapter 1 in mind) we uncovered that helped us zero in on companies and experts to interview.

FACTS

There are over 150 computer manufacturers, but just six control over 50 percent of the market.

There are five keyboard suppliers to the personal computer manufacturers who manufacture over 90 percent of all the keyboards used for personal computers.

There are hundreds of chip manufacturers who supply microchips to the personal computer manufacturers. The 10 leading chip companies capture only 15 percent of the entire market.

LESSON

The six leading computer manufacturers probably know a lot about the market, since they control virtually one half of it.

The keyboard manufacturers, although not direct sellers to the consumer, know a lot about the market—and know an awful lot about the leading manufacturers since they probably sell to them.

On the other hand, no one chip supplier is likely to know very much about the market or a particular company, because there are so many chip companies, each with a small share of the market. The chances of any one chip supplier coming into regular contact with your chosen target company is very small. Hence, chip suppliers will likely be poor sources of company intelligence in this industry.

WAR STORY 2 *(Continued)*

RESULT

1. Our interviewing of industry mavens quickly told us who controlled different phases of the personal computer market.

2. When we learned who controlled the market, we also knew who most likely had the vital information on the target company.

3. We interviewed each of the leading personal computer companies and keyboard suppliers and discovered that these controllers of the market knew a good deal about our target company.

---

1. To show you how to speak to each of these groups. It will help you understand how their organizations work, and who or what within each organization may have the answer for you.

2. To show you how to find the companies and organizations within each group—especially, how to find the companies that are in your target industry.

Seven industry groups are discussed in this section: the media, trade organizations, consumer groups, consultants and analysts, retailers, distributors, and manufacturers and suppliers.

The Media

Some industries have hundreds of publications, making any one magazine or newspaper a poor source of specific company data. On the other hand, many industries will only have a handful of trade magazines representing them. In such cases, editors of trade magazines become excellent company intelligence sources.

Tips for Using the Media

1. *Ask for the editor by topic.* If you don't have the editor's name, ask for an editor by the topic or industry segment your target company represents.

2. *Ask for the publisher's library.* If the editor cannot give you a satisfactory answer, ask to speak to the magazine's librarian. Often, trade magazines—especially from publishers who produce more than one magazine—will catalog all their articles. No one editor or writer can hope to remember every article that ever appeared in his or her magazine.

3. *Is there a special issue?* Find out if the magazine has published a yearly special issue that may have covered the company you are interested in (e.g., "The 100 largest. . ." or "The 50 Industry Leaders").

4. *Use an old article as a reference.* An article you dug up in your search may not answer your questions, but it can provide you with a conversation opener when interviewing a trade editor. (See "Milking an Article for All It's Worth" later in this chapter.)

5. *Go for the magazine with the largest circulation.* The directories listed below will tell you which magazines or newspapers have the largest circulation. The largest circulation magazines have the largest staff, and in turn have the largest information base—this means they probably have the best chance of knowing something about your target company. The one exception is the local town newspaper, which can often glean a good deal of information on a regional company.

Key Media Sources

Editor & Publisher International Yearbook (Editor & Publisher). Lists newspapers in the United States and in foreign countries. It contains information on a newspaper's circulation, prices, advertising rates, and so on.

The IMS Ayer Directory of Publications (IMS Press). One of the best media directories you can buy. It lists consumer, business, technical, trade, and farm publications for the United States and Canada. Aside from circulation figures for each publication, it also lists the editors and their titles.

The Newsletter Yearbook Directory (Newsletter Clearinghouse). One of the only directories of its kind. No other directory has as complete a list of specialty newsletters on an industry. Newsletters listed here range in subject from general news to high-technology publications. In some newly formed industries, newsletters may be the only source of company and industry information. The newsletters are indexed by subject and by state as well as alphabetically.

Business Publications Rates and Data (Standard Rate and Data Services). Part I contains a directory of U.S. and international business publications; Part II deals with direct response media.

Standard Periodical Directory (Oxbridge Communications). One of the most complete periodical directories available. It provides the reader with a description of the magazine as well as its circulation count, address, and editor. I have used this directory often to track down an esoteric journal that covers a target company's industry.

WAR STORY 3

Will the Real Information Source Please Stand Up?

We had been trying to locate some estimates of blank cassette tape production, both in the United States and abroad. The researcher had thumbed through the Encyclopedia of Associations (mentioned below) and came up with two or three key associations.

The calls were placed. The researcher managed to reach the information officer in each association, only to find out that they could only release the information to members.

After pressing the point a little more with one association, the information officer admitted that although they had the data, they were not really the ones responsible for compiling the information. The officer referred the researcher to a trade magazine, stating that the magazine was actually the source.

When the magazine editor was contacted, he said that, "Yes, we are the ones who collect the data. But I wouldn't place money on its validity."

What is the lesson in all this? Trade associations often just collect government statistics or regurgitate data given to them by other sources. Be careful when you ask them for statistics, and always ask them for their source.

Ulrich's International Periodical Directory (R.R. Bowker). This directory runs neck-in-neck with Oxbridge's (above). Well-indexed, it gives the reader an excellent overview of the periodicals in the industry under study.

Willings Press Guide (Thomas Skinner Directories). This directory is an international list of newspapers, periodicals, and annuals. It is indexed alphabetically by country.

The Working Press of the Nation (National Research Bureau). Divided into business, farm and agricultural, and consumer publications. It has one of the more complete listings of reporters and editors, and is a work similar to Ayer's (mentioned earlier in this list).

Trade Organizations

A trade organization may not want to give you very much data about its members, but it is usually happy to discuss its industry. Very often, it has assembled information packets, or has an officer handy to answer your probings about its market.

Most trade organizations are nothing more than lobbying groups. That is why you will find most of them with headquarters in Washington, D.C.

Their chief concern is to represent their members in halls of government. Many are also their industry's public and consumer relations voice. Because of their positions, trade associations must marshal the facts about their industries (but not necessarily about their member companies).

If you can find a trade association that represents a large portion of an industry's manufacturers, suppliers, or another industry segment, you have a valuable information source. Again, keeping the personal computer example in mind, where a small number of manufacturers or trade associations hold a large share of the market, they become excellent intelligence sources.

The directories mentioned later in this section are designed to point out which trade associations are dominant in their respective industries. By locating the largest and most powerful associations, you will have also located a likely intelligence source.

Tips for Using Trade Organizations

1. *Do not expect trade associations to give you company-specific information.* They represent their members, not you—a probing researcher. They will be happy to supply you with general industry information, but may be less than cooperative when asked for company-specific data. By giving you "insider" information about their membership, they could be compromising their membership.

2. *Ask for the information officer.* In associations where the staff is greater than five, you will probably find an information officer. Otherwise, the association's president often doubles as the public affairs or information officer.

3. *Ask for their annual study or report.* Most associations have published some sort of annual review of their industry. This study is usually available for free or for a nominal charge. Here you will find industry statistics and market share analyses.

4. *Check the data they supply you.* Many times, trade associations cannot afford to hire market research firms and instead use government data. You may have to look very carefully to find the footnotes that state that the information is from a government source. Also, make sure that the industry breakdown they are offering is the one you are looking for. For example, do you want the number of plastics manufacturers, or only those who produce polyurethane?

5. *Be prepared for smug or ignorant answers.* Although most trade associations are extremely helpful, some will discourage your research efforts. In our research, we have discovered that when one trade association

claimed that no one had the information, another association was able to give us the answer. If you feel you are not being given the information you expect, then maybe you are speaking to the wrong person in the organization. You could also be speaking to the wrong association. If this is the case, return to one of the directories listed in the next section and try again.

6. *Look for the organization with the largest membership and the largest staff.* Trade groups with the largest staff usually support a library and maintain statistics for the industry. Large size also indicates that the organization is likely to be one of the older, more established trade groups— meaning that it may have the greatest number of contacts in the industry.

Key Trade Organization Sources

Directory of Associations in Canada (University of Toronto Press). This is the alphabetical list of Canadian associations, containing the address and CEO of each association.

Directory of European Associations (CBD Research, distributed by Gale Research). A two-part work, this reference set lists over 9000 national organizations and regional groups of national significance. In addition, it also covers 6000 technical societies. Excluded are Great Britain and Ireland.

Directory of British Associations and Associations in Ireland (CBD Research, distributed by Gale Research). Similar to the above, but covering just Great Britain and Ireland.

Encyclopedia of Associations (Gale Research). This is the granddaddy of association guides. You will find it in almost every public and most private libraries in the United States. Now in its 18th edition, it contains entries for over 16,000 associations and societies. It is thoroughly indexed and numbers over 1600 pages. This book should be on every business researcher's shelf.

National Trade and Professional Associations of the United States and Canada and Labor Unions (Columbia Books). Indexed by keyword, location, executive, and budget, this directory is a list of approximately 4700 national trade and professional associations.

World Guide to Trade Associations (R.R. Bowker). An international trade association directory, listing trade associations and chambers of commerce. The associations are arranged by country.

Consumer Groups

Nonprofit clubs and societies can be an enormous treasure trove of valuable industry and company information.

As a timely example: Computer clubs are springing up everywhere. The Boston Computer Society, for instance, is one of the largest of its kind in the United States, with thousands of members. Here the researcher can find out how many new models are on the market and where the users are buying their machines. The Boston Computer Society is, in effect, a giant network of computer users who can supply the researcher with valuable insights into the market.

The second part of this section deals with market research firms that produce the market research studies describing the market and the consumers involved in it.

Tips for Using Consumer Groups

1. *Shop around for information.* Consumer groups and market research companies offer a wide variety of reports and findings. To the researcher in search of market data, finding the right group with the best information can be frustrating—and expensive. You may find that the data you need is free for the asking.

2. *Join consumer groups and professional societies.* Membership fees are often nominal, especially for nonprofit groups. Join the club or the society, assuming you qualify. These groups need more than just good will to survive. You will be amazed at the number of doors that will suddenly open when you become a member.

3. *Ask for the library or resource center.* The larger clubs and societies have been established for many years and will likely have information centers and files. The industry data you need will be found here.

Key Consumer Group Sources

Civitan International Club Directory (Civitan International). A directory that restricts itself exclusively to clubs in the United States and foreign countries. The book is organized geographically.

Cumulative List of Organizations (Internal Revenue Service/Treasury Department). This is the definitive U.S. list of nonprofit organizations. Over 186,000 organizations are listed. There is no subject index.

Findex (Find/SVP). This is a directory of market research studies that have been published. Price, publisher, and a description of the study are provided. The reports are indexed by subject and by publisher. Generally, the reports listed here are sold through Find/SVP. Reports vary in price from ten dollars to thousands of dollars. Included in this directory are reports published by Nielsen, SAMI, Frost & Sullivan, and many other well-known research houses.

Yellow Pages (local telephone operating company).   You will find a club or society under one of two headings—the Association's heading, or the heading or category of the industry itself.

Consultants and Analysts

Consultants abound in the business world. When a problem arises, you don't have to look far to find a consultant to solve it.

Consultants are entrepreneurial by nature and have marshaled a wealth of experience and contacts that make them extremely valuable for company research. Any consultant who has been in business for many years has accumulated hundreds, if not thousands, of contacts. Why not use this expertise to your advantage?

Tips for Using Consultants and Analysts

1. *As a company, a consultant sees you as a prospective client.*   Use this position to your advantage. Market research firms have a hard time getting data from other research firms because they are the competition. But as a company, you become a prospective client. You do not have to mislead the consultant; like anyone else, a consultant will soon see through a ruse. But by just being straightforward and explaining your position—that you are doing research on a company—you will find many a consultant offering you free information. After all, the consultant feels that this small favor will make you think of him or her in the future when you may want to hire an outside expert.

2. *Consultants appreciate receiving as well as giving information.*   Swap what you've got before you ask for too much. Information is a consultant's bread and butter, a commodity to buy and sell. Add to the consultant's storehouse and he or she will be happy to give you some information you may not already have.

3. *Narrow down your field as much as possible.*   Particularly in the technical fields, consultants find their own niches. Frequently these fields are so specialized that other consultants, even in a related area, may not have heard of these specialties. Directories like the ones listed in the next section will help you locate the consultant of your choice.

4. *Articles will help you find consultants.*   A consultant's best advertising vehicle is plain, good old publicity in the relevant field's trade magazine or newspaper. If you are having a hard time finding a consultant in your field of interest, search for an article in that field and watch the consultants pop out—as the article's author or as its subject.

WAR STORY 4

The Solution Was Just Cosmetic

The cosmetics industry is both very secretive and at the same time flashy. Yet, with all this flashiness and Madison Avenue glitter, it is still difficult to pinpoint particular distribution channels for one or two competitive products. Our assignment was to determine how a company's product line was distributed. Was it 50 percent department stores and 10 percent discount outlets? How has the distribution changed over time? These kinds of questions immediately told us we had to find an expert or noted consultant in the industry.

After reviewing trade articles on the subject, we identified two consultants who appeared to have collected this type of data.

The first consultant refused to help us. The second one agreed to give us some data, provided we promised to exchange some of our findings with him. We felt this was fair and he gave us invaluable data—information we would have found impossible to obtain anywhere else (see "Interviewing Techniques" later in this chapter for suggestions on swapping information).

---

5. *Consultants are great sources of management background.* They are privy to insider information about a company; they also hear almost every rumor to come down the industrial pike. When you are looking for nonfinancial information about a company, turn to a consultant.

Key Consulting Sources

Bradford's Directory of Marketing Research Agencies and Management Consultants in the United States and the World (Bradford's Directory of Marketing Research Agencies). Lists over 500 research agencies and management consultants in market research. Each entry offers the name, address, region of coverage, and description of services.

Consultants and Consulting Organizations Directory (Gale Research). Gale once again succeeds in producing one of the best reference sources in the field. The directory contains thousands of consultants in over 135 fields. The fields included in this work vary from advertising and agriculture to real estate and taxes.

Directory of Management Consultants (Kennedy and Kennedy). This directory contains over 550 management consultants from across the country. Consultants are indexed by services offered, manufacturers served, and geographical location.

Institute of Management Consultants—Directory of Members (Institute of Management Consultants). The directory lists 800 management consultants in a variety of specialties. The volume is indexed geographically.

Directory of Member Firms (New York Association of Consulting Management Engineers). A directory of engineering firms, with a fairly extensive description of each firm.

Directory of Research Services (Marketing Research Associates). Contains over 400 market research firms in the United States and Canada. Indexed geographically.

Who's Who In Consulting (Gale Research). Offers the reader biographies on leading consultants. Each reference appears in three separate issues throughout the year and the directory itself contains over 1000 biographies.

Retail Trade

Department stores, discount houses, and just plain mom and pop retail stores will offer you some extremely valuable information on your competition. Although your competitor may have already made certain moves that you could have caught earlier on in the business cycle, you can still learn many details by interviewing the retailers carrying your competitor's products.

Here is some of the competitive information you can learn from a retailer.

1. Where is a product positioned in the store?
2. Has your competitor designed a special display for the product?
3. What are its price points? Do discount stores price the product differently?
4. Has your competitor tailored the product to fit different markets? Is it sold in two types of packages, one to appeal to the mom and pop shop and another for the mass merchandiser?
5. What is the product's retail market share?
6. Is the competitor shipping the product on time, or are there delays? Do these delays differ between small stores and large discount chains, for example?
7. Is the retailer being supported with manufacturer's co-op advertising?

Tips for Using Retailers

1. *Speak to the department manager.* The manager is likely to know such items as a product's market share in his or her department (in other

---

WAR STORY 5

An Order Is an Order

A new consumer electronics product had just been announced. The trouble was that this product was not due for shipping for at least another year. Our client, however, wanted to know what the intended shipping amount was going to be. The press had no idea.

We spoke to a buyer for a large department store chain. The buyer happened to be located within 20 miles of the target company's headquarters. The buyer said he was in contact with the target, and gave us a rough idea of what he had heard the expected shipment was going to be.

---

words, how that product is selling in that area), product price points, and packaging and display information. The manager will also be able to tell you service and warranty conditions and where the nearest service dealership is located.

2. *Buyers are everything to a retailer.* These are backshop executives who make all the buying decisions for either the store or an entire chain. They see the factory salespeople, independent representatives, and distributors. Aside from pricing, they may also have inside knowledge of a company, its management, and how it operates. Because they price-shop, they know who the industry leaders are and a market's concentration—probably better than anyone else.

Unfortunately, they are also busy people and most, when you speak with them, sound as if they are in a rush. Tell the buyer that the questions you have to ask will take no more than a minute (and stick to your promise), and that you will swap information on the company. Usually this will open some more doors for you.

3. *Walk through the store.* There is no better way to understand how a store positions and displays the product.

4. *Speak to more than one chain store.* Although the competitor's product is being sold in an entire chain of stores, how it is displayed and marketed can differ widely from store to store.

5. *Contact the store's receiving room.* Those stocking the shelves can tell you if they have received the product for a new promotion, and how often they restock the product.

Note—If you are looking for the corrugated box manufacturer who produced the boxes a product is shipped in, the shipping department is the department to ask (for further details see "Corrugated boxes" in Chapter 14.

Key Retail Trade Sources

Directory of Discount Department Stores (Business Guides).   A directory listing over 480 companies. Each reference points out chain headquarters, and reviews store square footage and gross sales.

Fairchild's Department Manual of Retail Stores (Fairchild Publications).   Fairchild publishes many leading trade newspapers for the retail industry and knows the retail trade well. This directory provides the name, address of, and financial information on leading retail chains.

National Association of Chain Drug Stores—Membership Directory (National Association of Chain Drug Stores).   This directory lists 200 drug chains and 400 of their key suppliers. Each entry includes firm name, headquarters address and telephone, number of company-owned and leased pharmacies, and names of key executives.

Phelon's Discount and Sheldon's Jobbing (Phelon, Sheldon and Marsar).   One of the most detailed of retail store directories, it actually lists close to 2000 discount stores and self-service stores. It also lists 8000 jobbers, rack jobbers, and catalog showrooms.

Retail Tenant Prospect Directory (National Mall Monitor).   Lists over 2000 retail stores and chains deemed by the publisher to be interested in locating their stores in shopping malls. The book lists the chains alphabetically, by retail group.

Sheldon's Retail Stores (Phelon, Sheldon and Marsar).   This text is considered one of the best retail store reference sources. It covers approximately 1800 independent department stores, 500 large junior department stores, 100 large independent and chain home furnishings stores, and 750 independent women's clothing stores. The book is arranged geographically, with an alphabetical index also included.

Stores of the World Dictionary (Newman Books).   A terrific directory if you are looking for the buyers for each chain. It lists the buyers by specialty. The directory covers department stores, discount chains, superstores, co-operatives, buying groups, and other retail chain stores. It is truly a worldwide directory and an excellent source.

Vending Times—International Buyers Guides and Directory Issue (Vending Times).   A different kind of retail directory. Instead of covering the retail stores themselves, it deals with vending equipment suppliers. Since the retailers may by unaware of the volume of business their vending machines are doing, or which are the better machines, your best bet is to turn to these suppliers for market information. The companies are listed alphabetically by machine grouping (e.g., music, game devices, or food vending machines.)

Distributors

How a product is distributed can tell the researcher a good deal about the manufacturer and its marketing plans. Some companies will distribute their own products (for example, Radio Shack). Other companies may use outside, independent distributors or trucking fleets.

By tapping into these lines of distribution you, as a researcher, can learn how much a company is shipping and how it is promoting one product, for example.

When I talk about distributors, I mean railroads, trucking firms, and warehouses. In the less strict sense, these distributors can include the non-manufacturing industries, as mentioned above, such as insurance brokers, licensee banks, and health care delivery services. These are all elements in the distribution network.

Let's say in one research case you are able to find out that the industry you are studying has only three distributors covering 90 percent of the industry. This should tell you that speaking to a distributor can tell you a good deal about any of the manufacturers in that industry.

Tips for Using Distributors

1. *Check to see if your target company uses an independent trucking fleet.* Many smaller manufacturers cannot afford to maintain an entire fleet of trucks. Here is where truck leasing can play an important role in your search. Like corrugated boxes, rented trucks are another incidental intelligence source. Find the leasing company and you may have found a source of production and shipping information on your target company.

2. *Speak to a retailer to find out how the company ships its products.* Retailers can tell you how long it takes a company to deliver an order and if the company is back-ordered. Because retailers are sensitive to customer needs, they are inclined to keep on top of their supplier's delivery and service.

3. *Distributors can tell you which products move best.* If a distributor feels a product is not moving, it will drop that particular item quickly. Conversely, should a distributor detect that an item is turning over fast, the distributor will be sure to hop onto the bandwagon before demand overtakes

the manufacturer's ability to supply the product and the distributor gets caught short.

4. *Ask for a distributor's line card.*   Independent market representatives and distributors issue what are known in the trade as line cards. These cards describe what product lines each distributor carries and mention the products in some detail. Line cards vary in size and detail. For example, some distributors will print their line card on the back of their business card. Others may design their card as a file folder, with the products and marketing information written on both the inside and outside of the folder. Line cards allow the researcher to quickly gauge the size of a manufacturer's product line, as well as to discern which products move the best. By ordering a number of line cards from competing distributors, you can determine which types of products are the most popular.

Key Distribution Sources

Air Freight Directory (Air Cargo).   A directory of companies affiliated with a private company called Air Cargo. These are companies that work with this air carrier to deliver and pick up freight.

Air Freight Carriers Conference—Routing Guide (Air Freight Motor Carriers Conference).   This publication lists trucking firms by the cities in which they operate. Like the above directory, this book only lists motor carriers that make connections with air freight carriers.

American Warehouseman's Association—Membership Directory (American Warehousemen's Association).   Lists over 500 warehouse companies that store and handle nonrefrigerated merchandise.

Directory of Alternative Delivery Systems (Circulation Systems).   In this case, we are talking about a highly specialized distributor: a company that delivers newspapers and magazines. Possibly a highly useful source for locating circulation patterns for competing publications. Each entry offers a good deal of data on the delivery service, including methods of delivery, area serviced, and major accounts (a great way to directly locate the distributor for your target publisher).

Directory of Public Refrigeration Warehouses (International Association of Refrigerated Warehouses).   A directory that lists over 600 refrigerated warehouses, as well as companies that supply to this segment of the warehouse industry.

Distribution Worldwide—Distribution Guide Issue (Chilton).   A special issue of the magazine, it covers rail services, ports, trucking companies, warehouses, and lessors of transportation and distribution equipment. Entries will include name, address, contact's name, and some description of the products or services offered.

International Warehouse and Storage Directory (IPC Industrial Press). One of the largest directories of its kind, it lists over 5000 warehouse companies. Included in each listing are company name, address, telephone, telex, capacity, and description of facilities.

National Distribution Directory (Local and Short Haul Carriers Conference). Contains names and addresses of local warehouses and distribution services throughout the United States. The directory is arranged geographically.

Quick Frozen Foods Directory of Food Processors (Harcourt Brace Jovanovich). Lists over 3000 food processors, refrigerated warehouses, trucking companies, and rail freight haulers that carry and handle frozen products. The book is arranged both geographically and by product.

Thomas Grocery Register (Thomas Publishing Company). This is the single best company directory for firms in the food business. There are three volumes, the first of which contains over 4000 brokers and 4200 wholesalers and distributors, divided by their specialty (meats, institutional, general merchandise, rack jobbers, and so on). We have used this source many times to track down competitors in the same geographic areas. In one instance, the Grocery Register allowed us to locate a company whose owner was formerly employed by the target company. This former employee told us about the target's expansion plans, its product line, and names of current customers.

U.S. Trade and Transport Directory (Trade and Transport Company). A directory that contains 20,000 companies involved in shipping, trucking, or other transportation services.

Manufacturers and Suppliers

Throughout this text I discuss sources of manufacturing and manufacturer information—sources such as the Thomas Register, the Dun & Bradstreet Million Dollar Directory, and Standard & Poor's corporate directory. We will not go into depth here about the pros and cons of each source. These sources will be covered in Chapter 4.

Since manufacturers are in the center of the product cycle, they can tell a researcher about an industry's suppliers, distributors, consultants, government offices, trade press, and, of course, the competitors.

Aside from gleaning names from such sources as the Thomas Register, there is one book that is indispensable for determining the size and makeup of your target industry: the *U.S. Industrial Outlook Handbook*. (Again, here we are talking about manufacturing companies, not service firms. For a list of specific industry sources, see Chapter 5.)

The *U.S. Industrial Outlook Handbook* explores and reports on hundreds of U.S. industries, giving the reader the number of companies, their concentration, and their geographical distribution. It will describe the industry's growth rate and product trends. At the end of each section, it offers a brief bibliography of other sources you may want to refer to. In addition, it states the name and phone number of the Department of Commerce analyst who compiled the report. The Handbook is published by the Government Printing Office and appears annually.

MILKING AN ARTICLE FOR ALL IT'S WORTH

Searching through business literature can be a frustrating experience for someone who desperately wants to locate details on a company. Why? Because most of the time that person has unrealistic expectations of what the literature can offer. Also, people generally do not understand an article's true potential.

There are two major problems with searching for corporate information in an article:

1.   Your question may be too narrowly focused. No publisher in its right mind would publish an article on a very narrow subject that might interest only two or three readers. You don't sell papers that way. An article can *hint* at your subject, but that is all.

2.   Likely as not, you need timely information about your competition. That often means that the event may have occurred literally yesterday or last week. Apart from daily publications, this kind of deadline is difficult for trade magazines to meet.

Monthly and weekly magazines may have a six-month waiting list for certain articles. So, keep in mind that although an article appears on a particular date, it may have been written six months earlier, and researched months before that. Timeliness is not usually a trade magazine's highest virtue.

 Yet, what can you use an article for? You should turn it uspide down and inside out for valuable leads. Leads come in the form of names of experts,

Homespun Madness: Crazy Quilts Now Fetch Crazy Prices

* * *

Heirlooms and New Creations
Become Fit for a King
After Bicentennial Revival ◆

By CLAUDIA RICCI
Staff Reporter of THE WALL STREET JOURNAL

Later this year, when Maria McCormack-Snyder of Baltimore sells five of the quilts she has designed and stitched, she figures the proceeds will be sufficient for a down payment on the house she is building.

In Modesto, Calif., artist Yvonne Porcella makes quilts and then fashions them into one-of-a-kind clothing priced in the four-figure range.

Two years ago, Sotheby Parke Bernet Inc., the New York auctioneers, sold a colorful early-20th century quilt depicting a bustling Illinois farm scene for $10,000—one of the highest prices ever paid for a quilt at auction.

The homespun quilt has transcended its ragbag origins to become a luxury item. Whether delicate heirlooms or vividly colored contemporary creations, quilts today spell big business. They have acquired such cachet that quilters by the tens of thousands—rural seamstresses doing piecework, suburban homemakers hunched over dining-room tables and artists working in urban lofts—can't cut, piece, stuff and stitch fast enough to satisfy demand.

Wide-Ranging Interest

Their handiwork often fetches thousands of dollars at glitzy galleries, boutiques and department stores, and more modest sums at church fairs or craft shows from Maine to Marin County. The explosion of interest in quilts and quilting has spawned numerous classes, workshops, how-to books, magazines and newsletters, not to mention quilting-supply businesses like Jeff Gutcheon's in Manhattan, which will gross about $1 million this year—five times his sales three years ago. All told, quilt-making has become a $50 million to $100 million business, though for the quilters themselves, it is more a labor of love than money.

"Quilts are a link to past generations and a link to future generations," says Karey Bresenhan, who owns a quilt shop and runs a national trade show for quilt-store owners in Houston every year. "They are statements of quality, they are statements of beauty, they are something that lives after you."

At a time when much of the art market is mired in a recessionary slump, gallery owners and auctioneers say that antique quilts continue to command steep prices. Patchworks from pioneer beds survive today as sought-after folk art, and are likely to be found gracing gallery walls, corporate corridors and sumptuous contemporary homes.

Floating Sale

In August, more than 450 quilt fanciers crowded aboard a Circle Line sightseeing boat to bid on antique bedding while cruising around Manhattan. The sale, sponsored by Guernsey's Country Auction of New York, took in over $40,000 for 135 quilts. Barbara Mintz, Guernsey's owner, says the auction house has been selling an average of 100 quilts a month, for several hundred dollars each.

The swift rise in quilt prices has taken some collectors by surprise. A few years ago, Robert L. Williams, a New York tax attorney, bought an Amish quilt dating from the 1920s. He did so behind his wife's back, for she had thought its $800 price outrageous. Mr. Williams, who sneaked the quilt

---

Figure 2.1 Intelligence leads in the quilting industry (underscoring added). (*Wall Street Journal*, October 11, 1982. Printed by permission of the *Wall Street Journal*,© Dow Jones & Company, Inc. 1981. All Rights Reserved.)

into his Long Island home while his wife was asleep, recalls that later "when she came home with a new dress and a couple of pairs of shoes, I felt safe enough to unveil my purchase." Today, Mrs. Williams is delighted with the quilt, a highly prized type of patchwork that now would probably sell for between $3,000 and $5,000. "What else can you use as an investment that you can also take to bed with you?" Mr. Williams asks with a chuckle.

Quilts have become gifts fit for a king. A New York banker recently purchased one, made for the 1876 U.S. Centennial, as a gift for Spain's King Juan Carlos. President and Mrs. Reagan have presented quilts to heads of state while on trips abroad. And, when Prince Charles and Princess Diana's son was born this June, the Reagans gave them a baby quilt made by Kentucky craftswomen.

Quilts are no longer confined to the bedroom. Corporations, for example, have found them ideal for adding touches of homey warmth to hard-edged office environments. Quilts adorn walls at International Business Machines Corp. facilities in Franklin Lakes, N.J.; Essex Junction, Vt., and Mechanicsburg, Pa. Chase Manhattan Bank in New York boasts 49 American quilts in its extensive art collection. The San Francisco office of Esprit de Corp., a sportswear manufacturer, was designed expressly to display the company's collection of 200 quilts valued at $500,000.

The resurgence of interest in patchworks began as part of the general interest in folk art and Americana that accompanied the 1976 U.S. Bicentennial. But the history of quilting reaches much farther back than Colonial America. Some evidence suggests that the Egyptian Pharaohs, as far back as 3400 B.C., wrapped themselves in quilts for warmth. And in the Middle Ages, crusaders visiting the Near East took to wearing quilts as protective padding beneath their armor. When they returned home, the technique of quilting spread rapidly through Europe.

Queen Elizabeth I wore quilted gowns, richly embroidered in gold, silver and pearls. Catherine Howard was given 23 silk quilts when she married King Henry VIII in 1540. And an elaborate bridal quilt given to Marie Antoinette indirectly led to her demise: The French Revolutionary tribunal held up the flower-and-cupid-bedecked quilt as an example of her extravagance.

But the craft of quilting culminated in Colonial America, when a chronic shortage of cloth and harsh conditions forced the early settlers to fall back on their ingenuity and needlecraft skills. Cotton wasn't yet being manufactured in the Colonies, and it took months to turn flax and fleece into linen and wool. Women recycled scarce fabrics repeatedly—first as garments and finally, when only scraps remained, as quilts.

Quilting was one of the only creative outlets then available for women. Little girls learned the craft as soon as they could handle a needle, and by the time they married, were expected to have pieced together a dozen patchwork tops. When a girl became engaged, family and friends would assemble to finish the blankets at a marathon quilting bee. These gatherings, like barn raisings, corn huskings and church picnics, offered welcome respite from the isolation of frontier life. (To a lesser extent, boys, too, helped quilt. Both Dwight D. Eisenhower and Calvin Coolidge admitted in later years to having helped cut and piece patchworks in their youth.)

Callus Problem

Unlike their forebears, contemporary quilters are blessed with a surfeit of fabric from which to stitch their creations. Yet they do fall victim to age-old quilters' ailments, such as heavily callused forefingers, where the tiny quilting needles come to rest again and again.

Judy B. Dales, a Mountain Lakes, N.J., quilter who also teaches the craft, says she suffers from arthritis, a pain in her right hand so intense she can barely hold a pencil. Other quilters complain of sore hips from too many hours of sitting. "I tell all my students they'll end up hunchbacked and blind," Mrs. Dales says with a smile.

They are also likely to end up poorly paid. So time-consuming is the work that even those who produce quilts that sell for several thousand dollars often labor for the less than the minimum hourly wage. Sue H. Rodgers of Mountain Lakes, N.J., recently sold a pair of her quilts for $2,300. But it took her more than 1,200 hours to complete the intricate, trapunto-style bed coverings.

Big quilt retailers often farm out work to seamstresses in rural areas or in foreign countries. Near Bell Buckle, Tenn., about 40

Figure 2.1. *(Continued)*

local women produce quilts in their homes for shipment to stores across the nation.

A group of Mennonite women in the Lancaster, Pa., area produce quilts for a Madison Avenue boutique called The Gazebo. The store charges between $400 and $600 for each quilt, more than double what it pays to the group producing the quilt.

But most of The Gazebo's quilts are made in Haiti, where about 60 women working at a small factory earn only a few dollars a week. The store started its Haitian operation six years ago, when the Pennsylvania quilters couldn't meet burgeoning demand.

'Supplemental Income'

Quilt-making provides "very good supplemental income," says Nancy Puentes, executive director of the Quilt Institute, a trade organization of quilt-shop owners. "But it's certainly not producing (anyone's) living."

Clearly, the rewards of quilting are found elsewhere. Quilters say they enjoy the intricate, painstaking stitching that some might regard as tedious. "It's therapy in a way," says Ann Ralph, a New York quilter who recently moved from California. "It's almost like meditation."

Quilters are equally reverent about the end product—whether their own handiwork or that of a long-forgotten pioneer seamstress who whiled away bleak prairie winters stitching something of beauty. So it was with much indignation that they greeted fashion designer Ralph Lauren's fall collection, featuring $1,000 skirts and $700 petticoats, all fashioned from antique quilts. "You wouldn't take a fragment of a fine painting and make a Christmas tree ornament out of it," snaps Bonnie Leman, editor of Quilter's Newsletter Magazine in Wheatridge, Col. Though Mr. Lauren insists his patchwork designs were cut from ripped and damaged quilt remnants, Mrs. Leman suggests the scraps might more properly have been framed as art.

For those who love them, every quilt is a tangible fragment of history. Karey Bresenhan of Houston is especially fond of a quilt begun back in the 1930s by her great-grandmother, who had learned the craft by candlelight in a tent on the Texas prairie. A few weeks before Mrs. Bresenhan was married in 1963, 15 of her great-aunts, cousins and other kinfolk gathered to finish the quilt as a wedding present. It was a three-day quilting bee that Mrs. Bresenhan remembers with particular fondness.

"We worked 24 hours a day, sleeping in shifts," she says. For Mrs. Bresenhan, the finished product, with its pattern of five pastel-colored stars, has no price tag. "It's not the most valuable quilt I own," she says. "And it's not the most beautiful. But Howard Hughes didn't have enough money to buy this quilt. I wouldn't sell it for anything."

Figure 2.1. *(Continued)*

companies, suppliers, and so on. These are live experts, not names that have been lying in some directory or randomly assembled. These names have a direct link to your target company. Use them. Some typical types of sources you will find in a business article are authors, competitors, suppliers, distributors, end-users, similar products, and industry experts.

Articles are especially useful when dredging up information on a company in a new and little-known industry.

Let's look at a whimsical example of such an industry: the quilting industry. I have taken an article from the *Wall Street Journal* (Figure 2.1)

TABLE 2.1. Intelligence Leads

Cited Sources	What You Can Learn
Quilters	
Maria McCormack-Snyder Baltimore, MD Yvonne Porcella Modesto, CA Judy B. Dales Mountain Lakes, NJ Ann Ralph New York, NY	1. Number of quilts personally manufactured each year 2. Average price of a quilt 3. Who buys the quilts 4. Source of materials 5. Immediate market group 6. Other quilters' names 7. Cost of production 8. End uses
Auction Houses	
Sotheby, Parke Bernet, Inc. New York, NY Guernsey's Country Auction New York, NY (Barbara Mintz, owner)	1. Number of quilts auctioned annually, either at Sotheby or at other auction houses 2. Average age of "collectible quilts" 3. Source of quilts 4. Potential for market
Retailers	
Jeff Gutcheon New York, NY Gazebo New York, NY Karen Bresenhan Houston, TX	1. Production, output 2. Sizes, styles 3. Trends 4. Consumer profile 5. Cost of production
Corporate Buyers	

IBM
  Franklin Lakes, NJ
  Essex Junction, VT
  Mechanicsburg, PA
Chase Manhattan Bank
New York, NY
Esprit de Corps
San Francisco, CA
	1. Market details from purchasing agent (source of quilts)
	2. Leads for other sources
	3. Reasons for purchase
	4. Awareness of other corporate buyers

Trade Organization	
Quilt Institute (Nancy Phentes, Executive Director)	1. Statistics on sales, number employed, sales outlets, price points

TABLE 2.1. (Continued)

Cited Sources	What You Can Learn
	2. Market growth
	3. Cost of operation
	4. Referral list
Reporter	
Claudia Ricci	1. Leads for all of the above

and then listed (Table 2.1) all the possible contacts that you can glean from this fairly short piece.

If you had even a handful of similar articles on the company you wish to investigate, think how fruitful your search would be if you milked them for all they're worth.

INTERVIEW TECHNIQUES

The telephone is the researcher's most valuable tool, allowing one to go outside the narrow confines of a particular city or company. In just a few brief minutes the caller can solicit answers to questions from a wide variety of sources—that is, if he or she is skilled in getting the answers.

Knowing when and how to ask the right questions takes a combination of instinct and experience. The dos and don'ts that follow are culled from Information Data Search's experience in the field. They are not completely foolproof. Sometimes you may hit a string of successful calls; other times you may strike out.

Our apologies for making some of the suggestions sound almost too simple. But sometimes it may pay to belabor the obvious. After all, one man's forest is another man's trees. By employing these suggestions, you will be well on your way toward using the telephone as a powerful information-gathering tool.

Explain who you are and why you are calling. Play it straight. Tell who you are and why you are calling. By doing so, you become more than just a disembodied voice on the other end of the line. You become a person, accountable to some corporation or organization. You establish credibility, and put the contact at ease.

Have a name at hand.   Ask for a specific person. By knowing the names and titles of knowledgeable sources, you eliminate fishing for experts and avoid runarounds.

When in doubt, ask for public relations or personnel.   If you don't know who to talk to, ask for public relations. PR people generally know who's who and what's what in a company. They can either put you in touch with the experts in their firm or direct you to outside sources. They can also dig up organizational data or industry statistics in a hurry.

If public relations is of no help, ask for personnel. This area's strength is in locating the right department. It has organization charts handy, as well as divisional or group locations.

Don't be a know-it-all; don't act tough.   Most people love to talk about their areas of expertise, and will respond nicely to a disarming interviewer. Come on too strong, however, and the contact will go on the defensive and clam up. No one who feels threatened is going to offer information. Likewise, no one will talk freely if you appear to already have all the information you need, or can easily get it elsewhere.

Smile when you dial.   This is an old sales trick that also applies to any research setting. If you have a smile on your face when you talk on the phone, your voice carries that message to the person on the other end. And human nature being what it is, people are always more receptive to exuberance than they are to ennui.

Be humble, be naive.   Play it smart by acting dumb. By claiming to know little or nothing about the subject—but desperately wanting to learn— you will probably get a respondent to offer more information. Or else, the person may feel sorry for you and refer you to another source.

This technique also allows the researcher to ask questions until the information is clearly understood. In research, the only dumb question is the one that isn't asked.

To get a response, feed information.   Remember you are calling people out of the blue. To help orient their thought and adjust them to your thinking, tell them some of what you have found out to date and what you still need. Tell them about some of the industry gossip you have heard. Also, mention the gaps that your research still has.

Bracket data.   Many professionals refuse or feel hesitant in offering numbers or statistics off the top of their heads. They would rather refer to a textbook—which, of course, is never handy when you are calling.

Help them along by giving them a range of numbers to work with. For example: "Do you think sales are between $10 and $15 million, or are we talking more in the range of $50 to $75 million?" Another example might be: "Are we talking about five types of wiring or 50 types?"

Say you were referred. Referrals are door-openers. Whenever you call someone based on a referral, make sure that the first thing you tell that person is who referred you.

Exchange information. The maxim "You get nothing for nothing" holds very true when it comes to research.

You will encounter a lot of resistance if you are pestering someone who will gain nothing from your questions. No one likes to feel milked. U.S. government analysts may be the only exception; they are specifically hired to answer a taxpayer's questions.

For everyone else, however, swap information or offer to send them a small portion or summary of your results (without sacrificing confidentiality or disclosing too much of the report). This is an especially effective technique when soliciting information from service professionals (marketing consultants, management consultants) who make their living dispensing advice. They are not likely to give you any information unless you can offer something in return.

Your Sense of Timing, or How to Make Sure You Reach Your Expert

Bracketing your data and swapping information are excellent tips to use in order to make your interview successful. Of course, this assumes you are able to reach the interviewee in the first place. In order to better insure your getting through, I recommend following this advice.

Don't call on Mondays. Mondays are the best time to reach experts and the worst time for getting them to talk to you. Imagine your own situation. You probably have left a number of pressing needs hanging from your Friday departure. In addition, you are not yet in the frame of mind to be interviewed by anyone. The expert feels the same way.

Mornings are better than afternoons. By Tuesday, a person is in the workweek frame of mind. So, aside from Monday mornings, the early part of the workday is often the best time to reach executives. They have the fewest intrusions early in the day.

Try the contact twice, then call back once more. Three times should be enough. Your time is precious, too. If you do not find a potential respondent cooperative, then move on to the next one. Remember, there is always more than one expert.

WAR STORY 6

"Hello, Mr. Chairman"

A client had asked us to conduct a specialized series of interviews with a select group of CEOs, some of whom were heads of Fortune 500 corporations.

Now, when you think of the Fortune 500, you may imagine a monolithic skyscraper, on top of which is the executive suite. In that executive suite, you have visions of a mammoth office interior with an phalanx of secretaries guarding the CEO's sanctum sanctorum.

That all may have been true when we undertook the survey. Yet we still achieved a relatively high success rate. The reason was our timing.

Instead of calling during normal business hours (9 A.M. to 5 P.M.), we chose to call the CEOs at 7 or 7:30 A.M. Even the most devoted secretary had not yet appeared to screen the call. Security had answered the switchboard phone and just passed us through to the head of the company.

Don't overkill. Although many people admire persistence, few welcome pests. Do not make yourself a nuisance. People may refuse you because they just do not have the time to give that week. Should you create ill will at this first encounter, you may be closing doors to any future contact or additional surveys you will have to conduct.

Set up a call-back time.   If you set up a time to call back, the respondent will expect to hear from you and at least has to have some kind of answer to your questions. Generally, a respondent appreciates that you respect his or her time enough to schedule the interview.

Tell the respondent how long the interview will be.   Never say the interview "will take a few minutes." Any of you who have ever received one of these consumer telephone survey calls realize that the "few minutes" stated by the interviewer can often run into a half hour or more. Meanwhile, your supper has gone cold and your anger has heated up.

Keep your surveys relatively short, but always state an accurate time.

Also, it is always better to give an exact time, or one that sounds fairly precise. For example, state "This survey will take approximately two minutes and thirty seconds."

The Mason-Dixon Factor

The Mason-Dixon factor is one of those unspoken phenomena in corporate intelligence-gathering that is worth noting here.

I usually find Southern contacts far more friendly and approachable than those from the North. Now, this may be a gross generalization that will offend those from the North and will appear condescending to Southerners. But I find it a hard point to deny. After all, it was Benjamin Franklin who said something to the effect that "Generalizations are generally true."

It becomes an especially difficult factor to ignore when you have gotten 10 turn-downs from Northern contacts and then pick up the telephone again to call a Georgian or a Texan. All of a sudden, people start talking. You're asking the same questions in the same tone of voice. This time, the only difference is that people are talking to you—and they're nice, too!

There are exceptions to every rule. I have also found, for example, that larger Southern cities may be just as unfriendly as their Northern counterparts.

Yet, in general, those experts south of the Mason-Dixon line seem to have more time to spend, or at least give the researcher the courtesy of a thoughtful answer.

THE VALUE OF QUESTIONNAIRES

Questionnaires should be used as a matter of course when organizing even the simplest of projects. Usually associated with political pollsters, the questionnaire is one of the most effective tools for collecting competitor information.

One of the first steps a researcher should take when beginning a project is to design a survey form to use on the telephone. A survey form gives the interviewee a point of reference and a place from which the interviewer can branch out and ask other questions.

Because the intelligence-gathering process is such a precarious one, and you can never be certain where the answer will actually come from, a written questionnaire will help guide the researcher to the most likely places. It will take the person being interviewed step by step, hopefully leading to the answer you are seeking. In short, a well-written survey will insure that:

Everyone involved in the project is speaking the same language and asking the same questions.

The person being interviewed is being led logically through the area of interest.

At the project's end, the answers collected can be easily organized and sorted.

In this section we will discuss two fundamental questionnaire formats: linear and grid. Each serves a different purpose, and can be designed in open or closed-ended style. Table 2.2 describes each style. Samples of linear closed-ended and open-ended questionnaires follow.

A Grid Survey

Let's say you are handed an assignment to collect data on six competitors in the same industry. You realize that calling the same contacts back six times for each of the target companies would be ridiculous, not to mention a waste of your contacts' time. By the third call, you can be sure your contact will hang up on you. The result: not only have you lost a present contact, but you have also closed the door to any future inquiries with this contact.

A partial solution to this dilemma is the grid survey. The grid allows the researcher to pigeonhole the data into the right slot. It permits the researcher to quickly cover all the target companies and categories.

Drafting the grid is simple. In the leftmost column you list the companies you are studying. On the top row across you label each of the categories or topics you are covering (e.g., product pricing, size of salesforce, plant expansion). See the sample that follows.

The grid survey is a quick-and-dirty method for collecting preliminary data. It is not a good tool for in-depth inquiry, because of the limited space allotted for information on the grid itself. It also requires a researcher who is more attuned to the assignment than the researcher using the straightforward, linear questionnaire discussed in the first part of this section.

TABLE 2.2.   Types of Questionnaires and Their Uses

Type of Questionnaire	Advantages for Intelligence-Gathering
Linear, open-ended	Flexibility
	A conversation opener
	Allows for the unknown
	Doesn't box the interviewer in
Linear, closed-ended	Easy—doesn't require industry knowledge
	Contains listings of products
	Useful for quantitative data
	Allows for quick response time
Grid	Covers many companies in one interview
	Permits shorter answers (yet not as controlled as a linear questionnaire)

Linear, Closed-Ended Questionnaire—The Data Gatherer

Hello, my name is _____ and I am calling from Information Data Search. We are an independent research firm based in Cambridge, Massachusetts.

Could you give me a few minutes of your time to answer questions on the oil valve industry and a few companies that are in it?

[If YES, continue.] Thank you.

[If NO, thank the person for his or her time.]

1. Have you ever purchased products from either Marko-Valves, Lead Valves, or Excel-Valve? _____ YES _____ NO

2. In the past year, did you buy:

    _____ 1–5 valves

    _____ 6–10 valves

    _____ 10–20 valves

    _____ 20–50 valves

    _____ 50 or more (if so, how many? _____)

3. If you could estimate Marko's regional sales (in your region), would they be:

    _____ between 50 and 100 million

    _____ between 100 and 125 million

    _____ between 125 and 150 million

4. Do you feel that the last recession:

    _____ caused Marko to lay off workers

    _____ caused Marko to shut down its plant on occasion

    _____ had no effect on Marko's operations

    _____ caused its sales to climb

5. Do you think _____'s [mention one of the above companies] market share was:

    _____ 10% or less

    _____ between 10 and 15%

    _____ greater than 25%

Thank you for your time. Should I have any other questions, may I call you back? _____ Also, whom can you refer me to who might have dealt with Marko or any of the other companies in the past? Is there another company that may have purchased a large number of their valves in this area? Whom in Excel's sales department can you recommend I speak to?

Linear, Open-Ended Questionnaire—The Opinion Gatherer

Hello, my name is _____ and I am calling from Information Data Search. We are an independent research company based in Cambridge, Massachusetts.

Could you give me a few minutes to answer a half-dozen questions on the oil valve industry and some companies in it?

[If YES, continue.] Thank you.
[If NO, thank the respondent for his or her time.]

1. Have you ever used Marko-Valves, Lead Valves, or Excel-Valve products?

2. What do you think of their service?

3. Does this company send its salespeople out to you more than once a year? _____ If so, exactly how often? What do you think of its salesforce?

4. Do you know how many salespeople operate out of this office?

5. Tell me, do you know the salesforce size for _____ and _____ [the other two not discussed above]?

6. How many Marko-Valves have you bought in the past year?

7. Do you feel that Marko's market share in this line is greater than 50% or less than 50%? _____ How much less or more?

8. How do you think _____ [mention one of the above companies] weathered the recession? Were there layoffs, plant shutdowns?

Thank you for your time. Should I have any more questions, may I call you back? _____ Also, whom can you refer me to who might have dealt with Marko in the past? Is there another company that may have purchased a large number of their valves in this area? Whom in Excel's sales department can you recommend I speak to?

The sample grid questionnaire helped the interviewer investigate over six competitors and dozens of product lines—all on one page. Although the information entered in each box was limited, it did provide a quick means of comparison. Also, because one competitor's data fell right next to another's, the researcher could catch nuances in the data and return rapidly with further questions for the expert being interviewed.

Some Tips for Drafting an Intelligence Questionnaire

1. Always provide an introduction, where the researcher gives his or her name and affiliation, along with the project description.

2. Limit the questionnaire to five to ten questions and no more. After

Grid Questionnaire—The Data Gatherer for More Than One Company

Hello, my name is _____ and I am calling from Information Data Search. We are an independent research firm based in Cambridge, Massachusetts.

Could you give me a few minutes of your time to answer one or two questions on the oil valve industry and its product lines?

[If YES, continue.] Thank you.

[If NO, thank the person for his or her time.]

1. Have you bought any Marko, Excel, or Lead Valves in this past year?

[If YES, continue.]

2. I would like to go down a brief list of companies and their product lines. Can you tell me, to the best of your recollection, exactly how many valves you may have bought?

Company	2″ Valve	5″ Automatic Control Valve	2″ Valve with Filter
Marko			
Excel			
Lead			
U.S. Valve			
Lockwood			
Tennessee			
Treasure			

Thank you for your time. Should I have other questions, may I call you back? _____ Also, whom can you refer me to who might have dealt with Marko or any of the other companies in the past? Is there another company that may have purchased a large number of their valves in this area? Whom in Excel's sales department can you recommend I speak to?

all, if the person on the other end of the phone wants to talk, the questionnaire will act as a springboard to further questions. (Don't limit yourself to the questions on the sheet. Don't feel tied down by the survey's structure. Use it as a starting point. You may want to have a list of additional questions on the side in case you find an extremely valuable and talkative source.)

3. Always get the respondent's name and the title or position.

4. Incorporate familiar industry terminology into the questionnaire. Make the survey as conversational as possible.

This basic questionnaire should be used when you have one or two companies as a target, as in the sample grid questionnaire. In the instance where you must analyze a host of competitors using the same interview sources, then you should use a grid survey rather than a linear or simple questionnaire.

LEARN THE LINGO: KNOWING INDUSTRY JARGON

Learning an industry's catchall phrases and jargon can be one of the most difficult aspects of researching a company whose industry you know very little about. Have the fundamental terms at your fingertips. The experts you interview may have little patience for someone they perceive as coming to them unprepared.

The following are the best three ways you can quickly "get up to speed" on this new industry.

1. *Speak to an industry analyst.* This doesn't mean stockbrokers, for they will not have the time to explain the intricacies of an industry. After all, their job is to sell stock, not lecture to a new student.

Better yet, find a government analyst. The U.S. Department of Commerce has scores of them in Washington. To find the one that specializes in your category, look in the U.S. *Industrial Outlook Handbook* (a publication that is available at your local Government Printing Office bookstore).

2. *Locate a few key trade magazines and speak to their editors.* As long as you don't bend their ears too much, these editors will be happy to explain certain basics about their industry and its leaders. Also, it would help if, before calling them, you could read a handful of general articles on the subject and company you are investigating.

3. *Use an industry dictionary.* Almost every industry has one. This may contain the special production and technical terminology you will need when asking questions or writing your final report. Trade associations can steer you to the better reference sources. In addition, a well-equipped university library may have a collection of these special dictionaries. Many of the major dictionaries are mentioned in various industry sections throughout this book.

WHO IS AN EXPERT AND WHERE TO FIND ONE

Information Data Search conducted a survey of marketing and corporate planning executives back in 1982, asking them, among other things, whom they considered an expert.

Each executive had a variety of characteristics that he or she felt best described an expert. But the one characteristic that almost all mentioned was experience. Almost every respondent stated that an expert must have a certain number of years of experience in a field. The average number of years mentioned was 10 for a business generalist (such as a stockbroker or insurance executive) and 5 years or more for a technical expert (such as a computer programmer, electrical engineer, or chemist).

Respondents thought that a technical expert concentrates in one field almost from the start of his or her career and rapidly gains the necessary expertise; that is why 5 years is all that is needed. For example, an engineer who has worked on a computer language for 5 years will know that language thoroughly by the time 5 years have passed. On the other hand, a business generalist or business professional may take more years to gain the insight and overall wisdom of an industry. Because the generalist's area of learning is far broader, his or her learning curve takes that much more time.

Keeping the above in mind, Information Data Search then ran the above results against U.S. Department of Labor statistics and discovered that almost one-half (48.9 percent) of all technical professionals currently employed had been in their professions for at least 5 years, making them experts. Almost one-third (29.7 percent) of all general business professionals were employed 10 years or more, according to Department of Labor statistics.

This should tell the reader that experts are far easier to find than one might first suspect. And very often these experts are employed within one's own organization.

FRIENDLY VERSUS UNFRIENDLY SOURCES

A researcher gathering intelligence must realize that just as there are sources that will not talk, there are probably an equal number of sources that will supply the answers. But what usually occurs as the research begins is the following:

1. A researcher begins lining up contacts and starts making telephone calls.

2. By midday the researcher has not learned anything new, since most contacts turned him or her down flat.

3. By the day's end, the researcher concludes that it is impossible to get the information.

No company is an island unto itself. Chances are there are many more contacts this researcher has not yet reached who would be perfectly happy to answer questions. All the researcher has to realize is that for every unfriendly source, there is probably a friendly one. It's only a matter of *finding* that friendly source.

What Makes a Source Friendly?

A source that is friendly to a manufacturer may be totally unfriendly to a market research firm. Here is an example. A market researcher for a manufacturing firm needed to collect data on her competitors. So, she decided to call everyone and everybody in the industry for information. Here is a list of whom she contacted and their reactions:

Contact	Reaction to inquiry
Competing company	Unfriendly
Distributor	Friendly
Market research firm	Friendly
A competitor's sole-source supplier	Unfriendly
Government agency	Friendly

The reasons that the distributor, market research firm, and government agency were friendly were because they were an impartial observer (the government agency), saw a potential business relationship (the market research firm or distributor), or did not feel threatened (the distributor).

The reason that the competitor and the competitor's sole-source supplier felt threatened was because the source saw a direct threat (to the competitor), or the source would compromise an existing, competing relationship (with the sole-source supplier).

By taking a step back from your research and examining which sources you used, you will quickly distinguish between the friendly and unfriendly sources. To give yourself a better sense of perspective and a realistic sense of who will speak to you when you make contact, draft a list of all potential sources and tag them "friendly" or "unfriendly." This little exercise will save you time, frustration, and a lot of wasted energy.

STEPS IN SETTING UP A RESEARCH PROJECT

Once you have assembled your research team, how do you insure that your project will follow a smooth and efficient path? Here are some steps you can take to establish and organize your projects:

1. *Get the request in writing.* This applies whether your client is an in-house supervisor or an outside company. When the client places the questions down on paper, he or she is forced to think clearly and will more likely spell out the details of the project. Once you have the request in writing, pass out the request to all team members.

2. *Hold a first meeting.* At an initial meeting all team members can discuss the project. That will insure that everyone hears the same problem and project objectives.

3. *Hold end-of-day meetings.* To keep tight reign on the project and to make sure everyone is remaining locked on to the project's objectives, hold individual meetings at the end of the day to review progress and redesign part of the strategy, if necessary.

4. *Begin your library and field research at the same time.* Do not wait. This seems like a strange way to go about intelligence-gathering. Your first reaction might be: "Well, can't we learn what we need to know from either the field or the library research? Why do both at the same time?"

The answer lies in the nature of the work. Both the library work and the field work will offer you different results. Limiting yourself to just library research can severely restrict your view of the company, leaving you little insight as to other avenues to pursue and people to contact.

Just as damaging to your project's success would be the attitude that all you need to do is interview a few choice experts and then you will have your answer. You might find that after spending 10 hours on the phone, a single news article would have answered the question, if only you had looked for it in the first place.

> If there is any common problem in getting industry analyses underway, it is that researchers tend to spend too much time looking for published sources and using the library before they begin to tap field sources. . . . Published sources have a variety of limitations: timeliness, level of aggregation, depth, and so on. Although it is important to gain some basic understanding of the industry to maximize the value of field interviews, the researcher should not exhaust all published sources before getting into the field. On the contrary, clinical and library research should proceed simultaneously. They tend to feed on each other, especially if the researcher is aggressive in asking every field source to suggest published material about the industry. Field sources tend to be more efficient because they get to the issues, without the wasted time of reading useless documents. Interviews also sometimes help the researcher identify the issues. This may come, to some extent, at the expense of objectivity. *

5. *Use one depository for literature.*   Any literature you collect should go into one common filing folder or bin. When researchers get the notion that they can begin accumulating literature in their own personal files, you will begin seeing duplication and wasted effort.

6. *Keep track of the experts.*   Once you have found a contact who proves to be a valuable source of information, don't lose this person. Maintain that list of key contacts and later, after the project has ended, enter these names onto a central list.

7. *Use a single outline.*   Before starting, make sure everyone involved uses the same outline and understands the questions to be answered.

THE IMPORTANCE OF DEBRIEFING

Look back on any intelligence-gathering project you completed. Think of all the sources you leafed through or called. They may number in the dozens or in the hundreds.

---

* Michael E. Porter, *Competitive Strategy* (New York: The Free Press/Macmillan, 1980), p. 371.

Project Debriefing Form

Project title_____

Project _____ Analyst's name _____

Total billable time _____   _____

STATISTICS

Number of telephone calls attempted: _____

Number of telephone calls completed: _____

Number of valuable calls: _____

VALUED SOURCES

What were some of the most productive and valuable sources you used for this assignment? (You can include: data bases, newspapers, directories, certain contacts you made.)

Valued Source   Why?

_____   _____

_____   _____

_____   _____

_____   _____

_____   _____

_____   _____

_____   _____

NEW SOURCES

What were some of the new and unusual sources you could recommend for future projects (e.g., government agencies, new data bases, types of directories)?

New Source   How best used?

_____   _____

_____   _____

_____   _____

_____   _____

New Source   How best used?

_____   _____

_____   _____

_____   _____

GENERAL COMMENTS

Based on your experience with this assignment, how can future projects be more efficiently run? Was there an aspect of this assignment and the way it was carried out that was highly inefficient?

_____

Now, ask yourself what will occur when you are asked six months down the road to research a similar company. In those six months you have undertaken other assignments; your mind has gone to other important matters. So, you begin to research this new company, and you begin scratching your head. "Wasn't there a source we used last time that was very effective? Yes, I think there was, except I can't remember what it was or whom to call."

If this sounds familiar, you are in very good company. Even the meticulous researcher fails to keep perfect notes. That is why you should, at the end of every project, debrief yourself and every other researcher who participated in the project.

A thorough debriefing can serve these purposes:

It can record vital research statistics such as the number of phone calls made for a project. This collected data, when compared to data in other projects, can assist researchers in estimating the amount of time they may expect to spend on subsequent projects or how many phone calls need to be made in order to achieve success.

A good debriefing will teach others which sources prove most valuable and why.

Almost invariably, every company investigation will turn up one or two new sources that you found extremely worthwhile. The debriefing will bring these new gems out.

By the same token, there will be sources or techniques that were time-wasters and resulted in many unproductive hours. This kind of information should also appear on a debriefing form.

On the preceding pages is a sample format you may want to use in a debriefing. A debriefing should not be a long and arduous talk that consumes hours of a researcher's time. It should take no more than a half hour to fill out, and should tell the reader at a glance exactly what went right and what went wrong with the research.

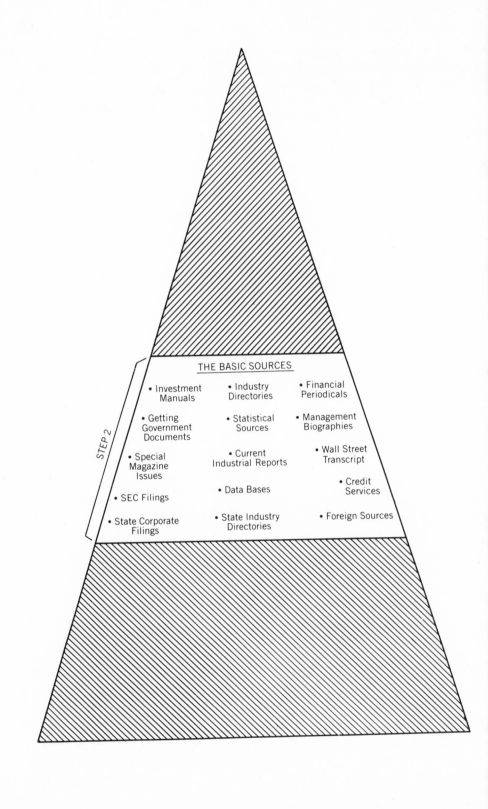

STEP 2

THE BASIC SOURCES

- Investment
  Manuals

- Industry
  Directories

- Financial
  Periodicals

- Getting
  Government
  Documents

- Statistical
  Sources

- Management
  Biographies

- Special
  Magazine
  Issues

- Current
  Industrial Reports

- Wall Street
  Transcript

- SEC Filings

- Data Bases

- Credit
  Services

- State Corporate
  Filings

- State Industry
  Directories

- Foreign Sources

PART 2

THE BASIC SOURCES OF INTELLIGENCE

This book is filled with many unusual intelligence sources, sources that will often get you the answers to such difficult questions as plant capacity or marketing plans. But remember, do not forget the obvious!

Wouldn't it be embarrassing to have spent days on the telephone trying to find the number of employees at a competitor's plant or office, only to discover that the information was already contained in an article in an industry trade magazine?

That is the pitfall this section hopes to help you avoid, the pitfall of "Wouldn't-it-be-embarrassing." In a series of annotated lists and descriptive sections, I will take you through a wide variety of vital sources you will need to begin your intelligence-gathering. These sources range from federal and state filings to specialty magazines, investment manuals, and data bases. In each case, I have included only those sources that offer company-specific information.

Learn from my embarrassing moments. Use the basic intelligence sources before you jump too quickly into the exotic and unusual sources. Save that for Part 3, Creative Sources and Techniques.

CHAPTER 3

FEDERAL, STATE,
AND LOCAL SOURCES

FINANCIALS FROM UNCLE SAM'S LIBRARY

There are literally hundreds of published sources that offer financial histories of companies. Some simply list the income statements and balance sheets; others will present full write-ups on the company along with a description of the officers and any acquisitions or mergers that may have taken place. This section brings all the commonly known as well as some of the lesser known sources together.

Public Filings—Federal, State, and Local

SEC Filings. Whenever you ask researchers where they would go to find company financials, the first question they ask is: "Do you have an SEC filing on the company?"

Since 1934, when the Securities and Exchange Commission was established, publicly traded companies have come under ever increasing scrutiny. Because corporations are accountable to the Federal Government, they must file highly detailed accounts of their performance.

When researching a publicly traded company, the first place you should turn for a historic analysis of the company is one of over a dozen types of SEC reports, whether it be a 10-K (annual financial report), 10-Q (a quarterly financial filing), proxy (special event report given to stockholders to vote on), or one of the lesser-known filings.

Until the mid-1970s, there was only one basic way to locate and retrieve an SEC report: write the Commission and wait two to three weeks to receive the report. Today you have many alternatives. Here are your options:

WRITE TO THE SEC.　This is the slowest but least expensive route you can take. For no more than the cost of a postage stamp you can receive as many reports as you wish—but the order may still take weeks to arrive. To order a report, write:

Securities and Exchange Commission
1100 L Street, N. W.
Washington, DC 20549

GO TO THE SEC REFERENCE ROOM.　If you are in Washington, you can pore over the SEC documents yourself. They are located at:

Securities and Exchange Commission Building
Public Reference Room
500 North Capitol Street, N. W.
Washington, DC 20549

There are also regional SEC offices with limited collections. These too are available for public inspection. Their locations are as follows:

Everett McKinley Dirksen Building
219 S. Dearborn Street　　　　　　　　　10960 Wilshire Boulevard
Chicago, IL 60604　　　　　　　　　　　Los Angeles, CA 90024
312–353–7433　　　　　　　　　　　　　213–473–4511

26 Federal Plaza
Room 1100
New York, NY 10007
212–264–1614

FOR SPEEDY SERVICE, USE DISCLOSURE.　Disclosure, Inc. is a private company that is the SEC's sole vendor for the private reproduction and distribution of its report filings. This company has made SEC reports easy to find and easy to retrieve. The service's features include:

An 800 number, to check where and when a particular SEC report was filed. Disclosure's operators are extremely helpful and will answer your questions almost immediately.

Disclosure will either make paper copies of the report for you at a cost of less than 35 cents per page or accept an order for the entire filing on microfiche for $10 per report.

For even faster service, you can retrieve the 10-K and 10-Q financials and company description on-line, through Disclosure's data base.

To contact Disclosure, call or write:

Disclosure, Inc.
5161 River Road
Bethesda, MD 20816
800–638–8241

SEC Filings and What They Reveal

Filing Type	Filing Period	Contents	How It Is Used
10-K	Annually (company's fiscal year)	Income statement Balance sheet Sales by product line Application of funds Auditor's name and opinion Debt structure Management analysis Depreciation and other schedules Dilution factors Earnings per share	Financial analysis Strategic planning and marketing changes Changes in product line

Filing Type	Filing Period	Contents	How It Is Used
		Foreign operations	
		Plants and property	
		Securities structure	
		Subsidiaries	
		Industry description	
		Discussion of new developments in the industry	
		Major court suits	
N-1R	Annually, for management investment companies	Portfolio operations	Investment company structure
		Income statement	
		Balance sheet	
		Debt sheet	
		Earnings per share	
		Family affiliations	
		Company staffing	
10-Q	Quarterly reports by publicly traded companies	Income statement	Observe quarterly changes in company
		Balance sheet to date (statements unaudited)	
		Earnings per share	
		Dividends paid	
Proxy statement	For shareholders to vote	Holdings and compensation of officers, directors, and insiders	Locate officers' earnings
Prospectus	When company first issues stock	Auditor's name	Learn about a new company
		Company history	

Filing Type	Filing Period	Contents	How It Is Used
	or offers new issues	Debt structure	and financial history before it was publicly traded
		Depreciation and other schedules	
		Identification, holdings, and compensation of officers	
		Legal counsel	
		Product-line breakout	
		Securities structure	
		Subsidiaries	
		Underwriters	
Schedule 13-D	Major stock acquisition (5% or more of the company's stock)	Transactions purchased	Trace major stock shifts and purchases
		Securities description	
		Issuer's background	
		Number of shares owned	
Schedule 14-D	Tender offer	Reason for offer	Discover reason for rejection of tender offer
		Description of issuer and the security	
		Information on any transactions between the two parties	
6-K	At time foreign stock is publicly traded in the U.S.	Income statement	Conduct a financial analysis on company
		Balance sheet	
		Major company changes	
		Officers' backgrounds	

The Weakness of Government Sources

Competitor intelligence, by definition, is timely. Government information too often is not.

If you can find your answer in time to make a business decision, then the intelligence you have gathered is invaluable. Should you miss that deadline, or provide dated information, then all your efforts could be wasted. For example, state, and federal filings are usually published months or years after the fact.

Government reports are useful sources of historical data, but do not rely on them for up-to-the-minute information. In some cases, government reports may be the only source you have, period. I am thinking of EPA or FCC filings, which we will discuss later on in the book.

This is the principal rule of thumb for retrieving intelligence from government sources:

A company will only disclose what it is forced to. Nothing more.

Government sources are weakest for management background, financials on privately held corporations, change in organization structure, marketing plans, new product introductions, foreign competitors, and subsidiaries of publicly traded companies.

Government sources are best used for plant size (square footage), environmentally regulated production processes, publicly traded corporations, and general historical data on an industry.

As I keep stating throughout the book, always do your homework and never overlook the obvious sources. That includes government sources. They may only supply you with 10 percent of your valuable intelligence—but that may be the 10 percent you could not find anywhere else.

STATE YOUR CASE: STATE CORPORATE FILINGS

While all 50 states require corporations to file annual reports and other financially related documents, very few of these filings will do you, the researcher, any good. Most are no more than a yearly registration form. All they ask for is name, address, and names of officers. For such a monumentally auspicious name—Annual Report—they deliver very little.

Fear not. There are the exceptions that make every rule. A number of states do require that their incorporated companies file far more than just the company's name and address.

Figures 3.1 and 3.2 give examples of state annual report forms.

APPROVED

By _____

Date _____

Amount _____

_____ **FORM 7**

Annual Statement of Proportion of Capital Stock

O ANTHONY J. CELEBREZZE, JR.
ecretary of State,
olumbus, Ohio.

_____ , 19____

_____ , a corporation organized under the laws

_____ , with its principal office at _____

nd its Ohio office located at _____ , having assets

Ohio located in the counties of _____ ,

nd having assets located without the State at _____ ,

compliance with Section 1703.07 of the Ohio Revised Code makes the following statement:

Said corporation holds license No. _____ , issued on _____ , 19____

Said corporation's purpose is _____

This report is made as of _____ , which is *the date of the ending of*
(Date)

the corporation's accounting period in the preceding calendar year. (See Note No. 2 on reverse side).

The book value (exclude goodwill) of Ohio assets is _____
(See Note No. 4 on reverse side).

Amount of business transacted in Ohio last year was _____

  Sums of Items 4 and 5 _____

Book value (exclude goodwill) of all assets is _____

Total business transacted in last year was _____

  Sums of Items 6 and 7 _____

a. Number of authorized shares _____

b. Number of issued shares _____

Notice of fees due may be mailed to _____

0. Corporation's statutory agent in Ohio is _____

Agent's address is _____

Issued Shares	_____
Decimal	_____
Present Prop.	_____
Prior Prop.	_____
Increase	_____
Fee Due	_____
Penalty (15%)	_____
Total	_____

DO NOT USE THIS SPACE

(Signed) _____

By _____
(Must be an officer of corporation)

TATE OF _____
} s.s.
OUNTY OF _____

Personally appeared before me, a notary public, in and for said county and state, this _____

ay of _____ , 19____ , the above named _____
ho, being duly sworn, did depose and say that he was authorized to make the foregoing statement and
hat the averments therein are true and correct according to his best knowledge and belief.

Witness my hand and official seal on the day and year last aforesaid.

(SEAL)   Notary Public.

INSTRUCTIONS ON REVERSE

Figure 3.1. Examples of two state corporate annual reports.

DO NOT WRITE IN THIS SPACE

CORPORATION
ANNUAL REPORT
1982

George Firestone
Secretary of State

FLORIDA DEPARTMENT OF STATE

DIVISION OF CORPORATIONS

Read Notice and Instructions on Other Side Before Making Entries
► **Filing Fee of $10 Required — Make Checks Payable To:** *Secretary of State* ◄

1. Name and Address of Corporation Principal Office:	2. Enter Change of Address of Corporation Principal Office, P.O. Box Number Alone is NOT Sufficient.
⌐ ¬	Street Address
	P.O. Box No.
	City
L ⌐	State Zip Code
If above address is incorrect in any way, enter the correct address in Item 2. Include Zip Code.	

3. Date Incorporated or Qualified To Do Business in Florida	4. Federal Employer Identification Number (FEIN)	5. Date of Last Report

6. Names and Street Addresses of Each Officer and Director

Names of Officers and Directors	Title	Street Address of Each Officer and Director (Do NOT Use Post Office Box Numbers)	City and State

Registered Agent Information

7. Name and Address of Current Registered Agent	8. Name and Address of New Registered Agent
	Name
	Street Address (Do NOT Use P.O. Box Number)
	City, State and Zip Code

9. Pursuant to the provisions of Sections 607.034 and 607.037, Florida Statutes, the undersigned corporation, organized under the laws of the State of Florida, submits this statement for the purpose of changing its registered office or registered agent, or both, in the state of Florida.

Such change was authorized by resolution duly adopted by its board of directors on: _____

SIGNATURE _____ DATE _____
(Registered Agent Accepting Appointment)
$3.00 additional fee required for Registered Agent changes.

10. *See signature restrictions under instructions on reverse side of this form.*

I Certify That I Am An Officer of the Corporation, the Receiver or Trustee Empowered to Execute This Report as Required by Chapter 607 F.S.
I further Certify That I Understand My Signature On This Report Shall Have The Same Legal Effect As if Made Under Oath.

Signature	Date
Typed Name of Signing Officer	Title	Telephone Number

COR 620 (11-81)

Figure 3.1. *(Continued)*

FOREIGN LIMITED PARTNERSHIP ANNUAL REPORT
(Please read instructions before completing this form.)

1. The name of the Partnership _____

   The mailing address of the Partnership _____

BALANCE SHEET

2. Complete the Balance Sheet for the limited partnership:

   Balance sheet as of _____
   (Tax closing date)

ASSETS   LIABILITIES AND INVESTED CAPITAL

(Do not write in shaded areas.)

	AMOUNT	TOTAL		AMOUNT	TOTAL
a. Cash			o. Accounts payable		
b. Trade notes and accounts receivable • Less allowance for bad debts			p. Mortgages, notes, bonds payable in less than 1 year		
c. Inventories			q. Other current liabilities		
d. Government obligations: • U.S. and instrumentalities • State, subdivisions, thereof, etc.					
e. Other current assets			r. Loans from partners		
f. Loans to partners			s. Mortgages, notes, bonds payable in 1 year or more		
g. Mortgage and real estate loans					
h. Other investments			t. Other liabilities		
i. Buildings and other fixed depreciable assets • Less accumulated depreciation			u. Total liabilities		
j. Depletable assets • Less accumulated depreciation			v. Invested capital:		
k. Land (net of any amortization)			• Limited partners		
l. Intangible assets (amortizable only) • Less accumulated amortization			• General partners		
			w. Total invested capital		
m. Other assets					
n. TOTAL ASSETS			x. TOTAL LIABILITIES AND INVESTED CAPITAL		

3. Complete the reconciliation of the partners' capital accounts:

a. Capital account at beginning of year	b. Capital contributed during year	c. Ordinary income (loss)	d. Income not included in column c. plus non-taxable income	e. Losses not included in column c. plus unallowable deductions	f. Withdrawals and distributions	g. Capital account at end of year

Figure 3.2. Foreign limited partnership annual report.

WAR STORY 7

One Telephone Call and 2000 Pages Later

Ninety-nine out of one hundred times a search through the state corporate records is a pro forma task that yields poor results.

In this case, we needed to retrieve an Illinois company's financials and amendments for the past five years. When we received a letter back from the office of corporations in Illinois we were shocked—shocked to find that it could retrieve and copy over 2000 pages of documentation, if we were willing to spend approximately $250 in copying fees.

Some of this material offered detailed balance sheet and income statements.

Note—This was a fruitful search, but only because we knew which forms or reports to ask for. All too often you will encounter clerks who will not give you the time of day, let alone assist you in finding the desired filing. Have someone at the corporate office list the documents that are on file or send you a packet of sample documents. With sample documents in hand, you can see at a glance what categories the state requires corporations to file and the necessary details.

Information Data Search surveyed each state for the reports each requires. The results are given in the state corporate filings list later in this section. Where a state's Office of Corporations did not request data other than name and address or did not offer an adequate explanation of its forms, we offer no description in the list. In cases where states demand a more lengthy report from resident companies, we listed the report's name and its features.

Should you need further details about the forms and reporting requirements, contact the appropriate office mentioned on the list. Generally speaking, states have the following types of offices, each containing the type of information indicated:

Corporations Office.   Most state corporate offices require resident companies to file these documents, which can be found in the corporations office:

Articles of incorporation.

Amendments to articles.

Consolidation notices.

Merger announcements.

Corporate name changes.

Franchiser filings.

Occupational Safety Office. This office can be useful when you need to find out the types of machinery and processes that operate in a plant. This office will record state inspections and reports of dangerous machinery.

State Securities Office. This office acts as a state SEC, requiring each company offering a certain amount of stock within the state to file a prospectus.

Uniform Commercial Code Office. This office will be described in some detail in Chapter 14. Its primary duty is to record all commercial loans within the state. The UCC office maintains records that contain the borrower's name, the loan's purpose, and its maturity date.

State Corporate Filings

ALABAMA

Corporate Filings	Occupational Safety Filings
Office of the Secretary of State Corporate Division 524 State Office Building Montgomery, AL 36130 205–832–6855	Labor Department 64 North Union Street Montgomery, AL 36130 205–832–6270

Securities Filings	UCC Filings
Alabama Securities Commission 100 Commerce Street Montgomery, AL 36130 205–832–5733	Office of the Secretary of State UCC Division State Office Building, Room 536 Montgomery, AL 36130 205–832–3572

ALASKA

Report Type	Special Features
Annual report	Primary, secondary, and tertiary SIC codes. Authorized shares and par value.

Report Type	Special Features
	Issued shares: class, series, and par value.
	Names and addresses of officers and directors.
	Names, addresses, and nature of relationship between corporate and alien affiliates.
	Name and address of person having direct ownership or control of at least 50% of any class of shares.

Corporate Filings	Occupational Safety Filings
Department of Commerce and Economic Development Corporation Section Pouch D Juneau, AK 99811 907–465–2531	Division of Occupational Safety and Health Department of Labor Box 630 Juneau, AK 99811 907–465–4855

Securities Filings	UCC Filings
Division of Banking, Securities and Corporations Department of Commerce and Economic Development Pouch D Juneau, AK 99811 907–465–2521	Department of Administration Uniform Commercial Code P. O. Box 3336 Juneau, AK 99811 907–274–0212

ARIZONA

Report Type	Special Features
Annual report	Aggregate number of shares.
	Number authorized, class series, and par value.
Merger/consolidation (required listing—no standard form)	Names of stockholders who own at least 20% of stock.

Report Type	Special Features
	Names and addresses of officers and directors with date on which each assumed office.

Corporate Filings	Occupational Safety Filings
Corporate Commission 1200 West Washington Street P. O. Box 6019 Phoenix, AZ 85005 602–255–3026	Division of Occupational Safety and Health Industrial Commission of Arizona P. O. Box 19070 Phoenix, AZ 85005 602–255–5795

Securities Filings	UCC Filings
Securities Commission 1210 West Washington Street Suite 210-E Phoenix, AZ 85009 602–255–4242	Secretary of State 1700 West Washington Street Phoenix, AZ 85007 602–252–8221

ARKANSAS

Corporate Filings	Occupational Safety Filings
Secretary of State Corporation Division State Capitol Building Little Rock, AR 72201 501–371–5151	Department of Labor Security Division 1022 High Street Little Rock, AR 72202 501–375–8442

Securities Filings	UCC Filings
Securities Department No. 1 Capitol Mall Suite 4B-206 Little Rock, AR 72201 501–371–1011	Secretary of State UCC Division State Capitol Building Little Rock, AR 72201 501–371–5078

CALIFORNIA

Corporate Filings	Occupational Safety Filings
Secretary of State Corporate Filing Division 1230 J Street Sacramento, CA 95814 916–445–0620	Division of Occupational Safety and Health P. O. Box 603 San Francisco, CA 94101 415–557–1946

Securities Filings	UCC Filings
Department of Corporations 600 South Commonwealth Avenue Los Angeles, CA 90005 213–736–2741	Secretary of State UCC Division P. O. Box 1738 Sacramento, CA 95808 916–445–8061

COLORADO

Report Type	Special Features
Annual report	Federal employer ID number. Issued and authorized shares, par value. Names and addresses of directors.

Corporate Filings	Occupational Safety Filings
Secretary of State Corporations Division 1575 Sherman Street Denver, CO 80203 303–866–2361	Division of Labor Department of Labor and Employment 1313 Sherman Street, 3rd Floor Denver, CO 80203 303–866–2782

Securities Filings	UCC Filings
Division of Securities 1575 Sherman Street Denver, CO 80203 303–866–2607	Secretary of State UCC Division 1575 Sherman Street Denver, CO 80203 303–866–2563

CONNECTICUT

Corporate Filings	Occupational Safety Filings
Office of the Secretary of State Corporation Division 30 Trinity Street Hartford, CT 06101 203–566–3216	Occupational Safety and Health Administration Connecticut Department of Labor 200 Folly Brook Boulevard Wethersfield, CT 06109 203–566–4550

Securities Filings	UCC Filings
Securities Division State Banking Department 165 Capitol Avenue State Office Building Hartford, CT 06106 203–566–5783	Office of the Secretary of State UCC Division 30 Trinity Street Hartford, CT 06115 203–566–4020

DELAWARE

Corporate Filings	Occupational Safety Filings
Secretary of State Corporations Department P. O. Box 898 Dover, DE 19901 302–736–4221	Industrial Accident Board Division of Industrial Affairs Department of Labor State Office Building 820 North French Street Wilmington, DE 19801 302–571–2884

Securities Filings	UCC Filings
Office of the Securities Commissioner State Office Building 820 North French Street, 8th Floor Wilmington, DE 19801 302–571–2515	Secretary of State Uniform Commercial Code Division P. O. Box 793 Dover, DE 19901 302–678–4279

FLORIDA

Report Type	Special Features
Annual report	Federal employer ID number.
	Date of incorporation.
	Date of last report.

Corporate Filings	Occupational Safety Filings
Secretary of State	Industrial Safety Section
Division of Corporations	Bureau of Workmen's Compensation
Capitol Building, Room 2001	Department of Labor and
Tallahassee, FL 32304	Employment Security
904–488–9000	2551 Executive Center Circle, West
	204 Lafayette Building
	Tallahassee, FL 32301
	904–488–3044

Securities Filings	UCC Filings
Division of Securities	Secretary of State
Capitol Building, Suite 1402	UCC Division
Tallahassee, FL 32304	P. O. Box 5588
904–488–9805	Tallahassee, FL 32301
	904–488–1010

GEORGIA

Report Type	Special Features
Annual report (domestic and foreign)	Incorporation date.
	Date of last report.

Corporate Filings	Securities Filings
Secretary of State	Secretary of State
Corporations Department	Securities Division
200 Piedmont Avenue	2 Martin Luther King Drive
Atlanta, GA 30334	State Capitol, Room 216
404–656–2185	802 West Tower
	Atlanta, GA 30334
	404–656–2894

UCC Filings

Securities Division
2 Martin Luther King Drive
State Capitol, Room 216
802 West Tower
Atlanta, GA 30334
404–656–2894

HAWAII

Report Type	Special Features
Annual report	Stock—paid-in capital Authorized stock par value and par share.

Corporate Filings	Occupational Safety Filings
Business Registration Division Department of Regulatory Agencies P. O. Box 40 Honolulu, HI 96810 808–548–6521	Occupational Safety and Health Division Department of Labor and Industrial Relations 677 Ala Moana Boulevard, Suite 910 Honolulu, HI 96813 808–548–7511

Securities Filings	UCC Filings
Business Registration Division Department of Regulatory Agencies P. O. Box 40 Honolulu, HI 96810 808–548–6521	Bureau of Conveyances P. O. Box 2867 Honolulu, HI 96803 808–548–3108

IDAHO

Report Type	Special Features
Annual report	Federal employer number. Corporate number.

Corporate Filings	Occupational Safety Filings
Secretary of State Corporations Division State House, Room 203 Boise, ID 83720 208–384–2300	Industrial Commission 317 Main Street State House Boise, ID 83720 208–384–3250

Securities Filings	UCC Filings
Securities Division Department of Finance State House Boise, ID 83720 208–384–3684	Secretary of State UCC Division State House, Room 205 Boise, ID 83720 208–384–2300

ILLINOIS

Report Type	Special Features
Annual report	Officers: names and home addresses.
	Number of shares authorized and issued.
	Stated capital and paid-in surplus.
	Value of property in and out of Illinois.
	Gross amount of business transacted by corporation elsewhere.
	Gross amount of business transactions in Illinois.
	Location of principal places of business in each state where authorized, and amount of business transacted in each state.
Articles of merger/consolidation	Plan of merger/consolidation.
	Number of shares outstanding, assignation of class entitled to vote, number of shares of such class.
	Number of shares additional in treasury.

Report Type	Special Features
	Number of shares for and against merger/consolidation.

Corporate Filings	Securities Filings
Secretary of State Corporation Department Centennial Building Springfield, IL 62756 217–782–7880	Secretary of State Securities Department 151 Bruns Lane Springfield, IL 62756 217–782–2256

UCC Filings	
Secretary of State UCC Division Centennial Building, Room 300 Springfield, IL 62756 217–782–7518	

INDIANA

Report Type	Special Features
Corporate report	Number of shares authorized and issued with par value, no par value, par value per share, series. Share dividend.
Articles of merger (two companies into one)	Manner of adoption and vote. Statement of changes in authorized stock.
Articles of merger (subsidiary into parent)	Plan of merger. Shares outstanding.

Corporate Filings	Occupational Safety Filings
Secretary of State Corporation Division State House, Room 155 Indianapolis, IN 46204 317–232–6576	Department of Occupational Safety and Health Division of Labor State Office Building, Room 1013 Indianapolis, IN 46204 317–232–5845

Securities Filings	UCC Filings
Securities Division State House, Room 102 Indianapolis, IN 46204 317–232–6681	Secretary of State UCC Division State House, Room 106 Indianapolis, IN 46204 317–232–6393

IOWA

Report Type	Special Features
Articles of merger/consolidation	No standard form, must be drawn up from Code of Iowa referring to the appropriate chapter of incorporation laws.
Annual report (foreign)	Stock issued and authorized.
	Entire amount of stated capital.
	Fair and reasonable value of all property used in Iowa.
Annual report (domestic)	Directors' names and addresses.
	Stock authorized and issued.
	Entire stated capital amount.

Corporate Filings	Occupational Safety Filings
Secretary of State Corporation Division Hoover Office Building Des Moines, IA 50319 515–281–5204	Bureau of Labor 307 East 7th Street Des Moines, IA 50319 515–281–3606

Securities Filings	UCC Filings
Securities Division Lucas State Office Building Des Moines, IA 50319 515–281–4441	Secretary of State UCC Division Hoover State Office Building Des Moines, IA 50319 515–281–3226

KANSAS

Report Type	Special Features
Annual report	Original certificate of good standing must accompany form.
	Last election data for officers and directors.
	Names and addresses of directors, officers.
	Authorized and issued stock, par value.
	Value of properties owned.
	Balance sheet.
	Farming land owned.
Articles of merger/consolidation	No standard form.
Foreign limited partner	Assets and liabilities.
	Reconciliation of partners' capital accounts.

Corporate Filings	Occupational Safety Filings
Secretary of State Corporate Department The Statehouse, 2nd Floor Topeka, KS 66612 913–296–2236	Industrial Safety Section Division of Labor Management Relations Department of Human Resources 512 West 6th Street Topeka, KS 66603 913–296–4386

Securities Filings	UCC Filings
Securities Commission 109 West 9th Street Topeka, KS 66612 913–296–3307	Secretary of State UCC Department The Statehouse Topeka, KS 66612 913–296–4587

KENTUCKY

Corporate Filings	Occupational Safety Filings
Office of the Secretary of State Corporate Division Capitol Building, Room 154 Frankfort, KY 40601 502–564–7330	Occupational Safety and Health Department of Labor U. S. 127 South Frankfort, KY 40601 502–564–7360

Securities Filings	UCC Filings
Division of Securities Department of Banking Securities 911 Leawood Drive Frankfort, KY 40601 502–564–2180	Office of the Secretary of State Corporate Division Capitol Building, Room 154 Frankfort, KY 40601 502–564–3490

LOUISIANA

Corporate Filings	Occupational Safety Filings
Secretary of State Corporate Division P. O. Box 44125 Baton Rouge, LA 70804 504–925–4704	Occupational Safety and Health Department of Labor P. O. Box 44094 Baton Rouge, LA 70804 504–342–3126

Securities Filings	UCC Filings
Commissioner of Securities 325 Loyola Avenue State Office Building, Room 315 New Orleans, LA 70112 504–568–5515	UCC filings are not required in Louisiana.

MAINE

Report Type	Special Features
Articles of merger (Maine corporation into Maine corporation)	Plan of merger. Number of shares outstanding, entitled to vote, voted for and against each corporation.

Report Type	Special Features
	Designation and number of shares in each class, and number voted for and against for each corporation.
	Designation of class, number of shares outstanding before merger and after merger.
Articles of merger (Maine subsidiary into Maine parent company)	Number of outstanding shares, designation of class, and percent of shares owned by surviving parent.
	Date of mailing of merger plan to shareholders.
Articles of merger (domestic and foreign companies)	Plan of merger.
	Number of outstanding shares, number entitled to vote, number voted for and against for each corporation.
	Designation of class, number of shares, number for and against for each corporation.
	Designation of class, number of shares outstanding before and after merger.
Articles of merger (parent-subsidiary merger of domestic and foreign corporations)	Plan of consolidation.
	Number of stocks outstanding, number of shares entitled to vote, number voted for and against for each corporation.
	Designation of class, number of shares, number voted for and against for each corporation.

Corporate Filings	Occupational Safety Filings
Secretary of State Corporation Division State Office Building Augusta, ME 04333 207–289–3676	Department of Manpower Affairs Bureau of Labor State Office Building Augusta, ME 04333 207–289–3331

Securities Filings	UCC Filings
Securities Division	Secretary of State
Bureau of Banking	UCC Division
Department of Business Regulation	State Office Building
State Office Building	Augusta, ME 04333
Augusta, ME 04333	207–289–3676
207–289–2261	

MARYLAND

Report Type	Special Features
Assessments and Taxation Department—Annual report	Names, addresses of officers.
	Total cost, depreciation rate, and book value of furniture, fixtures, and equipment.
	Value of physical inventory at cost or market of raw materials and supplies.
	Ships, vessels, floating equipment, and water craft of all kinds over 100 feet long.
	Livestock.
	Motor vehicles.
	Tools, machinery, and equipment for manufacturing and other purposes.
	Supplies and tangible personal property.

Corporate Filings	Occupational Safety Filings
State Department of Assessment	Occupational Safety and Health
301 West Preston Street	Advisory Board
Baltimore, MD 21201	Division of Labor and Industry
301–383–3720	Department of Licensing and Regulation
	501 St. Paul Place
	Baltimore, MD 21202
	301–659–4195

Securities Filings	UCC Filings
Division of Securities 501 St. Paul Place Baltimore, MD 21202 301–576–6360	State Department of Assessment and Taxation 301 West Preston Street Baltimore, MD 21201 301–383–3330

MASSACHUSETTS

Report Type	Special Features
Articles of merger	Total number of shares authorized, par value and dollar amount.
	Description of each class of stock, with preferences, voting power, qualifications, and special privileges.
	Names, residence, and post office addresses of officers.
	Stockholders' meeting date.
Annual report	Federal identification number.
	Class of stock—number authorized and number of outstanding shares.

Corporate Filings	Occupational Safety Filings
Secretary of State Corporations Division 1 Ashburton Place, 17th Floor Boston, MA 02108 617–727–9640	Department of Labor and Industries Executive Office of Economic Affairs 100 Cambridge Street Boston, MA 02202 617–727–3455

Securities Filings	UCC Filings
Secretary of State Securities Division 1 Ashburton Place, Room 1719 Boston, MA 02108 617–727–7190	Secretary of State UCC Division 1 Ashburton Place, Room 1711 Boston, MA 02108 617–727–2860

MICHIGAN

Corporate Filings	Occupational Safety Filings
Department of Commerce Corporation and Securities Bureau P. O. Box 30054 Lansing, MI 48909 517–373–2901	Bureau of Safety and Regulation Department of Labor P. O. Box 30015 7150 Harris Drive Lansing, MI 48909 517–322–1814

Securities Filings	UCC Filings
Department of Commerce Corporation and Securities Bureau P. O. Box 30222 6546 Mercantile Way Lansing, MI 48909 517–373–0485	Secretary of State UCC Unit 7064 Crowner Drive Lansing, MI 48918 517–373–0810

MINNESOTA

Report Type	Special Features
Annual report (foreign)	Must hold "Certificate of Authority to Transact Business in MN." Name, title, and address of officers and directors. Net income.
Articles of merger	Must be filed by merging corporation.

Corporate Filings	Occupational Safety Filings
Secretary of State Corporation Division State Office Building, Room 180 St. Paul, MN 55155 612–296–2803	Occupational Safety and Health Administration Department of Labor and Industry 444 Lafayette Road St. Paul, MN 55101 612–296–2116

Securities Filings	UCC Filings
Securities Division Department of Commerce Metro Square Building, Room 500 St. Paul, MN 55101 612–296–6325	Secretary of State UCC Division State Office Building, Room 180 St. Paul, MN 55155 612–296–2434

MISSISSIPPI

Report Type	Special Features
Annual report (domestic and foreign)	Name and address of directors and officers.
	Aggregate number of shares authorized by class, par value, no par value, and series within class.
	Aggregate number of issued shares by class, par value, no par value, and series within class.
	Amount of stated capital.
Articles of merger/consolidation (domestic)	Plan of merger, consolidation.
	Total number of shares outstanding, designation of class entitled to vote and number of shares of such class for each corporation.
	Total number of shares voted for and against merger for each corporation, and within each class.
Articles of merger/consolidation (domestic and foreign)	Plan of merger/consolidation.
	Total number of shares outstanding and entitled to vote in each corporation.
	Total number of shares voted for and against plan by corporation.
Articles of merger (subsidiary into parent)	Class, number of shares outstanding and number of shares owned by parent.
	Date plan of merger mailed to stockholders.

Corporate Filings	Occupational Safety Filings
Secretary of State Corporation Division P. O. Box 136 Jackson, MS 39205 601–354–1350	Occupational Safety and Health Division State Board of Health 4443 I-55 North Frontage Jackson, MS 39206 601–982–6315

Securities Filings	UCC Filings
Secretary of State	Secretary of State
Securities Division	UCC Division
P. O. Box 136	P. O. Box 136
Jackson, MS 39205	Jackson, MS 39205
601–354–1379	601–354–1379

MISSOURI

Report Type	Special Features
Articles of merger (parent-subsidiary merger)	How outstanding shares are exchanges for shares of surviving company.
Articles of merger (domestic corporations—to be filed by attorney)	Date of shareholders' meeting, and number of shares voted for and against merger.
	Plan for exchange of shares.

Corporate Filings	Occupational Safety Filings
Secretary of State	Division of Labor Standards
Corporations Division	Department of Labor and Industrial
P. O. Box 778	Relations
Jefferson City, MO 65102	1001D Southwest Boulevard
314–751–4153	Jefferson City, MO 65101
	314–751–3403

Securities Filings	UCC Filings
Secretary of State	Secretary of State
Division of Securities	UCC Division
1001 Industrial Drive	112 State Capitol
Jefferson City, MO 65101	Jefferson City, MO 65101
314–751–4136	314–751–2360

MONTANA

Report Type	Special Features
Annual report	Authorized and issued stock class, series of stock.
	Shareholders (for professional corporation).

Report Type	Special Features
	Property statement (foreign companies).
Articles of merger/consolidation	Use "Montana Code Annotated" for guidelines.

Corporate Filings	Occupational Safety Filings
Secretary of State Corporation Department State Capitol Helena, MT 59620 406–449–3665	Division of Workers' Compensation Bureau of Safety and Health 815 Front Street Helena, MT 59620 406–449–3402

Securities Filings	UCC Filings
Investment Division State Auditor's Office P. O. Box 4009 Sam W. Mitchell Building Helena, MT 59601 406–449–2040	Secretary of State UCC Department State Capitol Helena, MT 59620 406–449–2034

NEBRASKA

Report Type	Special Features
Annual report (foreign and domestic)	Value of property owned and used by corporation in state.
	Occupation tax free.
Articles of merger/consolidation	No standard form, use "Nebraska Book of Statutes," Chapter 21 as guideline.

Corporate Filings	Occupational Safety Filings
Secretary of State Corporation Division State Capitol Lincoln, NE 68509 402–471–2554	Division of Safety Department of Labor P. O. Box 95024 550 South 16th Street Lincoln, NE 68509 402–471–2239

Securities Filings	UCC Filings
Bureau of Securities Department of Banking and Finance P. O. Box 95006 Lincoln, NE 68509 402–471–2171	Contact office of Secretary of State.

NEVADA

Corporate Filings	Occupational Safety Filings
Secretary of State Corporations Division Capitol Complex Carson City, NV 89710 702–885–5203	Department of Occupational Safety and Health 4600 Kietzke Lane Building F, Suite 153 Reno, NV 89510 702–784–6331

Securities Filings	UCC Filings
Secretary of State Securities Division 201 South Fall Street Capitol Complex Carson City, NV 89710 702–885–4270	Secretary of State UCC Division Capitol Complex Carson City, NV 89710 702–885–5207

NEW HAMPSHIRE

Report Type	Special Features
Annual report	Federal employee ID number. Directors.
Articles of consolidation (domestic and foreign companies)	Plan of consolidation. Number of shares outstanding. Number of shares voted for and against.

Report Type	Special Features
Articles of merger (foreign subsidiary into domestic parent)	Number of shares outstanding.
	Number of shares owned by surviving company.
	Plan of merger.
Articles of merger (domestic subsidiary into foreign parent)	Plan of merger.
	Number of shares outstanding.
	Number of shares owned by surviving company.
	Plan of merger mailed to shareholder.
Merger of foreign and domestic company	Number of shares outstanding.
	Number of shares owned by surviving company.
	Plan of merger.
	Par value of stock.
Merger (domestic into domestic)	Plan of consolidation.
	Number of shares outstanding.
	Number of shares voted for and against.
Merger (two domestic companies)	Number of shares outstanding.
	Number of shares owned by surviving company.
	Plan of merger.
	Par value of stock.

Corporate Filings	Securities Filings
Secretary of State Corporation Division State House, Room 204 Concord, NH 03301 603–271–3244	Securities Division Insurance Department 169 Manchester Street Concord, NH 03301 603–271–2261

UCC Filings

Secretary of State
UCC Division
State House, Room 203
Concord, NH 03301
603–271–3242

NEW JERSEY

Corporate Filings	Occupational Safety Filings
Secretary of State Commercial Recording Section State House CN 300 Trenton, NJ 08625 609–292–3790	Office of Safety Compliance Department of Labor and Industry John Fitch Plaza Trenton, NJ 08625 609–292–2424

Securities Filings	UCC Filings
New Jersey Bureau of Securities 80 Mulberry Street, Room 308 Newark, NJ 07102 201–648–2040	Secretary of State UCC Division State House CN 300 Trenton, NJ 08625 609–292–3799

NEW MEXICO

Report Type	Special Features
Annual report	NMSCC Certificate of Incorporation Number.
	NM Taxation and Revenue ID.
	Officers and directors' names and addresses.
	Next annual meeting date.
	Balance sheet.
	Capital stock.

Corporate Filings	Occupational Safety Filings
State Corporation Commission P. O. Drawer 1269 Santa Fe, NM 87501 505–827–4524	Occupational Health and Safety Program Environmental Improvement Division P. O. Box 968 Crown Building Santa Fe, NM 87504 505–984–0020

Securities Filings	UCC Filings
Securities Bureau Lew Wallace Building Santa Fe, NM 87503 505–827–7750	Secretary of State Legislative Executive Building, Room 400 Santa Fe, NM 87503 505–827–3700

NEW YORK

Corporate Filings	Occupational Safety Filings
Office of the Secretary Certification Division 162 Washington Avenue Albany, NY 12231 518–474–6200	Department of Safety and Health Department of Labor State Campus Albany, NY 12240 518–457–3518

Securities Filings	UCC Filings
State Attorney General Bureau of Securities 2 World Trade Center New York, NY 10047 212–488–7563	Department of State UCC Division P. O. Box 7021 Albany, NY 12231 518–474–4763

NORTH CAROLINA

Report Type	Special Features
Annual report	No reports required.
Merger (domestic company with domestic)	Number of shares outstanding, class, number of shares to vote.

Report Type	Special Features
	Number voted for and against merger.
Merger (domestic company with domestic)	Number of shares outstanding, class, number of shares to vote.

Corporate Filings	Occupational Safety Filings
Secretary of State Corporation Department 300 N. Salisbury Street Raleigh, NC 27611 919–733–4201	Occupational Safety and Health Administration Division Department of Labor 4 West Edenton Street Raleigh, NC 27601 919–733–4880

Securities Filings	UCC Filings
Secretary of State Securities Division Legislative Office Building 300 N. Salisbury Street, Room 30 Raleigh, NC 27611 919–733–3924	Secretary of State UCC Division 300 N. Salisbury Street Raleigh, NC 27611 919–733–4205

NORTH DAKOTA

Corporate Filings	Occupational Safety Filings
Secretary of State Corporation Department State Capitol Bismarck, ND 58505 701–224–2900	Department of Safety Workmen's Compensation Bureau Russel Building Highway 83 North Bismarck, ND 58505 701–224–2900

Securities Filings	UCC Filings
Securities Commissioner State Capitol, 9th Floor Bismarck, ND 58505 701–224–2910	Secretary of State UCC Department State Capitol Bismarck, ND 58505 701–224–2900

OHIO

Report Type	Special Features
Articles of merger/consolidation	No standard form, agreement drafted pursuant to "Ohio Revised Code."
Annual report (professional corporation)	List of shareholders.
Annual report (domestic and foreign)	Filed with tax department.
Annual report of proportion of capital stock (foreign companies)	Book value of assets.

Corporate Filings	Occupational Safety Filings
Secretary of State Corporation Division 30 East Broad Street State Office Tower Columbus, OH 43215 614–466–3910	Department of Industrial Relations 2323 West Fifth Avenue Columbus, OH 43216 614–466–3271

Securities Filings	UCC Filings
Division of Securities 180 East Broad Street, 13th Floor Columbus, OH 43215 614–466–3001	Secretary of State UCC Division 30 East Broad Street State Office Tower Columbus, OH 43215 614–466–3623

OKLAHOMA

Report Type	Special Features
Annual affidavit (foreign companies)	No par value stock—total authorized number.
	Minimum amount of capital now invested in state.
Statement of merger/consolidation (domestic with foreign)	Class, number, and series of shares outstanding.
	Names and addresses of principal officers.

Report Type	Special Features
Articles of merger/consolidation into Oklahoma corporation	Aggregate number of shares.
	Class, number, series authorized, and par value of authorized shares.
	Amount of stated capital.
	Class and number of authorized shares and consolidation received for new corporation.
	Number of directors in surviving/resulting corporation.
	Provisions limiting shareholders to acquiring additional shares.
	Provisions not consistent with law and regulation of affairs of corporation.
	Number of shares outstanding, number entitled to vote, class of designated shares of each constituent corporation.
	Names and addresses of directors and officers.
	Names and addresses; and percent of stock held by others, directors.

Corporate Filings	Occupational Safety Filings
Secretary of State Corporate Records Division State Capitol Building, Room 101 Oklahoma City, OK 73105 405–521–3048	Workmen's Compensation Board 2101 North Lincoln Boulevard Jim Thorpe Building Oklahoma City, OK 73105 405–521–8025

Securities Filings	UCC Filings
Securities Commission 2915 North Lincoln Boulevard Oklahoma City, OK 73104 405–521–2451	County Clerk 320 Robert S. Kerr Avenue Room 141 Oklahoma City, OK 73102 405–236–2727, ext. 402

OREGON

Corporate Filings	Occupational Safety Filings
State Corporation Commission	Accident Prevention Division
Commerce Building	Workmen's Compensation Department
158 12th Street, NE	Labor and Industries Building
Salem, OR 97310	Salem, OR 97310
503–378–4166	503–378–3272

Securities Filings	UCC Filings
Corporation Division	Secretary of State
Securities Section	UCC Division
158 12th Street, NE	Capitol Building, Room 132
Salem, OR 97310	Salem, OR 97310
503–378–4387	503–378–4146

PENNSYLVANIA

Corporate Filings	Occupational Safety Filings
Corporation Bureau	Bureau of Occupational and Industrial
Department of State	Safety
North Office Building, Room 308	Department of Labor and Industry
Harrisburg, PA 17120	1529 Labor and Industry Building
717–787–4068	Harrisburg, PA 17120
	717–787–3323

Securities Filings	UCC Filings
Securities Commission	Department of State Corporation
471 Forum Building	Bureau
Harrisburg, PA 17720	308 North Office Building
717–787–8061	Harrisburg, PA 17120
	717–787–8712

RHODE ISLAND

Corporate Filings	Occupational Safety Filings
Secretary of State	Division of Occupational Health
Corporation Department	Department of Health
State House, Room 218	75 Davis
Providence, RI 02903	Providence, RI 02908
401–277–3040	401–277–2438

Securities Filings	UCC Filings
Securities Division Banking, Insurance and Securities Administration 100 North Main Street Providence, RI 02903 401–277–2405	Secretary of State Division of UCC State House, Room 217 Providence, RI 02903 401–277–2357

SOUTH CAROLINA

Report Type	Special Features
Annual report	Names and addresses; and percent of stock held by others, directors.

Corporate Filings	Occupational Safety Filings
Secretary of State Corporation Division P. O. Box 11350 Columbia, SC 29211 803–758–2744	Division of Occupational Safety and Health Department of Labor P. O. Box 11329 3600 Forest Drive Columbia, SC 29211 803–758–3080

Securities Filings	UCC Filings
Securities Division Keenan Building, Room 816 Columbia, SC 29201 803–758–2833	Secretary of State UCC Division P. O. Box 11350 Columbia, SC 29211 803–758–2744

SOUTH DAKOTA

Report Type	Special Features
Annual report (domestic)	Directors.
	Issued and authorized shares, par value of shares.
Annual report (foreign)	Directors.

Report Type	Special Features
	Issued and authorized shares, par value of shares.
Articles of merger/consolidation	No standard form—must be formulated by attorney.

Corporate Filings	Occupational Safety Filings
Secretary of State Corporation Division 500 East Capitol Pierre, SD 57501 605–773–3537	Occupational Safety and Health Administration Department of Health Vital Statistics Foss Building Pierre, SD 57501 605–773–3355

Securities Filings	UCC Filings
Division of Securities State Capitol Building Pierre, SD 57501 605–773–4823	Secretary of State UCC Division 500 East Capitol Pierre, SD 57501 605–773–3537

TENNESSEE

Report Type	Special Features
Franchise and excise Foreign tax return	Balance sheets.
	Income statement.
	Book value of property (beginning and year-end).
	Franchise and excise tax computations.

Corporate Filings	Occupational Safety Filings
Secretary of State Records Section James K. Polk Building, Room 1014 Nashville, TN 37219 615–741–2286	Division of Occupational Safety Department of Labor 501 Union Building Nashville, TN 37219 615–741–2793

Securities Filings	UCC Filings
Department of Insurance Securities Division State Office Building, Room 114 Nashville, TN 37219 615–741–2947	Secretary of State Commercial Code Division James K. Polk Building, Suite 500 Nashville, TN 37219 615–741–3276

TEXAS

Report Type	Special Features
Public Information Department (part of Franchise Tax report)	Companies that reporting company owns interest of ten percent or more. Corporations that own ten percent of reporting company.

Corporate Filings	Occupational Safety Filings
Secretary of State Corporations Division P. O. Box 13701 Austin, TX 78711 512–475–2916	Division of Occupational Safety Department of Health 1100 West 49th Street Austin, TX 78756 512–458–7287

Securities Filings	UCC Filings
State Securities Board P. O. Box 13167 Austin, TX 78711 512–474–2233	UCC Division Capital Station P. O. Box 13193 Austin, TX 78711 512–475–3457

UTAH

Report Type	Special Features
Articles of merger	No standard form, articles of merger and plan of merger must be sent to Secretary of State. Name and address for directors.

Report Type	Special Features
	Issued and authorized shares.
	Par value of stock.
	Stated capital.

Corporate Filings	Occupational Safety Filings
Secretary of State Lt. Governor's Office P. O. Box 5801 Salt Lake City, UT 84114 801–533–4505	Occupational Safety and Health Division Industrial Commission 160 E. Third South Salt Lake City, UT 84110 801–530–6901

Securities Filings	UCC Filings
Securities Commission State Office Building, Room 5226 Salt Lake City, UT 84114 801–533–4239	Secretary of State P. O. Box 5901 Salt Lake City, UT 84110 801–530–6020

VERMONT

Report Type	Special Features
Corporate annual report	Aggregate number of shares authorized and issued.
	Names and addresses of corporate officers and directors.
	Copy of corporate tax return.
Trade name registration	Name and address of all individuals, copartners, and members.

Corporate Filings	Occupational Safety Filings
Secretary of State Corporations Office 109 State Street Montpelier, VT 05602 802–828–2363	Division of Occupational Safety Department of Labor and Industry 120 State Street Montpelier, VT 05602 802–828–2765

Securities Filings	UCC Filings
Securities Division	Secretary of State
Department of Banking and Insurance	UCC Office
120 State Street	109 State Street
Montpelier, VT 05602	Montpelier, VT 05602
802–828–3301	802–828–2363

VIRGINIA

Report Type	Special Features
Articles of merger or consolidation of Virginian and foreign companies	Number of shares outstanding.
	Number of shares entitled to vote as class.

Corporate Filings	Occupational Safety Filings
Clerk's Office	Division of Industrial Safety
State Corporation Commission	Department of Labor and Industry
P. O. Box 1197	P. O. Box 12064
Richmond, VA 23209	Richmond, VA 23241
804–786–3671	804–786–2391

Securities Filings	UCC Filings
Division of Securities	UCC Division
11 South 12th Street	State Corporation Commission
Richmond, VA 23219	P. O. Box 1197
804–786–7751	Richmond, VA 23209
	804–786–3689

WASHINGTON

Report Type	Special Features
Articles of merger/consolidation	No standard form—must send articles of merger and plan of merger to Secretary of State.

Corporate Filings

Secretary of State
Corporation Division
Legislative Building
Mail Stop AS22
Olympia, WA 98504
206–753–7115

Occupational Safety Filings

Industrial Safety and Health Division
Department of Labor and Industries
P. O. Box 207
Olympia, WA 98504
206–753–6500

Securities Filings

Securities Division
Business and Professions
Administration
P. O. Box 648
Olympia, WA 98504
206–753–6929

UCC Filings

Department of Licensing
UCC Division
P. O. Box 9660
Olympia, WA 98504
206–753–2523

WEST VIRGINIA

Corporate Filings

Secretary of State
Corporation Division
State Capitol
Charleston, WV 25305
304–348–0262

Securities Filings

Securities Commission
State Auditor's Office
W-118 State Capitol
Charleston, WV 25305
304–348–2257

UCC Filings

Secretary of State
UCC Division
State Capitol
Charleston, WV 25305
304–348–3000

WISCONSIN

Report Type

Information report (domestic)

Special Features

Number of shares of capital stock
authorized and issued.

Directors' names and addresses.

Report Type	Special Features
Annual report (foreign)	Directors' names and addresses.
	Authorized and issued stock, par value of stock.
	Number of Wisconsin shareholders.
	List of states and countries where company is licensed to do business.
	Proportion of capital represented in Wisconsin as of last fiscal year.
	Use for par stock and no-par stock.
Reinstatement report	Directors' names and addresses.
	Number of shareholders.
	Stock authorized and issued with par value.

Corporate Filings	Securities Filings
Secretary of State Corporation Division P. O. Box 7846 Madison, WI 53707 608–266–3590	Commissioner of Securities P. O. Box 1768 Madison, WI 53701 608–266–3431

UCC Filings
Secretary of State UCC Division 201 East Washington Ave. P. O. Box 7847 Madison, WI 53707 608–266–3087

WYOMING

Report Type	Special Features
Annual report	Directors' names and addresses.
	Nature of assets and dollar value.

Corporate Filings	Occupational Safety Filings
Secretary of State	Occupational Health and Safety
Corporation Division	200 East 8th Avenue
State Capitol, Room 110	Cheyenne, WY 82002
Cheyenne, WY 82002	307–777–7787
307–777–7311	

Securities Filings	UCC Filings
Secretary of State	Secretary of State
Securities Division	Corporate Division/UCC
State Capitol	State Capitol, Room 109
Cheyenne, WY 82002	Cheyenne, WY 82002
307–777–7370	307–777–7311

CURRENT INDUSTRIAL REPORTS: YOUR GUIDE TO INDUSTRY SIZE AND MARKET SHARE

For years the U.S. Department of Commerce has published detailed industry analyses. As the order booklet states:

> The Current Industrial Reports of the Bureau of the Census present timely data on the production, inventories, and orders of approximately 5,000 products, which represents 40 percent of all U. S. manufacturing.

How can you use these reports for specific company profiles?

You can determine market share. These booklets supply the number of companies and the amount their industry produces. If you have an idea of your target company's production, you can estimate market share for the firm.

You can better understand which are the strongest selling products for a particular industry segment.

Because the Current Industrial Reports track historical production information for an industry, you can see if your target is following general industry trends.

The reports use standard industry terminology and offer reasonably detailed breakdowns of each industry by major product groupings.

Some of the charts you would typically find in a Current Industrial Report are:

1. Shipments summary—shipments by year for the past five or six years.
2. Shipments by specified type of product—shipments by month for the past three or four years, according to product type.
3. Shipments by number and value shipped.
4. Shipments, exports, imports, apparent consumption by quantity and value.
5. Product description by specification.

The Current Industrial Reports appear monthly, quarterly, or yearly, depending on the industry studied. The industries covered are listed in the following pages. The code number appearing next to each report title is the report's series number. To order, simply ask for the report by its series number.

Food

Flour Milling Products M20A
Confectionery M20C
Fats and Oils—Oilseed Crushings M20J
Fats and Oils—Production, Consumption, and Stocks M20K

Textile Mill Products

Finished Fabrics M22A
Woolen System, Worsted Combing M22D
Stocks of Wool and Related Fibers MA-22M
Textured Yarn MA-22F.1
Spun Yarn MA22F.2
Narrow Fabrics MA-22G
Knit Fabrics MA-22K
Consumption on the Cotton System M22P
Carpet and Rugs MQ-22Q

Broadwoven Fabrics Finished MA-22S

Broadwoven Fabrics (Gray) MQ-22T

Sheets, Pillowcases, and Towels MQ-23X

Apparel

Gloves and Mittens MA-23D

Men's and Boys' Outerwear MA-23E

Women's and Children's Outerwear MA-23F

Underwear and Nightwear MA-23G

Brassieres, Girdles, and Allied Garments MA-23J

Footwear M31A

Wood, Paper, and Related Products

Hardwood Plywood MA-24F

Softwood Plywood MA-24H

Lumber Production and Mill Stocks MA-24T

Office Furniture MA-25H

Pulp, Paper, and Board MA-26A

Selected Office Supplies and Accessories MA-26B

Converted Flexible Materials MQ-26F

Business Forms, Binders, Carbon Paper, and Inked Ribbon MA-27A

Pens, Pencils, and Marking Devices MA-39A

Chemicals and Petroleum Products

Inorganic Chemicals M28A, MA-28A

Sulfuric Acid MA-28B

Inorganic Fertilizer Materials M28B

Industrial Gases M28C, MA-28C

Paint, Varnish, and Lacquer M28F, MA-28F

Pharmaceutical Preparations, Except Biologicals MA-28G

Asphalt and Tar Roofing and Siding Preparations MA-29A

Rubber and Plastics Products

Rubber Productions Shipments and Inventory MA-30A
Rubber and Plastics Hose and Beltings MA-30B
Shipments of Selected Plastics Production MA-30D
Plastic Bottles M30E

Glass, Clay, and Related Products

Flat Glass MQ-32A
Refractories MQ-32C, MA-32C
Clay Construction Products M32D
Consumer, Scientific, Technical, and Industrial Glassware MA-32E
Glass Containers M32G, MA-32G
Fibrous Glass MA-32J

Primary Metals

Iron and Steel Castings M33A
Steel Mill Products MA-33B
Inventories of Steel Mill Shapes M33-3
Nonferrous Castings M33E
Magnesium Mill Products MA-33G
Inventories of Brass and Copper Wire Mill Shapes M33K
Insulated Wire and Cable MA-33L
Aluminum Ingot and Mill Products M33-2
Copper Controlled Materials ITA-9008
Titanium Mill Products, Ingot and Castings ITA-991

Intermediate Metal Products

Plumbing Fixtures MQ-34E
Closures for Containers M34H
Steel Shipping Drums and Pails MQ-34K
Selected Heating Equipment MA-34N
Aluminum Foil Converted MA-34P

Machinery and Equipment

Farm Machinery and Lawn and Garden Equipment MA-35A
Construction Machinery MQ-35D, MA-35D
Mining Machinery, Mineral Processing Equipment MA-35F
Selected Industrial Air Pollution Control Equipment MA-35J
Internal Combustion Engines MA-35L
Air Conditioning and Refrigeration Equipment MA-35M
Fluid Power Products Including Aerospace MA-35N
Pumps and Compressors MA-35P
Antifriction Bearings MA-35Q
Computers and Office and Accounting Machines MA-35R
Tractors (Except Garden Tractors) M35S
Vending Machines (Coin Operated) MA-35U
Metalworking Machinery MQ-35W
Backlog of Orders for Aerospace Companies MQ-37D
Aircraft Propellers MA-37E
New Complete Aircraft and Aircraft Engines, Except Military M37G
Truck Trailers M37L

Electrical and Electronics

Switchgear, Switchboard Apparatus, Relays and Industrial Controls MA-36A
Electric Lamps M-36D, MQ-36B
Fluorescent Lamp Ballasts MQ-36C
Electric Housewares and Fans MA-36E
Major Household Appliances MA-36F
Transformers MA-36G
Motors and Generators MA-36H
Wiring Devices and Supplies MA-36K
Electric Lighting Fixtures MA-36L
Radio and Television Receivers, Phonographs, and Related Equipment MA-36M
Selected Electronic and Associated Products MA-36N

Selected Instruments and Related Products MA-38B

Selected Atomic Energy Products MA-38Q

To order a Current Industrial Report, write:

Data User Services Division
Customer Services (Publications)
Bureau of the Census
Washington, DC 20233

Each report costs $1.50. Orders of 100 copies or more will receive a 25 percent discount.

TIPS ON RETRIEVING GOVERNMENT DOCUMENTS

Federal

There are many copy services available in the Washington, D.C. area. You can either tell the services exactly the document you need and they will retrieve it, or you can ask them to search for the materials when you are not sure of their catalog number or location.

I can recommend three retrieval firms providing government documents; they are reasonable and quick:

The Downtown Copy Center
1114 21st Street, NW
Washington, DC 20026
202–833–1654
Specializes in FCC documents, but will also do other agencies.

Fairpress Service
Box 19352
20th Street Station, NW
Washington, DC 20036
202–463–7323
Specializes in FCC documents, but will retrieve from other agencies.

Washington Service Bureau
1225 Connecticut Avenue, NW
Washington, DC 20036
202–833–9200
Will retrieve almost any government document.

State

Many state capitals have copy services located near their archives. These are private services, much like the copy centers mentioned above. Your best bet in locating one is to call one of the larger law firms in town. They will usually know of services that retrieve court documents or other state and municipal filings.

In addition, most state corporate filing offices (such as the ones listed in the "State Your Case" section earlier in this chapter) will copy documents and send them for a small fee.

Local (Municipal)

For a small fee, town assessors' offices will, in most cases, send documents upon request. Often, especially in smaller towns, the town clerk will give you most of the needed information over the telephone.

CHAPTER 4

CORPORATE INTELLIGENCE IN PRINT

Do you remember ever having seen an annual issue or special directory that had exactly the type of industry or financial information you needed, but you were not able to recall exactly where it was? Various sections in this book will list special trade magazines that make it their business to track down just that kind of corporate information.

The present section is more general. It offers you the basic directories, newspapers, and annual issues that every researcher should have access to when beginning to look into an industry.

I have divided this section into three parts: (1) financial periodicals and annuals, (2) general industry directories, and (3) investment manuals and services.

Remember! This is just the beginning of your homework, but never overlook it. I can't tell you how often I have seen researchers hunt for days for a company's sales only to find it right under their nose in an industry directory. Don't let this happen to you.

This section spells out the obvious and the basic. Yet, you need to know the obvious and the basic before you can go ahead and use corrugated boxes or sophisticated telephone techniques to sleuth out corporate information.

FINANCIAL PERIODICALS AND ANNUALS

Advertising Age: 100 Leading National Advertisers (Crain Communications). Far more than just a list, each of the 100 entries is actually a profile on the advertiser's activity over the past year. It discusses which division and agency were responsible for a particular product line. The advertisers are chosen based on advertising expenditures as a percent of sales within industry groups. The expenditures are listed for the past three years. This is an excellent summary of a company's advertising campaign, and can provide insight into a company's marketing strategy.

American Banker: Mid-Year Review Issue (American Banker). A review of leading U.S. banks, with a discussion of their financials. This is the premier newspaper for the banking industry. Appearing daily, the newspaper covers company news events and background on recent developments in the banking industry. It also discusses banking legislation and overall news on the national and international banking scene, and offers the latest bank stock quotations.

American Banker: 100 Largest Credit Unions in the U.S. (American Banker). An annual roster of the largest credit unions in the United States, ranked by asset size. Also included under each entry is a particular credit union's total member savings, share drafts, number of regular share accounts, and number of share draft accounts. The data for each credit union listed covers two and one-half years.

American Banker: 100 Largest Domestic Bank Holding Company Systems (American Banker). Similar to the list above, but instead it ranks bank holding companies. Also ranked by assets, the list provides the following details on each bank holding company: change in rank from previous year, listing of assets for the past two years, total deposits for two years running, number of controlled banks, name of the largest controlled bank, and number of branches.

American Banker: 100 Largest Finance Companies (American Banker). Covers the nation's 100 largest finance companies, contains two years of data on each company's total capital funds, capital and surplus, assets, receivables net, net income, deferred income, receivables acquired, and amount of bank credit at the end of each year.

American Banker: 100 Largest Mutual Savings Banks (American Banker). Contains details on the 100 largest U.S. and the 300 largest international savings banks. Information covers two years. Each entry contains the number of accounts, range of interest rates, as well as asset and deposit data.

American Banker: 100 Largest Real Estate Investment Trusts (American Banker). This may be the only list of its kind for real estate trusts. It contains the name and location of the advisor, total assets for two years, total number of loans and investments, reserve for loss, and share equity.

Barron's (Dow Jones). A weekly business newspaper, published by the same people who bring you the *Wall Street Journal.* A paper I would recommend be on your library shelf. It often has far meatier articles than does the Journal. The paper covers all industries. Its company profiles are among the best written and most valuable around. Keep in mind that this is a paper written for educated businesspeople. For exactly this reason *Barron's* explores its subject in-depth, assuming that its readers are already familiar with the superficial news—as might be provided in the Journal. Because it is a weekly, it can truly explore its subjects. In addition to the news reporting, it regularly offers stock and bond prices and mutual fund data.

Best's Flitcraft Compendium (A. M. Best). Contains annuity data on 50 life insurance companies. The insurance industry considers Best publications as the industry's record-keeper.

Black Enterprise: The Top 100 Black Enterprises (Earl G. Graves Publishing Company). A listing of the 100 leading black-owned companies. Each listing mentions the company's chief executive officer, its sales, assets, and number of employees.

Business Week R&D Scoreboard (McGraw-Hill). A list of the companies with the largest research and development expenditures in the United States. R&D data remains one of the most difficult pieces of corporate information to find. Although much of *Business Week's* data is culled from public filings, the fact that you can now find it all in one place makes the Scoreboard an invaluable reference source.

Chain Store Age—General Merchandise: Top 100 Chains (Lebhar-Friedman). *Chain Store Age* magazine has three editions: *Merchandise, Executive,* and *Supermarkets.* Each is considered one of the key trade publications for the retail industry. Annually, a number of special issues list the leading companies in the retail business, ranking them by sales. Among these other issues are:

Annual Census of American Chain Stores. This list contains each company's earnings, total number of outlets, and number of employees for each of the top 50 chain stores.

Chain Store Age Executive: Big Builders. As the name implies, this list contains new construction information for the leading U.S. retail chain stores. It covers the chains' capital expenditures and number of new stores built, as well as their size.

Chain Store Age Executive: Retailing $100 Million Club. The largest retail outlets ranked by sales.

Chain Store Age General Merchandise: Top 20 Departments. An excellent tool for figuring square footage income for a retail store you may be studying. This list will provide benchmark numbers on department sales within large chain stores.

Chain Store Age Supermarkets: Nielsen Review of Retail Grocery Store Trends. Discusses new products and their performance. Its most useful aspect for the corporate researcher is its listing of market shares for brand names. You would ordinarily pay hundreds if not thousands of dollars to a research house for the market share information provided here.

Chain Store Age: Supermarket Sales Manual. Will provide the researcher with insight into how food sells within a supermarket. This issue lists units sold per store, share of total unit movement by product type, and sales of generic, private label, and brand name products for the leading food chains.

Commercial and Financial Chronicle (National News Service). A weekly newspaper and the best single source for national stock prices. Its stock listings have the most complete over-the-counter listings.

Dun's Review: Best Managed Companies (Dun & Bradstreet, National Credit Office Division). This yearly issue analyzes what, in its opinion, are the best-managed companies of the past year. Contained in each profile are the company's dividends, growth record, current yields, revenues, and earnings per share.

Dun's Review: Top Corporate Performers (Dun & Bradstreet, National Credit Office Division). Similar to the above list, but the criterion this time is dividend yield. Each profile contains stockholder equity, current yield, earnings per share, return on sales, sales, and stock prices.

Electronic News: Financial Fact Book & Directory (Fairchild Publications). Each directory entry contains a detailed review and profile of a company's activity. An industry bible, it lists company forecasts, income, balance sheet data, stockholders' equity, officers, divisions, subsidiaries, number of employees, and plant footage.

Financial World: America's Top Growth Companies (Macro Communications). A type of Fortune 500 list that gives data for top-growth companies with sales of over $500 million or under $500 million (there are two lists). Data entered for each company covers the past 10 years. The publication lists each company by industry. Included in the list are a company's dividends, revenue, earnings growth rate, and sales.

Financial World: Industry Forecasts (Macro Communications). A yearly review of 600 major corporations, with each entry containing company forecasts, dividends, P/E, yield, and stock prices. The publication lists each company by its industry. A useful source for the researcher just beginning to examine a company in an industry he or she knows little about.

Financial World's 500 American Top Money Makers (Macro Communications). Companies are ranked by sales and income, similar to the Fortune 500 listing below.

Forbes: Annual Directory Issue (Forbes). It divides the 500 leading companies into five lists, ranking them by sales, profits, assets, market value, and alphabetically. The alphabetical listing contains number of employees, headquarters, and stock exchange on which a particular company is traded.

Forbes Annual Report on American Industry (Forbes). Probably the best single compendium on a broad selection of industries. This annual issue is for the researcher who needs a thumbnail sketch on an industry and the companies within it. Usually appearing in one of its January issues, the issue lists over 1000 companies (publicly traded) with $450 million or more in sales. The issue covers 46 industries and offers 5 years of financial data for each company. Financial data includes: income, dividends, sales, and stock price.

Fortune: The 500 Largest U.S. Industrial Corporations (Time). Also publishes the Second 500 Largest listing. This is the mother list that begat all other corporate listings. Companies are ranked by sales. Each entry contains an income statement, dividends, assets, number of employees, growth rate, and sales. All companies here are publicly traded.

Fortune: The Fortune Service 500 (Time). Treats service companies the same way it does industrials. There is an alphabetical index. The 500 companies are broken up into 100 diversified service firms, 100 largest commercial banks, 100 diversified financial companies, 50 largest life insurance firms, 50 largest retailers, 50 largest transportation companies, and the 50 largest utilities. Like its industrial brother, this list contains each company's income, dividends, assets, number of employees, stock price, and sales.

Inc.: The Inc. 100 (Inc. Publishing Company). A list of the 100 fastest growing small publicly traded companies. The leading companies are profiled. In general, companies discussed in Inc. are not found in Forbes or Fortune. Inc.'s turf is smaller companies, and it does an excellent job of reporting on their activities. Inc. also has a special issue, the *Inc. 500*, the 500 fastest-growing private companies in the United States. A competing publication, *Venture*, covers similar topics and also does in-depth write-ups on smaller companies.

Journal of Commerce (Twin Coast Newspapers). A daily, not quite as popular as the *Wall Street Journal*, but serving a similar function. It appears to have different editorial criteria than the Journal. Its stress is on commodities, and shipping. I have found, in many instances, that the *Journal of Commerce* will cover stories that the *Wall Street Journal* just does not have space to cover or does not feel important enough to its readership. The Journal of Commerce is an excellent news source to add to your library. Its weekly special edition, the *Journal of Commerce Import Bulletin*, lists all cargo entering the United States.

The New York Times (The New York Times Company). A business reporter from the Times once confided to me that the *Wall Street Journal* is now considered the newspaper of record for the business community. Although this appears to be the case, based on circulation figures alone, the Times is still one of this country's great dailies. With this greatness comes considerable in-depth reporting on corporations. This paper is well worth a look-see before beginning any interviewing. Researching your target company and doing your homework in intelligence-gathering means retrieving those news articles. In addition to stock prices, the newspaper will publish company earnings statements, management changes, acquisitions, mergers, and plant openings.

United Mutual Fund Selector (United Business Service Company). A newsletter that offers performance data on mutual funds.

Wall Street Journal (Dow Jones). Last but far from least, this newspaper is recognized as the preeminent business information source in the country. While there are often glaring gaps in its coverage, considering its nationwide scope, it supplies more consistently accurate corporate intelligence than any other single paper today. Its concentration is on publicly held companies. Each issue contains earnings reports, stock prices, news of management changes, and so on. Each week there are special sections on marketing, technology, and advertising. The Journal is often the business news trendsetter. When an article appears in the Journal, you will often find other newspapers and radio stations soon reporting on the same subject. If your office subscribes to no other newspaper or reference source, it should at least order the Journal. Because the Journal is so well indexed by so many data bases and manual library indexes, it can be considered a reference work in itself.

INDUSTRY DIRECTORIES

Million Dollar Directory (Dun & Bradstreet).   Someone who is asked to locate information on a company will often head straight for this directory. While not by any means the most comprehensive general directory, it does offer such features as sales, number of employees, stock exchange, senior executive officers, and directors. To receive a listing in the directory a company must have a net worth of over $500,000.

This directory only lists headquarters locations, or addresses of a corporation's major subsidiaries. It does not list each plant location. A new version of the directory, the *Billion Dollar Directory*, lists all parent-subsidiary relationships and addresses for all companies with a worth of $500,000 or more.

A recommendation to any corporate researcher: Although D&B produces somewhat high-priced reference books, they are often one of a kind. They are also constantly spinning off new texts from their data base of over five million companies. Place yourself on their mailing list, or contact their sales representative.

News Front: 30,000 Leading U.S. Corporations (Year).   Public companies are ranked by sales, and privately held corporations are arranged by sales and geographic area. Tables include top performing companies by sales categories. Information contained on many of the companies includes assets, long-term debt, depreciation, P/E ratio, and stockholders equity.

North American Register of Business and Industry (Global Marketing Services).   This text contains the 5000 largest companies in North America. The companies are ranked by sales volume. In addition to sales, each entry lists number of employees.

Rand McNally International Bankers Directory (Rand McNally).   This hefty tome contains information on 15,000 U.S. banks and 33,000 branches of U.S. banks, as well as on foreign banks and their branches. The text also contains economic and financial data for over 1000 U.S. cities. Each entry offers amount of deposits held with that institution, other balance sheet information, the bank's principal officers, bank branches, and its directors.

Standard Directory of Advertisers (National Register Company).   On the surface, this is a book meant only for the advertising industry. But in fact it is an excellent reference tool for general business research. The book has a roster of over 17,000 companies that are major advertisers. Each entry lists the company, its advertising agency, the products, and the media used. The Directory also comes with a complementary Geographic and Trademark volume, from which you can cross-check a company by its location or its product trademark names.

Standard & Poor's Register of Corporations, Directors and Executives (McGraw-Hill). There are three volumes in this excellent set. While it contains only one half of the companies mentioned in D&B's *Million Dollar Directory*, the companies it does cover are covered well—with excellent indexing. The heart of the book, volume one, is an alphabetical listing of all the companies in the text. Each entry contains name, address, officers, directors, sales (where available), number of employees (also where available), and stock exchange. The other volumes index the text by geographical area and industry. It also has a parent-subsidiary directory, where the researcher can quickly spot who owns whom. The second volume sketches brief biographies of many of the key executives mentioned in volume one, under their company name. A relatively inexpensive set as reference works go, and well worth the money. (At the time of this printing the three-volume set leases for $270 for one year).

Thomas Grocery Register (Thomas Publishing Company). If you ever have to find a food store or a food wholesaler, this is the book to turn to. It lists almost 6000 companies in the food business. Aside from name and address, it also offers a company's estimated asset size and brief description of its product line. The types of companies mentioned are distributors, discount stores, food brokers, exporters, manufacturers, importers, equipment suppliers, and other services related to the food industry.

Thomas Register of American Manufacturers and Thomas Catalog File (Thomas Publishing Company). Probably the least expensive and one of the most effective corporate directories. Sixteen volumes long, it lists manufacturers' products and services by product. Companies are indexed by product. The product index itself serves two very important purposes: (1) it uses standard industry terminology, which will make looking up your industry group that much easier; and (2) the fact that Thomas uses industry lingo also makes the text a de-facto dictionary. You will find that the company advertisements, interspersed throughout the set, will quickly tell you how competitors are marketing their products and the extent of their product line. The last few volumes in the set are samples of company catalogs. Again, this will serve as a means to gauge the competition's product line. Another index, on yellow paper, has an extensive trademark listing. While not a true trademark register, it does cover thousands of commonly used manufacturers' trademarks.

Like the *Thomas Grocery Register*, this text will offer company name, address, telephone number, and an estimate of its asset size. This set sells for $120. Along with the Yellow Pages and the *Wall Street Journal,* you should consider Thomas a necessity for your research library.

INVESTMENT MANUALS AND SERVICES

Bank & Quotation Record (National News Service). A compilation of American, New York, and four other regional stock exchanges, including over-the-counter, government bonds, and foreign exchange rates. It is a monthly publication.

Barron's Quarterly Mutual Fund Record (Dow Jones). A listing of mutual funds and related financial data published quarterly.

Best's Insurance Reports: Life-Health (A. M. Best). This volume covers U.S. and Canadian health and life insurance companies. It contains income statement and balance sheet data as well as company history. The volume also discusses new businesses. As mentioned earlier, Best's is the insurance industry's bible. Whether or not you agree with its assumptions, you should turn to it to understand how the industry thinks and what it thinks of its competitors.

Best's Insurance Reports: Property-Liability (A. M. Best). This text examines the other side of the insurance coin: property and liability. It treats stock companies and mutual companies in the same manner as it does in the Life-Health manual listed above. Companies covered are located in the United States and Canada.

Bond Guide (Standard & Poor's/McGraw-Hill). A simple but fairly comprehensive listing of bond prices for American corporate bonds (this includes convertibles). Some Canadian bonds are also listed.

Capital Changes Reports (Commerce Clearing House). As the title implies, this five-volume set shows the changes a publicly traded company has gone through in its financial history. It will offer a brief company history and dates of merger or consolidation. All stock splits are also recorded.

Daily Stock Price Record (Standard & Poor's/McGraw-Hill). One of the only sources that lists a company's stock prices as they appeared during each day of trading (high, low, and closing prices). This collection comes in three sets—NY Stock Exchange, Over The Counter, and American Stock Exchange. Companies are alphabetically listed. All stock splits, dividends, and trading halts are indicated. It is a quarterly compilation and bound in hard cover.

Financial Dynamics (Investors Management Sciences). Published in looseleaf format, it analyzes the leading companies in over 100 industries. Taking a different approach to examining these companies, it uses financial ratios instead of actual financials. It reviews dozens of ratios for every company.

Financial World: Independent Appraisals of 1900 Stocks and Mutual Funds (Macro Communications). A compact summary of trading activity of all companies listed on the New York and American exchanges. The listing is alphabetical. The tables summarize a company's liquidity, earning power, and market price. Data for each company covers the past 10 years.

Investment Dealers' Digest: Mutual Fund Directory (Dealers' Digest Publishing Company). A summary of a mutual fund's history, sales, stock prices, and dividends. Published semiannually.

The M/G Financial Weekly (Media General Financial Services). One of the most complete weekly summaries of stock trading. Over 3400 companies are covered. Earnings per share, financial position, trading volume, and market trends are stated for the stocks listed. The newspaper also offers tables on stock options and commodities.

Money: The Top American Stock Exchange and OTC Stocks (Time). Ranks the leading companies on both exchanges. Data is for the past two years. Contains both yield and stock prices for each stock.

Money: The Top New York Stock Exchange Stocks (Time). Contains the same information as the above list, but includes only New York Stock Exchange issues.

Moody's Bond Record: Municipals, Corporates, Governments, Convertibles & Preferred (Moody's Investors Service). When you think of municipal bonds and their ratings, the first name you will probably come up with is Moody's. Long associated with bond ratings, this text can be considered the best possible starting point for exploring a bond's history. This compilation contains over 19,000 bond issues.

Moody's Bond Survey (Moody's Investor Service). One step ahead of the Bond Record mentioned above. The Survey offers investors recommendations to buy or sell bonds. It also tracks and discusses trends in the marketplace.

Moody's Dividend Record (Moody's Investors Service). Along with the equivalent Standard & Poor's volume, this is an excellent source of dividend declarations and payments. The semiweekly volumes are also compiled into an annual volume.

Moody's Handbook of Common Stocks (Moody's Investors Service). Offers a financial profile of 1000 commonly traded stocks over a 10-year span.

Moody's International Manual (Moody's Investor Service). Although more foreign financial sources will be mentioned in the foreign sources section, Moody's has compiled this single volume on leading international and multinational corporations (publicly traded only). Like Moody's Industrial and OTC Manuals, this one also reviews a company's corporate history, financials, businesses, annual stock prices, and so on.

Moody's Investors Manuals—Transportation, Public Utilities, Municipal and Government OTC, Industrial, Bank and Finance (Moody's Investors Service). Highly recommended set of books for any research library. When you do not have an annual report or a 10-K handy, these are the best substitutes. Each entry includes a company history, history of acquisitions, principal businesses, income statement, balance sheet, stock price history (yearly), officers, directors, and subsidiaries and their locations. Expanded report entries include a five to ten-year financial history, rather than the normal two-year comparison.

There are a couple of other sections to make note of: One set of blue pages will tell the reader if a company dropped out of the Moody's listing because it was acquired. This section will also record corporate name changes. Another blue section will offer a ten-year price range of stocks and bonds.

Should you need back issues, Moody's offers these volumes on microfiche.

Mutual Funds Almanac (The Hirsh Organization). A reference work that monitors the performance of over 600 mutual funds. The book tracks seven years of data.

National Monthly Stock Summary (National Quotation Bureau). Let's say you heard that a company had over-the-counter stock, but you could not find it mentioned in any of the standard investment reference texts. This would be the source you would turn to. For the unusual or little-traded OTC issue, this summary is the last word. The citations are brief, only mentioning the stock's bid and offered prices for the past six months. Also included in the listing is the dealer who traded the stock. Take note— Once you know the primary dealer's name, call this person up; he or she is an excellent source of intelligence on the company.

The Outlook (Standard & Poor's/McGraw-Hill). Follows publicly traded companies and offers buy or sell recommendations.

Over-The-Counter Securities Review (Review Publishing Company). Covers news on OTC stocks, including income, dividends, and general performance statistics.

Research Service/Paine Webber Mitchell Hutchins (Paine Webber Mitchell Hutchins). Reviews the financial activity of a select group of companies. This is issued in a looseleaf binder and is updated regularly.

Research Service/Smith Barney (Smith Barney). Similar to the Paine Webber service, it covers a broad assortment of publicly traded companies, offering financials as well as discussion of company activity.

Security Owner's Stock Guide (Standard & Poor's/McGraw-Hill). A compact book that reviews 5000 common and preferred stocks. Each entry discusses a company's earnings, dividends, stock price, and S&P rating.

Standard Corporation Records (Standard & Poor's/McGraw-Hill). Offers both a financial and written profile of publicly traded and some unlisted companies. This set has similar features to the Moody's Investor's Manuals.

Standard & Poor's Dividend Record (Standard & Poor's/McGraw-Hill). Serves the same purpose as the Moody's dividend report listed above, and is organized in a similar fashion.

Stock Reports (Standard & Poor's/McGraw-Hill). There is a separate set for each of the major trading groups—AMEX, NYSE, and OTC. The reports, in looseleaf notebooks, are concise and printed on two pages. Each report contains a stock performance chart and summary of the company's financial history. These reports are updated regularly, and should there be a major change in the company's position, new pages are issued to replace the older reports.

Value Line (A. Bernhard & Company). An in-depth analysis of over 1800 stocks in over 70 industries. Each report is one page long and is packed with data. In addition, to clearly presenting a company's 10-year financial history, the report graphs the stock's performance and reports on corporate developments (e.g., product line changes, acquisitions, and management shifts). The service groups companies by industry. At the beginning of each section the entire industry is reviewed. This one-page summary can give the corporate researcher a quick snapshot of the industry and companies in that industry.

Wiesenberger Investment Companies (Wiesenberger Services). A crucial source for the researcher who needs to find out about the companies that invest in other companies. What makes these investment firms tick? It profiles major U.S. and Canadian investment companies and mutual funds.

CHAPTER 5

HANDY SOURCES FOR SPECIFIC INDUSTRIES

Statistical Sources, Directories, and Associations

The other chapters in this book offer general sources and techniques for locating company information. This chapter concentrates on the valuable materials already in print on a wide variety of industries. The data appears in many different forms—as statistics, full-length prose, and simple directory listings.

In the following pages, I have summarized those key sources that in many cases supply general data about an industry and the companies within it. Each list is divided into statistical sources, directories, and associations.

Data bases will be covered in Chapter 7; in addition, industries not included in these bibliographies are mentioned in Chapter 6.

ADVERTISING

Statistical Sources

1. *Leading National Advertisers (Leading National Advertisers).*   This major corporate intelligence source is able to answer the question: "How much did company X spend on advertising this quarter or year?" This publication tracks thousands of products and an almost equal number of companies, and the advertising expenditures associated with the products. The reference allows you to look up ad dollars spent by company or by product name. The dollars reported are divided into different media groupings (TV, radio, newspaper, magazines, and so on).

2. *Standard Rate & Data Service (Standard Rate & Data Service).*   Another excellent advertising intelligence source. If you were trying to gauge the competitive advertising rates charged by one radio station or newspaper, this is the source you would turn to. Each edition contains an alphabetical index as well as the subscription rate, circulation data, and advertising rates charged. SRDS appears in a number of different versions, describing different media. You will find an SRDS directory in almost every newspaper, TV station, radio station, direct mail firm, and magazine in the United States. No advertising sales department can afford to be without one. Whenever a newspaper has to set its rates, it turns to SRDS first to compare its prices with that of a major rival. SRDS issues a number of updates on the rates charged.

   SRDS publishes the following directories:

   Business Publication Rates & Data
   Consumer Magazine and Farm Publication Rates & Data
   Direct Mail List Rates & Data
   Medical/Paramedical Publication Rates & Data
   Network Rates & Data
   Newspaper Rates & Data
   Print Production Data
   Spot Radio Rates & Data
   Spot Television Rates & Data
   Transit Advertising Rates & Data
   Weekly Newspaper Rates & Data
   Newspaper Circulation Analysis

British Rates & Data

Canadian Advertising Rates & Data

Directories

1. *Standard Directory of Advertising Agencies (National Register Company)*. This directory offers a brief, insightful view of U.S. advertising agencies, including name, address, account executives, annual billings, accounts, and a breakdown of the media placed or used. This last item can tell you if an agency has a great deal of experience in TV versus newspapers, for example. Some ad agencies place their clients' ads solely in newspapers or magazines, while others are known for their expertise in TV ads.

2. *Advertising Age: U.S. Agencies (Crain Communications)*. The U.S. agency issue appears in February of each year and the International agency issue appears in March. The U.S. agency issue is a somewhat smaller version of the Standard Directory mentioned above, with over 650 agencies and their accounts listed. This edition also states an agency's new accounts, as well as those dropped. Other special issues appearing in Advertising Age during the course of the year:

Marketing Reports (August) on the 100 leading national advertisers.

National Expenditures in Newspapers (June) tabulates ad expenditures for companies spending more than $10,000 for their brands in national newspaper space.

Profiles of Top 100 Markets in the U.S. (December) describes the economic activity in each of the 100 Top SMSAs.

3. *Membership Directory (International Advertising Association)*. A large listing of key executives on the international advertising scene.

Associations

1. *American Association of Advertising Agencies (New York)*. This is considered THE association for the advertising industry. The AAAA, as it is known in the trade, has a research service for its members that can retrieve articles or gather advertising information.

2. *American Advertising Federation (Washington, DC)*. A public affairs association for the industry with a large membership of over 22,000 members.

3.   *Business/Professional Advertising Association (New York).*   An agency devoted to business communications, publishing a number of newsletters in the business communication and advertising research field. It also conducts seminars for business communicators.

AEROSPACE INDUSTRY

Statistical Sources

1.   *Aerospace Facts & Figures (Aerospace Industries Association of America).*   This is an annual volume, offering statistics on aircraft production, trade, industry employment, R&D, and various military and federally sponsored programs.

2.   *Handbook of Airline Statistics (U. S. Civil Aeronautics Board).*   With airline deregulation, airlines will probably disclose less and less information as the years go by. This text, appearing once every two years, is the statistical source book for data on air carriers. This is the master reference source for the industry; the CAB publishes other more frequent and more specialized texts.

Directories

1.   *World Aviation Directory (Ziff-Davis Publishing Company).*   This text is far more than just a directory of manufacturers, suppliers to the industry, and air carriers; it is also a buyers' guide.

2.   *Interavia ABC: World Directory of Aviation and Astronautics (Interavia SA).*   The directory supplies names, addresses, and operating information for companies in all phases of the international aviation industry.

Associations

1.   *Aerospace Industries Association of America (Washington, DC).*   The primary association for manufacturers of military and civilian aircraft in the United States. The AIAA is extremely active in providing services to the industry. It publishes a quarterly magazine called *Aerospace*, as well as a statistical annual mentioned above. To obtain industry contact lists and names of key sources in the industry, I recommend that you order their annual committee directory.

2.   *American Institute of Aeronautics & Astronautics (New York).*   The largest technical membership association of its kind for scientists and en-

gineers in the industry, with over 32,000 members. It publishes almost a dozen magazines and journals; most are highly technical. Because of its membership size, it is an excellent opportunity for the researcher to begin networking with his or her contacts. The membership list can be an extremely valuable contacts directory.

3. *General Aviation Manufacturers Association (Washington, DC).* Its membership consists of manufacturers of general aviation components.

APPAREL

Statistical Sources

1. *Fairchild Fact File: Textile-Apparel Industries (Fairchild Publications).* Fairchild publishes some of the major "books" for the industry, including the bible: *Women's Wear Daily.* It publishes a number of these fact files, which combine original research with government statistics. It is a valuable compendium of data not easily gathered or collected elsewhere. Unfortunately, the Fact File appears irregularly.

2. *Focus: Economic Profile of the Apparel Industry (American Apparel Manufacturers Association).* This text concentrates primarily on the industry's economics and production. It does, however, also discuss corporate investments and capital investments—but again, on a macroscopic level, without concentrating on specific companies.

Directories

1. *National Apparel Contractors and Suppliers Directory (Apparel Industry Magazine).* The publication includes almost 5000 suppliers and contractors to the apparel industry.

2. *American Apparel Manufacturers Association Directory (American Apparel Manufacturers Association).* A directory containing over 800 member manufacturers and suppliers of goods and services. A product index is included.

Associations

1. *American Apparel Manufacturers Association (Arlington, VA).* There are scores of trade and union associations for this industry in the United States. This is one of the more influential associations, representing 450 manufacturers. It issues over a dozen publications. Its 25-odd committees

could provide an entry into an industry that is filled with thousands of ma
and pa shops and almost as many specialties.

2. *Apparel Manufacturers Association (New York).* Because of its strategic location—the heart of the garment industry in the United States—
the APA is another association whose opinion and advice you should seek
when beginning to research the industry.

APPLIANCES

Statistical Sources (Special Magazine Issues)

1. *Appliance 10-Year Statistical Review (Dana Chase Publications).*
Each April, *Appliance* magazine offers a ten-year review of appliance shipments and sales.

2. *Merchandising Marketing Report (Billboard Publications).* A superb review of the appliance and consumer merchandising scene. It appears
in the March issue of *Merchandising* and offers sales and growth statistics
for individual appliances. Many of these statistics are gathered by *Merchandising*'s staff and are not rehashed government statistics.

Directories

1. *Appliance Purchasing Directory (Dana Chase Publications).* Contains those companies that supply appliance manufacturers. Each entry
includes name, address, and products offered.

2. *Appliance Manufacturer—Annual Directory Issue (Cahners Publishing Company).* Lists approximately 3500 appliance manufacturers,
suppliers to the industry, and mass merchandisers. There is also a product
index.

Associations

1. *Association of Home Appliance Manufacturers (Chicago).* A primary association for appliance manufacturers. Membership directory is
available. It is published annually.

2. *Gas Appliance Manufacturers Association (Arlington, VA).* Over
250 members, including producers of commercial, industrial, and residential gas appliances. The association has separate divisions for each of the
major gas product groups.

AUTOMOBILE INDUSTRY

Statistical Sources

1. *Automobile Facts & Figures (Motor Vehicle Manufacturers Association of the United States).* To gauge a manufacturer's market share, you first need some accurate market size data. This is what the Facts book offers. It contains statistics on auto production, registrations, and automobile usage.

2. *Ward's Automotive Yearbook (Ward's Communications).* This is another one of those industry bibles. Ward's is the keeper of the industry statistical flame. This particular book offers statistics on industry trends, imports, auto parts, and registrations. The volume also contains a manufacturers' directory.

3. *Automotive News, Almanac Issue (Detroit).* A statistical compendium, offering data on U.S. car and truck production. It is literally an automobile shopping guide, presenting pictures of late models and their prices.

Directories

1. *Ward's Who's Who Among U.S. Motor Vehicle Manufacturers (Ward's Communications).* This directory lists over 8000 industry executives, including those involved in the manufacturing, associations, government agencies, unions, and trade magazines.

2. *Automotive Age Buyers Guide Issue (Feed-Crown Publishing Company).* An industry buyers' guide, appearing annually.

Associations

1. *Automotive Information Council (Southfield, MI).* For the researcher, this is a major automotive information center. Remember that this association, like others, is formed by its members. So do not expect the association to reveal confidential information about its membership. Still, it could prove a valuable source of contacts and advice. Its members include other trade associations, companies, and automotive entrepreneurs.

2. *Automotive Market Research Council (Toledo, OH).* Members of this association are primarily market researchers and analysts in the automotive parts, components, and service industries.

3. *Automotive Service Industry Association (Chicago).* Its members number over 8500 and include parts wholesalers, distributors, manufacturers

representatives, and remanufacturers. Its membership directory can provide you with a backdoor approach to learning about the industry or about a particular company. These are the very manufacturers who know about model changes, parts information, and competitor production. This association is no different than any other similar member organization, and its members are probably not more talkative than any other group's membership. But the idea is there: use the membership to provide you with a network of contacts that will lead to getting the intelligence you seek.

BANKING

Statistical Sources

1.   A *Profile of State-Chartered Banking (Conference of State Bank Supervisors)*.   A handbook of banking laws and regulations. In addition, this text offers data on the assets and operations of state-chartered banks.

2.   *Finance Facts Yearbook (National Consumer Finance Association)*.   Information on consumer spending and data on the consumer credit business.

3.   *Savings and Home Financing Source Book (Federal Home Loan Bank Board)*.   This annual reference source offers statistics on home loan bank boards.

4.   *Mortgage Banking: Financial Statements & Operating Ratios (Mortgage Bankers Association of America)*.   A text that presents operating data on mortgage banks.

5.   *Federal Reserve Bulletin (U.S. Board of Governors of the Federal Reserve System)*.   This is an eclectic banking reference source. It contains data for commercial banks, government securities, and federal bank statistics.

6.   *Savings & Loan Factbook (United States League of Savings Associations)*.   When you need an overview of the savings and loan industry, this is the appropriate text. The book explores the economic conditions (e.g., new construction and mortgage financing), and lists statistics on the savings and loans themselves.

Directories

1.   *American Bank Directory (McFadden Business Publications)*.   In this two-volume set, the researcher can find every bank in the United States, its address, financials, and officers.

Associations

1. *American Bankers Association (Washington, DC).* There are dozens of banking associations, both regional and national. But the ABA is considered the most influential and probably the best known of the lot. Its membership consists of commercial banks and trust companies. It has a large number of educational programs and an excellent reference collection. The ABA can provide the researcher with much esoteric information on the banking industry.

2. *Bank Administration Institute (Rolling Meadows, IL).* A purely educational organization whose job it is to conduct research and educate its constituents on bank operations.

3. *Independent Bankers Association of America (Washington, DC).* This organization represents relatively small-sized banks and may offer the researcher a different perspective on the banking industry.

BEVERAGE INDUSTRY

Statistical Sources

1. *Beverage Industry—Annual Manual (Magazines for Industry).* A combination industry directory and statistical yearbook. The directory is indexed by product and brand name.

2. *The Liquor Handbook (Jobson Associates).* This is considered a marketing handbook for wines and malts. It offers sales data for the past 15 years, as well as consumer demographics and advertising expenditures.

Directories

1. *Beverage World—Buyers Guide (Keller Publishing Corporation).* This guide is a product of one of the industry's key trade magazines. Suppliers are listed by product.

2. *National Beverage Marketing Directory (Beverage Marketing Corporation).* This should be considered one of the major industry directories, with over 16,000 entries. The directory covers producers, trade associations, and government agencies, and has an executive listing containing over 20,000 names. The volume covers company franchises, sales volume for bottlers, and brands handled by distributors.

Associations

1. *Distilled Spirits Council of the United States (Washington, DC)*. Publishes a Fact Book and other industry benchmark publications. It is established as a public information source.

2. *National Soft Drink Association (Washington, DC)*.   With a membership of over 1500, this is one of the major industry trade groups. Its primary purpose is to improve its members' operating procedures and research.

CHEMICAL INDUSTRY

Statistical Sources

1. *The Kline Guide to the Chemical Industries (C. H. Kline & Company)*.   Kline publishes a number of different industry directories and statistical sources for a number of heavy industries. This guide contains an analysis of the chemical industry. It also has estimated sales, by product line, for each of over 450 chemical companies. A key source for identifying plant capacity and equipment.

2. *Chemical Statistics Handbook (Manufacturing Chemists Association)*.   This book contains data on sales and production of synthetic organic and inorganic chemicals.

Directories

1. *Directory of Chemical Producers (SRI International)*.   A detailed directory of manufacturers in the chemical industry.

2. *ODP Chemical Buyers Directory (Schnell Publishing Company)*.   This guide is offered by the Chemical Marketing Reporter, a leading industry trade magazine.

Associations

1. *American Chemical Society (Washington, DC)*.   Probably one of the largest professional societies, with over 120,000 members and a staff of over 1500. It produces both technical and nontechnical literature and pamphlets.

2. *Chemical Manufacturers Association (Washington, DC).* An association that offers seminars and promotes the industry. Its approximately 200 members are manufacturers of basic chemicals.

3. *National Association of Chemical Distributors (Dayton, OH).* This association offers a somewhat specialized directory that lists only distributors. The NACD also compiles statistics.

DATA PROCESSING

Statistical Sources

1. *Computer Business News Stock Index (C. W. Communications).* Assembles, on a weekly basis, final stock prices for computer and computer-related publicly traded companies.

2. *Statistical Reference Book—Data Entry/Terminal Market (International Data Corporation).* IDC specializes in the computer industry. This text offers growth rates and projections for the industry.

3. *EDP Industry Report: Review and Forecast (International Data Corporation).* Unlike the above IDC report, this volume breaks out individual manufacturers' shipments and ranks the manufacturers by their shipments. Other valuable competitor data: number of installed machines and unit prices.

Directories

1. *Association for Data Processing Service Organization Membership Directory (Association for Data Processing Service Organizations—ADAPSO).* This directory of just under 500 members covers companies in this specific service niche.

2. *Data Communication: Buyers Guide (McGraw-Hill).* Mentions all companies involved in data communications: carriers and equipment manufacturers, including manufacturers of terminals and disk drives.

3. *Data Sources (McGraw-Hill).* A superbly organized and sweeping directory of the data processing and computer industries. It not only gives name and address but also product line and number of employees. The publisher, recognizing that this is a fast-changing industry, has chosen to offer four editions per year.

Associations

Note—There are literally dozens of associations, with more springing up each year. This section mentions a few of the major groups. Because of the crossover of communications, electronics, and computers, a number of the major computer associations are actually electronic and telecommunications industry groups. These related associations will be mentioned in other bibliographies that follow.

1. *Computer Communications Industry Association (Arlington, VA)*. This association represents mainframe vendors. Maintains a library and can be a valuable industry source.

2. *Association for Computing Machinery (New York)*. Probably the oldest of the computer associations, founded in 1947. With thousands of members and a number of influential scholarly and technical publications, it is one of the industry's strongest voices. It is not so much a lobbying group as an educational organization.

3. *Association of Data Processing Service Organizations—ADAPSO (Arlington, VA)*. As mentioned above, an organization that serves the data processing service companies. It does maintain a library and may be an excellent source for your inquiries on software and computer time-sharing services.

DRUGS AND COSMETICS

Statistical Sources

1. *Prescription Drug Industry: Factbook (Pharmaceutical Manufacturers Association)*. Offers company earnings, stock prices, and shipments for over 10 years. Has sections on market projections and trends. Also reviews the industry's imports and exports.

2. *Product Marketing's Annual Consumer Expenditure Study (Charleson Publications)*. Examines consumer expenditures on health and beauty products. The study is published yearly, in July.

Directories

1. *Soaps, Cosmetics, Chemical Specialties Blue Book: Reference and Buyer's Guide (MacNair-Dorland Company)*. A fairly comprehensive directory of companies that manufacture health and beauty aids products.

2.   *American Drug Index (J. B. Lippincott).*   This is the directory a researcher may want to use when trying to find the manufacturer of a particular type of drug. It is the equivalent of a trademark directory that is specifically geared to the pharmaceutical industry.

3.   *Drug and Cosmetic Catalog (Harcourt Brace Jovanovich).*   This text will allow the researcher to locate all those companies that serve the pharmaceutical and cosmetic houses. Companies included here are consultants, manufacturers of machinery and processing equipment, and key magazines and associations in the field.

Associations

1.   *Pharmaceutical Manufacturers Association (Washington, DC).*   A large and active association with an extensive library. Its members consist of manufacturers of ethical drugs and medical products and devices.

2.   *National Wholesale Druggists' Association (Alexandria, VA).*   This is a wholesalers'—not a manufacturers'—association. It is concerned only with the movement and sale of merchandise, not manufacturing aspects.

ELECTRONICS INDUSTRY

Statistical Sources

1.   *Electronic Market Data Book (Electronic Industries Association).*   The statistics generated by the EIA and contained in this book are often accepted as benchmarks for the industry. This work offers production and sales data for almost every electronic product category, from semiconductors to CB radios, televisions, and lasers.

2.   *Electronics (McGraw-Hill).*   Each January this publication offers a special issue on the state of the electronics industry. It presents table upon table of sales and shipment data for countries across the globe, concentrating on the U.S., Japanese, and European markets. While the magazine does not discuss specific companies, it does go into considerable depth on each of the product groups.

Directories

1.   *Electronic News Financial Fact Book and Directory (Fairchild Publications).*   Offers company profiles, including name, address, officers,

products, stock exchanges, ticker symbol, plant size, and some financial data.

2. *Electronic Industry Telephone Directory (Harris Publishing Company).* As the name implies, this is a handy reference book, listing names and phone numbers of U.S., Canadian, and foreign firms.

3. *Electronic Marketing Directory (National Credit Office/Dun & Bradstreet).* In addition to a statistical section, the directory does what D&B does best. It offers a nicely organized listing of electronic equipment manufacturers.

Associations

1. *Electronic Industries Association (Washington, DC).* A valuable resource. The EIA publishes a number of leading guidebooks in the industry, and also has an excellent library and information center that the press calls upon often for charts and data. Through its various directories, the corporate researcher should be able to begin understanding the industry and develop the necessary contacts. Its greatest strength is in consumer electronics.

2. *American Electronics Association (Palo Alto, CA).* Perhaps less well known than the EIA, this is an important group to contact when researching the manufacture of electronic components or their research and development. The association sponsors seminars and publishes a membership directory.

ENVIRONMENTAL ENGINEERING INDUSTRY

Statistical Sources

1. *Chemical Engineering Deskbook: Environmental Engineering (McGraw-Hill).*

Directories

1. *American Academy of Environmental Engineers—Roster of Diplomates (American Academy of Environmental Engineers).* Lists almost 1800 environmental engineers and is indexed geographically.

2. *World Environmental Directory (Business Publishers).* A broad di-

rectory, listing over 7000 manufacturers and other firms or organizations that are involved with environmental work. Aside from name and address, each entry also includes the firm's product or area of activity.

Associations

1. *American Academy of Environmental Engineers (Rockville, MD).* Publishers of the above directory, this association has established standards for environmental engineers. Its members specialize in air pollution control, industrial hygiene, radiation protection, solid waste management, water supply wastewater, as well as general environmental topics. The association itself is affiliated with a number of other groups, making it a nexus for information on the industry.

FOOD AND GROCERY INDUSTRY

Statistical Sources

1. *Almanac of the Canning, Freezing, Preserving Industries (E. E. Judge & Sons).* A collection of data compiled from government agricultural department statistics, as well as from a variety of other sources. A good source to use to gauge industry size.

2. *Chain Store Age Supermarkets Sales Manual (Lebhar-Friedman).* Packed with sales and product data on the supermarket industry, also offers comparative data from past years. The volume includes valuable supermarket operating information (e.g., profit margins), that may help you compute or compare your target's profitability.

3. *Chain Store Age Supermarkets Edition, July Issue (Lebhar-Friedman).* This magazine reviews a few dozen major product categories each year, naming names and providing insight to the latest sales activity—identifying the leaders and hot sellers on the grocery shelf.

4. *Supermarketing—Annual Consumer Expenditures Survey, September Issue (Gralla Publications).* One of the only regularly published studies of its kind. It offers highly specific sales figures for scores of products sold in food stores. The issue presents the data with a three-year history, and includes everything from batteries to spaghetti.

Directories

1. *IFT World Directory & Guide (Institute of Food Technologists).* The book to go to when you need contacts in the food-processing industry. This directory contains names of engineers and managers in the business of food processing. Another handy section offers names of suppliers and consultants to the industry. This book is available to Institute members only.

2. *Thomas Grocery Register (Thomas Publishing Company).* We already discussed this text in an earlier section. For under $100 this three-volume set should be in every corporate researcher's library, especially if that research takes you into the food industry. You will find names of small food brokers and distributors that you cannot possibly locate through any other single source. Because this is an industry of spinoffs and small ma and pa operations, a directory such as this one can lead you to former employees who have started their own operations or competitors who know your target very well.

Associations

1. *Institute of Food Technologists (Chicago).* A technical association with 20,000 members. Aside from its many technical committees, it publishes *Food Technology* and the *Journal of Food Science.* It is the major industry group devoted to developing and applying the latest engineering advances in the food-processing industry.

2. *National Association of Retail Grocers of the United States (Reston, VA).* A 40,000-member organization of independent food retailers. It can provide a wealth of information on food store operation.

HEALTH AND MEDICAL SCIENCES

Statistical Sources

1. *Hospital Indicators Monthly Statistics (American Hospital Association).* This semimonthly booklet contains operating information on hospitals nationwide. It reports on hospital activity, measuring salary levels, occupancy rate, and number of admissions.

2. *Medical, Marketing & Media (CPS Communications).* This magazine concentrates on the marketing and advertising of medical and health

care products. It has special issues and editions throughout the year that review advertising expenditures and marketing trends in the industry.

3.   *Modern Healthcare (Crain Communications).*   A glossy periodical that concentrates on the trade rather than on the technical aspects of the industry. It provides a wealth of data found nowhere else on subsegments of the health care industry. One example is a special issue on nursing homes that appears each year, offering data on sales, number of units, and growth trends.

Directories

1.   *The Hospital Phone Book (U.S. Directory Service).*   This is the comprehensive directory of hospitals throughout the United States. There are over 7500 hospitals listed.

2.   *Medical and Health Information Directory (Gale Research).*   A terrific health care industry reference source. It primarily lists health care agencies, not corporations. Over 12,000 groups are listed. Entries are also cross-indexed many different ways for easy access.

Associations

1.   *American Hospital Association (Chicago).*   A large organization with over 6000 member health care institutions. It studies the entire health care industry and publishes surveys in the field. It has a large library and publishes a good deal of statistical material. If you needed to locate a hospital administrator, this might be the group to approach first.

2.   *American Health Care Association (Washington, DC).*   Its members are involved in the nursing home industry, an industry made up of many small independent operators. This is one of the central information clearinghouses for this segment of the health care industry. It compiles otherwise hard-to-get statistics.

HOTEL AND LODGING INDUSTRY

Statistical Sources

1.   *Trends in the Hotel Industry—USA and International Editions (Pannell Kerr and Forster).*   These two volumes concentrate on operating information for hotels and motels. You, as a researcher, can in turn use this

data to assess your target. Is your target, for example, profitable? If so, by how much? How does your target compare to the rest of the industry?

2. *U.S. Lodging Industry: Report on Hotel and Motor Hotel Operations (Laventhol and Horwath).* Offers data similar to the above text. In addition, discusses trends.

Directories

1. *Directory of Hotel & Motel Systems (American Hotel Association Directory Corporation).* Covers 300 chains, listing name, address, telephone, information on hotel sites, and number of rooms.

2. *Official Hotel & Resort Guide (Ziff-Davis Publishing Company).* A worldwide listing of hotels and resorts. Each entry contains a brief description of each hotel or motel, as well as the name of the facility's manager.

3. *Hotel & Motel Management—Buyer's Guide (Robert Freeman Publishing Corporation).* This directory contains names, addresses, and services offered by 900 suppliers to the hotel and motel industry. The Guide appears in the February issue of *Hotel and Motel Management.*

Associations

1. *American Hotel and Motel Association (New York).* An organization of other hotel and motel associations. One of the largest and oldest national hotel associations; aside from promoting the lodging industry, it compiles statistics and conducts seminars on the industry.

INCENTIVES AND PREMIUM PRODUCTS INDUSTRIES

Statistical Sources/Special Magazine Issues

1. *Incentive Marketing—Facts Issue (Bill Communications).* Provides sales by product category, in addition to discussing industry trends.

2. *Premium Incentive Business—Annual Industry Report (Gralla Publications).* Similar to the above.

Directories

1. *Incentive Marketing—Directory of Incentive Sources (Bill Communications)*. This directory lists names of companies who manufacture or distribute pens, calendars, and other items used as advertising or promotional incentives. There are over 1000 companies listed in this directory. Each entry offers some description of the product or service. The issue appears in January of each year.

2. *Premium Incentive Business—Directory of Premium Suppliers and Services (Gralla Publications)*. A listing similar to the above but with over 300 suppliers. Suppliers are classified by product. The issue appears each February.

3. *Salesman's Guide Nationwide Directory: Premium Incentive & Travel Buyers (Salesman's Guide)*. This is a reverse directory and one that could prove extremely valuable to a corporate researcher in the industry. This directory lists the buyers—not the manufacturers—of premiums. Imagine if you had to find out competitive pricing or marketing information for a target company? This would be the perfect directory to turn to. The buyers are arranged geographically (just as a premium salesman would want it) and each listing contains the names of buyers and the type and dollar amount of the premiums purchased. This edition appears annually with three supplements.

4. *Premium Merchandising Club of New York/Directory (Premium Merchandising Club of New York)*. A regional directory, listing over 250 executives who both buy and supply incentive products.

Associations

1. *Incentive Manufacturers Representatives Associations (Philadelphia)*. IMRA is a group of manufacturers' representatives who sell premiums. It may provide the basis for a network of contacts in the premium business in the Northeast.

2. *Promotional Marketing Association of America (New York)*. An organization representing a broad cross-section of companies involved in the premium industry—companies such as service firms, sales incentive organizations, consultants, and manufacturers.

3. *Specialty Advertising Association International (Irving, TX)*. One of the largest incentives organizations in the country. In addition to seminars

and its monthly *Specialty Advertising Business* publication, it also compiles statistics and conducts research.

INDUSTRIAL ARTS

Statistical Sources

1. *Forecast (Annual) American Printer and Lithographer (MacLean Hunter Publishing).* The annual issue reports revenues and trends in the printing industry. It forecasts as far as a decade, and discusses all branches of the publishing industry.

Directories/Special Magazine Issues

1. *American Ink Maker—Buyers Guide (MacNair-Dorland Company).* A directory of suppliers to the industry, including equipment manufacturers and ink and pigment suppliers. The issue appears in October.

2. *Graphic Arts Monthly—Buyers Guide (Technical Publishing Company).* An alphabetical list of manufacturers, suppliers, and distributors to the graphic arts industry. Product descriptions are included. The issue appears each June.

3. *Printing Impressions Special (Annual) Directory (North American Publishing Company).* Similar to the above directory, but also includes model name and description for the equipment listed with each supplier.

Associations

1. *Graphic Arts Technical Foundation (Pittsburgh).* An organization that serves the graphic arts industry by conducting seminars and publishing informational pamphlets for the public and its members. It does maintain a fairly extensive library in printing and graphic arts.

2. *National Association of Printing Ink Manufacturers (Harrison, NY).* A highly specialized industry association, serving ink manufacturers and representing them in the legislature. Because any one ink manufacturer is likely to know dozens of equipment manufacturers in the industry, this association's membership may be able to provide you with contacts throughout the industry.

3. *Printing Industries of America (Arlington, VA)*.   This association's membership consists of commercial printers and publishes extensive operating statistics on this segment. The PIA is a knowledgeable source for rate charges and union contracts.

INSURANCE INDUSTRY

Statistical Sources

1. *Best's (Best Publishing Company)*.   This publishing company produces the widest-read insurance industry tabloid. Many of its publications, including statistical editions, were discussed in an earlier section.

2. *Insurance Facts (Insurance Information Institute)*.   A source of property and liability insurance industry statistics.

3. *Life Insurance Fact Book (Institute of Life Insurance)*.   A statistical overview of the life insurance industry.

4. *Source Book of Health Insurance Data (Health Insurance Institute)*.   A source of data on health benefits and associated premiums.

Directories

1. *Agents & Buyers Guide (National Underwriter Company)*.   A directory listing companies that offer special insurance lines.

2. *Insurance Almanac (Underwriter Printing and Publishing Company)*.   A directory of insurance companies, insurance agents, and brokers. Each entry contains company name, type of insurance written, and company history. Another section presents a variety of industry statistics.

Associations

1. *Insurance Services Office (New York)*.   An excellent source of insurance industry statistics.

2. *Life Insurance Marketing and Research Association (Hartford, CT)*.   This organization is established as a research arm for its member

general life insurance companies. LIMRA compiles statistics and has a fairly good-sized reference library.

LABORATORY DIAGNOSTIC SUPPLIES INDUSTRY

Statistical Sources

1.   *Clinical Lab—Diagnostic Instrumentation (Theta Technology Corporation)*.   A market study that offers data on leading companies, production, and company descriptions. Historical and forecast data are also presented.

2.   *Clinical Laboratory Reagents and Test Kits (Frost and Sullivan)*.   As the name implies, this report offers forecast information in various segments of the clinical testing industry.

Directories

1.   *Clinical Laboratory Reference (Medical Economics Company)*.   A directory of manufacturers of reagents, tests, and related equipment. Each listing includes company name, address, and products offered.

2.   *Directory of Medical Products Distributors (McKnight Medical Communications)*.   Instead of manufacturers, this directory focuses on distributors. A useful source because of its detailed entries, which contain the number of salespeople, geographical areas covered, and some financial information for each distributor.

3.   *Health Devices Sourcebook: A Directory of Medical Devices and Manufacturers (ECRI Shared Service)*.   A listing of products and their manufacturers.

Associations

1.   *American Society for Hospital Purchasing and Materials Management (American Hospital Association, Chicago)*.   A branch of the AHA. An association for buyers of medical equipment in hospitals and other health care institutions. With a membership of almost 1500, it may open up doors to the often inaccessible hospital purchasing community.

2.   *Health Industry Manufacturers Association (Washington, DC)*.   A group that represents domestic manufacturers of medical equipment. It publishes a directory of its members as well as technical reports.

LUMBER

Statistical Sources

1. *Current Monthly Domestic Production and Trade Statistics (National Forest Products Association).* This publication offers an overview of lumber industry production. Production data is reported monthly. The report also offers a regional production breakout on a quarterly basis. The regional data may be very useful in assessing a particular competitor's dominance of a specific market. Should one competitor dominate one region, it then becomes easy to estimate its output based on the report's regional figures.

2. *Statistical Yearbook of the Western Lumber Industry (Western Wood Products Association).* This annual volume offers statistics on lumber mills and sawmills, including employment, market data, shipments, and exports/imports. Companies are also identified by the number of acres owned. Historical consumption data is reported by type of demand.

Directories

1. *Crow's Buyers and Sellers Guide of the Forest Products Industries (C. C. Crow Publications).* A listing of over 5000 lumber, plywood, and miscellaneous wood products manufacturers. The text is indexed geographically, by product and by individual name.

2. *Forest Industries—Annual Equipment Catalog & Buyers' Guide Issue (Miller Freeman Publications).* An equipment buyers guide of suppliers of logging and manufacturing equipment. There is a product index.

Associations

1. *Hardwood Plywood Manufacturers Association (Reston, VA).* This association's membership consists of manufacturers and prefinishers of hardwood plywood. It publishes a number of newsletters and bulletins, including *Furniture Bulletin* and *Hardwood, Plywood and Veneer Imports Report.*

2. *National Lumber and Building Material Dealers Association (Washington, DC).* This group is actually an association of regional forest associations. All the associations that are members represent approximately 15,000 retailers. The association does compile statistics.

MACHINERY

Statistical Sources

1.   *Economic Handbook of the Machine Tool Industry (National Machine Tool Builders Association).*   This handbook offers general statistics on the machine tool industry, including shipments, trade information, and employment data.

Directories

1.   *American Machine Tool Distributors' Association Directory of Members (American Machine Tool Distributors' Association).*   This directory lists over 200 machine tool companies. Each entry includes the name, address, and senior executives.

2.   *Machine and Tool Directory (Hitchcock Publishing Company).*   The directory includes over 3000 manufacturers and distributors of all kinds of metalworking equipment. The directory is indexed by product.

Associations

1.   *Associated Equipment Distributors (Oak Brook, IL).*   A broadly defined organization, it represents manufacturers and distributors of various types of construction, road, and mining equipment. Very much a service-oriented organization, the AED compiles hard-to-find industry statistics.

2.   *Machinery and Allied Products Institute (Washington, DC).*   This organization's membership consists mostly of industrial and plant machinery manufacturers.

3.   *National Machine Tool Builders' Association (McLean, VA).*   Its members are manufacturers of machine tools. The association conducts various workshops throughout the year and would appear to be an excellent place to start making contacts within the industry.

MEAT PROCESSING

Statistical Sources

1.   *Meatfacts (American Meat Institute).*   A statistical summary of the U.S. production and consumption of meat and meat products.

Directories

1. *Meat Processing/Directory of Suppliers (Davies Publishing Company)*. An extensive listing of manufacturers of meat packing and processing equipment. Distributors are also listed. The directory is indexed by product.

Associations

1. *American Meat Institute (Washington, DC)*. One of the major industry associations, its membership consists of packers, processors, and canners of meat. This group may serve as an excellent starting point for any research you may want to conduct on the meat processing industry. It also publishes the above-mentioned *Meatfacts*.

2. *National Live Stock and Meat Board (Chicago, IL)*. This is an association of associations, representing some 30 organizations of meat suppliers, retailers, and other meat service firms. It is both a public relations arm for the industry and an information center.

MEDICAL/DENTAL SUPPLIES

Statistical Sources

1. *Facts about the Dental Market (American Dental Association)*. This publication offers the number of dentists by state and region. It also offers some information on the dental supply market.

Directories

1. *Health Devices Sourcebook (Emergency Care Research Institute)*. This is a directory of manufacturers that produce surgical and laboratory equipment and other hospital supplies. The volume is indexed by product and trade name.

2. *Health Industry Manufacturers Association Directory (Health Industry Manufacturers Association)*. A listing of producers of medical and diagnostic products.

3. *Hayes Directory of Dental Supply Houses (Edward N. Hayes)*. Not only does this directory list the company name, address, and phone number, but it also contains a credit rating for each entry.

4. *Hayes Directory of Physician and Hospital Supply Houses (Edward N. Hayes)*. This directory is similar to the above, but instead covers the hospital supply houses.

5. *Directory of Medical Products Distributors (McKnight Medical Communications)*. Directories like this one are key resources when looking for experts to interview. This particular directory is made to be used by buyers and, as such, lists distributors by region.

6. *Surgical Trade Buyers Guide (Surgical Business)*. An excellent resource for locating equipment manufacturers. Product groupings are fairly refined and offer the neophyte researcher a good feel for the finer distinctions among various types of medical equipment.

Associations

1. *American Surgical Trade Association (Chicago)*. Primarily an association for distributors of medical equipment and supplies. The association collects statistics and provides a number of publications, including a manufacturers directory.

2. *Health Industry Manufacturers Association (Washington, DC)*. A major industry association that provides statistics and industry information.

3. *American Dental Trade Association (Washington, DC)*. An association of manufacturers and distributors of equipment and supplies. It provides market research to its membership and produces operating ratios for distributors.

NONFERROUS METALS

Statistical Sources

1. *Non-Ferrous Metal Data (American Bureau of Metal Statistics)*. This annual study offers production, consumption, and pricing information for well over a dozen nonferrous metals.

Directories

1. *Non-Ferrous Founders Society/Buyers Guide & Directory (Non-Ferrous Founders' Society)*. A listing of nonferrous foundries in the United

States. Each listing is detailed—so detailed as to include the casting methods used and alloys handled by each foundry.

2. *Non-Ferrous Metal Works of the World (Metal Bulletin Books).* A worldwide listing of nonferrous plants. Each entry includes a description of the plant's equipment, products, and executives.

Associations

1. *American Bureau of Metal Statistics (New York).* As the name implies, its chief job is to compile and publish industry statistics. The yearbook mentioned above is one of its chief publications.

2. *Non-Ferrous Founders Society (Des Plaines, IL).* This group represents nonferrous manufacturers and publishes a number of publications, including the buyers' guide mentioned above.

PAPER

Statistical Sources

1. *Statistics of Paper and Paperboard (American Paper Institute).* This is a general compendium of aggregate industry statistics, including shipments, capacity, wages, prices, exports, and imports.

2. *Kline Guide to the Paper Industry (Charles H. Kline and Company).* Similar to the Kline Guide for the plastics industry, this volume reviews shipment data and analyzes industry trends. Over 400 manufacturers are listed, along with data on their production capacity.

3. *Monthly Statistical Summary (American Paper Institute).* A monthly review of production and expenditures.

4. *Newsprint Statistics (American Newspaper Publishers Association).* This annual review contains data on capacity and production for newsprint producers.

Directories

1. *Lockwood's Directory of the Paper and Allied Trades (Bulkey Dunton and Company).* This is considered by many researchers as the best single industry directory. It claims to list every mill and major user. Plant capacity is also reported for each facility.

Associations

1. *American Paper Institute (New York).* This is an association of pulp and paper producers. One of the premier paper associations, it acts as an information center for industry statistics and developments. It has numerous publications, both technical and general-purpose.

2. *Paper Industry Management Association (Arlington Heights, IL).* This organization of paper industry executives publishes a valuable directory of its 3000-plus membership.

PETROLEUM

Statistical Sources

1. *International Petroleum Encyclopedia (Penn Well Publishing Company).* Offers recent and historical drilling data by region. For example, it presents information on production by oil field, well counts, and costs of drilling and equipment. The book is organized geographically.

2. *Basic Petroleum Data Book (American Petroleum Institute).* The data here is broken down by category, such as drilling, production, and prices.

Directories

1. *Offshore Contractors and Equipment Directory (Penn Well Publishing Company).* An excellent and up-to-date list of every company in the offshore industry from the drilling contractors to geophysical companies. Firms here are listed by the equipment they use or their particular specialty.

2. *Oil & Gas Directory (Geophysical Directory).* This directory contains lists of drilling and exploration companies.

Associations

1. *American Petroleum Institute (Washington, DC).* The APT is a major industry organization that is often referred to in the press and relied upon for its industry statistics. It represents a broad cross-section of the industry, including suppliers, marketers, and refiners.

2. *Petroleum Equipment Institute (Tulsa, OK).* An association of companies that supply equipment to gas stations and other markets. I have found this group useful in locating information on the oil equipment industry.

PHOTOGRAPHY

Statistical Sources

1.   *Wolfman Report on the Photographic Industry in the United States (ABC Leisure Magazines).*   One of the few handy sources with historical statistics on the industry. Between two covers, it lays out employment, production, and consumption statistics on a variety of photographic products.

Directories

1.   *Photo Weekly—Buyers Handbook & Product Guide (Billboard Publications).*   This special issue of the magazine presents a listing of approximately 700 distributors and manufacturers in the photographic industry. The guide is indexed by product type.

2.   *Photographic Trade News—Master Buying Guide and Directory (PTN Publishing Corporation).*   One of the most complete industry guides available, with approximately 1500 entries of manufacturers. The guide is indexed by product and does list distributors, as well.

Associations

1.   *National Association of Photographic Manufacturers (Harrison, NY).*   This organization represents approximately 50 manufacturers and does assemble statistics on the industry.

2.   *Photographic Manufacturers and Distributors Association (New York).*   This organization represents a broad cross-section of wholesalers, importers, distributors, and manufacturers. Its membership directory, which is published annually, can prove to be an invaluable resource in networking throughout the industry.

PLASTICS

Statistical Sources

1.   *Kline Guide To The Plastics Industry (Charles H. Kline and Company).*   The Kline guides are excellent compilations of industry statistics

and trend analyses. This guide analyzes shipments, pricing, production, end-use markets, and major producers. The directory also includes a listing of hundreds of manufacturers and their estimated sales.

2. *Facts and Figures of the Plastics Industry (Society of the Plastic Industry).* A big-picture review of the industry. In addition to reporting on shipments and production, it ranks the major producers.

Directories

1. *The Society of the Plastics Industry, Inc. Membership Directory and Buyers' Guide (Society of the Plastics Industry).*   We have used this directory many times and have found it an extremely effective means to understanding the complex plastics industry. Entries not only include name and address but also discuss products and processes for each manufacturer.

2. *Plastics Manufacturing Handbook and Buyers' Guide (Bill Communications).*   This listing of plastics equipment and materials manufacturers provides specifics on product lines. The book is also indexed by trade name, a handy way to look up the product.

3. *Plastics Technology—Special Handbook and Buyer's Guide Issue (Bill Communications).*   This issue, which usually appears in June, concentrates on the machinery and supplies necessary in plastics processing.

4. *Plastics World—Plastics Directory (Cahners Publishing Company).*   A listing of manufacturers and suppliers to the industry. The indexes are both by product and by trade name. There are approximately 750 entries in all.

5. *Modern Plastics/Encyclopedia Issue (McGraw-Hill).*   One of the best guides to this industry. There are well over 4500 entries, which include just about every company in the industry, from manufacturers to industry suppliers.

Associations

1. *National Association of Plastics Distributors (Jaffrey, NH).*   This is an association exclusively devoted to distributors of plastics. The association does have a library.

2. *Society of the Plastics Industry (New York).*   Every industry has a granddaddy organization and this is one of them. Founded in 1937, the association consists mainly of plastics manufacturers. The group sponsors major conferences and collects statistics on the industry.

PUBLISHING

Statistical Sources

1. *Encyclomedia/Newspaper Edition (Decisions Publications).* A study of newspaper circulation and readership. In addition, the report studies advertising in magazines, television, radio, and various other advertising media. Also included is a directory of newspapers throughout the United States.

2. *Facts About Newspapers (American Newspaper Publishers Association).* A study that offers aggregate statistics on newspaper production and employment.

3. *Printing and Publishing/Quarterly Industry Report (Industry and Trade Administration, U.S. Department of Commerce).* A quarterly update on exports and imports of printed materials. Aside from statistical tables, the report includes some analysis of recent trends in the industry.

Directories

1. *Printing Trades Blue Book (A. F. Lewis & Company).* A directory that appears in various regional editions. It lists printing plants, typographers, paper producers, and almost everyone who is at all involved in producing printed materials. Each edition has thousands of listings. Each listing contains the firm's name, address, and chief buyer, as well as product or service offered.

The regional editions are: Delaware/Ohio Valley region, Northeast, New York, Southeast.

2. *American Ink Maker—Buyer's Guide Issue (MacNair-Dorland Company).* A directory of suppliers to the printing industry (e.g., inks, printing equipment, and chemicals).

Associations

1. *National Association of Printers and Lithographers (Teaneck, NJ).* A large and active organization with over 2700 members. It collects statistics and issues special wage and labor reports.

2. *National Association of Printing Ink Manufacturers (Harrison, NY).* This organization publishes a valuable trade name registry as well as other publications.

3. *National Printing Equipment and Supply Association (McLean, VA).*   Its members include manufacturers and distributors of equipment to the printing and graphic arts industries. The NPES does collect shipment data for the industry and has overseas connections.

4. *Printing Industries of America (Arlington, VA).*   One of the oldest printing associations, with almost 9000 members. Conducts ratio studies of the industry.

RUBBER

Statistical Sources

1. *Rubber Industry Handbook (Firestone).*   A historical review of tire and rubber industry production and consumption statistics. Employment, pricing, and capacity are also discussed.

2. *Rubber Statistical Bulletin (International Rubber Study Group).*   A bimonthly report that discusses production and consumption of rubber throughout the world.

Directories

1. *Rubber & Plastics World/Rubbicana Issue (Crain Communications).*   A detailed listing of rubber manufacturers and equipment suppliers. In addition to name and address, each listing includes type of ownership, products, annual sales, type of rubber used, and equipment employed.

2. *Rubber Red Book (Communications Channels).*   A listing of manufacturers and suppliers. Entries include a detailed list of senior executives as well as brand names.

3. *Rubber World Blue Book (Bill Communications).*   A directory of rubber industry suppliers. Each entry contains products and brand names listings.

Associations

1. *International Institute of Synthetic Rubber Producers (Houston).*   A watchdog organization for the industry, as well as a compiler of statistics. This organization maintains excellent international contacts in its industry. It also offers a membership directory.

SAVINGS AND LOAN

Statistical Sources

1. *Savings and Home Financing Source Book (U.S. Federal Home Loan Bank Board)*. A statistical report covering data on savings and loans, including asset, debt, and mortgage information. It organizes the S&L data by region.

2. *Savings and Loan Net Income (U.S. Federal Home Loan Bank Board)*. A semiannual study that examines net income as a percent of assets, and other operating ratios.

Directories

1. *Directory of American Savings and Loan Associations (T.K. Sanderson Organization)*. A detailed listing that includes 4800 Savings and Loan associations and their branches. Each entry includes the association's name, address, branch locations, and assets.

Associations

1. *American Savings and Loan League (Washington, DC)*. Sponsors seminars, collects statistical data on the industry.

2. *United States League of Savings Associations (Chicago)*. Monitors legislative changes that may affect the industry, and maintains an extensive library.

SOFT DRINKS

Statistical Sources

1. *Beverage Industry Annual Manual (Magazines for Industry)*. As an overview of the soft drink and beverage industry, this is one of the best compendiums I have come across. This publication ranks manufacturers and products. It states data for production, consumption, and advertising expenditures. This volume also serves as an industry directory, listing over 700 companies.

Directories

1. *Beverage World/Buyers Guide Issue (Keller Publishing Company)*. This annual September issue lists suppliers to those companies in the beverage industry.

2. *Beverage World/Soft Drink Franchise Company Directory Issue (Keller Publishing Company)*. This is a listing of soft drink companies that offer franchises. Each entry includes names of executives, brand names, and number of franchises.

3. *Beverages/Annual Buyers Guide Issue (All-Americas Publishers Service)*. The directory includes equipment and supplies manufacturers and their agents.

Associations

1. *National Soft Drink Association (Washington, DC)*. Members include manufacturers and industry suppliers. This organization concentrates on management issues in the industry.

2. *Society of Soft Drink Technologists (Washington, DC)*. As the name implies, this organization concentrates on the R&D and the production side of the soft drink industry. The organization does publish a directory and can be a good source of plant and operating information.

STEEL

Statistical Sources

1. *Metal Statistics (Capital Cities Media)*. See description below.

Directories

1. *Metal Statistics (Capital Cities Media)*. There are two major listings in this text—"where to buy" and "where to sell." These lists all deal with companies that buy and sell various metals, both ferrous and nonferrous.

2. *Directory of Iron and Steel Works of the United States and Canada (American Iron and Steel Institute)*. A key directory for this industry. Each entry lists name, address of each plant, senior executives, products, and equipment capacity.

3. *Iron and Steelmaker/Membership Directory Issue (Iron and Steel Society of AIME).* A directory of individuals who are involved with the technical processes and operations of the plants.

4. *Iron and Steel Works of the World (Metal Bulletin Books).* A detailed listing of iron and steel plants, including lists of key executives, plant capacities, expansion plans, headquarters addresses, equipment used, and sales office locations.

5. *Directory of Iron and Steel Plants (Association of Iron and Steel Engineers).* A large directory with over 1300 companies listed and approximately 15,000 individuals. Entries contain employment information, data on equipment used, and shipping and transportation facilities.

Associations

1. *American Iron and Steel Institute (Washington, DC).* A major information center for the industry. It publishes an annual statistical study, mentioned above, as well as other technical and general interest reports.

2. *Association of Steel Distributors (Cleveland).* This group deals with the wholesaling end of the industry and does its own industry research and collecting of statistics.

3. *American Society for Metals (Metals Park, OH).* An educational and research group with approximately 50,000 members. It maintains a library and publishes a number of important industry periodicals, including *Metal Progress* and *Metal Abstracts*.

TELECOMMUNICATIONS

Statistical Sources

1. *Independent Phonefacts (U.S. Independent Telephone Association).* An annual report on the trends in the independent telephone company market.

2. *Cable Services Report (National Cable Television Association).* Each year this association conducts and publishes an annual survey of cable television growth and activity.

3. *Statistics of Communications Common Carriers (U.S. Federal Communications Commission).* A yearly publication that reports on the activity of the telephone and telegraph companies and their related communications businesses.

Directories

1.   *Telecommunications/Reference Data & Buyers Guide Issue (Horizon House).*   A directory of telecommunications equipment manufacturers who produce such equipment as facsimile, CRT terminals, and switchboards. The directory is indexed by product.

2.   *Telephone Engineer & Management Directory (Harcourt Brace Jovanovich).*   A listing of suppliers to the telecommunications industry. Entries include information on plants, number of telephones currently in service, budgets for construction, and names of senior executives.

3.   *Telephony's Directory & Buyers' Guide (Telephony Publishing Corporation).*   A broad directory containing AT&T operating companies, independent telephone companies, and government offices.

Associations

1.   *National Telephone Cooperative Association (Washington, DC).*   Its membership consists of suppliers of telephone equipment, as well as independent telephone companies. The organization does compile statistics.

2.   *North American Telephone Association (Washington, DC).*   This organization consists of companies that deal with telephone interconnect equipment. The NATA does compile statistics.

TEXTILES

Statistical Sources

1.   *Textile Highlights (American Textile Manufacturers Institute).* Statistics on textile production and consumption. Industry plant and equipment expenditures also discussed.

2.   *Textile Organon (Textile Economics Bureau).*   This publication offers production statistics on a monthly and a quarterly basis.

Directories

1.   *Financial Performance Profile of Public Textile Companies (Kurt Salmon Associates).*   Salmon is one of the leading consultants in the industry. This volume on approximately 100 manufacturers includes company financials and analyses of each of the publicly held companies listed.

2. *Davison's Knit Goods Trade/The Red Book (Davison's Publishing Company)*. There are thousands of listings, including a nationwide listing of knitting mills. Each company's product or service is listed.

3. *Davison's Salesman's Book (Davison's Publishing Company)*. A long list of mills and other processors in the textile business.

4. *Davison's Textile Blue Book (Davison's Publishing Company)*. A comprehensive guide to plants in the textile industry, with over 18,000 companies listed.

5. *Davison's Textile Buyer's Guide/The Gold Book (Davison's Publishing Company)*. A directory of suppliers to the textile industry.

Associations

1. *Textile Information Users Council (Greensboro, NC)*. This association is tailor-made for the corporate researcher. Its mandate is to store and organize information on the textile industry.

2. *Textile Research Institute (Princeton, NJ)*. A technically oriented organization that issues publications such as *Notes on Research* and the *Textile Research Journal*.

CHAPTER 6

USING SPECIAL ISSUES

Trade and Business Magazines as a Key to Financial, Market, and Strategic Information

Trade and business magazines are often thought of in terms of the special issues they offer during the year. How many times have you caught yourself saying, "I know I saw an issue of a magazine that had just the list I need, only I have no idea where I can find the magazine, or even which magazine it is."

These special issues offer data and lists that truly cannot be found anywhere else. *Fortune* magazine publishes its famous list of 500 leading industrial companies. Yet, there is also *Inc.* magazine's own 500 leading companies list—this time, though, we are talking about the 500 fastest-growing privately held corporations, a much more difficult list to compile if you had to do it yourself.

What can special magazine issues offer you? Many issues have information on sales, a ranking of companies in an industry, a brief company history or description, news updates and analyses, explanations of why a company has been included or dropped from an issue, identifications of product lines, and discussions of company trends.

187

The following list of special issues is organized alphabetically by industry and includes a brief description of each issue's contents. Only special issues that in some way contain company-specific information are included.

ADVERTISING

Advertising Age/100 Leading Advertisers (Crain Publications). This issue appears in September of each year and outlines the 100 largest corporate advertisers in the U.S. It summarizes their past year's advertising campaigns, offers some projections on future advertising activity, and breaks down ad expenditures by medium. The issue also cites the advertising agency and account executives responsible for handling each account.

AEROSPACE

Aerospace (Aerospace Industries Association of America). The December issue offers an industry overview, including sales by industry sector. In addition—and this is what makes this an important issue for the corporate researcher—the December issue of Aerospace states exactly how far back-ordered certain manufacturers are.

Aviation Week and Space Technology (McGraw-Hill). Each August issue offers industry data as well as information directly relating to specific companies. Included are details on government contracts and contractors, the amount of the contract, the vendor, R & D expenditures, and allocation.

Exxon Air World (Exxon Corporation). This issue lists turbine engine manufacturers and the number of engines each produced for the past year.

Flight International (IPC Industrial Press). The September issue is a census of existing military aircraft. It identifies current aircraft by manufacturer. The magazine's January issue lists manufacturers of turbine engines for both commercial and military sectors. The August issue breaks down missile production by manufacturer.

Jane's All the World's Aircraft (Air Force Association). This single publication produces over half a dozen benchmark issues. Jane's is often referred to as the bible of the industry in terms of identifying pieces of equipment and their manufacturers. The issues appearing in February, April, June, August, October, and December offer details on the newest aircraft. Included in the description are the craft's features and specifications.

AGRICULTURE

Agri Marketing (Century Communications). The November advertising issue, called "Companies, Services, Agencies, Print, Broadcast, Associations," reports on the leading farm and agricultural equipment advertisers, the type of advertising they conduct, and their agencies. The issue covers both U.S. and Canadian companies.

AIR TRAVEL

Air Transport World (Penton/IPC). This periodical publishes a number of annual issues that involve analysis of specific companies in the airline industry.

Airline Marketing. Appears in June and tracks the past year's airline advertising dollars by company.

IATA Annual Statistics. Usually appearing in October, this issue prints the International Air Transport Association's statistics for the past two years. The data covers market share of member airlines, and rank orders the airlines based on their revenue.

Maintenance and Engineering. The maintenance and engineering issue covers over 60 airlines worldwide, and appears in July. The issue discusses airlines' current and planned maintenance expenditures.

Quarterly Tables. A quarterly analysis of U.S. airlines, including revenues, expenses, and other financial data.

Aviation Week and Space Technology (McGraw-Hill). Its quarterly issues contain income and operating information for passenger airlines, number of passenger airlines for leading air carriers, general information on miles traveled by the airlines, and statistics on miles traveled by aircraft type.

Business and Commercial Aviation (Ziff Davis Publishing Company). Each September, this magazine reviews the salaries for the airline industry.

Flight International (IPC Industrial Press). An annual review in the January issue of commercial aviation's accident reports. Carriers and date of the event are listed in this issue.

Traffic World (Traffic Service Corporation). Appearing in November, this issue provides route information for the leading airlines throughout the world.

APPAREL AND CLOTHING

Footwear News (Fairchild Publications). There are two special annual issues (December and July) that discuss and report financial information on the industry. But in general, *Footwear News* is the most comprehensive newspaper in the industry. It names names and reports on the latest developments. There are a number of magazines that cover general industry statistics, but few go into the depth that this newspaper does about specific companies and industry events.

APPLIANCES

Appliance (Dana Chase Publications). This publication presents statistics and company information in a concise and accurate manner. It makes corporate research in this field all the easier. Some of the special issues to be aware of are:

Ranges and Microwave Oven Report. A May issue on this segment of the industry and the manufacturers in it.

Portrait of the U.S. Appliance Industry. This is a crucial issue for anyone doing research in the appliance industry. It offers market shares, names private labelers and their asssociated product lines, and presents general industry sales statistics. The issue appears in September.

Profiles of Appliance Industry Suppliers. As the name implies, this issue presents descriptions of key suppliers to the appliance industry, including sales estimates. The issue appears in March.

Heating and Air Conditioning. The November issue treats this segment in a way similar to the above microwave report.

Appliance Manufacturer (Cahners Publishing Company). The January issue presents an overview of the appliance industry, including market share by brand name.

Mart Magazine (Morgan-Grampian). Throughout the year this magazine offers insightful articles on appliances and electronic consumer products. These articles mention market shares, sales, comments from industry experts, and new product introductions. The magazine recently spun off a new telephone magazine, offering special articles on the burgeoning telephone market and its key players.

Merchandising (Gralla Publications). Another important magazine in the appliance field. The November issue is packed with statistics on the industry in general. Other issues discuss specific product groups and cover sales and distribution information. This publication is similar to *Mart Magazine* in scope.

AUTOMOBILES

Automotive Industries (Chilton Book Company). The June issue provides a financial analysis and review of approximately 250 companies.

Automotive News (Crain Communications). Monthly, this publication offers sales and market share statistics for each automobile manufacturer. This is one of the two or three leading publications in the automobile industry. The magazine's Market Data Book, which appears sometime around April or May, offers extensive financial market information on the companies and the industry in general.

Chilton's Automotive Industries (Chilton Book Company). An annual (June) publication providing statistics and financial details on suppliers to the industry. The April edition offers market share and production data by product line.

Jobber Topics (Irving-Cloud Publishing Company). The annual market directory issue in July presents a myriad of statistics about the industry, as well as summary financial information on over 30 publicly traded automobile companies.

Ward's Auto World (Ward's Communications). This is one of the other important automobile trade magazines.

The Automotive Yearbook, an annual publication, presents data on the general industry, as well as specific automobile companies and the cars they produce.

BANKING

ABA Banking Journal (American Bankers Association). Each year, in May, this periodical offers a directory of congressional committees active in studying and regulating the banking industry. When researching any of the banks, especially with regard to bank mergers, these committee members may be able to direct you to the names, dates, and financials regarding that merger.

American Banker (American Banker).   This is one of the leading banking magazines, offering a wide variety of special issues on the banking industry. The following are the ones that would most benefit the corporate researcher:

Bank Holding Companies.   The holding company banks are ranked by the deposit size. This issue appears in April.

Correspondent Banking.   This December issue ranks correspondent banks deposit size. This issue appears in April.

Finance Companies.   This issue ranks almost 300 finance companies and offers a summary balance sheet for the 100 leading companies. Included in the list, usually appearing in June, are captive and independent finance companies.

First 5,000 Banks.   This is a 5000-bank listing, including abbreviated financials, of the largest commercial banks in the United States. The issue appears in June.

Largest Commercial Banks.   This February and August issue ranks the 300 largest commercial banks.

Largest Credit Unions.   Appearing in May, this offers a ranked list of the 100 largest credit unions. Ranking is again by asset size.

Largest Mortgage Companies.   In an October issue, a list is given of the 300 largest mortgage companies with accompanying financials.

Largest Mutual Savings Banks.   A ranking of the 100 largest mutual savings banks appears in a January issue.

Largest Savings Banks.   This August issue ranks the 100 largest U.S. mutual savings banks, as well as the 300 largest savings banks, worldwide.

Largest World Banks.   With deposit and other financial information, this July listing offers a ranking of the 500 largest banks in the world.

The Bankers (Financial Times).   Each June, this magazine offers a listing of the 500 leading world banks, with financials.

Bankers Monthly (Bankers Monthly).   Each May, this periodical offers an abbreviated balance sheet for more than 50 finance companies.

Bank News (Bank News).   The February and March issues offer complete financial reports on a variety of banks in Missouri, Kansas, Nebraska, Oklahoma, Texas, Colorado, New Mexico, Wyoming, and Illinois.

Business Week (McGraw-Hill).   The April issue contains the Bank Scoreboard. This list examines the assets and return on assets for the 200 leading U.S. banks.

Forbes (Forbes).   An April issue each year examines the 100 leading bank holding companies, including assets, deposits, loans, loan losses, and so on.

Magazine of Bank Administration (Bank Administration Institute). The August issue covers the largest income-earning banks.

Savings Bank Journal (Thrift Publishers). The March issue lists the 100 largest savings banks and offers financial information on each bank's number of deposits and the dollar amount of its total deposits.

Trusts and Estates (Communication Channels). Appearing each December, this issue lists the trust assets for approximately 5000 banks. These banks are located in both the United States and in Canada.

BEVERAGES

Advertising Age (Crain Publications). Throughout the year, this magazine discusses the advertising and marketing activities of the leading bottlers, brewers, and soft drink companies. A January issue, for instance, ranks the leading liquor manufacturers in the United States.

Beverage Industry (Magazines for Industry). One of the better industry magazines for reporting in-depth on the companies active in this sector. Its annual Manual offers market shares, as well as a host of tables and chapters on the overall industry. This Manual appears in September. Each year, around April, the magazine publishes a special issue on manufacturers and brands of soft drinks. It offers market share and overall sales for the category.

Beverage World (Keller Publishing Company). Another widely read publication in this industry, reporting on specific products and companies. Its July issue ranks the 100 leading beverage producers in the United States.

Modern Brewery Age (Business Journals). Its annual Blue Book offers brewery sales and production. Its February issue presents market and company production information.

Wines and Vines (Hiaring Company). The magazine's annual marketing issue (appearing in September) describes the wine industry, and discusses specific production information. The publication's January issue focuses on champagne and its producers.

BROADCASTING

Broadcasting (Broadcasting Publications). One of the magazine's January issues each year publishes a listing of which television and radio stations were bought or sold during the year. The surfeit of acquisition reporting makes this a valuable list. Purchase prices are also contained in this list.

Leading Formats Issue.   Appearing in June, this issue offers market share for the leading radio formats throughout the country.

Ranking of 100 Leading Electronic Communications Companies.   The January issue ranks the 100 leading communications companies (these are all publicly traded companies).

Weeks Worth of Earnings.   This appears each month, reporting on the revenues, net income, and earnings per share for publicly traded broadcasting companies.

Television Digest (Television Digest).   Annual ranking of the 50 leading cable television operators in the United States. Included in the ranking are the number of subscribers and data on planned growth (number of miles of cable to be added over the next year).

BUILDING AND CONSTRUCTION

Automation in Housing and Systems Building News (CMN Associates).   In addition to providing general industry data, this August issue ranks the leading 100 home builders by their sales and number of houses constructed.

Building Design and Construction (Cahners Publishing Company). Each July this magazine publishes a study analyzing the 300 largest construction and design companies in the United States. Company profiles are also included.

Chemical Engineering (McGraw-Hill).   This issue is offered twice a year (October and May), and describes new facilities planned or in progress in the United States, Canada, and Mexico. Aside from manufacturer's name and address, the listing includes the projected capacity for each chemical processing plant.

F. W. Dodge (McGraw-Hill).   The Dodge books and annuals on the construction industry are considered the bibles of· construction costs. The monthly *Dodge Construction Potentials Bulletin* presents information on new construction throughout the United States. The semiannual *Dodge Digest of Building Costs and Specifications* offers details on recently bid projects.

Electrical Contractor (McGraw-Hill).   This publication offers a number of special issues during the year. Here are the ones that would most interest the corporate researcher:

400 Largest Contractors. Appearing in April, the list contains sales information in the form of contract dollars awarded, number of contracts, and a brief description of each firm.

Leading International Contractors. A ranking of the leading international contractors. Included are contract awards, profits, and other background about these international firms. This issue appears in July.

Specialty Construction Firms. Sales and contract information for approximately 300 of the largest specialty contractors in the United States. The issue appears each August.

Offshore (Penn Well Publishing Company). Each November, an issue reports on construction in the offshore oil well industry on a worldwide basis. Contained in this special issue are data on construction in progress, construction planned, platform locations, and expected completion dates.

Oil and Gas Journal (Penn Well Publishing Company). In October and in May of each year special issues appear on the planned and current construction of wells, refineries, and pipelines in the petroleum industry.

Pipe Line Industry (Gulf Publishing Company). This January issue presents the pipeline construction for over 200 companies. The list is extremely detailed. Aside from naming names, it presents construction costs and gives a description of the project.

Professional Builder and Apartment Business (Cahners Publishing Company). The July issue lists the leading home construction contractors in the United States. The list contains approximately 400 companies and presents sales, company description, and address. Companies are ranked by sales.

BUILDING MATERIALS

American Glass Review (Ebel-Doctorow Publications). Appearing each February, this issue lists manufacturers of flat glass and other glass products. In addition to telephone number and address, it also states the brand names or trademark names the glass is sold under.

Floor Covering News (Maclean Hunter). Each January, leaders in the Canadian floor covering market present their opinions on the market.

Modern Concrete (Pit and Quarry Publications). The January issue lists production statistics for the industry, as well as information on wages and plant expenditures.

Pit and Quarry (Pit and Quarry Publications). In addition to general data on concrete and cement building materials, each July an issue offers income and production information for leading producers of concrete and cement.

Cement Plant Production. The January issue offers plant-by-plant production and capacity information, where available.

Financial Reports Round-up. Twice a year, *Pit and Quarry* offers revenue information on the leading cement and concrete companies in the United States.

BUSINESS, GENERAL

Business Week (McGraw-Hill). A number of invaluable special issues are published throughout the year. Many corporate researchers consider these issues to be mini-reference volumes unto themselves.

Corporate Scoreboard. Lists over 800 corporations and their first-quarter earnings and sales. Subdivided by industry group, the Scoreboard also offers comparative figures from the past year. It appears in May.

International Corporate Scoreboard. Appearing in July, this issue reviews over 700 foreign corporations in over 50 countries. It offers information similar to the above U.S. *Corporate Scoreboard.* A valuable source of foreign corporate data. Financial data, though, is for the previous year.

Investment Outlook. In a January issue, the Outlook analyzes earnings and performance for major U.S. corporations for the previous calendar year.

R&D Scoreboard. Drawing on SEC filings and derived estimates, this July issue offers R&D expenditures for over 700 companies for the previous calendar year. R&D information is hard to come by. This may prove a priceless issue for the researcher needing R&D data.

California Business (California Business News). This regional business magazine has two special issues of interest to the corporate researcher. One is entitled "California's 100 Fastest Growing Companies" and the other, "California's 500." These list the 100 fastest-growing California companies (names of corporate officers and revenue for past two years are included), and the 500 leading California companies by revenue produced.

Canadian Business (CB Media). This magazine issues a special edition each July called "Canada's Top 500 Companies." Similar to the Fortune 500, but for Canadian companies.

Colorado Business (Titsch Publishing). Titsch publishes "The Top 300 Companies in the Rocky Mountain West," a regional listing of the 300 top revenue-producing companies in that area. These companies are ranked by assets, revenues, and earnings. There is also an alphabetical listing.

Dun's Review (Dun & Bradstreet). Each year Dun's publishes issues of interest to the corporate researcher. "Top Corporate Performers" lists the leading corporations ranked by dividends earned. "Five Best Managed Companies" gives an in-depth examination of five companies.

The Financial Post (Maclean Hunter). In June of each year, the Post compiles and publishes a ranking of Canada's 500 largest companies. Unlike the Fortune 500, which deals with industrial companies exclusively, the Post 500 ranks service, financial, real estate, and industrial concerns in the same list.

Financial World (Macro Communications). A list of the leading growth companies in the United States. This issue ranks the companies by sales and groups companies by industry. The issue appears sometime in August.

Forbes (Forbes). This magazine publishes its own Forbes 500 list, similar to the Fortune list. The issue appears in May. Another special issue, the "Scorecard on Capital and Labor," appears in May and ranks companies by number of employees as well as by sales and assets. A third special report that Forbes produces is a sweeping review of American industry. This issue, which is published in January of each year, describes the state of various industries. Each description reports on trends and major shifts in an industry. It also offers a chart for each industry that lists the leading companies with a financial summary of the past year's performance. This is one of the most concise and easy-to-read summaries of American industry.

Fortune (Time). Aside from *Fortune's* 500 and second 500 list of industrials (appearing in May and June), the publication also offers the following special issues:

The Top 50 Exporters. Appearing in September, it ranks the companies by export dollars.

World Business Directory. A listing of the world's largest industrial corporations (excluding the United States). Companies are ranked by sales. Details supplied for each company include number of employees, assets, net income, products, and stockholders' equity.

Inc. (United Marine Publishing Company). This magazine has a number of special issues, listing companies not grouped elsewhere. The companies on these lists are privately held or publicly traded start-up companies. The issues include the Inc. 100 (the 100 fastest growing companies in the

United States), appearing in May of each year. Also, there is the *Inc. 500*, a December year-end tally of the 500 fastest growing private corporations.

New England Business (Yankee). There are two June issues: one a ranking of the leading 200 industrial firms in the region by sales, and the other a sales ranking of the top 200 service firms in New England.

New Jersey Business (New Jersey Business and Industry Association). Called the "Top 100 Employers," the May issue of this magazine lists the leading 100 firms by employment size.

News Front/America's 500 Most Profitable Medium Sized Corporations (Ward Publications). Unlike other 500 listings, this one ranks the companies by profit-to-sales ratio, and offers data on stockholders' equity.

The South Magazine (Southern Business Publishing Company). Each July, this magazine offers an issue titled "200 Corporate Winners: The Top 200 Companies in the South." Information contained in this listing includes sales, earnings, earnings per share, equity, and assets.

CHEMICALS

Chemical and Engineering News (American Chemical Society). This is a listing of the top 50 producers in the United States. Sales and profit information is presented. This issue appears in May. A list of the second 50 appears a month later in the June edition. Other special issues include:

Capital Spending. Issues usually appearing in October and December report on the leading chemical producers and their plant and equipment expenditures.

Foreign Sales. This annual report reviews American chemical companies' sales abroad. The issue appears in May.

R&D. This July issue provides otherwise hard-to-find Research and Development information on chemical companies and affiliated universities, and their chemical R&D programs.

Chemical Engineering (McGraw-Hill). A twice-yearly report on plant and equipment construction and installation for chemical plants in the United States, Mexico, and Canada. Plant addresses and expected capacities are given.

Chemical Week (McGraw-Hill). This publication offers a number of annual review publications each year. They are:

Chemical Week 300. In April, it ranks the leading chemical companies by sales and provides other useful financial information.

100 Top Foreign CPI Terms/Annual Financial Survey. This August issue ranks the 100 leading foreign manufacturers and gives accompanying financial information.

Modern Plastics (McGraw-Hill). This is an unusual special issue. Its focus is new products and the manufacturers who make them. Should a researcher review each year's version of this annual issue, he or she might learn company trends or strategies. The issue appears in September.

COMPUTERS AND DATA PROCESSING

Computerworld (CM Communications). The December and January issues offer forecasts on the marketplace and identify new systems and software.

Datamation (Technical Publishing Company). This publication is one of the key magazines in the data processing and computer industry. It monitors trends and offers detailed surveys on the DP workforce and employment trends. Among the special issues that would be of interest to the corporate researcher are:

Analysis of the Computer Industry in the U.S. This issue usually appears in January, and offers valuable information on marketing strategy and new products in the field.

Minicomputer Survey. An annual survey and profile of minicomputer manufacturers, with market segmentation and market share information included. This issue appears in November.

The Top 50 Data Communication Industry Manufacturers. This appears in June and ranks the leading companies by sales. It also discusses the leading technologies in the data communication sector.

User Surveys. Throughout the year, *Datamation* conducts surveys of system and software users. These studies appear in January (Brand Preference Study of the Data Processing Industry), December (Software Evaluations), January (Budget Survey), and April (Salary Survey).

Dun's Review (Dun & Bradstreet). A review of the computer industry, appearing in August. This issue discusses specific companies and the market structure.

Mini-Micro Systems (Cahners Publishing Company). An annual issue on printers and a series of articles examining the industry's growth, market structure, and shipment data. This issue appears in January.

DRUGS AND COSMETICS

Drug and Cosmetic Industry (Harcourt Brace Jovanovich). An annual issue that is in effect a buyers' guide to suppliers of manufacturing and processing machinery to the drug industry. Product names are given.

Medical Marketing and Media (Technomic Publishing Company). Each April, this issue offers the brand names of the most widely prescribed drugs of the past year. Over 200 products are listed.

Pharmaceutical Technology (Pharmaceutical Technology). The fall issues offer summary information on the latest industry trade shows.

ELECTRICAL EQUIPMENT AND POWER

Electrical World (McGraw-Hill). This magazine is one of the key trade periodicals for the electric power industry. Its yearly special issues include:

Capacity. New generating plant construction is covered in this January issue.

Statistical Report. Aside from general market statistics (e.g., power consumption, capital expenditures), this issue also covers financial data of the major utilities. The issue appears in March.

Transmission and Distribution Construction Survey. This August issue tracks and records the latest construction plans for United States utilities with power transmission and distribution.

Power Engineering (Technical Publishing Company). This issue offers specific operating information about new generating plants. The issue appears in April.

Public Power (American Public Power Association). This periodical offers a number of annual issues, most of which cover aggregate data rather than company-specific information. Among the issues that corporate researchers might find useful are Bond Sales (March) and Plant Construction and Improvements Expenditures (November).

ELECTRONICS

Electronic Business (Cahners Publishing Company).   In the half dozen
or so years that this publication has been around, it has established itself as
a major supplier of industry statistics and corporate news. Among its special
issues are:

Electronic Business 100.   A listing of the 100 leading electronic businesses, ranked by sales.

Events Calendar.   An unusual issue offering a monthly listing of trade
shows and industry conferences throughout the coming year. The Calendar appears in January.

Electronic Engineering Times (CMP Publications Company).   This January issue offers general forecasts for the industry, as well as interviews with
corporate executives.

Electronic News (Fairchild Publications).   A fairly in-depth review of
the top 50 U.S. companies (along with approximately one dozen foreign
competitors). In addition to financial information, each profile reviews the
company's product line and marketing efforts. The issue appears in July.

Electronics (McGraw-Hill).   Aside from its excellent annual market review (appearing in January), it has a number of detailed company issues
each year. One of the key issues that you should consider is:

Technology Update.   Each October, the magazine offers a review of the
latest products and processes in the electronics industry.

Power Engineering (Technical Publishing Company).   Aside from being
a directory of engineering firms involved in the building of power plants,
this May issue also lists new plants and their power generating capacity, as
well as information on projected plants.

ENGINEERING

Contract (Gralla Publications).   An interesting review of companies in
the contract-specifying segment of the engineering industry. The publication
ranks them according to the amount of square footage designed. In addition,
it offers names of executives, sales of the firms, and current projects. The
issue appears in September.

Engineering News-Record (McGraw-Hill).   Another magazine-bible. A widely read periodical, it offers two key issues of interest to the corporate researcher. They are:

Leading 500 U.S. Design Firms.　Appearing each May, this has become the "Fortune 500" listing for the industry. Each entry includes billings, number of employees, and specialty.

Top U.S. Construction Firms With Foreign Billings.　This July issue lists the approximately 150 leading construction design firms that do business worldwide.

FOOD PROCESSING

Candy & Snack Industry (Magazines for Industry).　Aside from its buyers' guide, the January issue of Candy & Snack presents plant-by-plant information as well as information on mergers in the industry.

Food Engineering (Chilton Book Company).　The October issue ranks the leading 50 food companies by capital expenditures—not sales.

Food Processing (Putnam).　This magazine offers the leading 100 food-processing companies in the United States ranked by sales. The issue usually appears in December.

Food Product Development (Magazines For Industry).　The July issue is a directory of pilot food-processing plants. The December issue presents similar information, but for plants producing food additives.

Processed Prepared Food (Gorman Publishing Company).　This trade magazine has a couple of issues of interest to the researcher:

50 Leaders.　In February each year, the editors rank the leading 50 companies by sales volume for various food product groups.

Warehouse Locations.　In July, the magazine covers the locations of warehouses and warehouse chains and the space each has available.

Restaurant Hospitality (Penton/IPC).　The January issue lists the companies supplying the restaurant industry.

Snack Food (Harcourt Brace Jovanovich).　Each year, in June, this magazine publishes one of the only reviews of the snack food market. While other publications touch on this market segment, Snack Food specializes in this analysis—and the specialization pays off. The "State of the Snack Food Industries Report" not only offers general market statistics, but also presents market share by company, and dollar sales by manufacturer in many categories.

GAS (NATURAL)

Oil and Gas Journal (Penn Well Publishing Company).   This journal has a number of detailed, company-specific issues. They are:

Gas Processing Report.   This July issue offers statistics on facilities, production, and consumption.

Pipelines.   This issue offers both an industry-wide and a company-by-company review of the market, with new pipeline construction and company revenues.

Pipeline and Gas Journal (Harcourt Brace Jovanovich).   Every quarter, the magazine reports on oil and gas company financial statements. Another issue is devoted to reporting on pipeline construction worldwide (October).

HEALTH CARE

Modern Healthcare (McGraw-Hill).   The August issue offers statistics and background information on the contract-management segment of the health care industry. The April issue analyzes the size and growth of American multi-hospital systems. A May or June issue does a similar analysis of the nursing home system or chains.

HOTELS AND RESTAURANTS

Fast Service/Family Restaurants (Harcourt Brace Jovanovich).   The October issue offers a report on the leading fast food chains, including revenues, units, and extent of franchising.

Lodging Hospitality (Penton/IPC).   The August issue offers statistics as well as operating information on the leading companies.

Restaurant Business (Bill Communications).   The March issue covers operating details on the leading franchise systems.

Restaurants and Institutions (Cahners Publishing Company).   A detailed listing of the 400 largest food service companies in the United States. This is another one of those invaluable works. The food service industry is comprised of literally thousands of "ma and pa" companies, none of which controls an overwhelming share of the market. For this reason, it becomes difficult to locate any information on food service companies. This issue also offers marketing insight into the various company operations in pithy one- or two-line statements. This issue appears in July.

Restaurant Hospitality (Bill Communications). The June issue does for restaurants what *Institutions* does for food service. It ranks the 500 leading independent restaurants and offers sales and employment information.

Service World International (Cahners Publishing Company). The June issue presents the 100 largest hotel chains and provides some financial and descriptive information on each.

HOUSEHOLD AND INSTITUTIONAL FURNITURE

Contract (Gralla Publications). The January annual issue lists manufacturers in the contract-design market. But more important for corporate researchers, this same issue has organized a list of showrooms and exhibits that are open during the year.

INSURANCE

Best's Review (A.M. Best Company). The Best series of trade magazines on the insurance industry is the epitome of the industry bible. There are many special issues. Those key to corporate research are mentioned below:

Accident and Health Premiums. The 300 insurance companies that write the greatest dollar amount of accident and health policies; in the August issue.

Leading Life Insurance Companies. This July issue ranks the 100 leading companies in three separate categories.

Ten-Year Dividend History. A January issue comparing the dividend histories for over 70 insurance companies.

Best's Life and Health Edition (A.M. Best Company).

Company Changes. This March issue reports on life insurance companies' financial changes.

Executive Earnings. Appearing in November, this issue offers comparative salaries for industry executives.

125 Companies by Assets. This October issue ranks the companies by their asset values.

Ranking of Leading Life Insurance Companies. The June issue.

Best's Property and Casualty Edition (A.M. Best Company).

Corporate Changes. The March issue covers new companies or changes with established companies.

Insurance Stock Trends. Each February, Best reviews the stock performance of insurance companies.

Leading Auto Insurers. The August issue.

Leading Property and Casualty Companies. This is an annual ranking of the 200 leaders. The issue appears in June.

Marine Insurance Companies. The November issue lists and analyzes the leaders in the field.

Institutional Investor (Institutional Investor Systems). A directory of pension funds and the companies that manage them. The issue appears in January.

National Underwriter (National Underwriter Company). Among its special issues are:

Leading Life and Health Insurance Companies. A ranking of the leaders, appearing in a May or a June issue.

Year-End Analysis of Property and Casualty Companies. Analysis of insurers that appears sometime in January.

Pensions and Investments (Crain Communications). A listing of the 100 largest pension funds in the United States. Assets are included in this ranking. The issue appears in January.

Pension World (Communications Channels). An analysis of the pooled pension funds. This issue appears in May.

INVESTMENT BANKING

Bankers Monthly (Bankers Monthly). An annual financial breakdown of investment banking and brokerage firms. The issue appears in May.

Financial World (Macro Communications). Based on a survey, a ranking of the top brokers and brokerage firms in the United States. The issue usually appears in December.

Forbes (Forbes). Usually appearing in the September issue is a ranking and analysis of U.S. mutual funds.

Institutional Investor (Institutional Investor Systems). A listing of the

300 leading investment institutions. The ranking is based on investment assets, and appears in August.

Pensions and Investments (Pensions and Investments). Each March, the magazine lists the top equity funds for various financial institutions.

Leading Investment Management Organizations. This March issue profiles the 400 largest investment management organizations in the United States.

Trusts and Estates (Communications Channels). The May issue offers a selection of the approximately 50 most popular common stocks held by U.S. common trust funds.

IRON AND STEEL

Iron Age (Chilton Book Company). A general statistical review of the steel and nonferrous industries, offering general statistics as well as detailed information on the leading manufacturers. In addition, weekly the magazine reports on prices for iron, steel, and other metals. On a quarterly basis, the magazine presents earnings reports on the leading companies.

MACHINERY

Appliance (Dana Chase Publications). This March issue profiles suppliers to the appliance industry.

Construction Equipment Maintenance (Cahners Publishing Company). This May issue ranks the leading companies in the field of equipment maintenance.

Electrical World (McGraw-Hill). A breakdown of boiler manufacturers, offering numbers of orders, market shares, and other financial information. The issue usually appears in December.

Gas Turbine World (Pequot Publishing). This magazine publishes an annual handbook that contains order and installation information on gas turbines. Aside from company listings, it contains the numbers of machines installed and the installation sites.

Plastics World (Cahners Publishing Company) The February issue reviews the new equipment in the industry and offers a description of the machinery.

Precision Metal (Penton/IPC). A general statistical review that discusses capacity and sales information in the metal-forming industry. The issue appears in November.

METALS

Iron Age (Chilton Book Company). The magazine's forecast issue (January) offers statistics on the future of the market and includes a section on new products and the manufacturers who make them.

Metal Progress (American Society for Metals). Its annual January issue presents statistics on the future of the industry. Like *Iron Age*'s annual above, *Metal Progress* also describes new products, their sales activity, and the companies affiliated with the technology.

MINING

Engineering and Mining Journal (McGraw-Hill). This January issue covers new mines throughout the world. Included in each description of new mines or expansion of existing mines are the amount of capital invested and the expected capacity.

Nuclear Exchange Monthly Report (Nuclear Exchange Corporation). The August issue deals with sources of nuclear consumption, where the plants are, and where they will be. The November issue explores the industry from the perspective of production, providing information on current and future production facilities.

Skillings' Mining Review (David N. Skillings). Annual review of iron ore production, categorized by company and site.

World Mining (George O. Miller Freeman Publications). The annual September issue reports on all mineral mines and production by company.

PACKAGING AND CONTAINERS

Beverage World (Keller Publishing Corporation). The June issue details the major companies that manufacture bottles and cans.

Modern Packaging (Morgan-Grampian).　In addition to a buyer's guide, the December issue also offers articles on the industry.

PAPER

Paperboard Packaging (Magazines for Industry).　The January issue analyzes capital expenditures by region.

Paper Trade Journal (Vance Publishing Corporation).　This periodical offers a number of significant special issues:

Quarterly Sales.　On a quarterly basis, the magazine reports sales and earnings for a few dozen U.S. and Canadian companies.

Top 50 Paper Firms.　Appearing each June, this is a listing of the leading 50 paper companies. It includes financial information on the leading companies.

Presstime (American Newspaper Publishers Association).　Both the May and November issues report on newsprint plants' expansion plans and capacity.

Pulp and Paper (Miller Freeman Publications).　This is a key source for information on the paper industry. The magazine contains some of the most frequently published and detailed data about paper companies. Among its special issues are:

Capital Expenditures.　Each January the magazine offers a listing of new plant construction and expansion.

Company Profiles.　Usually appearing in the June issue are charts describing the leading U.S. and Canadian companies.

Foreign Leaders.　The October issue presents the 25 foreign leaders in the paper industry, and includes production and sales information.

Quarterly Summaries.　Each quarter, the publication presents tables of sales and earnings for the leading U.S. and Canadian manufacturers.

Southern Pulp and Paper (Ernest H. Abernethy Publishing Company).　This issue presents detailed plant and equipment information about Southern paper mills, supplied by the mills themselves. The issue appears in October.

PETROLEUM

Energy Magazine (Business Communications Company).　The quarterly issues detail production data for oil and gas.

Fuel Oil, Oil Heat and Solar Systems (Industry Publications). This annual publication offers details on another segment of the oil and gas industries—that of fuel oil delivery companies. Included in the September issue is information on company size and managment.

National Petroleum News (McGraw-Hill). Each quarter, the magazine lists the earnings for over 20 petroleum companies.

Ocean Industry (Gulf Publishing Company). The October and March issues have a detailed listing of current and planned offshore wells and drilling platforms. The September issue is a worldwide directory of offshore drilling rigs, identifying the actual ships and vessels used in the exploration and drilling.

Offshore (Penn Well Publishing Company). During the course of the year, this periodical offers a number of detailed lists of activities within the industry:

Deepwater Wells. The June issue contains a directory of deepwater wells throughout the world.

Marine Pipeline Report. A listing of pipeline projects, current and planned. The issue appears in July.

Oil and Gas Journal (Penn Well Publishing Company). This magazine, too, has a number of special issues that are published on a regular basis:

Capital Expenditures. The February issue discusses actual outlays and planned capital expenditures for over 25 companies in the United States.

Gas Processing. A July issue offers worldwide capacity data on gas and petroleum plants.

Pipeline Projects. Each January, an issue lists the amount of pipeline under construction or planned.

Refinery Report. The March issue presents refinery capacities and operating information.

Worldwide Issue. This issue, usually appearing at the end of December, offfers production statistics as well as company-specific information.

Pipeline and Gas Journal (Harcourt Brace Jovanovich). The quarterly issues present financial data on approximately 100 oil and gas companies.

Platt's Oil and Petroleum Directories and Special Publications (McGraw-Hill). Platt's is to the oil and gas industry what F.W. Dodge is to the construction industry. The series of Platt's publications offers the researcher details on pricing and leglislation.

A list of some key Platt publications and services includes:

Platt's Bunkerwire (telexing service on marine fuel prices).

Platt's LP Gaswire (telexing service on liquified petroleum gas prices).

Platt's OHA Digest.

Platt's Oilgram Legislative Service.

Platt's Oilgram Marketscan.

Platt's Oilgram News.

Platt's Oilgram Price Report.

Platt's Oil Marketing Bulletin.

Platt's Oil Price Handbook.

World Oil (Gulf Publishing Company). The annual issue, usually appearing in August, provides a detailed listing of oil sites and production. It is one of the most extensive reviews of petroleum industry production to appear in any magazine.

PHOTOGRAPHY

Modern Photography (ABC Leisure Magazines). One of the two or three major slick photography magazines that offers tips and advice to photographers. In its annual December issue it presents the leading cameras, their specifications, and the names and addresses of the manufacturers.

Photomethods (Ziff Davis Publishing Company). The annual June issue discusses new products as well as industry news.

PLASTICS

Modern Plastics (McGraw-Hill). Throughout the year, this trade magazine is considered an extremely valuable source of general industry data as well as specific company information. The January issue is particularly useful—it is a compendium of statistics on usage of plastics materials and actually charts the resin capacity of each producer.

Plastics World (Cahners Publishing Company). The January issue lists the leading 400 plastics plants in the United States, including names, the processes used, and the product lines offered.

PUBLISHING

Editor and Publisher (Editor and Publisher). One of the key magazines in the publishing industry. Each month, with information supplied to it by Media Records, Inc., *Editor and Publisher* offers linage statistics for major U.S. newspapers.

Folio (Folio Magazine Publishing Corporation). Another important industry trade source, this magazine provides in its January issue a listing of the 400 best-selling magazines, including their sales, and circulation statistics.

Printing Impressions (North American Publishing Company). Each July the magazine offers a listing of companies in the publishing and printing industries based on their stock market performance. Included in each listing is a company's income, earnings per share, and stock prices.

Publishers Weekly (R.R. Bowker). Along with *Folio* and *Editor and Publisher,* this is a crucial magazine covering the industry. Its annual yearly review issue (usually appearing in March) presents capsules of industry news, naming names and citing the best-selling books for the past year.

RAILROADS

Modern Railroads Rail Transit (Cahners Publishing Company). Each quarter, this magazine offers earnings and operating reports on the U.S. Class I railroads.

Railway Age (Simmons-Boardman Publishing Company). The January Outlook issue covers the industry during the past year and offers insights by industry executives. This issue also covers industry and company statistics and financials.

RETAILING

Automotive News (Crain Communications). Semiannually the publication reviews imported car sales, ranking the market leaders. Each quarter it reviews the number of dealerships by manufacturer.

Chain Store Age (Lebhar-Friedman). As we mentioned earlier, this publication actually appears in three editions: Executive, General Merchandise, and Supermarkets. It is a wonderful source of product trends and discussion—on a national level—of various chain operations. Below are listed some of the key annual publications that present company-specific information. If you are going to do extensive research on the retail industry, this is one of the first magazines you should pick up.

Executive Edition. The following two special issues appear as indicated:

Census of Chain Stores. Each August, it ranks the leading chain stores by sales. Other information is included, such as number of facilities and number of employees.

Building. The September issue profiles the leading builders among chain store operators.

General Merchandise Edition. The two special issues below appear as shown:

Leading Department Stores. This issue appears each May.

Leading 100 General Merchandise Chains. This ranking appears each June.

Supermarkets. The two special issues listed below appear as indicated:

Financial Performance. The June issue is a financial review of leading supermarket chains.

Sales Review. Each July, the magazine reviews the leading products and their sales. In addition, it covers the leading wholesalers and chains and their performance.

Convenience Stores Magazine (Progressive Grocer). The October issue ranks convenience stores by their sales.

Discount Merchandiser (Discount Merchandiser). The January, May, and October issues offer general product sales data without mentioning specific product names. The June issue ranks the leading discount stores with annual sales of over $100 million.

Discount Store News (Lebhar-Friedman). A September issue offers a ranking and discussion of the leading 100 discount store chains in the United States.

Drug Store News (Lebhar-Friedman). An April issue annually reviews the latest mergers and market shares for drugstore chains. An annual July report offers a brand name and market share study for the most profitable and active products sold in drugstores.

Drug Topics (Medical Economics Company). A December or a January issue forecasts the expected performance of leading drug chains, in addition to reviewing the past year.

The Griffin Report (Griffin Publishing Company). A regional publication that covers New England food stores, including convenience stores and supermarkets. An annual issue ranks regional supermarkets.

Marketing and Media Decisions (Decisions Publications). There are two major issues that discuss advertising expenditures of toy manufacturers. The December issue offers a breakdown of product by medium, and the July issue ranks the top 200 brands by advertising dollars spent.

Merchandising (Gralla Publications). Throughout the year, this publication offers statistics (March, August, and September) on the electronics and appliance industries. Its January issue reviews and speculates on consumer electronics products, naming names and presenting general industry statistics.

National Mall Monitor (National Mall Monitor). Each July, this magazine ranks mall retailers by sales.

Progressive Grocer (Progressive Grocer). The April issue gives the reader a statistical and narrative overview of the market. In addition, it presents rankings of leading companies in the grocery store market, from wholesalers to retailers.

Stores (National Retail Merchants Association). Each July, the magazine ranks the top 100 department stores.

Supermarket Business (Gralla Publications). A ranking and analysis of the leading supermarket chains. The issue appears in October.

Supermarket News (Fairchild Publications). Once a year, usually in August, the newspaper profiles major supermarket chains in almost two dozen metropolitan areas.

RUBBER

Modern Tire Dealer (Bill Communications). The January issue offers a directory and a statistical summary of tire shipments and plant capacity.

TELECOMMUNICATIONS HARDWARE

Cablevision (Titsch Publishing). This January issue discusses and identifies new plant construction and additions of equipment by cable television companies.

TELEPHONES

Telephony (Telephony Publishing Corporation). One of the leading magazines on the telephone industry, it presents monthly stock prices and earnings reports on the leading telephone companies. A January issue goes into depth on the telephone companies, discussing plants and equipment.

Note—With the deregulation and divestiture processes accelerating, there are a number of newsletters and magazines being created just to serve this rapidly changing market. During the next few years, expect dozens of magazines and special newsletters to appear, meeting this upsurge in activity.

TOBACCO

Advertising Age (Crain Communications). The December issue is a market-share listing of the leading cigarette manufacturers.

Business Week(McGraw-Hill). Appearing in a December issue is a market-share analysis and description of the current state of the cigarette industry.

Tobacco International (Lockwood Trade Journal Company). One of the July issues details tobacco production, as well as export and import activity.

Tobacco Reporter (Harvest Publishing Company). Another valuable publication, especially in the complex and secretive world of the tobacco industry. True, consumers may be aware of various cigarette brands, but that does not mean that they know a good deal about the companies that produce them. The April issue of *Tobacco Reporter* goes into some depth, explaining company structures and corporate relationships within the tobacco industry.

TOILETRIES AND COSMETICS

Drug and Cosmetic Industry (Harcourt Brace Jovanovich). The July issue presents a ranking and profiles of the leading U.S. producers of various cosmetics products.

Product Marketing (Charleson Publications). In each issue, this magazine publishes the results of independently conducted brand studies. These studies provide brand preference data.

TRANSPORTATION (TRUCKING FLEETS)

Chilton's Truck and Off-Highway Industries (Chilton Book Company). The July issue examines the manufacturers and production of trucks. It offers production and market-share statistics. The June issue (*100 Largest Motor Carriers*) ranks the 100 top Class I truck fleets and offers data on income, number of employees, and number of shipments.

Metropolitan (Bobit Publishing). An annual statistical review of city bus systems, with number of operating buses and employees listed for each system.

Quick Frozen Foods (Harcourt Brace Jovanovich). Statistics and specific company information on refrigerated trucking fleets. The issue appears in January.

WOOD AND LUMBER

Forest Industries (Miller Freeman Publications). The January issue reviews capital expenditures and construction in the forest industry.

CHAPTER 7

USING DATA BASES FOR CORPORATE INTELLIGENCE

Starting in the early 1970s, publicly available data bases became a popular research tool with both corporate and academic librarians. Since then, data bases have proliferated. At this writing there are well over 5000 data bases that the researcher can tap into through a timesharing terminal and a telephone line.

This section deals with data bases as a corporate research tool, as a means to get information on specific companies. Wherever a data base may have some company information to offer, we will point it out and offer tips on how best to employ this data base for corporate research purposes.

DATA BASES: A DEFINITION

What is a data base? Without veering into computerese, a data base is simply a collection or pool of information that is recorded, indexed, and stored on a computer. In other words, it is nothing more than a computerized reference book.

Through a computerized index, you, the researcher, have an almost unlimited ability to find the information you are looking for. In contrast, the traditional library indexes you may be used to (e.g., the *Readers' Guide to Periodical Literature*, the *Wall Street Journal* newspaper index, *The New York Times* Index) are hardbound books, with fixed index terms. If the term or concept you are looking for cannot be found in the printed index, then you have little chance of locating the information you need. A data base permits the researcher to try whatever term he or she wants, letting the computer program search throughout the data base's records—from title, to author, to abstract, to index terms—to find the words that the researcher requested.

A data base does not need a fixed index. In practice, bibliographic data bases—that is, data bases that house abstracts of articles—allow the researcher to search under any term. The program will do the rest of the work. Should the term exist in the data base, then the program will match those records that contain the term.

HOW CAN A DATA BASE HELP THE CORPORATE RESEARCHER?

Because a data base is so flexible, and because you can scan any portion of a data base record, there is little chance that you will miss a company name or product, if filed.

A data base search can help answer the following questions:

1. Which articles were written on this market?
2. Which companies are associated with this product group?
3. What patents are available for this technology?
4. Which are the major magazines or texts in this industry?
5. What are the chances that I will find something in print on the target company?
6. How many companies are in the same industry as the target company?
7. Which reporters study this industry?
8. How can I be updated on industry and company events without having to constantly request the information?
9. How can I compile a list of the leading experts in the industry and the key institutions they are associated with?

DATA BASE LIMITATIONS

Instant information does not mean current information. The fact that data comes spewing out of your terminal with lightning speed does not mean that it is current. For the corporate researcher in need of current data on the competition, a data base may not always be your perfect solution. Too often a data base may contain information that may be as much as a month or even a year old.

When gathering corporate information through a data base, here are some of the data base limitations you should be aware of:

1. *The age of a periodical.* By the time an article citation appears in a data base, the original material and information in that article may be a year old. This is because when an article is submitted to a magazine (especially a scholarly journal), it may be six months to a year before the article is printed. In addition, once the data base supplier receives the journal or magazine article, it may be another one or two months before the article is entered into the data base.

2. *Data bases are selective.* Although a data base states that it indexes articles from a certain magazine, be careful! Because data base suppliers have limited space and limited time in which to enter the abstracted articles, they often do not include the entire issue of the magazine. Bibliographic data bases commonly omit advertisements, events calendars, editorials, personnel announcements, help-wanted advertisements, charts, graphs, photographs, and stock prices.

3. *Priority lists.* Sometimes, when a data base supplier sees news articles from different periodicals duplicating one another among the magazines and newspapers that it abstracts, he will enter only one of the articles. This may mean, in instances where two newspapers cover the same news event, that only one of the two articles may be entered into the data base. The result: you can lose sources of information. Although both may have covered national events, each reporter interviewed different sources. Because the data base supplier chose only one of the articles for its data base, you are only seeing part of the picture.

4. *Missing the update cycle.* This can occur most often in financially oriented data bases. For instance, let's say that a data base was updated once every three months. If a company's reporting period ends on the week following the last update, the data base will not catch the updated financials for another three months. A researcher needing up-to-the-minute compet-

itor financial reports cannot rely on such a data base for absolutely current information.

HOW A DATA BASE SYSTEM WORKS

This section may be addressed more to a librarian than to a manager. Nevertheless, you, the manager, should understand how and why you have access to so many data bases.

A Brief Explanation

The data base supplier is nothing more than a publisher. But instead of printing the work on paper, the supplier places it on an electronic medium (a disk or tape). From there the tape is sent or electronically transmitted to the distributor or timesharing service. The timesharing service may have more than one data base from more than one supplier. The timesharing service has created a common search language so that a librarian can search more than one data base from any number of suppliers.

Timesharing services charge the user by the time spent on the system. Some services will require an additional subscription fee, and others allow users to pay as they go. In other words, a user pays only for the time spent on the system.

Most services, such as Dialog or SDC, require that the user attend one of their system training sessions before using the system. The sessions cost approximately $100, but usually pay for themselves with the free search time given by the service to attendees. By all means sign up. The time you waste on the computer system will translate into lost dollars—dollars that could have been better spent attending the service's training seminar.

To find an appropriate data base, first contact the timesharing services themselves (listed later in this chapter). After you have done that and have received piles of literature, also call your local library or library school. Speak to the person in the reference section who does the searching. Ask him or her what the pros and cons of each data base system are and ask which is the best system for you based on your needs and budget.

DATA BASE SEARCHING TIPS

Data bases are black boxes as far as intelligence-gathering is concerned. They may have a lot of data, but you may not know how the data are stored or indexed. Here are some data base searching lessons that we have learned in the course of our research. Not all of these tips apply to all the data bases you may use; I present them here as a general rule of thumb.

1 *Find out how much of a periodical a data base abstracts.* As I mentioned earlier, most bibliographical data bases do not abstract events calendars, editorials, or product announcements. If you use one data base often, call or write the supplier. It will tell you what material is included and excluded from the publications indexed.

2 *Get a publications list.* Each data base supplier should be able to send you a list of indexed publications.

3. *Look for a company field.* If a data base has designated a special field just to list the company or companies mentioned in the records, that is a tip to the researcher that this data base is geared to collecting and indexing company information. (Every data base uses fields. A field is a category of information in a data base record. For example, an article title is given a field; so too, the publication date is given a field. Each major category is given a field.)

A sample record of a search conducted on one of the PTS F&S data bases appears on page 222. The abstracts' bottom lines list all the companies mentioned in the article (see Figure 7.1).

4. *Avoid four-digit SIC codes.* Any data base that only goes as far as identifying an industry by its four-digit SIC tag can possibly lead the searcher in the wrong direction or, even worse, give misleading information.

Market share based on a four-digit SIC code can be entirely wrong. For example, a company manufacturing microchips may have a large share of the market in its specific industry (13 percent), but it may have a far smaller share (0.1 percent) when compared to the entire electronics industry.

On the other hand, the data base that will allow the searcher to define the industry as far as a seven-digit SIC grouping is a far better source. Again, the PTS F&S data bases are examples of a source that defines an industry to seven digits.

5. *Collect synonyms.* The industry you are searching may have more than one name. Use the industry dictionaries and speak to a few analysts and experts to make sure you are searching under all possible categories. (Remember! A data base is a black box. You may not know what is inside.)

6. *Have the data base help you search for synonyms.* Data base systems such as Dialog and SDC allow you to print out the index terms that most

```
1031307
  An image problem for Detroit.
New York Times (National Edition)   May 21, 1984   p. 21,32

     General Motors and Ford are paying record bonuses to their execs, an
example to some of management high-handedness--since the firms are enjoying
protection from Japanese competition--that could cause political problems for
all US corporations. Execs in the auto firms acknowledge that they expected a
hostile reaction to the payments, which put the compensation of top officers of
GM and Ford Motor well over $1 mil each for 1983, but contend that high pay for
key execs is standard in US business and that to leave auto execs' compensation
below the levels of other manufacturing industries would risk seeing their most
talented people find better pay elsewhere.
     LA Iacocca of Chrysler will hold Chrysler bonuses to top execs to about 50%
of those paid at Ford and GM. Iacocca, who cut his own pay to $1/yr during
Chrysler's financial crisis, feels that the public relations value of
Chrysler's gesture outweighs any risk of an exodus of top managers. Automakers
face a special image problem: the profits that generated the bonuses are partly
due to govt restraints on imports of Japanese cars, and the public remembers
that the US carmakers opposed such social goals as cleaner air and greater fuel
economy. A Natl Academy of Engineering study in 1982 identified public
resentment toward Detroit's operating style as 1 reason for the popularity of
imported cars. The bonuses are expected to affect negotiations with the UAW,
which complains that an exec can be paid more money in 1 yr than a worker will
earn in a lifetime of factory toil.

*1USA *United States *3711100 *Automobiles  *21  *mgmt development;  *General
    Motors; Duns No: *00-535-6613; Ticker: *GM; CUSIP: *370442
1USA  United  States 3710000 Motor Vehicles &  Parts 21 mgmt development;  Ford
    Motor; Duns No: 00-134-4746; Ticker: F; CUSIP: 345370
```

Figure 7.1.   From data base to you.

closely resemble the ones you are using. Let's say we were to use the ABI/
Inform data base on the Dialog system. We wanted to search for articles
on General Motors marketing programs, but we weren't sure how ABI/
Inform classified the term "marketing" and what other terms it may use to
index articles.

We took the word "marketing" and asked the Dialog system to pull out
other terms that are close to "marketing." The resulting printout included
other terms such as "marketing research" and "marketing strategy," which
should be used when doing a thorough search on GM's marketing programs.

7. *Buy the data base thesaurus.*   Buy the thesaurus for any data base
you use often. Many suppliers will not only give you a thesaurus but will
include search tips to help you through their data base. A quick scan of the
thesaurus will tell you the scope of the data base. For instance, does the
data base concentrate on management issues or more on new product announcements? Most thesauri cost under $50.

8. *Look for both a primary and secondary industry.*   When searching,
keep in mind that the data base may have listed your company or companies

under another industry. When examining companies in an industry, prepare to gather more than just one or two industry categories.

Let's say you wanted to find companies that manufactured personal computers. You would want to search not only under "personal computers" but also under "home computers," "microcomputers," "transportable computers," "portable computers," and so on.

9. *Ask yourself whether you need historical data or current data.* Some data bases are better and more comprehensive suppliers of historical information than of information that may be only three months old. The data base supplier tells you in its descriptive literature how often the data base is updated.

10. *If you have already found an ideal article, use it for your search.* If you have an article in hand that supplies you with just the information you need, find out which data base indexes that magazine or newspaper. Then, punch in that exact title. Print out the record that appears—with the index terms used. By printing it out with the index terms, you have now learned how that supplier indexes the articles you are looking for. Next, simply take those same index terms and punch them back into the data base and you will receive all other articles that pertain to your industry and companies.

An example is given in Figure 7.2. Here we wanted to receive all articles on the IBM-Hitachi espionage case, plus other related articles. First we asked for an article on the case by requesting articles that mentioned IBM and Hitachi together.

11. *Limit your company search by financial size.* In data bases that track company financials, you can often limit your search. For instance, you can limit all companies in the search to those with sales between $50 and $100 million.

12. *The number of times a magazine or periodical appears on a search will indicate its interest in and knowledge of the industry.* Although a search may not yield an article that answers your question, it can indicate which magazine, editor, or author may be the best to interview.

```
1636972 /5
1636972  EDP  83/11/21   P1   SRCE:002055   ABSTRACT:6988727    (1usa)
  Fujitsu Pays IBM for copyright violations of operating software
  Intnl  Business  Machines  Gets  $300mil  from Hitachi for rights to IBM-like
operating software

  1usa United States    7372001 System Software    370 Patents & Copyrights
```

Figure 7.2. IBM-Hitachi search.

DATA BASE SEARCH FORM

The following form provides you with the categories and questions you should address when searching a data base for information about a corporation.

General industry and product lines: _____

1. Synonyms for product type, technology, or industry:

    a. _____

    b. _____

    c. _____

    d. _____

    e. _____

2. How current must the information be? (e.g., within the last month, year, etc.)

3. Are you looking for a data base that offers primarily:

    _____ narrative

    _____ statistics

4. What is the primary industry you are searching for?

    _____

5. What is the secondary industry that might be appropriate?

    _____

6. Do you have an ideal article that fairly well represents the information you are looking for? Can you supply the following about it:

    Title: _____

    Publication: _____

    Date the article appeared: _____

7. If you were unable to find an ideal article, what would be the title of the ideal article as you would imagine it? Please write in this imagined title below:

    _____

    _____

```
355902
  GENERAL MOTORS CORP. (U.S.)    820923

  Employees at Canadian Unit Ratify Labor Contract

    Sept.   20,   1982,   press reports from Toronto,  Ont., stated that 33,600
  employees of General Motors of Canada Ltd.,  subsidiary,  represented  by  the
  United  Automobile,  Aerospace &  Agricultural Implement Workers of America had
  approved a two-year labor contract,  which provided wage increases and cost  of
  living adjustments averaging about 9%  in the first year and 7%  in the second.
  Such employees currently earn an average of $11.83 an hour.
    Contract also provided more life insurance coverage,  training  guarantees
  for skilled trade workers, and a plant closing severance pay plan for employees
  with ten or more years seniority, through which such employees would be granted
  between $10,500 and $17,500 in the event of a plant closing.
    (Standard & Poor's NEWS)
```

Figure 7.3. Information from an S&P data base. (Reprinted with permission from Standard & Poor's News Online.)

SDI: A DATA BASE REMINDER SERVICE

Selective Dissemination of Information (SDI) is a service offered by several data base services, such as Dialog or SDC. SDI allows the researcher to place a company name or a subject of any type into a data base and receive regular reports whenever the data base is updated.

SDI frees the executive from constantly having to request the same information from the corporate library each week or month. The system will automatically send the executive a new list of articles each time it is updated.

For example, let's say that a researcher queries Standard & Poor's data base for a weekly update on General Motors. Each time the S&P data base is updated, the computer prints out and sends the new General Motors information to the researcher. Figure 7.3 gives an example of such a printout.

LOCATING EXPERTS THROUGH DATA BASES

Technical experts in highly specialized areas are difficult to locate. Word of mouth may be helpful in finding leads (and perhaps just the right contact). But chances are you may waste a lot of time on fruitless hunches.

Data bases can help, provided they are used judiciously. Any bibliographic data base will list articles and their respective authors. However, in some instances these authors are free lance or ghost writers for company senior officers—they are not the authors. Technical or scientific data bases,

```
0778025    82223025
Catheter  modification  to  improve  the  performance  of  aorto-ileo-femoral
examinations.
  Abaskaron M
  Department of Radiology, University of Louisville, Ky.
  Radiology (UNITED STATES)    ,Jul 1982,    144 (2)    p420,    ISSN  0033-8419
Journal Code: QSH
  Languages: ENGLISH
  Journal Announcement: 8210
  Subfile: AIM; INDEX MEDICUS
  Tags: Human
  Descriptors: Aged; *Aorta; *Catheterization--Instrumentation (IS);  Contrast
Media--Administration and Dosage (AD); Extremities--Radiography (RA); *Femoral
Artery--Radiography (RA); *Iliac Artery--Radiography (RA)
```

Figure 7.4.   Information from MEDLINE data base.

where ghosting is almost nonexistent, are better for locating experts. So, take a data base and let it create a directory of experts for you.

In the example shown in Figure 7.4, an expert on femoral catheters was located through MEDLINE, the National Library of Medicine data base.

WHICH DATA BASE SYSTEM TO CHOOSE

A data base system is a computer timesharing service that stores and makes available data bases to users of this service.

One system may have 200 or more data bases available. The Dialog system is an example. It carries data bases that cover the arts, literature, engineering, patents, and even the Yellow Pages.

The researcher can tap into each system with a search language that was designed by the system engineers. The same search language can be used on any of the data bases in the system. Each system, however, has a unique language, which means that the researcher has to learn a different language for each data base system.

To gain access to the system all you need is a dumb terminal (that is, a terminal without memory, or the ability to store information) and a modem or telephone connection to hook your terminal into the timesharing network. Each data base system may require different types of terminals. Contact the system company directly for details.

The four leading bibliographic systems and their key strengths are listed below:

1.   *BRS.*   (Bibliographic Retrieval Service, 1200 Route 7, Latham, NY 12110, 518–783–1161.) This service requires users to pay a monthly subscription fee. For that fee, it offers immediate discounts on all the data bases

in its system. Also, the search language is popular among librarians and lay users alike, and is considered an easy language to learn.

2. *DIALOG*. (3460 Hillview Avenue, Palo Alto, CA 94304, 415–858–3785.) This system has the largest selection of data bases, currently numbering over 200. The data bases available cover a broad assortment of technical and general interest fields. Dialog offers a volume discount for high volume users. Its documentation, used to explain various data base contents, is clear and well thought out.

3. *NEXIS*. (Mead Data Central, P. O. Box 933, Dayton, OH 45401, 513–859–1611.) Mead also produces a data base well known in law firms and law school libraries, called LEXIS. The Nexis system contains entire articles, not just abstracts, a characteristic not generally found on the other three systems mentioned here. Aside from the full-text option (a big plus, where you cannot find a library that carries the article), Nexis also offers a large newspaper selection. Its acquisition of The New York Times Information Bank substantially added to its newspaper coverage. Inexperienced searchers also consider its language easy to use.

4. *SDC/Orbit*. (Systems Development Corporation, 2500 Colorado Avenue, Santa Monica, CA 90406, 213–820–4111.) This system is best known for its scientific and technical data bases. Its Derwent data bases are thought of as the most complete collection of patent information available. The system offers over 80 data bases in all.

There are other timesharing vendors mentioned throughout the list later in this section. Their names and addresses are:

Newsnet
945 Haverford Road
Bryn Mawr, PA 19010

Control Data Corporation
Business Information Services
500 West Putnam Avenue
P.O. Box 7100
Greenwich, CT 06836

Dow Jones/News Retrieval
P.O. Box 300
Princeton, NJ 08540

Data Resources, Inc.
Data Products Division Headquarters
1750 K Street, NW Suite 1060
Washington, DC 20006

I.P. Sharp Associates
Box 418
Exchange Tower
2 First Canadian Place
Toronto, Ontario M5X 1E3, Canada

GTE Information Systems, Inc.
East Park Drive
Mount Laurel, NJ 08504

Chase Econometrics/Interactive Data
486 Totten Pond Road
Waltham, MA 02154

Securities Data Company, Inc.
62 William Street, 6th floor
New York, NY 10005

A LIST OF DATA BASES FOR THE CORPORATE RESEARCHER

This section lists only data bases that in some way offer corporate information. This list does not contain data bases that present general economic data or market-trend information (although some data bases mentioned here may indeed also offer that kind of information).

Each entry contains the data base name, the name of the supplier, a description of the corporate information the data base offers, and advice on how you can best use the data base in your company research.

ABI/Inform (Data Courier). A business data base that indexes feature articles from over 500 business publications. Its focus is on management issues and business decisions. It generally omits specific plant and equipment articles, as well as personnel announcements. Yet it is excellent as a source for locating significant trends within companies and industries through articles published in the business press. The data base is indexed by company name as well as by issue or subject. The abstracts are usually more than 50 words, which makes it ideal for free text searching and increases your likelihood of finding the article you are looking for, even though the topic did not fall under an index term. ABI/Inform is especially good for retrieving information on the banking and insurance industries.

Accountants Index (American Institute of Certified Public Accountants). This covers the major accounting literature. Occasionally, an article will reflect on a company's particular accounting practices.

Active Well On-Line Data (Petroleum Information Corporation). This data base's records go into great depth on active oil wells in the Rocky Mountain area of the United States. An excellent source for the researcher doing any investigation of the oil supply business. Records typically contain the well's production, depth, and overall characteristics. Each record also lists the well's operator.

Adtrack (Corporate Intelligence). A relatively new data base, with information beginning in 1980. This data base abstracts and indexes advertisements of at least a quarter page that appear in approximately 150 consumer magazines.

We have used the data base to locate where a particular company has advertised. If, because of the results of an Adtrack search, we spotted one magazine as a major advertising source, we would often call up the editor and the advertising department of the magazine for more details. This is because if an advertiser does a considerable amount of advertising with one magazine, that magazine will be certain to try to attract other advertisers in the same industry. To do that it must conduct research on the industry. The advertising research departments of many of these magazines are excellent resources of advertising intelligence on competing advertisers. In addition, the editors of a magazine receiving heavy advertising from one company or industry will be sure to provide more news copy on that industry and will probably know a considerable amount about the companies in the industry.

The data base is indexed by company name, publication, publication date, product name, and even by product code. So you can limit your search by combining any of these fields (e.g., you could limit your search by selecting only ads that appeared in a particular magazine between certain dates for a single product or advertiser).

AMI (The New York Times). This data base is now distributed through Mead Data Central. It is a data base constructed for marketing and advertising executives, and abstracts articles from approximately 60 marketing and advertising publications. It is useful for understanding advertising strategies and the direction recent ad campaigns have taken. Beware—this data base is highly selective and may only accept one article per subject, although other publications may have done a piece on the same topic.

APIPAT (Central Abstracting and Indexing Service of the American Petroleum Institute). Similar to APLIT in subject matter, but concentrates on patents issued by the United States, Belgium, Canada, France, Germany, Great Britain, Holland, Japan, and South Africa.

APLIT (Central Abstracting and Indexing Service of the American Petroleum Institute). This data base, going all the way back to 1964, covers research and events in the petrochemical industry. Each author's company affiliation is given. The abstracts are fairly detailed and manage to pull out the substance of the article. This is an excellent source for leads to R&D information on the industry.

Arthur D. Little/Online (Arthur D. Little Decisions Resources). An index of market studies and reports offered by this research and consulting company. Each record presents a report's summary, table of contents, and author.

Australian Stock Exchange Indices (Sydney Stock Exchange). A listing of stock, bond, and commodity prices on the Australian exchanges. A prime source of trading information for companies located down under.

Automotive News Data Bank (Crain Automotive Group). This data base tracks over 2000 forecasts and historical statistics in the automobile industry. The information is derived from the magazine *Automotive News* and is a valuable source of competitor production data.

Banker (Bell & Howell).   This data base indexes articles that appear in *American Banker*, one of the leading banking publications. By default this is one of the leading data bases covering the banking industry. Note—The records are short, and index terms are specific. Be sure you have the correct index terms before searching. If you need assurance on your search strategy, call the data base system you are using; its customer service line can often answer your question. Also, many systems have a built-in dictionary that will assist you in selecting other appropriate terms that you may not have thought of in advance.

A.M. Best Data Bases (A.M. Best Company).   Like their printed counterparts, Best data bases represent the single most complete company-specific data and aggregate insurance industry data available. Company data is offered by state and product line. Over 3000 firms are included in the data base.

BHRA Fluid Engineering (BHRA Fluid Engineering).   On the surface this appears to be an engineering-related data base with little to offer the corporate researcher. In truth, data bases like BHRA (and we will show you others) present patent information on the field and corporate or university affiliations of the researcher whose paper or patent appears in the data base. We have used these data bases to generate lists of experts based on certain specialties.

Billboard Information Network (Billboard Publications).   This is the only source that a researcher can turn to for quick record sales statistics and for finding out how much air time songs receive. Some of this information is available in *Billboard* magazine. A retailer or radio station would find this an excellent source for tracking the record market.

BIOSIS Previews (BioSciences Information Service).   Another scientific data base. Biosis reviews over 9000 journals, institutional reports, and other research literature in the fields of biology and medicine. The data base currently contains well over 3 million records. Although primarily a data base designed for scientific research, Biosis can be a source of experts for the corporate researcher.

Biotechnology (Derwent Publications).   Like Medline, this data base was designed for the scientist, not the corporate researcher. But also like Medline, the corporate researcher may find this a highly powerful data base when studying the field of biotechnology and genetic engineering. The data base represents major journals and conference proceedings from around the world. Patents are also included. The articles cover both theoretical and applied research.

Books In Print (R. R. Bowker).   Never overlook the obvious. The hard-cover version of this data base has long been a stock book of local libraries and bookstores. The fact that it is now on a data base makes searching through its contents that much easier. The data base contains books in print from over 12,000 publishers. Who knows? The information you may be looking for could be in a book already in print.

The one limitation of this data base is the lack of an abstract. That means that you would have to either know the title of the book or get a very close hit when searching; otherwise, the book you may be looking for may not appear in your search.

CA Search (Chemical Abstracts Service).   Containing over 5 million records, this data base contains a wide variety of information on the chemical industry, including patents, journal articles, monographs, and conference proceedings in the field. This data base can provide you with the latest chemical patent information as well as with experts in the field. You can search the data base by patent number, country, journal name, or institution.

Catfax (Grey House Publishing).   Another source to locate suppliers of unusual products. The data base lists over 4000 mail-order catalogs, along with each catalog publisher's name and address. This data base can be used to determine how many catalogs carry a particular product line.

Chemical Industry Notes (Chemical Abstracts Service).   A data base that specializes in chemical business magazines and journals. Articles that this data base references include plant capacity and product information. There are approximately 500,000 records on file.

CIS (Congressional Information Service).   This data base indexes congressional working papers including hearings, committee reports, and documents published as a result of special investigations. Unknown to many researchers, there is often a wealth of corporate information to be had from CIS. This is especially the case with companies that are in highly regulated industries, or industries that are under investigation for some reason. Each record on the data base contains a brief abstract, reference date, and number. To receive a complete copy of the document referred to in the record, contact the Congressional Information Service. They place the original documents on microfiche. CIS will also tell you which library in your area is a subscriber of their microfiche service. Most major cities will have libraries that are either full or partial subscribers.

Coffeeline (International Coffee Association).   The ultimate coffee data base. This data base tracks the latest news and events in the coffee industry, from the agricultural aspects to health reports. The data base also names company names and, as a result, is excellent source for tracking competitors worldwide.

Compendex (Engineering Information). This is the computerized version of the paperbound *Engineering Index.* We have used this data base many times to locate companies or experts who specialize in certain areas of engineering. Although there are a large number of engineering directories and buyers' guides available through associations and trade magazines, they still cannot match the versatility of a specialized data base such as this one.

Here are some key advantages to using Compendex:

1. The name and organization of the author are clearly identified.
2. There is an abstract that will explain the context of the citation.
3. The data base indexes over 3500 journals in disciplines ranging from control engineering to aerospace. Currently Compendex claims to have more than 1.1 million records.

Comp-U-Store (Comp-U-Card of America). In the consumer market it may be hard to establish true retail discount prices, especially anything beyond manufacturers' suggested list prices. This data base is set up for the purpose of at-home shopping. But the astute researcher can use the Comp-U-Store data base to locate prices for thousands of products. Prices are usually well below standard list prices. Comp-U-Store can also reveal formerly unknown competitive brands to the researcher first exploring the marketplace.

Conference Papers Index (Cambridge Scientific Abstracts). This is a unique collection of scientific and technical papers indexed from over 1000 meetings each year. Each listing contains the author's name and affiliated institution, as well as the address and ordering price of the paper being discussed. In many instances these papers can reveal which companies specialize in certain areas of research. Although sometimes dated, the papers found in this data base cannot be located elsewhere.

DAAS/Drilling Activity Analysis System (Petroleum Information Corporation). An extremely detailed set of records on oil and gas wells. Records include data on site, depth of well, potential yield, and class of the well. Other information is also supplied on the operator and the geological factors of the site.

Data Processing and Information Science Contents/DISC (BRS). Instead of abstracting articles, DISC provides you with tables of contents for major magazines in the microcomputer and minicomputer industries.

Datastream (Datastream International). A superb financial data base on thousands of companies in the United States, South Africa, Japan,

Canada, and Europe. Included in the data base are company financials, stock prices, and country economic indicators.

D&B—Dun's Market Identifiers 10 + (Dun's Marketing Services). This data base is one of the most complete company listings available on line. Through one data base, the researcher can locate over 1.2 million companies, plants, or branch locations. This data base takes *Thomas' Register* one step further: it not only offers headquarter locations but the subsidiary or branch locations as well. Among the pieces of information available in most records are company name, company address, SIC code, sales, number of employees, executive officers, and type of location (e.g., branch, headquarters).

D&B Million Dollar Directory (Dun's Marketing Services). Similar to the above, but only includes companies whose net worth is over $500,000. There are over 121,000 companies in the data base. Each record's features are similar to that of the Multi-Market data base.

D&B Principal International Businesses (Dun & Bradstreet's International Marketing Services). Similar to the above, but includes only foreign companies. There are over 57,000 companies on file from over 133 countries. The features are similar to those described in the D&B Market Identifiers data base described above. Sales are listed both in local and U.S. currency.

Disclosure II (Disclosure Incorporated). This data base contains summaries of 10-K, 10-Q, 8-K, and 20-F corporate *Securities and Exchange Commission* filings. There are over 8000 public companies on file. As was mentioned in an earlier section on SEC filings, these reports have detailed financial and management information on publicly traded companies monitored by the SEC. Aside from the summary information available from this data base, each abstract contains the Disclosure order number, which allows the researcher to order the original documents from Disclosure itself. The reports can be ordered either on microfiche or on paper copies.

Because the data base allows you to search both by SIC code and by product line, you can usually pull out companies that fit your description. This flexibility gives you the ability to create lists of companies that you will not find cataloged anywhere else. Most corporate directories are only indexed by the limited four-digit Standard Industrial Code. This means that by using the Disclosure data base you can pick out manufacturers of "hybrid integrated circuits"; whereas a search through a standard corporate directory would allow you to get only as far as "electronics components."

Disclosure also allows the experienced searcher to select companies based on financial ranges—for example, you could say "Give me all companies with sales between $50 and $100 million." If you wish to further narrow the resulting list, you can cross-index the request by city, state, or product group.

Dodge Construction Potentials Data Bank (McGraw-Hill Information Systems). This data bank can identify specific construction projects, detailing the nature and the size of each project along with the name of the builder.

Dow Jones News/Retrieval (Dow Jones). For late-breaking financial and general news, this is an excellent data base. The researcher can retrieve both news stories and stock prices. Since Dow Jones is the publisher of the *Wall Street Journal*, a searcher can often find information on the data base a day in advance of its appearing in the newspaper.

EI Engineering Meetings (Engineering Information). Similar to the Compendex data base, except that EI catalogs only meetings, not articles from technical journals. There is some overlap with Compendex. Yet this data base does not present abstracts; rather, it offers a listing of the papers presented at each conference.

EIS Digests of Environmental Impact Statements (Information Resources Press). An important data base for any researcher exploring plant operations in the chemical process industries. This data base has managed to record all EPA environmental impact statements filed since 1970.

EIS Industrial Plants (Economic Information Systems). This data base contains approximately 150,000 plants that have a total sales of over $500,000. The file is smaller than D&B Market Identifiers, although you may find a plant here that is not listed in D&B. Each record offers name, address, estimated sales, market share, the number of people employed at the plant, and a cross-reference to the headquarters location.

This file is weakest when presenting sales and market-share information. We have generally found market-share data to be off, possibly because the companies with narrow product lines are filed under a general SIC code category. The result is a market share that does not reflect the company's true, more narrow industrial group.

EIS Nonmanufacturing Plants (Economic Information Systems). This file contains nonmanufacturing locations that employ more than 20 individuals. There are over 250,000 establishments on file. The record structure is similar to that of records in the EIS Manufacturing Plants file discussed above.

Electronic Yellow Pages (Market Data Retrieval). The Yellow Pages section in this book emphasizes the directory's importance to the corporate intelligence gatherer. While you can purchase a hard copy collection of Yellow Pages from throughout the country, this data base version can save you a lot of space—as well as offering you far more flexibility in searching for company listings.

With the paperbound copy you are restricted by the categories and indexing in each volume. In addition, you will have to page through each volume to compile listings city by city. This electronic version permits you to conduct a broad search on a national scale quickly and economically.

What makes this data base such a wonderful search tool? Here are some ways we have used this source:

1. You can search for companies not only by subject, but by Standard Industrial Code as well.

2. You can limit your search by the county in which the companies are located, to identify neighboring competitors or suppliers.

3. You can limit the companies you search for by their estimated asset size.

4. Let's say you wanted to locate only those stores serving a metropolitan area of a certain population density. This data base allows you to limit your search to areas of one size or another.

5. You can select the addresses by headquarters or branch location.

There are some limits, however. While the publisher states that it takes the listings from most of the Yellow Pages throughout the United States, we have found gaps. For instance, in one search for a retail chain that we knew had over 800 outlets, the data base listed only 600. According to our latest searches using this data base, we find that it contains an average of 50 to 80 percent of all the possible listings. At times we have also found 100 percent of all expected entries.

Also, we have found that the data base does not as yet cover all categories. But based on the rapid growth we have witnessed in this file, you will probably find many of these gaps soon closed. Here are the categories covered by the Electronic Yellow Pages: construction, finance, manufacturers, professionals, retailers, services, and wholesalers.

Encyclopedia of Associations (Gale Research Company).   The hard-copy version of this data base is a keystone to almost every public, corporate, and university library collection in America. Containing over 16,000 records, this data base provides you with far more flexibility (there's that word again) than does the text. You can search by industry, subject area, or free text.

As part of your homework when researching any company, always contact the affiliated association to order its industry membership directory or buyers' guides. These can become excellent networking tools. Also, you will find that these associations are often trade magazine publishers as well. Speak to the editor and he or she will guide you to other industry experts who may help you in your corporate quest.

Energy Data Base (Technical Information Center). This data base extensively covers technical literature and patent information in the energy field. Each entry lists the "organization source," which means the author's corporate or institutional affiliation. There are over 800,000 records to date.

Energynet (Environment Information Center). This data base publisher specializes in energy and environmental information. Energynet is an electronic telephone directory of experts and organizations in energy and the energy industry. There are approximately 3000 records. Organizations and individuals mentioned come from both the private and governmental sectors.

Equity (Securities Data Corporation). A wonderful source for tracking specific stock offerings for over 5000 common stocks and 800 preferred issues (collected since 1970). A typical record might contain the stock's offering price, current price, book value, and the name of the underwriter.

Excerpta Medica (Excerpta Medica). This, along with Medline, is the leading medical data bases. We have used this source to collect expert names in a particular technology. Since the articles that are abstracted here also include the author's name as well as the affiliated institution, Excerpta Medica in effect becomes an international medical science directory.

Fast Permits On-Line (Petroleum Information Corporation). Within days of an oil well drilling permit being issued, this data base has recorded the data about that well. Each record includes the well operator, the operator's address, and well depth. The data base can be used effectively by both competitors and equipment suppliers to determine activity in a region.

Federal Index (Capitol Services International). The key phrase here is "Contract Awards." This data base abstracts and indexes information on federal rulings and legislation from the *Congressional Record, Federal Register*, and the *Washington Post*. But it also records who wins certain contract awards—a crucial bit of information when examining companies that rely on government contracts for business.

Federal Register Abstracts (Capitol Services International). This data base concentrates on the *Federal Register* only and performs a function similar to that of the Federal Index, mentioned above.

Financial Post Securities (Financial Post Investment Databank). A data base devoted to the Canadian stock exchanges. The Securities data base monitors 3000 stocks and includes for each entry the high and low price and daily trading volume. The data base also includes selected New York and American exchanges' securities.

Financial Times Company Information Database (Information Industries). This data base cites and abstracts articles from both the London and the Frankfurt edition of the *Financial Times*. For those who have not read the paper, it is a cross between *The New York Times* and the *Wall Street Journal* in content and business coverage. It is considered one of the leading European financial papers.

Financial Times Share Information (Financial Times Business Information). This data base can almost claim comprehensive coverage of stocks traded on the London Stock Exchange. The data base is updated a number of times each day. A very complete and current data base.

Findex (Find/SVP). An excellent source for locating market studies and research reports published by market research houses as well as by Wall Street analysts. You can search Findex by publisher, subject, or date of the report. There are over 6000 reports on file from over 300 publishers.

Foods Adlibra (Komp Information Services). This data base covers both food trade and technical journals. It includes patents, new product announcements, and studies on the food industry and its products. We have found that this data base manages to stay current and that it effectively covers almost any significant announcement in the food-processing industry.

Foreign Traders Index (U.S. Department of Commerce). Since there are too few listings of foreign companies, the Foreign Traders Index may provide you with foreign company names that were formerly unavailable. FTI lists almost 150,000 companies from 130 countries that either import U.S. goods or would like to. The names are originally funneled through the foreign embassies, then fed to the U.S. Department of Commerce.

Each entry lists the company name, address, year established, size estimate of the firm, number of employees, chief executive officer, product codes, and a further description of the product lines they are interested in.

Globe and Mail (Info Globe). This is a full-text edition of the *Globe and Mail* Canadian newspaper. The data base is as current as the edition that appears on the newsstand. It is updated each day. A superb source of Canadian business and general news.

GPO Monthly Catalog and GPO Publications File (Government Printing Office). These two files tell the researcher what documents and reports are available through the Government Printing Office. Each entry includes the originating agency and cost of each item. In many instances, the citation also has a small abstract describing the document's contents. When doing any corporate research relating to government activities or legislation, these data bases may give you details on hearings that the company has attended, or general information regarding its industry.

GML (GML Information Systems). An important data base for a researcher exploring computer hardware. GML provides on-line access to technical specifications on over 12,000 computers and computer parts and accessories. The record will also display the product's price and availability. An excellent source for developing lists of competitive hardware in this fast-changing aspect of the computer industry.

Harfax Industry Data Sources (Harfax Database Publishing). This data base version of the hardbound copy offers references to market studies, special magazine issues, related industry data bases, and other published material relating to 65 industries. This is an excellent source for the researcher just beginning to examine a company. It can quickly pull together many of the key sources on industry and on related companies in that industry.

Harvard Business Review (Wiley). All the articles from 1971 to the present (with the exception of the book reviews and letters to the editor) that have appeared in the *Harvard Business Review* are contained here in abstracted form. The data base has also included a number of articles that appeared in the HBR before 1971. The *Harvard Business Review* is a superb source of management and strategic information on companies. Also, the authors are often considered experts in their fields. So, should the articles themselves not pan out, you may want to contact those who wrote them.

INSPEC (Institution of Electrical Engineers). A huge data base of international citations from journals and conference proceedings in physics, electrotechnology, computers, and control. Although this is not a patent data base, it does list and discuss patents. It also lists the corporation or conference from which the article stemmed. This is an excellent source of experts worldwide. The data base could also lead you to the companies or institutions that are responsible for the most active R&D efforts in a particular field.

Insurance Abstracts (University Microfilms). This data base covers over 100 publications. An excellent source for the latest news on the industry.

International Auto Data Bank (Data Resources). This data bank contains detailed current and historical production data on specific automobiles throughout the world. Records reveal details on make and model, number of cars, new car production by model, domestic sales, and export data.

International Pharmaceutical Abstracts (American Society of Hospital Pharmacists). The pharmaceutical industry in many ways is discreet and extremely secretive in its activities. Trying to locate areas of experimentation can be difficult. The IPA data base allows you to discover which companies are using which types of drugs and how they are experimenting with them. Be aware, though, that by the time the article reaches this data base, it is likely to be somewhat dated itself—and the information therefore may not be extremely timely or useful. Each citation lists the corporate source and the names of individuals who wrote the article referred to.

International Software Database (Imprint Software). Since software is the driving force in microcomputers, a data base that provides you with suppliers of this software can be an invaluable source of expert names. Those who supply the software often know a great deal about the companies whose machines they are servicing. For example, a company producing third-party software for an Apple microcomputer may have heard a good deal about Apple's activities and marketing plans. In some instances, the software supplier may be a direct subcontractor to Apple. Locate the software and you may have found an expert corporate intelligence source.

Investext (Business Research Corporation). Full-text coverage of over 3000 publicly traded company research reports published by investment banking houses worldwide. The reports cover companies in the United States, Canada, Europe, and Japan. Each report includes financials and company analysis. You can locate a company on the data base any number of ways: by company name, stock exchange ticker symbol, industry code, or product name. This becomes an even more valuable data base since brokerage houses have begun to charge for their formerly free research reports. Also, by just scanning the table of contents of any report you will be able to tell whether or not you are wasting your time in choosing this report. Should you find that the contents don't meet your needs, you can skip over the report and move on to another.

ISMEC (Cambridge Scientific Abstracts). A data base that concentrates on journals from the fields of mechanical engineering and production. Since the data base does list the author's name and the affiliated institution or corporation, you can assemble a list of experts in these fields fairly easily.

Kompass-France (Société Nouvelle d'Éditions Industrielles). An online listing of approximately 60,000 French manufacturers. Each record contains name, address, telephone number, telex, lines of business, senior executives, products, and bank affiliations. This is an on-line version of the printed book.

LC MARC (United States Library of Congress). A listing of all books cataloged by the Library of Congress, including volumes on companies. This data base begins with 1968.

Legal Resource Index (Information Access Company). This data base covers topical news items that have appeared in law journals and law newspapers. The index offers reports on court cases and litigation that the lay reader will find easy to understand. The data base can unearth company information that could be buried in court records and case books. The data base begins in 1980.

Licensable Technology (Dvorkovitz & Associates). When entering the high-technology field, a new venture may want to determine if there is not already an invention or device that may be open for licensing. This data base contains over 10,000 inventions and processes that can be licensed.

Magazine Index (Information Access Corporation). For those of you who have used the *Readers' Guide to Periodical Literature*, that classic index used by high schoolers across the nation to write term papers, now its equivalent (by a different publisher) is in data base form. Magazine Index covers over 400 publications, including *Forbes, Fortune,* and *Business Week.* If all you need is a quick review of company activities as reported in the general press, this is a very useful data base.

Management Contents (Management Contents). Similar to ABI/Inform, this index reviews management and business literature, citing feature articles in business management and administration.

Marquis Who's Who (Marquis Who's Who). This classic biographical directory is now on-line. There are over 75,000 records. Chances are you will not find biographies of CEOs of smaller corporations on this data base, but you will probably locate CEOs of many Fortune 500 companies.

Medline (United States National Library of Medicine). This data base begins in 1966 (fairly old by data base standards) and has over 4 million records. The data base covers medical literature throughout the world, and is considered the preeminent medical data base. Because it lists company or institutional affiliation along with each article, we have found that it can provide us with an accurate worldwide list of experts in extremely narrow disciplines.

Mergers and Acquisitions (Securities Data Company). While no data base or printed text can claim to cover all mergers and acquisitions that do occur, this data base makes a valiant attempt. There are approximately 1300 records on file. A typical record includes the number and type of securities that have changed hands, the location of the companies involved, and any other financial data.

METADEX—Metals Abstracts/Alloys Index (American Society for Metals). Here is another of those little-known specialty data bases that can prove highly useful when exploring the field of metallurgy. The journal citations contain corporate affiliation, author's name, and a fairly detailed abstract of the article. The data base also abstracts certain industry patents.

Microcomputer Index (Microcomputer Information Services). A data base that covers articles in 40 microcomputer journals. This is considered more of a popular literature data base than a technical one. Journals indexed include *Byte, Personal Computing,* and *Infoworld.*

Monitor (Bell & Howell). This data base covers the *Christian Science Monitor,* including articles from all of its regional editions. The data base was begun in 1979. Regional coverage here is the key. Unfortunately, what occurs in many data bases is the omission of regional data in favor of national information.

National Newspaper Index (Information Access Corporation). This is an excellent cover-to-cover index of the *Wall Street Journal, The New York Times,* and the *Christian Science Monitor.* There is virtually no abstract, but all company names or individuals mentioned in the article are provided with index terms or "descriptors" as they are known in data base lingo. The data base began in 1979 and now has over 600,000 citations. Note—the data base does omit stock quotations, weather reports, crossword puzzles, and horoscopes.

Newsbeat (GTE Information Systems). A news data base that draws its information from the Dow Jones News service. The articles are complete, not abstracted. The records are also indexed by industry or company code for more accurate retrieval.

Newsnet (Newsnet). A data base of over 100 newsletters, all available in full-text on-line. This is unusual. The only other system offering a fairly extensive newsletter collection is the Nexis package. This data base, though, specializes in newsletters. The current file is known as Newsnet and the historical collection of newsletters is called the Library. The newsletters in the system range from technological to financial and governmental.

Newspaper Index, Index to Black Newspapers (Bell & Howell). Here is another data base with a regional slant. It includes 10 major U.S. newspapers, as well as 11 black newspapers. There are no abstracts accompanying citations, but the coverage is unusually broad—in some ways paralleling the efforts of the former New York Times Information Bank before it was purchased by Mead Data General.

Newsearch (Information Access Company). This is a daily updated data base of articles that have appeared in legal, popular, and trade literature. After each month the citations are spun off into other data bases mentioned in this section (National Newspaper Index, Magazine Index, Legal Resource Index, Management Contents, and Trade and Industry Index). The big advantage of this data base is its timeliness.

NEXIS (Mead Data Central).   Nexis is more than one data base. In fact, it is dozens of data bases, each covering one publication or wire service. What makes the Nexis data bases highly useful is their full-text format. You, the researcher, can search through just one publication, or through a family of publications, or through the entire system at once with one search strategy.

There are four major data base groups: newspapers (of which there are 11 to date), magazines (of which there are 30 to date), newsletters (of which there are 27 to date), and wire services (of which there are 9 to date). The newspapers range from *American Banker*, the *Japan Economic Journal*, and the *Manchester Guardian Weekly* to *The New York Times*. The magazines include ABA *Banking Journal*, *Business Week*, *Defense and Foreign Affairs*, *Electronics*, *Inc.*, and *U.S. News & World Report*. Newsletters include *Advertising Compliance Service*, *Banking Expansion Reporter*, the *Dorvillier News Letter*, *East Asian Executive Reports*, and *World Financial Markets*. The wire services include the Associated Press, Reuters, Jiji Press Ticker Service, and United Press International.

NTIS (National Technical Information Service).   NTIS is a branch of the U.S. Department of Commerce and records any government-sponsored research. All information contained here is declassified. We have found that by the time we locate news from NTIS, it's old news. Corporate research might best be done through other sources. But NTIS may be useful in a historical vein, telling you which corporations have historically had a relationship with the federal government in a research area.

Paperchem (Institute of Paper Chemistry).   No other data base that I have found provides such extensive coverage of the paper and pulp industry. The data base abstracts articles from approximately 1000 periodicals written in 20 languages. Corporate or institutional affiliation is given. The data base includes coverage from 1968.

Patdata (BRS).   This patent data base specializes in abstracting utility patent filings only. The data base begins with patents issued in 1971.

PESTDOC (Derwent Publications).   One of the series of Derwent patent and research data bases. This one concentrates on the scientific and patent literature for the pesticide and herbicide industries. It lists corporate source and author. Note—the person conducting the search on a Derwent data base should have some knowledge of chemistry or chemical structure and nomenclature. Otherwise, he or she is liable to miss crucial citations. The

SDC system, which offers the Derwent patent data bases, offers special training classes in their use.

Philadelphia Daily News/Philadelphia Inquirer (Philadephia Newspapers). Full-text data base of feature and news articles appearing in these two newspapers. The data base does not include stock exchange data.

PTS (Predicasts). The series of data bases I will discuss below is produced by PTS and is considered by most corporate librarians to be the best first source of published corporate information available. What makes these data bases so useful is their indexing. Predicasts employs SIC (Standard Industrial Codes) down to the seven-digit level. This allows the researcher to probe into highly specific product lines and product areas.

PTS Annual Reports Abstracts. This is a fairly new entry for Predicasts. This data base offers annual report summaries for 3000 publicly held U.S. companies.

PTS F&S Indexes. This data base has over 2 million citations from over 5000 publications worldwide. Each article either has a brief one-line synopsis of the contents or a descriptive title. The citations are heavily indexed to include all companies mentioned in the article. What makes this a wonderful data base to use is its lack of selectivity. It not only indexes the feature articles, but it abstracts many of the product announcements and contract award articles as well.

PTS International Forecasts. With over 400,000 citations, this index offers forecasts in tabular format, giving the reader the information in visual form, by column and row.

PTS PROMT. PROMT takes selected articles from 5000 publications in the F&S Indexes and supplies large abstracts. Although this data base is somewhat more selective, with approximately 600,000 citations as opposed to 2 million for F&S Indexes, you may have more luck finding your corporate information. The reason is in the abstract. The abstract will have many more terms in it and may have the phrase you are searching for; whereas the F&S Indexes are abbreviated and force you to either hit the right SIC or the correct index term. We have found the PROMT abstracts so well-written that we did not need to see the complete articles from which they were abstracted.

PTS U.S. Forecasts. This data base covers industry forecasts for the United States in tabular form, much like the International Forecasts data base.

PTS United States Time Series. Similar to the F&S International Forecasts, but for specific product groups in the United States.

RINGDOC (Derwent Publications).   Another Derwent special. This patent data base, available on the SDC system, covers scientific literature in the pharmaceutical industry. The RINGDOC data is divided into two files. Again, along with the author, the data base states the corporate or institutional affiliation.

Robotics Information (Cincinnati Milacron Industries).   This unusual data base scans the technical literature for robotics information and developments.

SAE (Society of Automotive Engineers).   Should you be looking for experts on the technical side of the automotive industry, this is the data base for you. This data base includes conference papers presented at the Society for Automotive Engineers conferences. Author's name and corporate affiliation are given, along with a brief abstract.

Scisearch (Institute for Scientific Information).   A huge data base with over 4.5 million records in the fields of science and technology. The citations are somewhat meager and do not have abstracts. But Scisearch makes up for this by claiming to have covered over 90 percent of the world literature in these fields. In addition, citations are cross-indexed to other articles published by the same author. This data base does list the author's affiliated institution or corporation. The corporate researcher can therefore use this data base to derive names of experts as well as the R&D their companies are undertaking.

Spectrum (Computer Directions Advisors).   Spectrum takes a different look at the publicly traded corporation. It offers searchers a review of a company's major stockholders and institutional investors.

SSIE Current Research (National Technical Information Service).   Here is a data base that was designed with the intelligence-seeker in mind. It cites current scientific research projects undertaken through government or private sponsorship. For those looking for R&D information on a company, this may be the perfect place to start your hunt. The data base started in 1978. Most of the research (an estimated 90 percent) reported here is government-sponsored. Citations are indexed in a number of very useful ways: by sponsoring organization, by the institution performing the work, and by the dollar size of the project.

Standard & Poor's Compustat (Standard & Poor's Corporation).   This data base provides financial information on over 6000 publicly traded corporations. The file has a good deal of depth, with financials available for the past 10 years.

Standard & Poor's General Information File (Standard & Poor's Corporation). This file reviews and profiles approximately 3000 publicly held companies. A typical record contains a company's address, senior officers, net sales and income, earnings per share, and the latest company developments.

Standard & Poor's News and News Daily (Standard & Poor's Corporation). This is a superb data base for catching the press and earnings announcements of over 10,000 publicly held companies. Each announcement has an accompanying abstract. Many times the announcement is taken in its original form. We have found that this data base can be the quickest and most current source for quarterly earnings reports, information on plant expansion, information on personnel, new product announcements, stock splits, and dividend reports. The Daily version of this data base contains weekly updates of the News version.

Technotech (Control Data Corporation). This is a very current data base that tracks technologies that can be licensed. There are approximately 16,000 records on the data base at any one time. Technotech is an excellent tool for investigators who need to research state-of-the-art technologies and those companies that might be producing them.

Telegen (Environmental Information Center). This data base concentrates on the fields of genetic engineering and biotechnology. Because the corporate or institutional affiliation is listed, you can compile a list of experts in the field.

Textile Technology Digest (Institute of Textile Technology). The data base to use if you are attempting to explore products and processes in the textile industry.

Textline (Finsbury Data Services). An English-language data base of European business news. All citations and abstracts are in English, no matter what language the article was originally written in.

Trade and Industry Index (Information Access Corporation). The literature used for this data base comes from much of the popular business and trade literature, such as the *Wall Street Journal, Advertising Age, Coal Age, Byte,* and *Electronic Design.* There are over 275 magazines indexed.

Trademarkscan (Thomson and Thomson). Although you will need a patent and trademark attorney to determine if a trademark is unique, this data base may provide the researcher with an initial sweep of many of the available marks already on file—over 600,000 of them. This data base contains the trademark name, a brief description of the mark and how it is used, the government classification, the date of issue, and the mark's owner.

Tulsa (University of Tulsa).   Tulsa is a data base specializing in petroleum exploration and production. Among the topics covered are geology, geophysics as it relates to petroleum exploration, drilling, well logging, well completion, oil and gas production, reservoir studies, and storage. There are approximately 300,000 records to date. The data base also tracks patents in the industry. Author is always mentioned. Corporate affiliation is only occasionally cited, but can always be found in the article itself.

Ulrich's International Periodicals Directory (R. R. Bowker).   This online version of the famous periodical directory is an excellent data base for locating trade magazines or newsletters in a wide variety of industries and disciplines.

UPI News (United Press International).   This data base indexes the full-text version of UPI stories that have appeared since April 1983.

U.S. Patent Classification (Derwent).   This data base does not so much supply information on the patent as display the classsification of the patent. Cross-reference patent classifications are also presented.

U.S. Patent Copies—USPA, USP77, USSP70 (Derwent).   These three data bases cover inventions with patent numbers in the United States from 1970. There are over 900,000 patents on file in these data bases. Along with a description of the patent, the citation contains the assignee's name, patent date, and number. While no data base search can guarantee 100 percent success, I recommend that you approach this data base first when seeking patent information on U.S. inventions. Note—remember to use an experienced searcher, one who understands patent terminology and filing procedures.

Value Line (Arnold Bernhard and Company).   The hard-copy version of this data base has become a staple reference source in the Wall Street investment community. But where the hard-copy version may offer 10 years of historical financial data, the data base can present over 20 years of historical financials. There are approximately 1700 publicly traded companies in the data base.

What distinguishes Value Line from other financial data bases is the way it treats the income and balance sheet data. Instead of simply representing straight income, expense, and asset liability data, it manipulates the data via financial ratios. The data base version also presents industry composites.

VETDOC (Derwent).   A highly specialized data base that concentrates on veterinary medicine and drugs. It names names and mentions corporations involved in the research.

Ward's Autoinfobank (Ward Communications). Ward's is the printed source for automotive news in the United States. This data base is a supplement to the printed *Automotive News*. It has detailed inventory figures for the various manufacturers, and should prove a strong competitive tool and an intelligence boon to auto industry parts suppliers.

World Aluminum Abstracts (American Society for Metals). As the name implies, the specialty here is aluminum and its processing. The data base is drawn from over 1600 publications, conference proceedings, government reports, and dissertations. The institution or corporate affiliation is given. So if you are exploring the aluminum industry, this is one of the first sources you should tap.

World Patents Index/World Patents Index—Latest (Derwent). WPI and WPIL provide the searcher with over 2.5 million patent citations from 24 countries around the world. The patent name, description, and all pertinent patent information are there for the asking. Again—I cannot repeat it too often—use a searcher who is experienced in searching the patent literature and Derwent's patent data bases.

World Textiles (Shirley Institute). This is a worldwide textile data base which offers the corporate or institutional affiliation. Again, another excellent source for uncovering R&D information, as well as finding names of experts in the textile industry.

CHAPTER **8**

FOREIGN INTELLIGENCE FROM U.S. SOURCES

Researching Abroad While Staying at Home

Although the intelligence sources given in this chapter may have originated in a foreign country, you can gain access to every one of these sources without ever having to leave the United States. International publishing and advanced telecommunications have—at least from an intelligence-gathering standpoint—brought nations much closer to one another.

That is the point of this chapter. You can locate vital foreign corporate intelligence via telephone, telex, or a hop to a specialty library or consulate. Although there is no substitute for actually being on the scene (as described in Chapter 13), you can learn a good deal about a competitor's marketing strategy, plant and equipment, and delivery of services by understanding where to find the sources. Among the resources described in this chapter are foreign banks, corporate branch offices, securities brokers, the International Trade Commission, trade shows, consulates, public filings, foreign chambers of commerce, foreign financial texts and specialty magazines, and foreign library collections.

WAR STORY 8

Tracking Down a German Acquisition

In one case, we had to confirm a rumor about the acquisition of one German company by another German company. Instead of telexing the companies directly (which might not have given us the answer, and could have tipped off each of the parties involved), we called one of the major German banks in New York City and located the executive responsible for that industry group. She not only confirmed the rumor, but did an independent check for us through sources in her own country.

BANKS

Most major foreign banks have U.S. offices. New York City, the financial hub for worldwide business activity, is the home of most of these banks. They have libraries; their collections may contain annual reports and statistical collections not available elsewhere.

Some foreign banks serve dual roles—that of stockbroker and financier. West Germany does not have stockbrokers in the traditional sense; German banks serve in this capacity.

BRANCH OFFICES

Talk about networking—here is the best opportunity for you to begin establishing an intelligence network on any number of foreign companies. Even if it is a one-person operation, most foreign companies that do a sizable amount of business in the United States will at some point open an office here. Where business is conducted on a regional basis, one company may establish an office in each region or district. We have used such offices to sketch the competitive picture of these companies both in the United States and abroad. In certain cases, the branch offices contacted knew their competitors' plant capacity abroad.

To help you find these scattered offices, we have included a selection of directories of foreign companies with U.S. offices in the "Key Foreign Business Magazines and Directories" section in this chapter.

SECURITIES BROKERS

Here we are talking about U.S. brokerage houses that employ specialists on foreign companies. The brokers will often have on hand foreign annual reports and financial information on the companies they track regularly. You can find these brokers through banks, consulates, and the Wall Street community of brokers who have an active Old Boy network.

INTERNATIONAL TRADE COMMISSION

The ITC, through its embassy network abroad, has been able to compile a data base consisting of thousands of companies. The ITC uses the U.S. embassies to scout out these foreign companies for U.S. businesses that may want to do business with them. The embassies' reports are routed to the ITC and placed into the data bank. Called the World Traders Data Reports, they record credit data, contacts, and other information relating to the companies' export and import trades.

TRADE SHOWS

Many of the widely attended international trade shows do take place in the United States (with a number of notable exceptions). Not to be overlooked, they are valuable sources of competitor intelligence on foreign firms. See the trade show section in Chapter 14 for details.

CONSULATES

Never overlook the obvious. We have visited a number of consulates and discovered that they house some of the finest foreign corporate collections and experts. Much of a consulate's collection is unique.

For one assignment, we needed to ascertain the amount of glassware that one foreign competitor was exporting to the United States. We located the principal consulate in the United States and asked for their information and statistics office. The person in charge not only gave us the amount of glassware that the country was exporting to the United States, but also reported that approximately 90 percent of the exports were destined for the target company. This kind of intelligence would not have been available through U.S. Customs, since Customs does not track specific companies— only the countries themselves.

See "Foreign Consulates and Embassies" later in this chapter for a list of major foreign consulates located in the U.S.

PUBLIC FILINGS

The Securities and Exchange Commission, as well as many state governments, require that certain foreign companies operating in the United States file with their respective offices. See the SEC and state filings section of Chapter 3 for further information on the particular reports and filing requirements.

FOREIGN CHAMBERS OF COMMERCE

Partly established as a lobbying force for foreign companies doing business in the United States, these trade organizations are excellent referral centers for data on a foreign company. A list is given later in this chapter in the section "Foreign Chambers of Commerce and Associations in the United States." Many have published directories, telling the reader where foreign company branch offices are located in the United States. These directories are listed in this section under "Key Foreign Business Magazines and Directories."

NETWORKING THROUGH U.S. MULTINATIONALS

Just as foreign companies have embedded themselves in the U.S. economy, so too have U.S. corporations established corporate empires abroad. You should use them the same way you use foreign branch offices here in the United States. For various projects, we have called a U.S. multinational in the United States and asked to be put in touch with the executive who had experience in the target country of interest to us. This executive was savvy and could easily distinguish between official foreign published statistics and genuine data on the country or company we needed data on. If you can arrange for an information swap, this executive may go so far as telexing his or her foreign office to assist you in your assignment. You can find the U.S. companies you need, say those with extensive contacts in Europe or

Taiwan, by using the materials listed in the section "Key Foreign Business Magazines and Directories."

FOREIGN FINANCIAL TEXTS

Although often dated, and sorely lacking financial details by American standards, a number of corporate directories will offer basic revenue and balance sheet items. In certain cases, the texts will offer extensive financial data. The British Extel service is equivalent to the Moody's Investors manuals in the United States. Informations Internationales is similar to the Value Line service. However, mainly because foreign corporations do not have to file as often or as extensively as U.S. companies, financial details about them are skimpy.

Of all the foreign countries, West Germany, the United Kingdom, Canada, and France offer the best financial reviews of their own companies. Partly because of the language barrier and the markedly different reporting requirements, Far East corporations have little financial information to offer. Japanese companies, publicly traded in the United States and abroad, are the one exception.

You can find a list of foreign financial texts under the heading "Key Foreign Business Magazines and Directories" in this chapter.

FOREIGN LIBRARY COLLECTIONS

Many of the special directories and periodicals cited in this chapter can only be found in special libraries located in the United States. The librarians can guide you to other sources and information centers that may have the data you are looking for. A list of these libraries and their telephone numbers appears later in this chapter under "U.S. Libraries and Information Centers with Foreign Information Sources."

FOREIGN CHAMBERS OF COMMERCE AND ASSOCIATIONS IN THE UNITED STATES

AFRICA

African-American Chamber of
Commerce, Inc.
212–766–1343

ARGENTINA

Argentine-American Chamber of
Commerce
212–943–8753

ASIA

Association of Asian-American
Chambers of Commerce
202–638–5595

AUSTRIA

U.S.-Austrian Chamber of
Commerce, Inc.
212–571–0340

BELGIUM

Belgian-American Chamber of
Commerce in the U.S., Inc.
212–247–7613

BRAZIL

Brazilian-American Chamber of
Commerce, Inc.
212–575–9030

Brazil-California Trade Association
213–627–0634

CHILE

North American-Chilean Chamber of
Commerce, Inc.
212–288–5691

CHINA

Chinese Chamber of Commerce of
New York
212–226–2795

COLOMBIA

Colombian-American Association,
Inc.
212–233–7776

COSTA RICA

Costa Rica Export and Investment
Promotion Center
305–358–1891

DOMINICAN REPUBLIC

Dominican Republic Export
Promotion Center
212–432–9498

ECUADOR

Ecuadorean-American Association,
Inc.
212–233–7776

FAR EAST

Far East-American Chamber of
Commerce and Industry, Inc.
212–265–6375

FINLAND

The Finnish-American Chamber of
Commerce
212–832–2588

FRANCE

French-American Chamber of
Commerce in the U.S.
212–581–4554

GERMANY

German-American Chamber of
Commerce, Inc.
212–582–7788

German-American Chamber of
Commerce
202–347–0247

GREECE

Hellenic-American Chamber of
Commerce
212–943–8594

INDIA

India-America Chamber of Commerce
202–659–1700

INDONESIA

American-Indonesian Chamber of
Commerce, Inc.
212–344–1808

IRAN

Iran-American Chamber of
Commerce, Inc.
212–757–9704

Iran-American Chamber of Commerce
and Industry
213–967–2005

IRELAND

Ireland-United States Council for
Commerce and Industry, Inc.
212–751–2660

ISRAEL

American-Israel Chamber of
Commerce and Industry, Inc.
212–354–6510

ITALY

Italian Chamber of Commerce of
Chicago
312–427–3014

Italy-America Chamber of Commerce,
Inc.
212–279–5520

JAPAN

Honolulu-Japanese Chamber of
Commerce
808–949–5531

Japan Business Association of
Southern California
213–628–1263

Japanese Chamber of Commerce of
New York, Inc.
212–425–2513

KOREA

Korean-American Midwest Association
of Commerce and Industry
312–431–8315

U.S.-Korea Economic Council
212–749–4200

LATIN AMERICA

Central American Chamber of
Commerce in the U.S., Inc.
212–766–1348

Chamber of Commerce of Latin
America in the U.S., Inc.
212–432–9313

Latin American Manufacturing
Association
202–467–5803

Pan American Chamber of Commerce
and Trade Council
415–752–4093

Pan American Society of the U.S.,
Inc.
212–628–9400

LEBANON

United States-Lebanese Chamber of
Commerce
212–432–1133

MEXICO

Mexican-American Chamber of
Commerce of Chicago
312–762–5662

The Mexican Chamber of Commerce
of the U.S., Inc.
212–432–9332

Mexican Institute for Foreign Trade
212–371–3823

United States-Mexico Chamber of
Commerce
202–296–5198

U.S.-Mexico Quadripartite
Commission
212–888–1215

MIDDLE EAST

American-Arab Association of
Commerce and Industry
212–986–7229

American-Arab Chamber of
Commerce
713–222–6152

U.S.-Arab Chamber of Commerce
212–432–0655

U.S.-Arab Chamber of Commerce
(Washington)
202–293–6975

THE NETHERLANDS

The Netherlands Chamber of
Commerce in the U.S., Inc.
212–265–6460

NIGERIA

Nigerian-American Chamber of
Commerce, Inc.
212–766–1343

NORWAY

Norwegian-American Chamber of
Commerce, Inc.
312–782–7750

Norwegian-American Chamber of
Commerce, Inc.
212–421–9210

PAKISTAN

Pakistani-American Chamber of
Commerce, Inc.
516–488–4100

PERU

Peruvian-American Association
212–943–8753

THE PHILIPPINES

The Philippine-American Chamber of
Commerce, Inc.
212–972–9326

SPAIN

Spain-U.S. Chamber of Commerce
212–354–7848

SWEDEN

Swedish-American Chamber of
Commerce, Inc.
212–838–5530

TRINIDAD

Trinidad and Tobago Chamber of
Commerce of the U.S.A., Inc.
212–541–4615

UNITED KINGDOM

British-American Chamber of
Commerce
212–889–0680

British-American Chamber of
Commerce and Trade Center of the
Pacific Southwest
213–622–7124

VENEZUELA

The Venezuelan-American Association
of the U.S., Inc.
212–233–7776

FOREIGN CONSULATES AND EMBASSIES

Note—The following telephone numbers are all in the 212 area code.

AFGHANISTAN

Afghanistan Mission to the U.N.
754–1191

AFRICA

Organization of African Unity
697–8333

ALBANIA

Albanian Mission to the U.N.
722–1831

ARGENTINA

Argentina Consulate General
397–1400

Argentine Mission to the U.N.
688–6300

AUSTRALIA

Australian Consulate-General
  Information Service
  245–4000

  Trade Commission
  245–4000

Australian Mission to the U.N.
421–6910

AUSTRIA

Austrian Consulate General
737–6400

Austrian Mission to the U.N.
949–1840

Austrian Trade Commission
421–5250

BELGIUM

Belgian Consulate General
586–5110

Belgian Mission to the U.N.
599–5250

BOLIVIA

Consulate General of Bolivia
586–1607

BOPHUTHATSWANA

Bophuthatswana International Ltd.
686–5295

BOTSWANA

Permanent Mission of the Republic of
Botswana to the U.N.
759–6587

BRAZIL

Brazilian Mission to the U.N.
832–6868

Brazilian National Superintendency of
Merchant Marine-Delegation
943–9339

Consulate General of Brazil
757–3080

BULGARIA

Bulgarian Embassy Office of
Commercial Counselor
935–4646

Bulgarian Mission to the U.N.
737–4790

BURMA

Permanent Mission of Burma to the
U.N.
535–1310

CAMEROON

Cameroon Mission to the U.N.
794–2295

CANADA

Canadian Consulate Offices
586–2400; 757-4917

Canadian Permanent Mission to the
U.N.
751–5600

CEYLON

Ceylon Sri Lanka Tourist Board
935–0369

CHILE

Prochile Chilean Trade Bureau
466–1025

Chilean Mission to U.N.
687–7547

CHINA

Chinese Investment and Trade Office
752–2340

Consulate General of China
697–1250

COLOMBIA

Consulate General of Colombia
949–9898

CONGO BRAZZAVILLE

Congo Brazzaville Mission to the
U.N.
744–7840

COSTA RICA

Consulate General of Costa Rica
867–3922

Costa Rican Permanent Mission to the
U.N.
986–6373

CYPRUS

Cyprus Consulate General of the
Republic
686–6016

DENMARK

Danish Consulate General
697–5101

DJIBOUTI

Djibouti Mission to U.N.
753–3163

DOMINICAN REPUBLIC

Dominican Republic Consulate
265–0630

Dominican Republic Mission to the
U.N.
867–0833

ECUADOR

Consulate General
245–5380

Ecuador Mission to the U.N.
986–6670

EGYPT

Arab Republic of Egypt Permanent
Mission to the U.N.
879–6300

EL SALVADOR

Consulate General of El Salvador
889–3608

El Salvador Mission to the U.N.
679–1616

ESTONIA

Estonian Consulate General
247–1450

ETHIOPIA

Ethiopian Mission to the U.N.
421–1830

FIJI

Fiji Mission to the U.N.
355–7316

FINLAND

Consulate General of Finland
832–6550

Finnish Mission to the U.N.
355–2100

FRANCE

France Consulate General Office
535–0100

French Embassy
432–1820

French Mission to the United Nations
308–5700

FRENCH WEST INDIES

French West Indies Tourist Board
757–1125

GERMANY

Consulate General of the Federal
Republic of Germany
940–9200

Embassy of the German Democratic
Republic
490–8600

Permanent Mission of the Federal
Republic of Germany to the U.N.
838–2134

GHANA

Ghana Mission to U.N.
832–1300

GREECE

Consulate General of Greece
988–5500

Greek Consulate General
425–5764

Greek Mission to the U.N.
490–6060

GRENADA

Permanent Mission of Grenada to the
U.N.
599–0301

GUATEMALA

Guatemalan Permanent Mission to the
U.N.
679–4760

GUINEA

Guinea Permanent Mission to the
U.N.
697–6330

Papua New Guinea Mission to the
U.N.
682–6447

GUINEA-BISSAU

United Nations Mission
661–3977

HAITI

Haiti Consulate
697–9767

Haitian Mission to the U.N.
986–9686

HONDURAS

Consulate General of Honduras
889–3858

HONG KONG

Hong Kong Trade Development
Council
582–6610

HUNGARY

Consulate General of Hungary
879–4127

Embassy of the Hungarian People's
Republic
752–3060

ICELAND

Consulate General of Iceland
686–4100

Permanent Mission of Iceland to the
U.N.
686–4100

INDIA

India Consulate General
879–7800

Trade Development Authority of India
753–6655

INDONESIA

Indonesian Consulate General and
Information Office
879–0600

Indonesian Mission to the U.N.
286–8910

IRAN

Mission of Iran to the U.N.
687–2020

IRAQ

Iraq Mission to the U.N.
737–4433

IRELAND

Ireland Industrial Development
Authority
972–1000

Irish Consulate General
245–1010

Irish Export Board
371–3600

ISRAEL

Consulate General of Israel
697–5500

ITALY

Consulate General of Italy
737–9100

Italian Mission to the U.N.
486–9191

Italian Trade Commission
980–1500

IVORY COAST

Ivory Coast Visa Office
246–9577

JAMAICA

Jamaica Consulate General
935–9000

JAPAN
Consulate General of Japan
986–1600

Japanese Mission to the U.N.
421–9580

JORDAN

Jordan Consulate
759–1950

Jordan Mission to the U.N.
752–0135

KENYA

Kenya Mission to the U.N.
421–4740

KOREA

Korean Consulate General
752–1700

Korean Financial Attache
593–1852

Korean Mission to the U.N.
371–1280

LAOS

Laos Permanent Mission to the U.N.
986–0227

LEBANON

Consulate General of Lebanon
744–7905

United Nations Missions
335–5460

LESOTHO

Permanent Mission of the Kingdom of
Lesotho to the U.N.
421–7543

LIBERIA

Liberian Consulate General
687–1025

Liberian Mission to the U.N.
687–1033

LIBYA

Libyan Arab Republic Mission to the
U.N.
752–5775

LITHUANIA

Consulate General of Lithuania
877–4522

MALAGASY REPUBLIC

Malagasy Republic Mission to the
U.N.
986–9491

MALAYSIA

Malaysian Industrial Development
Authority
687–2491

MALI

Mali Permanent Mission to the U.N.
737–4150

MALTA

Malta Mission to the U.N.
725–2345

MAURITANIA REPUBLIC

Permanent Mission of the Islamic
Republic of Mauritania
697–2490

MAURITIUS

Mauritius Mission to the U.N.
949–0190

MEXICO

Consulate General of Mexico
689–0456

Instituto Mexicano De Comercio
Exterior
371–3823

Mexican Commercial Counselor
371–3823

Mexican Institute for Foreign Trade
371–3823

Mexican Mission to the U.N.
679–6416

MONACO

Consulate General of Monaco
759–5227

MOROCCO

Consulate General of Morocco
683–3062

Moroccan Mission to the U.N.
421–1580

NEPAL

Nepal Mission to the U.N.
986–1989

NETHERLANDS

Consulate General of Netherlands
246–1429

Netherlands Chamber of Commerce
in the U.S., Inc.
265–6460

Netherlands Mission to the U.N.
697–5547

NETHERLANDS ANTILLES

Netherlands Antilles Economic
Mission
765–3737

NEW ZEALAND

New Zealand Consulate General
586–0060

NICARAGUA

Consulate General of Nicaragua
247–1020

NIGER

Niger Mission to the U.N.
421–3260

NIGERIA

Consulate General of Nigeria
935–6100

Permanent Mission of Nigeria to the
U.N.
953–9130

NORWAY

Export Council of Norway
421–9210

Norwegian Mission to the U.N.
421–0280

OMAN

Permanent Mission of Oman to the
U.N.
355–3505

PAKISTAN

Consulate General of Pakistan
879–5800

Pakistan Mission to the U.N.
879–8600

PANAMA

Consulate General of Panama
307–0491

PARAGUAY

Paraguay Mission to the U.N.
687–3490

PERU

Consulate General of Peru
687–3490

Peruvian Mission to the U.N.
752–5990

PHILIPPINES

Commercial Attache of the Philippines
575–7925

Consulate General of the Philippines
764–1330

Philippine Mission to the U.N.
764–1300

POLAND

Consulate General of Polish People's
Republic in N.Y.
889–8360

Permanent Mission of the Polish
People's Republic to the U.N.
744–2506

Polish Commercial Counselor's Office
486–3150

PORTUGAL

Consulate General of Portugal
246–4580

Portuguese Government Trade Office
354–4610

United Nations Missions
759–9444

ROMANIA

Office of the Economic Counselor of
the Romanian Embassy
682–9120

Romanian Mission to the U.N.
682–3274

SAN MARINO

Consulate General Republic of San
Marino
737–3749

SAO TOME AND PRINCIPE

Permanent Mission of Sao Tome and
Principe
697–4211

SAUDI ARABIA

Consulate General of Saudi Arabia
752–2740

Saudi Arabian Mission to the U.N.
697–4830

SIERRA LEONE

Permanent Mission of Sierra Leone to
the U.N.
570–0030

SINGAPORE

Singapore Economic Development
Board
421–2203

Singapore Mission to the U.N.
826–0840

Singapore Trade Office
421–2207

SOMALIA

Somalia Mission to the U.N.
687–9877

SOUTH AFRICA

Consulate General of South Africa
838–1700

SOUTHERN YEMEN

Southern Yemen Mission to the U.N.
752–3066

SPAIN

Consulate General of Spain
355–4080

Spanish Commercial Office Embassy
of Spain
661–4959

Spanish Mission to the U.N.
661–1050

SUDAN

Sudan Mission to the U.N.
421–2680

SURINAM

Consulate General of Surinam
826–0660

Surinam Mission to the United
Nations
826–0660

SWAZILAND

Permanent Mission of Swaziland
371–8910

SWEDEN

Consulate General of Sweden
751–5900

Swedish Trade Office
593–0045

SWITZERLAND

Consulate General of Switzerland
758–2560

SYRIAN ARAB REPUBLIC

Permanent Mission of the Syrian Arab
Republic to the U.N.
752–4250

TANZANIA

Tanzania Mission to the U.N.
972–9160

THAILAND

Thailand Embassy
466–1777

Thailand Embassy Office of Economic
Counselor
466–1745

TOGO REPUBLIC

Togo Permanent Mission to the U.N.
490–3455

TRINIDAD AND TOBAGO

Consulate of Trinidad and Tobago
682–7272

TUNISIA

Tunisian Mission to the U.N.
988–7200

Tunisia Trade Office
489–6930

Consulate General of Tunisia
737–1062

TURKEY

Consulate General of Turkey
247–5309

Turkish Embassy
687–8395

Turkish Embassy Commercial
Counselor's Office
687–1530

Turkish Mission to the U.N.
949–0150

UNITED KINGDOM

British Government Office
Inquiry
752–5747

British Trade Development Office
593–2258

United Kingdom Mission to the U.N.
752–8400

URUGUAY

Consulate General of Uruguay
755–8193

Uruguay Delegation to the U.N.
752–8240

VENEZUELA

Consulate General of the Republic of
Venezuela
826–1660

Venezuelan Institute of Foreign Trade
421–3360

Venezuelan Mission to the U.N.
838–2800

WEST AFRICA

Gabon Mission to the U.N.
867–3100

Ghana Mission to the U.N.
832–1300

WEST INDIES

Permanent Mission of St. Vincent and
the Grenadines to the U.N.
687–4490

Saint Lucia Permanent Mission to the
U.N.
697–9360

YEMEN

Yemen Arab Republic Mission to the
U.N.
355–1730

YUGOSLAVIA

Vojvojanska Banka-Udrezena Banka
697–1960

Yugoslav Permanent Mission to the
U.N.
879–8700

U.S. LIBRARIES AND INFORMATION CENTERS WITH FOREIGN INFORMATION SOURCES

AFRICA

Library of Congress
African and Middle Eastern Division
Washington, DC 20540
202–426–7937

Stanford University
Hoover Institute on War, Revolution
and Peace
Library
Stanford, CA 94305
415–497–2058

University of California, Los Angeles
African Studies Center
Research Workshop and Reading
Room
10367 Bunche Hall
Los Angeles, CA 90024
213–825–2944

ASIA

American Academy of Asian Studies
Library
134–140 Church Street
San Francisco, CA 94119
415–863–4168

Asia Society
Library
112 East 64th Street
New York, NY 10021
212–751–4210

Asian Foundation
Library
550 Kearny Street
San Francisco, CA 94119
415–982–4640

Michigan State University
International Library
W309-316 University Library
East Lansing, MI 48824
517–355–2366

University of Texas, Austin
Asian Collection
General Libraries, MAI 316
Austin, TX 78712
512–471–3135

BRAZIL

Library of Congress
Hispanic Division
Library of Congress Building
Second Floor, East Side, Room 239E
Washington, DC 20540
202–426–5400

Oliveira Lima Library
Catholic University of America
Washington, DC 20064
202–635–5059

BULGARIA

Library of Congress
European Division
Thomas Jefferson Building
Fifth Floor
Washington, DC 20540
202–426–5413

CANADA

Canadian Consulate General
Library
1251 Avenue of the Americas
New York, NY 10021
212–586–2400

Canadian Embassy Library
1771 N. Street, N.W.
Washington, DC 20036
202–785–1400

CHINA

Chinese Information Center
Chinese Cultural Center Library
159 Lexington Avenue
New York, NY 10016
212–725–4950

George Washington University
Institute for Sino-Soviet Studies
Library
2130 H Street, N.W.
Washington, DC 20052
202–676–7150

Yale University
East Asian Collection
Sterling Memorial Library
New Haven, CT 06520
203–436–4810

CZECHOSLOVAKIA

Library of Congress
European Division
Thomas Jefferson Building
Fifth Floor
Washington, DC 20540
202–426–5413

DENMARK

Library of Congress
European Division
Thomas Jefferson Building
Fifth Floor
Washington, DC 20540
202–426–5413

EUROPE

European Community Information
Center Library
2100 M Street, N.W.
Suite 707
Washington, DC 20037
202–862–9500

Harvard University
European Studies Library
5 Bryant Street
Cambridge, MA 02138
617–495–4150

Library of Congress
European Division
Thomas Jefferson Building
Fifth Floor
Washington, DC 20540
202–426–5413

Stanford University
Hoover Institute on War, Revolution
and Peace
Library
Stanford, CA 94305
415–497–2058

EUROPE, EASTERN

Stanford University
Hoover Institute on War, Revolution
and Peace
Library
Stanford, CA 94305
415–497–2058

Yale University
Slavic and Eastern Europe Collections
Sterling Memorial Library
New Haven, CT 06520
203–436–0230

EUROPEAN ECONOMIC COMMUNITY
COUNTRIES

European Community Information
Service Library
2100 M Street, N.W.
Suite 707
Washington, DC 20037
202–862–9500

European Community Information
Service Library
245 East 47th Street
New York, NY 10017
212–371–3804

FAR EAST

Columbia University
East Asian Library
300 Kent
New York, NY 10027
212–280–4318

Far East Merchants Association
FEMAS Trade Library
1597 Curtis Street
Berkeley, CA 94103
415–565–3211

Stanford University
Hoover Institute on War, Revolution
and Peace
Library
Stanford, CA 94305
415–497–2058

FRANCE

French Institute/Alliance Française
Library
22 East 60th Street
New York, NY 10022
212–355–6100

Library of Congress
European Division
Thomas Jefferson Building
Fifth Floor
Washington, DC 20540
202–426–5413

GERMANY

German Information Center
Federal Republic of Germany
410 Park Avenue
New York, NY 10022
212–752–5020

Goethe Institute
Library
530 Bush Street
San Francisco, CA 94108
415–391–0370

Harvard University
European Studies Library
5 Bryant Street
Cambridge, MA 02138
617–495–4150

Library of Congress
European Division
Thomas Jefferson Building
Fifth Floor
Washington, DC 20540
202–426–5413

GREAT BRITAIN

British Consulate General
Library
120 Montgomery Street
San Francisco, CA 94104
415–981–3030

British Information Services
Library
845 Third Avenue
New York, NY 10022
212–752–8400

GREECE

Library of Congress
European Division
Thomas Jefferson Building
Fifth Floor
Washington, DC 20540
202–426–5413

ICELAND

Cornell University
Icelandic Collection
Olin Research Library
Ithaca, NY 14853
607–356–6462

Library of Congress
European Division
Thomas Jefferson Building
Fifth Floor
Washington, DC 20540
202--426–5413

INDIA

Consulate General of India
Information Department
3 East 64th Street
New York, NY 10027
212–879–7800

Embassy of India
Library of the Information Service of
India
2107 Massachusetts Avenue N.W.
Washington, DC 20008
202–265–5050

IRELAND

Ireland Consulate General
Library
580 Fifth Avenue
New York, NY 10036
212–245–1010

ISRAEL

Consulate General of Israel
Information Department
800 Second Avenue
New York, NY 10017
212–697–5500

JAPAN

Harvard University
Harvard Yenching Institute Library
2 Divinity Avenue
Cambridge, MA 02138
617–495–2760

George Washington University
Institute for Sino-Soviet Studies
Library
2130 H Street, N.W.
Washington, DC 20052
202–676–7105

Japan Society
Library
333 East 47th Street
New York, NY 10017
212–832–1155

Library of Congress
Asian Division
Thomas Jefferson Building
First Floor
Washington, DC 10540
202–426–5420

University of California, Los Angeles
Oriental Library
21617 University Research Library
Los Angeles, CA 90024
213–825–4836

Yale University
East Asian Collection
Sterling Memorial Library
New Haven, CT 06520
203–436–4810

KOREA

Columbia University
East Asian Library
300 Kent
New York, NY 10027
212–280–4318

George Washington University
Institute for Sino-Soviet Studies
Library
2130 H Street, N.W.
Washington, DC 20052
202–676–7105

Yale University
East Asian Collection
Sterling Memorial Library
New Haven, CT 06520
203–436–4810

LATIN AMERICA

Library of Congress
Hispanic Division
Library of Congress Building
Second Floor, East Side, Room 239E
Washington, DC 20540
202–426–5400

Syracuse University
E.S. Bird Library
Area Studies Department
Syracuse, NY 13210
315–423–4176

University of Florida
Latin America Data Bank Library
319 Grinter Hall
Gainesville, FL 32611
904–392–0375

University of Texas, Austin
Benson Latin American Collection
General Libraries
SRH 1.109
Austin, TX 78712
512–471–3818

MEXICO

Degolyer Foundation
Library
Box 396
SMU Station
Dallas, TX 75275
214–692–2253

NEAR EAST

Library of Congress
African and Middle Eastern Division
Washington, DC 20540
202–426–5421

Middle East Institute
George Camp Keiser Library
1761 N Street, N.W.
Washington, DC 20036
202–785–1141

Stanford University
Hoover Institute on War, Revolution
and Peace
Library
Stanford, CA 94305
415–497–2058

NETHERLANDS

Consulate General of the Netherlands
Press and Cultural Section
One Rockefeller Plaza
New York, NY 10020
212–246–1429

Library of Congress
European Division
Thomas Jefferson Building
Fifth Floor
Washington, DC 20540
202–426–5413

Netherlands Embassy
Library
4200 Linnean Avenue, N.W.
Washington, DC 20008
202–244–5300

NEW ZEALAND

New Zealand Consulate General
Library
630 Fifth Avenue
Suite 530
New York, NY 10020
212–586–0060

New Zealand Embassy
Library
19 Observatory Circle
Washington, DC 20008
202–265–1721

NORWAY

Library of Congress
European Division
Thomas Jefferson Building
Fifth Floor
Washington, DC 20540
202–426–5413

POLAND

Library of Congress
European Division
Thomas Jefferson Building
Fifth Floor
Washington, DC 20540
202–426–5413

Polish Institute of Arts and Sciences in
America
Research Library
95 East 66th Street
New York, NY 10021
212–988–4338

PORTUGAL

Library of Congress
Hispanic Division
Library of Congress Building
Second Floor, East Side, Room 239E
Washington, DC 20540
202–426–5400

Portuguese Continental Union of the
U.S.A.
Library
899 Boylston Street
Boston, MA 02155
617–536–2916

RUSSIA

George Washington University
Institute for Sino-Soviet Studies
Library
2130 H Street, NW
Washington, DC 20052
202–676–7105

Library of Congress
European Division
Thomas Jefferson Building
Fifth Floor
Washington, DC 20540
202–426–5413

New York Public Library
Slavonic Division
Fifth Avenue and 42nd Street
Rooms 216, 223
New York, NY 10018
212–790–6336

Radio Free Europe/Radio Liberty
Reference Library
30 East 42nd Street
New York, NY 10017
212–867–5200

Stanford University
Hoover Institute on War, Revolution
and Peace
Library
Stanford, CA 94305
413–497–2058

SPAIN

Library of Congress
Hispanic Division
Library of Congress Building
Second Floor, East Side, Room 239E
Washington, DC 20540
202–426–5400

SWEDEN

Library of Congress
European Division
Thomas Jefferson Building
Fifth Floor
Washington, DC 20540
202–426–5413

Royal Swedish Embassy
Library-Information Center
Watergate 600
Suite 1200
600 New Hampshire Avenue, N.W.
Washington, DC 20037
202–965–4100

Swedish Information Service
825 Third Avenue
New York, NY 10022
212–751–5900

TURKEY

Turkish Tourism and Information
Office
821 United Nations Plaza
New York, NY 10017
212–687–2194

SWITZERLAND

Library of Congress
European Division
Thomas Jefferson Building
Fifth Floor
Washington, DC 20540
202–426–5413

YUGOSLAVIA

Library of Congress
European Division
Thomas Jefferson Building,
Fifth Floor
Washington, DC 20540
202–426–5413

KEY FOREIGN BUSINESS MAGAZINES AND DIRECTORIES

Europe, Canada, and Australia

Australia

The Australian Financial Review (John Fairfax & Sons). Daily newspaper of Australian economic and financial events. Includes extensive stock market information and company-specific data.

Australian Journal of Management (The University of New South Wales). A semiannual journal of Australian management issues.

Australian Mineral Industry Annual Review (Bureau of Mineral Resources, Geology and Geophysics, Australian Government Publishing Service). Annual guide to Australian mining industry. Includes industry statistics and mineral analyses as well as company and mine information. For instance, it will report on a particular mine's production, its size, and where the ore is shipped.

Australian Marketing Researcher (Market Research Society of Australia). The semiannual journal of Australian advertising, marketing, and research issues. This magazine includes some company-specific information.

The Australian Share Market in Perspective (Roach Tilley Grice & Company). Annual guide to Australian stocks. Includes basic Australian economic statistics and industry analysis. Includes comments and recommendations on particular stocks and companies.

The Insurance Record of Australia and New Zealand (McCarron Bird). Monthly magazine of Australia and New Zealand insurance companies and industry events.

Jobson's Mining Yearbook (Dun & Bradstreet/Australia PTY). Annual guide to Australian mining, oil, and exploration companies and industry trends. The text includes predictions for the future of the industry. The directory also contains a listing of company directors.

Jobson's Yearbook of Public Companies of Australia & New Zealand (Dun & Bradstreet/Australia PTY). An annual guide to all publicly traded Australian and New Zealand companies. Gives general financial and historical information on each company, as well as company reviews.

Key Business Directory of Australia (Dun & Bradstreet/Australia PTY). Annual listing of 9000 of Australia's largest companies. The directory presents each company's address, estimated sales, and names of key executives. The directory is indexed by company, location, and product grouping.

Who Owns Whom—Australia & Far East (Dun & Bradstreet). Annual guide to parent companies, their subsidiaries, and affiliates registered in Australia, the Far East, and those linked to foreign parent corporations. The directory is organized by country and indexed by company name.

Who's Who in U.S. Business in Australia (American Chamber of Commerce in Australia). Guide to members and their companies' products and services. Organized by company name, executive's name, and the company's product or service. There is also information on U.S. businesses in Australia and Australian businesses in the United States. The directory lists each company's address and telephone number.

Belgium

Belgium (Belgium Foreign Trade Office). A quarterly review of Belgian economic and business issues.

Belgium Economic and Commercial Information (Belgian Foreign Trade Office). A quarterly magazine of Belgian industry, with special profiles of successful companies.

Belgium Economy and Technique (Publications Economiques Pour L'Etranger). Quarterly review of Belgian economy and industry. The magazine includes industry and company analyses.

Kompass (Kompass Belgium).   This Belgian volume is part of the Kompass series that covers countries throughout Europe, Latin America, and Asia. The Belgian volume contains name, address, and product information for those companies located in Belgium and Luxembourg.

Membership Directory/American Chamber of Commerce in Belgium (American Chamber of Commerce in Belgium).   Annual August issue of *Commerce in Belgium*. The directory gives each company's address, telephone number, key personnel, and products or services. Companies are listed alphabetically and are indexed by product or service.

Canada

Canadian Business (CB Media).   A monthly magazine of Canadian business events.

The Canadian Business Review (The Conference Board of Canada).   A quarterly journal of Canadian business issues.

Canadian Business Top 500 Companies (CB Media).   An annual directory that lists the top 500 Canadian companies, organized by sales size and indexed by company name. The directory lists financial information, including sales, assets, liabilities, equity, net income, and shareholder information for each company.

Canadian Grocer (MacLean Hunter).   This monthly magazine covers the Canadian grocery store industry, including food-processing, consumer goods, wholesalers, distributors, brokers, and retailers. Each issue discusses individual companies and their activities.

Canadian Key Business Directory (Dun & Bradstreet Canada).   Annual directory of the largest Canadian organizations, with 14,000 listings. Entries are indexed by Dun's number, location, and business grouping.

Canadian Mines Handbook (Northern Miner Press).   Annual guide to Canadian mining industry. The directory is organized by company name. It provides address, telephone number, president's name, bank affiliation, major shareholders, and a detailed listing of company-held properties. Maps are included to aid in the description of the properties and their locations.

Canadian Trade Index (Canadian Manufacturers' Association).   Annual comprehensive list of Canadian manufacturers. The directory is indexed by company, location, and industry.

Canadian Transportation and Distribution Management (Southam Business Publications).   A monthly magazine covering Canadian highway, marine, rail, and air transportation and transportation services (public warehousing, freight forwarding, and customs brokers) industries. The magazine contains numerous company analyses. Its annual *Transportation Guide* (appearing in July) contains contacts, addresses, office locations, and telephone numbers for all types of companies, indexed by province or (for those companies located in the United States) by state.

The Financial Post (MacLean Hunter). A leading weekly newspaper on Canadian business. The newspaper includes extensive stock market listings and news reports on companies in Canada.

The Financial Post Survey of Industries (MacLean Hunter). This directory offers details on operations, management, financials, subsidiary data, and stock price history for all publicly traded Canadian corporations.

Financial Times of Canada (Financial Times). A weekly newspaper covering Canadian business and economic events.

Foreign Investment Review (Foreign Investment Review Agency). Quarterly journal on investment conditions in Canada. It includes listing of capital investment projects in Canada, organized by industry and province. Each listing offers company name, project description, estimated completion date, cost, and location.

Metalworking Directory and Buying Guide (MacLean Hunter). Annual directory of manufacturers and distributors in the Canadian metalworking industry. The directory is organized by company name and indexed by product. Each listing provides address and telephone number.

Walker's Manual of Western Corporations (Walker's Manuals). This directory includes descriptions and financials for publicly owned companies in the 13 western U.S. states and Canada.

Denmark

Denmark Quarterly Review (Copenhagen Handelsbank). Journal of Danish economic, business, and political trends and events.

Export Directory of Denmark (Kraks Legat). Directory of Danish export firms, indexed by products and company name.

Kompass (A/S Forlaget Kompzas-Danmark). Register of Danish companies and foreign companies located in Denmark. The directory is indexed by company name. Also contained in each listing are each company's products or services and its industrial classification.

Nordisk Handels Kalender (Scan-Report). A comprehensive trade directory of the industry and wholesale trade of Norway, Iceland, Denmark, Sweden, and Finland. It is organized by country and indexed by type of product or service. Each entry gives address, telephone number, and basic product information.

Paper and Pulp Makers Directory of Sweden, Norway, Denmark and Finland (Wezata Forlag). An annual guide to pulp and paper companies of Sweden, Norway, Denmark, and Finland. Each entry offers basic data on companies, including mills and divisions. The directory is organized by country and indexed by company name.

Europe, General

Advertising Age's Focus (Advertising Age). The European version of the U.S.' *Advertising Age.* It is a monthly magazine that reports on specific European advertising and marketing campaigns.

Brown's Directory of North American and International Gas Companies (Harcourt Brace Jovanovich). An annual guide to international gas distribution and pipe companies. The directory is organized by company and indexed by country, U.S. state, or Canadian province. Each entry contains address, telephone number, and basic operating and financial data.

Business Eastern Europe (Banda House). A weekly report on Eastern European business issues, trends, policies, and corporate strategies.

Business Europe (Banda House). A weekly report on Western European business issues, trends, policies, and corporate strategies.

EFTA Bulletin (European Free Trade Association). A quarterly bulletin of the European Free Trade Association that reports on recent meetings, events, trends, and legislation. There are industry articles and some company-specific information.

Euromoney (Euromoney Publications). A monthly magazine on international capital and money market events.

Euromoney 500 (Euromoney Publications). Annual issue ranks the world's top 500 banks by total group shareholder funds. It gives the net profit and total assets for each bank. The directory also ranks banks by asset and equity growth.

European Banks (St. Gall Institute of Banking Studies). Annual analysis of 100 leading European banks organized by country and indexed by bank name. The directory gives a five-year balance sheet, five-year profit and loss statement, and five-year tracking of the number of branches and employees for each bank.

The Europa Yearbook (Europa Publications). The directory provides names, addresses, and key personnel for all banking, publishing, press, and trade associations in the world. The directory is organized by country.

Europe's 10,000 Largest Companies (Dun's Marketing Services). Companies are ranked by profit and are grouped by industry type (e.g., banks, advertising, hotels). Companies are indexed alphabetically.

Jane's Major Companies of Europe (MacDonald's & Jane's Publishers). Guide to over 1000 companies in 16 European countries. The directory gives general company data as well as detailed financial information. The directory is indexed by country and industry group.

Kelly's Manufacturers and Merchants Directory (Kelly's Directories). A directory listing approximately 90,000 British companies, manufacturing and nonmanufacturing. A typical entry includes the company's name, address, products, and telephone number. Companies are listed by industry classification.

Key Figures of European Communities (Investment Research Group of European Banks International EBK). This publication is offered three times a year and contains financial reports for top European companies. It is organized by country and indexed by industry.

Le MOCI (SNEI). A magazine of international business. It has extensive coverage of economic and industrial issues, organized by country.

Finland

Finnish Trade Review (The Finnish Foreign Trade Association). A magazine focusing on a different Finnish industry in each issue—for example, "Foodstuffs & Fisheries" or "Packaging." Specific companies and product information is included.

Kansallis-Osake-Pankki (Kansallis-Osake-Pankki). A semiannual review of the Finnish economy. Included are industry analyses and basic Finnish economic statistics.

Paper & Pulp Makers Directory of Sweden, Norway, Denmark and Finland. See description under Denmark.

State Owned Companies in Finland (State Owned Companies Advisory Board). Annual guide to Finnish stated-owned companies. Each entry includes income statements, balance sheets, and other background information on each company.

France

American Chamber of Commerce in France Directory (American Chamber of Commerce in France). Annual guide to firms in France. It is indexed by products, services, and standard industrial classification codes (SICs). Each entry includes company name, address, and telephone number.

American Subsidiaries and Affiliates of French Firms (Commercial Counselor to the French Embassy). Annual guide to American firms with a minimum of 50 percent ownership by a French company. Organized by French company name, the directory contains addresses for both parent and subsidiary, as well as the telephone number for the subsidiary.

French Company Handbook (French Company Handbook). An annual guide to key French firms. It is organized by industry and indexed by company name. It provides the address, telephone number, management, major activities, company history, and major known shareholders. A basic financial history of each company is also provided.

Kompass-France (SNEI). Another in the series of Kompass directories. It is an annual guide to companies in France, with each company classified by product, service, and company name. Each listing contains company name, address, telephone number, senior officers, trade names, and number of employees.

L'Expansion (L'Expansion). A biweekly magazine of French business events and issues.

Germany

American Subsidiaries of German Firms (German American Chamber of Commerce). An annual directory organized by U.S. subsidiary and indexed by German parent firm. It gives the name and address of both the subsidiary and the parent, the type of company, amount of stock held by parent, products, and the number of employees of the subsidiaries. There is also a geographical listing organized by state.

Aussenwirtschaft (Verlag Ruegger). A scholarly journal of international business.

BDI Deutschland Liefert Germany Supplies (Gemeinschaftsverlag). An export directory of German products. There is a product index and a listing of manufacturers.

Directory of American Business in Germany (Seibt-Verlag). Annual directory of German companies and their U.S. counterparts. It is organized by German company name, American company name, and type of product or service. Each listing provides address and telephone number.

Handbuch der Deutschen Aktiengesellschaften (Verlag Hoppenstedt). A directory of approximately 3000 German corporations.

Kompass/Switzerland and Germany (Kompass Schweiz Verlag).   Similar to all the other Kompass directories, it offers a listing of companies alphabetically. Each entry contains name, address, telephone number, and product description.

Great Britain

Anglo-American Trade Directory (American Chamber of Commerce U.K.).   Annual guide to members, organized by company name and indexed by type of product or service. Each entry gives address, telephone number, key manager name, product, and company affiliation. In addition the directory lists American consulates, embassies, and attachés in the United Kingdom. Coverage includes England, Wales, and Scotland.

British Exports (Kompass Publishers).   Annual guide to British exports organized by products, services, and company name. Each entry lists the company's products, address, telephone number, and technical information regarding the company's products or processes.

Britain's Top 1,000 Foreign Owned Companies (Jordan & Sons).   Annual guide to top 1000 British companies that are foreign-owned. Organized by sales size and indexed by company name, it gives financial information, including sales, profits, exports, and net assets. Also mentioned in each entry are the company's address, telephone number, chief executive officer, and number of employees.

Britain's Top Private Companies (Jordan & Sons).   Annual guide to top 2000 (with an additional 1000 available in another volume) private United Kingdom companies. Each entry gives a company's address, telephone number, chief executive officer, sales, profits, exports, and net assets. Companies are listed by sales size. There is also an index by company name.

Directory of British Associations (CBD Research).   Similar to the U.S. publication the *Encyclopedia of Associations* (Gale Research Company), this directory is a guide to British national associations, societies, and institutes in a wide variety of fields. The associations are listed alphabetically and are indexed by subject.

Financial Times of London (Bracken House).   This is the premier English-language business newspaper of Europe. It contains extensive stock listings, as well as reports on company events throughout Britain and Europe.

Investors Chronicle (Financial Times of London).   A well-indexed weekly magazine. It offers detailed company profiles and manages to stay current with press announcements put out by British companies. In addition, it supplies an index with each issue that allows you to locate company information by type. That means that you can see if a company income statement or acquisition was announced without having to comb through dozens of back issues or hundreds of pages. The magazine also publishes a quarterly cumulative index. In addition, it regularly prints interim income statements or balance sheets.

Kelly's Manufacturers and Merchants Directory (Kelly's Directories). This book provides the name, address, telephone number, and products or services for each of 90,000 United Kingdom companies. The directory is indexed by trade headings, company name, and product.

London Chamber of Commerce and Industry Directory (Guardian Communications). Annual list of members of the North American Chapter of The London Chamber of Commerce and Industry.

The Stock Exchange Official Year-Book (Macmillan Publishers). A superb directory with detailed entries for all companies traded on the London Stock Exchange. Company entries contain financials for past years, company descriptions, and information on stock movement.

The Times 1,000 (Times Books). A concise and easy-to-read annual guide to the 500 largest United Kingdom industrial companies and the 500 largest European companies. Detailed information is supplied on each company's products, sales, and other basic financials. There is also a listing of British banks. The information is presented in easy-to-read tabular form with additional narrative.

Trade and Industry (Crown). A weekly magazine of British trade and industry events and company activities.

Greece

Business Directory (American Hellenic Chamber of Commerce). A directory of American companies with manufacturing plants or offices in Greece.

Business and Finance (Financial Publishing Company). An English-language weekly magazine covering business and company information.

Economikos Tachydromos (Economikos Tachydromos). A weekly business newspaper, covering business and industry news.

ICAP Financial Directory of Greek Companies (ICAP Hellas). Somewhat similar in purpose to the Moody's Investment directories for American companies. Each listing offers a company's address, telephone number, balance sheet, income statement, and description of the products or services.

Iceland

Commercial and Industrial Directory for Iceland (Steindorsprent). A listing of Icelandic companies by products. The volume's indexes are in both English and Icelandic.

Nordisk Handels Kalendar (Scan-Report). See the description under Denmark.

Ireland

Business & Finance (Belends Publications). A weekly newspaper covering Irish commerce and finance.

Directory of American Business in Ireland (American Chamber of Commerce in Ireland). A directory of U.S. corporations located in Ireland.

Irish Business (Irish Financial Publications). A monthly business magazine that covers corporate and general industry news and issues. The magazine also issues special reports on various industries throughout the year.

Irish Independent (Independent Newspapers). A daily newspaper that reports on business events and company activities in Ireland.

Irish Press (Irish Press). A daily newspaper that reports on business events and company activities in Ireland.

Irish Times (Irish Times). Another daily newspaper that also covers business issues and company events. In addition, it publishes an annual listing of Ireland's 50 leading corporations.

Made in Ireland (Institute for Industrial Standards and Research). A listing of products and the companies manufacturing them. Also included is an index of products and trademarks.

Management (Irish Management Institute). A monthly magazine of Irish management issues.

Italy

American Chamber of Commerce in Italy Directory (American Chamber of Commerce in Italy). Annual directory of both American firms in Italy and Italian companies with U.S. ties. The directory is classified by company name and Standard Industrial Classification code.

Corriere Mercantile (Corriere Mercantile). A daily newspaper that offers extensive coverage of business and financial news.

Espansione (Espansione). A bimonthly magazine of Italian economic affairs and events.

Italian American Business (American Chamber of Commerce in Italy). A monthly magazine covering Italian-American business events. Issues include company profiles and personnel news.

Kompass Italia (Etas Kompass Periodici Tecnici). Annual guide to Italian industry and commerce classified by product or service and company name.

Liechtenstein

Kompass: Register of Industry and Commerce of Switzerland and Liechtenstein (Kompass Schweiz Verlag). A directory of Swiss and Liechtenstein businesses organized geographically and indexed by company name and by products or services.

Luxembourg

Annuaire des Societes Anonymes du Grand-Duche de Luxembourg/Stock Exchange Yearbook (Banque Internationale à Luxembourg). A directory of publicly traded companies on the Luxembourg Stock Exchange. Each entry includes name, address, and asset and liability financials.

Belgium and Luxembourg's 1000 Largest Companies (Dun & Bradstreet/Belgium). A directory of the largest companies in Belgium and Luxembourg. Besides address, each listing offers some financial information.

De Letzeburger Merkur (Luxembourg Chamber of Commerce). A monthly business magazine covering business issues and company information.

Kompass: Register of Industry and Commerce of Belgium & Luxembourg (Kompass Belgium). See listing under Belgium.

Le Courrier de Commerce (Le Courrier de Commerce). A monthly business magazine covering company and general information on various industries.

Quarterly Economic Review of Belgium, Luxembourg (The Economist Intelligence Unit). A journal of Belgium and Luxembourg business and business trends.

Netherlands

ABC Voor Handel En Industrie (ABC Voor Handel En Industrie). Annual register of Dutch companies, classified by product group.

De Financieele Koerier (De Financieele Koerier). A weekly newspaper that covers business and financial news in the Netherlands.

Dutch Companies and U.S. Affiliates (The Netherlands Chamber of Commerce in the U.S.).   Annual guide to U.S. affiliates and related Dutch companies. The directory is organized by Dutch firms and indexed by U.S. affiliate name. It provides names of the firms, their CEOs, addresses, and telephone numbers for each company and affiliate.

HET Financieele Dagblad (Gebouw Metropol).   A daily financial newspaper covering general business and company-specific news.

Kompass (Kompass Nederland).   A directory of companies in the Netherlands that is indexed by company name as well as by products or services.

Quarterly Economic Review of The Netherlands (The Economist Intelligence Unit).   A journal of Dutch business issues.

Van Oss' Effectenboek (Van Oss' Effectenboek).   A directory and financial listing of those companies publicly traded on the Amsterdam Stock Exchange. Each company entry offers fairly detailed financials.

Norway

Farmand (Ticon Industrier).   A magazine of Norwegian business activity.

Kompass (Kompass-Norge).   Similar to other Kompass directories mentioned, with a listing of Norwegian companies, their addresses, and their product or service lines.

Nordisk Handels Kalender (Scan-Report).   See the Denmark listing.

Norges Industri (Industriens og Eksportens).   A magazine of Norwegian business events.

Norway Exports (Export Council of Norway).   A monthly magazine that reports on the Norwegian export industry.

100 Largest Companies in Norway (A/S Okonomisk Literatur).   The 100 largest companies are ranked by sales, exports, profits, and employees.

Paper and Pulp Makers Directory of Sweden, Norway, Denmark and Finland (Wezata Forlag).   See the listing under Denmark.

Quarterly Economic Review of Norway (The Economist Intelligence Unit).   A journal of Norwegian business issues and events.

Portugal

Anuario Comercial de Portugal (Epresa Publica dos Jornais Noticias e Capital).   A directory of Portuguese corporations. Besides name and address, it also lists each company's product or service.

Quarterly Economic Review of Portugal (The Economist Intelligence Unit). A journal of Portuguese business issues.

Scotland

Anglo-American Trade Directory (American Chamber of Commerce U.K.). See listing under Great Britain.

Business Scotland (Holmes McDougall). A monthly magazine of Scottish business events and trends, with articles giving company-specific information.

Spain

Actualidad Economica (Actualidad Economica). A weekly magazine of Spanish economic, business, and company events. Industry analyses, government activities, and company-specific information appear regularly in the magazine.

Anuario Financiero y de Sociedades Anonimas de Espana (SOPEC). A directory of Spanish companies with detailed descriptions of each entry.

Informacion Commercial Espanola (Ministerio de Economia y Hacienda). A monthly magazine of Spanish economic events and issues. It includes industry analyses and company-specific information.

Kompass Espana (Kompass Espana). A directory of Spanish companies classified by company name and products or services.

Sweden

Affarsvarlden (Affarsvarlden). A magazine of Swedish business news and events.

Nordisk Handels Kalender (Scan-Report). See listing under Denmark.

Nordk Economic Outlook (Swedish Industrial Publications). Semiannual analysis of Nordic industries and economics, organized by country. Each analysis includes basic economic statistics for all Nordic countries.

1,000 Largest Companies in Sweden (A/S Okonomisk Literatur). A directory, similar to the Norwegian version, that lists the 1000 largest companies in Sweden.

Paper and Pulp Makers Directory of Sweden, Norway, Denmark and Finland (Wezata Forlag). See listing under Denmark.

Swedish Export Directory (Swedish Trade Council). Annual directory of Swedish exporting firms, indexed by company name, products, and services. It also gives information on Swedish trade councils, chambers of commerce, and consulting services.

Switzerland

Capital International Perspective (Capital International). A monthly guide to international stock market securities, arranged by industry. It gives valuation and performance for 1600 companies.

Finanz und Wirtschaft (Finanz und Wirtschaft). A semiweekly magazine covering Swiss businesses and general industry news.

Journal de Geneve (Journal de Geneve). A daily newspaper that includes reports on Swiss corporations and stock trading.

Kompass/Switzerland and Germany (Kompass Schweiz Verlag). See the listing under Germany.

Swiss-American Chamber of Commerce Yearbook (Swiss-American Chamber of Commerce Yearbook). Annual guide to members organized by company name. Each entry contains the address, telephone number, contact, and product. Coverage includes both American firms located in Switzerland and Swiss firms located in the United States.

Swiss Export Directory (Swiss Foreign Trade Office). A listing of approximately 7000 companies and Swiss government offices that are involved in the export of Swiss products.

Swiss Stock Guide (Union Bank of Switzerland). A directory with a detailed review of publicly traded Swiss corporations.

Switzerland's Largest Companies (Union Bank of Switzerland). Annual guide to basic financial information on Switzerland's largest industrial banks and insurance companies.

Yugoslavia

Trziste-Novac-Kapital (Institut Za Spoljnu Trgovinu). A bimonthly journal of Yugoslavian business issues and events.

Ekonomska Politika (Ekonomska Politika). A weekly business magazine that also offers an annual review of the leading Yugoslavian companies. It gives general background and financial information on each company.

Privredni Adresar SFJR (Privredni Pregled). A directory of Yugoslavian companies with their addresses, telephone numbers, and product descriptions. Each listing also includes directors' names and the bank affiliation.

Yugoslavia Export-Import Directory (Yugoslavia Chamber of Economy Council for Economic Relations Abroad). A directory of Yugoslav enterprises dealing in foreign trade and indexed by company name and type of product or service.

Asia, USSR, and China

Asia, Far East—General

Asia Corporate Profile and National Finance (Asian Finance Publications). Annual guide to Asia's 550 largest corporations. Organized by country and indexed by company name, the directory gives each company's address, telephone number, product description, basic balance sheet, bank, and senior executives. The directory also offers an overview of each Asian country's economic outlook.

Asia-Pacific Petroleum Directory (Pennwell Publishing Company). Annual guide to petroleum companies in Asia organized by country and indexed by company name. Each entry contains address, telephone number, business history, names of key personnel, and plant capacity.

The Asian Wall Street Journal (Dow Jones). A daily newspaper with extensive coverage of Asian economic, political, and financial issues and events. Much like its U.S. counterpart, this version of the Journal reports detailed stock market listings and company announcements.

The Bankers' Handbook For Asia (Asian Finance Publications). Annual reference book of 2000 domestic and foreign banks and finance companies. These companies are either headquartered or operating in Asia or Australia. The directory is organized by country. Each section opens with a "State of the Country" report.

Business Asia (Business International Asia/Pacific). Weekly journal for Asian and Pacific business events. Specific company news is offered.

Far Eastern Economic Review (Far Eastern Economic Review). This is a weekly magazine of Far Eastern business issues and events.

Who Owns Whom—Australia and Far East (Dun & Bradstreet). This is an annual directory of parent companies and their subsidiaries registered in Australia and the Far East or with offices there. The directory is indexed by company name.

China

The China Business Review (National Council for U.S.-China Trade). A bimonthly journal of Chinese business and economic issues.

The China Directory of Industry and Commerce and Economic Journal (Science Books International). Annual directory of Chinese economy and businesses. It is organized by product type and company name. Each entry contains company name, address, telephone number, chief executive, number of employees, and product description. Included also is an extensive review of the Chinese economy.

China's Foreign Trade (China Foreign Trade). A bimonthly magazine covering general Chinese trade issues and specific export companies. Extensive product descriptions, offered by company and by industry.

The China Phone Book (The China Phone Book Company). Annual directory to all Chinese organizations, including a wide variety of industries. The directory is organized geographically.

India

Bangladesh Directory and Year Book (SA Hasnat for Associated Book Promoters). Annual register of Indian exporters, indexed by industry, and of importers indexed by country.

Commerce (Commerce Publications). A magazine of Indian business events and issues.

The Economic Times (Bennet, Coleman & Co.). Annual guide to Indian and Asian business and economic issues. The directory includes specific industry analyses.

Foreign Trade Review (Indra Naratan Tadon). A quarterly journal of the Indian Institute for Foreign Trade. It contains scholarly articles on foreign trade issues with some company-specific references.

Handbook of Rupee Companies (The Colombo Brokers' Association). This text offers financial information and acreage for Rupee companies.

Journal of the Indian Merchants Chamber (TK Seshadri). A monthly journal of chamber and member activities. The text includes basic information on new members (with their names and addresses), as well as background on government legislation.

The Times of India Directory and Yearbook (Times of India Press). A guide to Indian business. It is indexed by industry and location. It includes a "who's who" section of administrative and diplomatic personnel.

Indonesia

Directory of U.S. Firms and Organizations in Indonesia (American Embassy, Jakarta). A directory of U.S. firms in Indonesia and a listing of the U.S. Embassy's economic and commercial officers located in Indonesia.

Israel

Dunsguide Israel (Dun & Bradstreet Israel).   Annual directory of companies—both domestic producers and exporters. Companies are listed alphabetically and are indexed by product or service.

The Israel Economist (Kollek & Sons).   A monthly magazine of Israeli businesses and corporations.

Israel Export Directory (Israel Overseas Publications).   Annual guide to Israeli export companies. The text is organized by company name and indexed by product type. Most entries contain the company's address, telephone number, and export product.

Japan

Business Directory of Hong Kong (Current Publications).   Annual guide to 11,000 manufacturers and business service firms. Companies are classified by product grouping or service category.

Cotton & Allied Textile Industry—Annual Statistical Review (Japan Spinners Association).   Annual industry review provides aggregate statistics on imports, exports, production, demand, raw materials, and equipment. Also has names and addresses of Japan Spinners Association members.

Directory of Foreign Capital Affiliated Enterprises (Business Intercommunications).   Annual guide to 23,000 corporations organized by Japanese company name and indexed by both the company's Japanese and foreign investors. Each company entry lists address, telephone number, name of Japanese investor, amount of foreign capital invested, and investment ratio.

Economic World Directory of Japanese Companies in the U.S.A. (Economic Salon).   Annual guide organized and indexed by company name. Each entry presents extensive information on senior personnel, company history, subsidiaries, and products. In addition, the entries contain addresses for plants and offices, as well as basic financial information.

Focus Japan (Jetro International Communications).   A monthly magazine on the Japanese economy and business issues. Jetro also publishes an annual directory of Japanese companies with U.S. offices. This directory is indexed geographically.

Japan Company Handbook (The Oriental Economist).   Semiannual guide to 1049 Japanese corporations, organized by stock exchange code number and indexed by company name. Each entry contains address, telephone number, bank, senior officers, and detailed financials. Included in the financials presented are historical operating results, sales breakdown, major stockholders, and stock price information.

Japan Directory (The Japan Press). Annual listing of corporations (including leading foreign and Japanese firms). The companies are indexed geographically.

The Japan Economic Journal (The Niiton Keizai Shimbun). Weekly newspaper of Japanese and international economic events. It includes industry analyses and company-specific articles. There are regular industry sections, securities summaries, and personnel announcements.

Japan Economic Yearbook (The Oriental Economist). Annual guide that includes a list of major companies. It gives the company's name, address, telephone number, bank, product line, and president's name. The listing is organized by product or service and is indexed by company name. Each entry presents basic financial data and a sales breakdown by product type.

Japan Electronic Buyers Guide (Dempa Publications). Annual guide to 1400 Japanese electronics manufacturers. It is organized both by company name and by 800 electronics products. It gives address, telephone number, product information, and basic sales information on each company. It is indexed by trade name and company name. It also provides basic data on 600 trading firms handling electrical and electronics products.

Japan Trade Directory (Japan External Trade Organization/JETRO). A guide to 2000 Japanese export and import companies organized geographically and indexed by company name and type of product or service. Each entry gives address, telephone number, president, bank, basic financials, and export products. Also contained in the directory is information on Japanese trade and industrial associations.

The Oriental Economist (The Oriental Economist). Monthly review of Japanese business issues, events, and companies. The magazine also lists Japanese economic indicators.

Jordan

The Industry of Jordan (The Amman Chamber of Commerce). Annual classified directory of industrial firms and products in Jordan. The directory also offers basic information on the country's economy, laws, and fiscal matters.

Malaysia

Malaysia International Chamber of Commerce & Industry Yearbook (Malaysian International Chamber of Commerce and Industry). Annual directory of the Malaysian Chamber of Commerce. Lists member companies and industry code. No other company details are listed. Also included are the names of Chamber of Commerce personnel, committees, and meetings.

Malaysian Trade Review (United Chamber of Commerce of Malaysia). Annual guide to Malaysian economy. The Review reports basic industry statistics as well as import-export data.

Middle East and Arabia

Arab Banking & Finance (Meed Group). Monthly magazine of Mideast business topics, with an emphasis on specific foreign investments.

Arab Oil & Gas Directory (Arab Petroleum Research Center). Comprehensive guide to Arab oil and gas activity. The text is organized by country and indexed by company name. It includes information on exploration, production, refining, exporting, and transportation activity.

The Meed Middle East Financial Directory (Middle East Economic Digest). A directory that lists central bank authorities, specialized and commercial banks, and other financial institutions for all Middle Eastern countries. Entries include the names of influential banking officials and major shareholders. The directory also provides a list of Middle Eastern financial institutions in foreign countries and headquarter offices of foreign associated banks, indexed by country.

The Middle East (Magazines Limited). Monthly magazine on Middle Eastern issues. Includes a regular business section. The magazine covers trade issues, industry trends, and company events and analyses.

Pakistan

Chamber's Trade Directory (Chamber of Commerce and Industry). Directory of major importers and exporters, indexed by commodity. The directory also lists Chamber of Commerce members who provide trade services.

Directory of Exporters and Manufacturers (Publishers International). Index to exporters, manufacturers, and import/export organizations in Pakistan. It is indexed by company name and commodity.

Pakistan Trade Directory and Who's Who (Barque and Company). Provides facts about the products, activities, and people involved in Pakistan industry. The directory is indexed geographically.

Philippines

Agricultural and Industrial Life (Agricultural and Industrial Life). Monthly magazine of Philippine industry and agriculture. It includes trade and company information.

Philippine Export Directory (Institute of Export Development). Annual guide to Philippine export firms, organized by company name and indexed by type of product. It provides address, telephone number, contact person, bank reference, and basic product information for each company.

Taiwan

Taiwan Buyer's Guide (China Productivity Center). Annual guide to Taiwanese manufacturers, classified by company name and product type. Exporters and importers are classified by their respective industries.

Thailand

The Industrial Directory (Advertising and Media Consultants). Annual buyers guide to Thai industry with sections on importers, manufacturers, and trade names.

The Investor (Thai Investment Publications Company). Monthly Thailand business and economic review. The magazine includes articles on government actions and interviews with Thai government officials.

Turkey

Turkish Trade Directory and Telex Index (Turkish Trade Directory and Telex Index). A listing of Turkish companies.

Union of Soviet Socialist Republics

Foreign Trade (USSR Ministry of Foreign Trade). Monthly magazine of Russian trade issues and events. The magazine contains some company-specific news and Russian plant and product descriptions.

Soviet Export (V/O Vneshtorgrecklama). Bimonthly magazine of Russian export, economic, industry, and company issues.

Latin America

Latin America, General

American Business in Argentina (The American Chamber of Commerce in Argentina). Annual guide organized by American company name. The directory gives address, telephone number, Argentine personnel, and products for most American companies. The directory is indexed by company, subsidiary name, and industrial code.

Business Latin America (Business International Corporation). A weekly report of Latin American countries' economic, financial, and political issues and events.

CEPAL Review (United Nations Economic Commission for Latin America). A magazine published three times a year covering Latin American economic issues. It includes specific country and industry analysis, and also contains extensive country financial and transnational enterprise coverage.

Latin American Petroleum Directory (Penwell). Annual guide to petroleum companies in Latin America. It is organized by country and indexed by company name. The directory provides address, telephone number, history, business activity, and key personnel for most companies. Also included in the book are the results of special industry surveys.

Major Companies of Argentina, Brazil, Mexico and Venezuela (Graham & Trotman). Annual directory of firms in these four countries. The book is organized by country and indexed by company name and industry.

Brazil

American Chamber of Commerce for Brazil Annual Directory (American Chamber of Commerce for Brazil). Alphabetical listing of member companies, officers, and directors. The directory includes members located in Rio De Janeiro, Brasília, Salvador, São Paulo, and other Brazilian cities, as well as members in the United States and other countries.

Comercio & Mercados (Orgao da Confederacao Nacional do Comercio). A monthly journal of Brazilian business topics.

Export Director of Brazil (Editora de Guias). Guide to Brazilian export companies. The directory is organized by type of goods or service and company name.

Industria e Produtividade (Confederacao Nacional da Industria Servico de Relacoes Publicas). A monthly magazine of Brazilian economic and political issues. The publication includes specific industry and company news.

Major Companies of Argentina, Brazil, Mexico and Venezuela (Graham & Trotman). See listing under "Latin America, General."

Chile

Chile Economic Report (Corporacion de Fomento de la Produccion). Monthly report on Chile's economy. The magazine includes articles on finance, investments, and business opportunities. It also reports specific company events.

Empresas Siderurgicas Y Ferromineras Latinoamericanas (Instituto Latinoamericano del Fierro y El Acero). A guide to companies in South America, organized by country. Entries present basic information on each company.

Colombia

Columbia Directorio De Exportadores (Proexpo—Export Promotion Fund, Banco de la Republica). Annual guide to Colombian exporting companies. The guide is organized by company name.

Cuba

Cuba Economic News (Chamber of Commerce of The Republic of Cuba). Monthly journal of Cuban business events. It includes industry articles and international events.

Mexico

American Chamber of Commerce/Membership Directory (American Chamber of Commerce of Mexico). The directory lists members alphabetically and by area of activity. The directory also lists members in the Guadalajara and Monterrey branches of the Chamber.

Major Companies of Argentina, Brazil, Mexico and Venezuela (Graham & Trotman). See listing under "Latin America, General."

Mexican-American Review (American Chamber of Commerce of Mexico). A monthly magazine of Mexican-American trade issues and events. There is a section on new products, as well as periodic information on particular companies.

Puerto Rico

The Commercial Directory—Puerto Rico & Virgin Islands (The Witcom Group). Directory lists wholesalers, business products, and service firms alphabetically. It also contains a consumer products section with whole-salers, retailers, and brand names. Finally, it lists types of business products and service firms followed by brand names and their distributors.

Puerto Rico Business Review (Government Development Bank for Puerto Rico). Monthly journal of Puerto Rican economic issues. It includes some industry analyses and company-specific information.

Venezuela

Business Venezuela (Venezuelan-American Chamber of Commerce and Industry). A bimonthly English-language magazine of Venezuelan business issues and events.

Major Companies of Argentina, Brazil, Mexico and Venezuela (Graham & Trotman). See listing under "Latin America, General."

Ven Am Cham Yearbook (Venezuelan-American Chamber of Commerce and Industry). Annual guide to members, including extensive "who's who" section. It is organized by company name and classified by business, product, or service. Each entry offers address, telephone number, basic products, key personnel, and representatives.

Africa

Kenya

East African Report on Trade and Industry (News Publishers). Monthly official journal of the Kenya Association of Manufacturers. It contains industry and economic information.

Nigeria

Business Directory of West Africa (Prestige Publications). Basic information on West African economics. The directory is organized by country and gives each major company's address and telephone number. The directory also contains information on government and diplomatic organizations and their scheduled events.

Major Companies of Nigeria (Graham & Trotman). A guide to major Nigerian companies, classified both by company name and by type of service product.

Management in Nigeria (Nigerian Institute of Management). Monthly journal of Nigerian management techniques and business issues.

Nigerian Business Review (Vdonkim & McOliver, Publishers). Bimonthly journal of Nigerian business and economic issues and events.

South Africa

Finance and Trade Review (Volkskas). Biannual journal of South African financial and economic issues.

Financial Mail (Financial Mail). Magazine of South African business issues and events. It includes coverage of company activities, as well as reports on industries and on the country itself.

Management (PTD Publishing Services). Monthly magazine of South African companies, business issues, events, and personalities.

The Stock Exchange Handbook (Flesch Financial Publications). A guide to the Johannesburg Stock Exchange, the traded companies, and the brokers. Companies are listed alphabetically.

Top Companies (Financial Mail). This is a special annual supplement to the *Financial Mail.* It presents detailed information on South Africa's 100 leading companies, organized by industry.

Zambia

Zambia Mining Yearbook (Copper Industry Service Bureau). Annual survey of Zambia mining companies. It offers extensive information on all Zambian mining companies, including a listing of directors, financials, and holding companies.

Zimbabwe

The Confederation of Zimbabwe Industries Buyers Guide (Thomson Publications). Annual guide to manufacturers, classified geographically and by product. There are also sections on brand and trade names, as well as a listing of chief executives.

CHAPTER 9

ADDITIONAL VALUABLE SOURCES

There are a number of basic intelligence sources that do not fit neatly into any of the previous categories. Typically, they are not magazines or other conventionally thought-of reference sources.

For example, in my competitor intelligence seminars I always ask the audience, which primarily consists of marketing executives and business planners, if they have ever heard of the *Wall Street Transcript*. At best, only half of the audience ever acknowledges having heard of the newspaper. It is a basic source, one every intelligence-gatherer should know about, yet few do.

Other basic sources and methods we discuss in this last part of the Basic Sources section include:

How to find a patent filing.

What a business school case study offers.

A new means to find regional data.

Where to find management biographies.

The usefulness of state business directories.

WAR STORY 9

Finding an Expert in Food Service

For anyone who has ever researched the food service industry, I'm sure you will agree that it is a highly fragmented market, with thousands of companies. No one company or group of companies controls even a small portion of the market.

We had to locate details on a number of competitors in the business. Unfortunately, since no one company controlled a sizeable market share, it also followed that no company knew very much about its nearest competitor— at least on the surface. Trying to find a knowledgeable individual was nearly impossible.

That is, until we turned to the Transcript. In one of its weekly Roundtable discussions, it covered the food service industry, mentioning dozens of experts throughout the transcribed interviews.

Aside from names, the Transcript also gave us a sense of the industry's dynamics. It told us, for instance, who were the most aggressive marketers out there and who were the most innovative.

WHAT DID THE CEO SAY? ASK THE TRANSCRIPT

The *Wall Street Transcript* is published weekly by:

The Wall Street Transcript Corporation
120 Wall Street
New York, NY 10025

Each issue contains analysts' reports, roundtable discussions of industries (Figure 9.1), quarterly earnings reports of publicly held companies, and transcripts of speeches made before groups of analysts.

The Transcript essentially takes company press releases and analysts' news reports and publishes them with little or no editing. Speeches made before financial societies and business roundtable discussions are published in their entirety. Each issue is a couple of hundred pages long and is indexed by company or industry. These indexes are cumulative, appearing on a monthly, quarterly, semiannual, and annual basis. An example is shown in Figure 9.2.

This is a prime source for updates on company trends. It also supplies

Telecommunications Equipment

Photo Courtesy of Avantek Inc.

A TWST Roundtable Discussion

MODERATOR:
Martha A. Curtis - Associate Editor

PARTICIPANTS:

Steven G. Chrust - Sanford C. Bernstein & Co., Inc.
Charles A. DiSanza, Jr. - Drexel Burnham Lambert Inc.
Clifford H. Higgerson - L.F. Rothschild, Unterberg, Towbin
Margaret O'Shea - Eberstadt Asset Management
Harry K. Rosenthal - Bear, Stearns & Co.
Aristide J. Vitolo - Century Capital Associates

PAST PERFORMANCE

(BJ018/00) TWST: Mr. Chrust, would you please sum up for us what's happened to the telecommunications stocks in the past six months?

Mr. Chrust: It's a rather general question; however, in the areas that I concentrate in, most of the stocks are seriously depressed relative to prices last year. In a large part relatively poor performance is a function of the market's realization that multiples were expecting rates of growth that were unrealistic. There were a number of examples of this. One of the most notable is **Digital Switch Corp.** But I should be quick to add it's not by any means alone; in the past six months many stocks have been cut in half. I'd say it's not happened in a vacuum in that the entire technology group has been pretty well depressed over the last six months.

TWST: Would anybody else like to comment on this?

Mr. Rosenthal: To back up what Steve said, we at Bear, Stearns generate internal statistics using April 30 as a base period which happens to be the beginning and end of our fiscal year. Of the stocks we cover in the technology group, the telecom group is down 37 percent according to our index, and is the worst performing of all in the technology area.

An interesting question I asked myself is why did the telecom group perform worse. One reason is earlier in the year we were looking for interest rates to go down and now we're looking for interest rates to stay the same or go up. Obviously, the market saw that before we did. But I think that the telecom group may have performed worse because of the incredible confusion and lack of conviction about the implications of the **AT&T** divesti-

(Continued on Page 73,202)

Figure 9.1. *Wall Street Transcript* roundtable discussion. (Copyright © 1984 by Wall Street Transcript Corporation.)

CORPORATE REGISTER

The Corporate Register consists of a compilation of essential source documents for the Investment Profile of individual publicly traded companies. Each firm sponsors and updates the publication of its own investment profile, which appears in the Corporate Register Section of The Wall Street Transcript as a service to the business and financial community throughout the world.

STONE CONTAINER CORP.

Annual Report, 12-31-80; Form 10-K, 12-31-80; First Quarter Report, 3-31-81; Form 10-Q, 3-31-81; Proxy Statement, 4-9-81; Second Quarter Report, 6-30-81; Form 10-Q, 6-30-81; Analyst's Reports: Corporate Reports 10-Q, 6-30-81	63,073 / 63,073
Ups. qtrly. div.; to make 3-for-2 stk. split	63,119
Record yr. ended 12-31-80	63,119
Record 1st qtr. ended 3-31-81	63,120
Realigns management	63,120
Plans waste-to-energy plant at mill	63,120
Record 2nd qtr. ended 6-30-81	63,120
Declares 138th consec. qtrly. div.	63,120
Sells health care products subsid.	63,120
Expects record 3rd qtr.	63,391
Record 3rd qtr ended 9-30-81	63,498
Southern Box finances plan expansion	63,598
Declares qtrly. div.	63,759
Completes financing for Mishawaka expansion	64,100
Third Quarter Report, 9-30-81; Form 10-Q, 9-30-81	64,123
Ups qtrly. div.	64,551
Record 4th qtr. ended 12-31-81	64,918
Annual Report, 12-31-81	65,283
New Phoenix corrugated container operation	65,446
Reports for 1st qtr. ended 3-31-82	65,477
Annual Report, 12-31-81; Form 10-K, 12-31-81; Proxy Statement, 4-9-82	65,651
Report of Ann. Mtg.	65,743
Declares 141st consec. qtrly. div.	65,743
First Quarter Report, 3-31-82; Form 10-Q, 3-31-82	65,839
Makes partial liquidation div. on Lypho-Med	66,714
Reports for 6 mos. ended 6-30-82	66,734
Declares cash distribution	66,807
Second Quarter Report, 6-30-82; Form 10-Q, 6-30-82	66,961
Makes $125 million bank credit pact	67,359
Reports for 3rd qtr. ended 9-30-82	67,674
Declares qtrly. div. with favorable tax treatment	67,788
To buy Samson Paper Bag	67,870
Third Quarter Report, 9-30-82; Form 10-Q, 9-30-82	67,893
Completes sale of tax benefits	68,262
Declares qtrly. div.	68,678
Reports for yr. ended 12-31-82	68,974
Files for comm. stk. offering	69,144
Frew elected pres. & COO	69,402
Reports for 1st qtr. ended 3-31-83	69,688
Annual Report, 12-31-83; Form 10-K, 12-31-83; Proxy Statement, 4-8-83	69,711
Declares 145th consec. qtrly. div.	69,930
Completes buy of Dean-Dempsey Corp.	70,018
First Quarter Report, 3-31-83; Form 10-Q, 3-31-83; Prospectus, 3-23-83	70,049
Declares qtrly. div.	70,307
Reports for 2nd qtr. ended 6-30-83	70,307
Talks with Continental Group re forest products buy	70,972
Second Quarter Report, 6-30-83; Form 10-Q, 6-30-83	71,127
Anti-trust waiting period on Continental deal expires	71,510
Completes buy from Continental	71,511
Reports for 3rd qtr. ended 9-30-83	71,715
Declares 147th consec. qtrly. div.	71,797
To offer comm. stk.	72,078
Third Quarter Report, 9-30-83; Prospectus, 12-7-83	72,309
Declares qtrly. div.	72,706
Reports for yr. ended 12-31-83	72,981

TRACOR INC.
See ROUNDUP (ELECTRONIC),
E. F. Hutton 73,008

TRANS WORLD AIRLINES INC.
See ROUNDUP (AIRLINES),
E. F. Hutton 73,010

TRANSCO ENERGY CO.
See TECHNICAL,
MKI Securities 73,126

TRITON ENERGY CORP.
See MON. MGR.,
Reilly 73,096

TROLLEY CHEF INC.
Gets franchise from
Rhode Island (CRF) 73,049

TRW INC.
See ROUNDUP (TRW),
Janney Montgomery Scott 73,093

TUCSON ELECTRIC POWER CO.
See ELEC. UTILITIES,
TWST Roundtable 73,037
TWST selects Theodore M. Welp,
Chief Executive Officer, Tucson
Electric Power Co., for Gold Award,
Electric Utilities 73,063

TURNER BROADCASTING SYSTEM INC.
See ROUNDUP (TURNER
BROADCASTING),
J. C. Bradford 73,120

UAL INC.
See ROUNDUP (AIRLINES),
E. F. Hutton 73,010
See ROUNDUP (UAL),
Smith Barney, Harris Upham .. 73,172

UNION CAMP CORP.
See ROUNDUP (PAPER),
Prudential-Bache 73,009

UNIVERSAL RESOURCES CORP.
Reports for 1st qtr.
ended 1-31-84 (CRF) 73,046
See ROUNDUP (ENERGY),
Kidder, Peabody 73,091

UNIVERSAL FURNITURE LTD.
Birr-Wilson 72,982

UNOCAL CORP.
See ROUNDUP (ENERGY),
Kidder, Peabody 73,091
See MON. MGR.,
Reilly 73,096
See ROUNDUP (PETROLEUM),
Dean Witter Reynolds 73,168

UPJOHN CO.
See ROUNDUP (UPJOHN),
Prudential-Bache Securities 73,170

URI THERM-X INC.
Joint venture with
Luxtron Corp. (CRF) 73,125

U S AIR GROUP INC.
See ROUNDUP (SURVEY),
Lehman Brothers Kuhn Loeb .. 73,170

U S AIR INC.
See ROUNDUP (U S AIR),
Dean Witter Reynolds 72,977
See ROUNDUP (AIRLINES),
E. F. Hutton 73,010

US WEST
D. A. Davidson 73,015

UTAH POWER & LIGHT CO.
See ROUNDUP
(ELECTRIC UTILITY),
Birr Wilson 73,015

UTL CORP.
Schneider Bernet & Hickman ... 72,994

VARIAN ASSOCIATES INC.
See ROUNDUP (ELECTRONIC),
E. F. Hutton 73,008

Figure 9.2. *Wall Street Transcript* cumulative index. (Copyright © 1984 by Wall Street Transcript Corporation.)

in-depth—and current—statements about an industry. A yearly subscription to the *Wall Street Transcript* costs $860.

THE PATENT HUNT

Obtaining information on patents and trade secrets requires two different types of research as shown in Figure 9.3.

This section deals with only patent research. It explains the distinction

	Patent	Trade Secret
Subject Matter	Specific and limited by statute (machines, articles of manufacture, processes and composition of matter)	Applies to broad range of intellectual property and business information
Requirements	Must be useful	Must provide competitive advantage
	Must be novel	Must not be generally known
	Must not be obvious	Must be kept secret
Definition	Defined strictly by language of the "claims"	Often difficult to define with equal precision, but can be as broad as the "equities" of a particular case require
Disclosure	Required	Any disclosure must be limited and controlled
Protection	Defined by narrow but specific statute	Varies depending on circumstances and court based on many theories
	Can prohibit use by anyone else	Protection only against "unfair" users; none against those who independently discover or reverse-engineer
Duration	17 years from issuance	Potentially unlimited as long as secret
Expense	Procuring policing infringement	Protecting from unauthorized disclosure or use
Risk	Invalidity	Independent discovery or inadvertent disclosure
Marketability	Licensing easier	Licensing more difficult, and requires policing of licensee security measures

Figure 9.3. Comparison of patent information and trade secrets. (Reprinted with permission from James Pooley, *Trade Secrets: How to Protect Your Assets*, New York: Osborne/McGraw-Hill, 1982.)

between patents and trademarks, and provides directions for manually searching for a patent abstract. A list of public government depositories in each state where full-text copies of the patents are available is included.

Many industrial data bases include information on patents, and are excellent sources for current information on new processes and products. A list of data bases is also included in this section. Some of the data bases listed contain only patents, and others are industrial data bases with bibliographic as well as patent information available.

How to Search for Patents

1. If the number of the patent is known, then look the number up in the *Official Gazette of the United States Patent and Trademark Office*. This is published weekly and is organized numerically by patent number. The abstract of the patent in the *Official Gazette* includes the following information:

   a. Patent number.

   b. Inventor's name and address.

   c. Assignee (person/corporation that has the right to use the patent).

   d. International classification number.

   e. United States class and subclass number.

   f. Number of claims against patent.

   g. Abstract of patent.

2. An example is shown in Figure 9.4. If the inventor or assignee of the patent is known, then go to the *Index of Patents, Part I: List of Patentees*, an alphabetical list of patentees. An example is shown in Figure 9.5. There is also an index of assignees. Under each assignee's name is the patent number.

3. If neither the patent number nor the inventor is known, then the search must be conducted by subject.

   a. Go to the *Index of Classification*, which is arranged by subject (Figure 9.6 shows sample entries). Choose the term that best represents the subject matter of interest.

   b. Once the pertinent class and subclass are determined, then the *Manual of Classification* should be checked. The Manual contains the entire classification schedule under each class (for an example see Figure 9.7), and will help determine the best subclass to use.

Re. 31,019
STRINGLESS ELECTRONIC MUSICAL INSTRUMENT
Fred J. Evangelista, 14 Linda La., Severna Park, Md. 21146
Original No. 4,177,705, dated Dec. 11, 1979, Ser. No. 973,801,
Dec. 28, 1978. Application for reissue Jun. 25, 1980, Ser.
No. 162,777
Int. Cl.³ G10H 1/00 1/02
U.S. Cl. 84—1.16   20 Claims

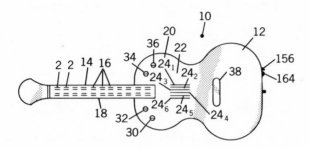

1. In an electronic musical instrument for simulating a stringed
instrument having a [body portion adapted to carry] tone generating means [and a neck portion adapted to carry a finger-board
assembly coupled to said tone generator means] and being op-
erable to vary the tonal output thereof, the improvement comprising.

tone generator means including an electrical oscillator circuit
[for each fundamental frequency desired to be simulated and]
including switch operated circuit means [operable from said
fingerboard assembly] for selectively changing [the] tonal
[output] frequency [of said oscillator circuit]:
[a respective] *an* output amplifier circuit coupled to said oscillator circuit and being energized in accordance with the
operative state of a player actuated switch device; and
said player actuated switch device [consisting of] *comprising* a
relatively thin [flexible blade-type] switch actuator member
[mounted on edge in a substantially upright position on the
outer surface of said body portion adjacent said fingerboard
assembly,] *having a pair of sides and* being adapted [thereby]
to be deflected bi-directionally [transverse] *transversely* [to
said upright position] when strummed, struck, picked or
plucked or bowed by a player, and at least one pair of electrical switch contacts located on each side of said actuator
[element] *member*, wherein deflection of said actuator [ele-
ment] *member* in either direction operates one of said pair
of switch contacts to energize said output amplifier circuit.

Figure 9.4. Example of patent abstract from *Official Gazette of the U.S. Patent and Trademark Office.*

Sweat Buddy, Inc.: *See*—
  Black, Henry C.; and Black, Ella J., 4,224,712, Cl. 15-209.00R.
Sweat, C. Downing, Jr.: *See*—
  Hebert, Chris J.; Hollister, Ralph T.; and Sweat, C. Downing, Jr., 4,220,170, Cl. 134-167.00R.
Sweat, George B.; and Warren, Alvin E. Tree climbing apparatus. 4,230,203, 10-28-80, Cl. 182-134.000.
Sweda International, Inc.: *See*—
  Goldstein, Amnon; Swett, Robert W.; and Greenwood, David L., 4,189,217. Cl. 354-7.000.
  Markkanen, Carl O.; Benson, William G.; and Goldstein, Amnon, 4,208,009, Cl. 235-475.000.
Swedo, Raymond J.; and Marvel, Carl S., to University Patents, Inc. Biphenylene polymers and resins and the production thereof. 4,197,393, 4-8-80, Cl. 528-173.000.
Sweeney, Kevin M., to Simulaids, Inc. Disposable protective sleeve, having a pneumatic action, for a rigid splint board or the like. 4,182,320, 1-8-80, Cl. 128-89.00R.
Sweeney, Lawrence J., to Franklin Steel Company. Drive cap. 4,190,118, 2-26-80, Cl. 173-130.000.
Sweeney, Michael T.: *See*—
  Moore, William T.; and Sweeney, Michael T., 4,234,240, Cl. 350-6.100.
Sweeney, Patrick E.; and Critcher, John J., to United States of America, Army. Directional fuze selector apparatus for artillery delivered mines. 4,205,609, 6-3-80, Cl. 102-8.000.
Sweeney, Ralph B.; and Verdouw, Albert J., to General Motors Corporation. Mount assembly for porous transition panel at annular combustor outlet. 4,191,011, 3-4-80, Cl. 60-39.320.
Sweeney, Richard F.; and Sukornick, Bernard F., to Allied Chemical Corporation. Process for producing halogenated hydrocarbons. 4,192,822, 3-11-80, Cl. 260-653.000.
Sweeney, Richard F.: *See*—
  Lockyer, George D., Jr.; Burd, Dennis E.; Sweeney, Richard F.; Sukornick, Bernard; and Ulmer, Harry E., 4,187,386, Cl. 585-367.000.

Figure 9.5.   Example of list of patentees.

c. The final check of the class and subclass is Classification Definitions. This is a series of detailed definitions that illustrate the kind of subject matter that can be found in each class and subclass.

d. Once the correct class and subclass are obtained, then the Official Gazette can be used. At the back of each weekly Gazette is an index ("Classification of Patents") by class and subclass with each patent number under that particular subject. At the end of this index is a table entitled "List of Patent, Design, Plant Patent, Reis-

Button	24	90+
Abrading cleaning shields	51	265
Design	D2	405+
Apparel, design	D2	449+
Art collection	425	801*
Attaching		
Processes	2	265
Sewing machine	112	104+
Bell buttons mechanical	116	172
Collar or cuff	24	101
Design	D2	405+
Lapel	D11	95+
Eyelet and rivet setting	227	55+
Fabric	24	92
Fastener making	29	4
Fasteners	24	90+
Feeder	227	31
Sewing machine	112	113
Fluorescent and phosphorescent	250	462
Hinged leaf	24	97+
Hole (See buttonhole)	24	202
Cutters	30	118+
Marking guides	33	190
Hook	D2	378.2
Loop	24	202.1
Making	79	
Making, metal	29	4
Metallic	79	3+
Pearl & composition	79	6+
Setting machine	227	55
Shank buttons	79	2
Strap or cable button	24	114.5
Switch	200	329+
Telegraph key	178	110
Whip	231	6
Work supports	79	18
Buttoner	24	40
Design, shoe	D2	378.3
Machine for shoes	12	58.3
Buttonhole	24	202
Cutting	83	905*
Hand tool	30	118
Marker	33	190
Sewing machines	112	65+
Processes and seams	112	264
Shoe closures	36	52
Stitch machine	112	157
Workholder in making	269	

Figure 9.6. Example of subject classification.

CLASS 9   BOATS, BUOYS AND AQUATIC DEVICES

1.1	BOATS, BOAT COMPONENTS OR ATTACHMENTS
1.2	. Wheeled landing or launching aid
1.3	. Circular
1.4	. Canoes or kayaks
1.5	. With protective covers or shields
1.6	. Boarding aids
1.7	. Deck or gunwale attachments
3	. Lifeboats
4 R	. . Inclosed
4 A	. . . . Even keel
5	. Hunting
2 R	. Sectional and folding
2 C	. . . Collapsible
2 F	. . . Foldable
2 S	. . . Sectional
2 A	. . . Inflatable
6 R	. Hull construction
6 M	. . . Metal
6 P	. . . Plastic
6 W	. . . Wood
6.5	. . Formers and framers
7	. Seats and foot supports
8 R	BUOYS
8 P	. . Offshore platform
8.3 R	. Illuminating
8.3 E	. . . Electrical
8.5	. Oil distributors
9	. Wreck indicating
10	. Safes
11 R	LIFE RAFTS
11 A	. . Inflatable
12	. Ship parts and furniture
13	. Mattress
14	LIFE-SAVING APPARATUS
15	RAFTING AND BOOMING
16	. Timber couplings
30	LIFE CRAFT HANDLING
31	. Conveying from storage position to launching position

Figure 9.7.   Example of class and subclass listing.

sue and Defense Publication Numbers Appearing in the *Official Gazette.*" This is a guide to the particular issue of the Gazette containing the specific patent number.

e.   If there is no number under the class or subclass, then there was no patent issued. If you cannot find the patent, then you have chosen the wrong class or subclass. Check the *Index of Classification* again.

4. Once the patent abstract is found, the patent can be ordered through the Patent Office in Washington, D.C.:

Commissioner of Patents
U.S. Patent and Trademark Office
Box 9
Washington, DC 20231.

The U.S. Patent Office also publishes a booklet called *General Information Concerning Patents*, which can help you in your patent search.

5. There are also 38 libraries nationwide that maintain a patent depository. They are open to the public and provide technical staff for assistance. A list of these libraries follows.

Reference Collections of United States Patents Available for Public Use in Patent Depository Libraries

State	Library name	Telephone number
Alabama	Birmingham Public Library	205–254–2555
Arizona	Tempe: Science Library, Arizona State University	602–965–7607
California	Los Angeles Public Library	213–626–7555
	Sacramento: California State Library	916–322–4572
	Sunnyvale: Patent Information Clearinghouse	408–738–5580
Colorado	Denver Public Library	303–571–2122
Delaware	Newark: University of Delaware	302–738–2238
Georgia	Atlanta: Price Gilbert Memorial Library, Georgia Institute of Technology	404–894–4559
Illinois	Chicago Public Library	312–269–2865
Louisiana	Baton Rouge: Troy H. Middleton Library, Louisiana State University	504–388–2570
Massachusetts	Boston Public Library	627–536–5400
Michigan	Detroit Public Library	313–833–1450
Minnesota	Minneapolis Public Library and Information Center	612–372–6552

State	Library name	Telephone number
Missouri	Kansas City: Linda Hall Library	816–363–4600
	St. Louis Public Library	314–241–2288
Nebraska	Lincoln: University of Nebraska–Lincoln, Engineering Library	402–472–3411
New Hampshire	Durham: University of New Hampshire Library	603–862–1777
New Jersey	Newark Public Library	201–733–7814
New York	Albany: New York State Library	518–474–5125
	Buffalo and Erie County Public Library	716–856–7525
	New York Public Library (The Research Libraries)	212–790–6524
North Carolina	Raleigh: D.H. Hill Library, North Carolina State University	919–737–3280
Ohio	Cincinnati and Hamilton County, Public Library of	513–369–6936
	Cleveland	216–623–2870
	Columbus: Ohio State University Libraries	614–422–6286
	Toledo/Lucas County Public Library	419–255–7055
Oklahoma	Stillwater: Oklahoma State University Library	405–624–6546
Pennsylvania	Philadelphia: Franklin Institute Library	215–448–1321
	Pittsburgh: Carnegie Library of Pittsburgh	412–622–3138
	University Park: Pattee Library, Pennsylvania State University	814–865–4861
Rhode Island	Providence Public Library	401–521–7722
South Carolina	Charleston: Medical University of South Carolina	803–792–2372

State	Library name	Telephone number
Tennessee	Memphis and Shelby County Library and Information Center	901–528–2957
Texas	Dallas Public Library	214–748–9071
	Houston: The Fondren Library, Rice University	713–527–8101
Washington	Seattle: Engineering Library, University of Washington	206–543–0740
Wisconsin	Madison: Kurt F. Wendt Engineering Library, University of Wisconsin	608–262–6845
	Milwaukee Public Library	414–278–3043

A Data Base That Is Patently Obvious

When using data bases, I discovered that a number of them index and track patent information in their fields. There are only a handful of data bases that solely monitor patents. Yet there are another 20 data bases that incidentally watch for new patent filings, although they are not called patent data bases. A list of those data bases follows. For a more complete description of a particular data base, see Chapter 7.

Computer Patent Sources

Data Base	Publisher	Description
APTIC	United States Environmental Protection Agency	Air pollution patents
BHRA Fluid	BHRA Fluid Engineering	British patents in fluid engineering
CA Search	Chemical Abstracts Service	Patent specification in chemistry
CAB	Commonwealth Agricultural Bureau	Agricultural patents
Chemsearch	Chemical Abstracts Service	Latest six weeks of chemical patents

Data Base	Publisher	Description
Claims/Citation	Search Check	Patent references cited during patent examining process
Claims/Patent Files	IFI/Plenum Data Co.	Engineering, chemistry, and mechanical patents
Claims/Uniterm	IFI/Plenum Data Co.	All United States chemical and chemically related patents, five foreign countries included
Coffeeline	International Coffee Organization	Patents for coffee
DOE Energy	United States Department of Energy	Patents for energy
Electronic Yellow Pages—Professional Directory	Market Data Retrieval	United States patent attorneys
Food Science and Technology Abstracts	International Food Information Service	Food patents from 20 countries
Foods Adlibra	K and M Publications	Patents in food industry
INPADOC	IFI/Plenum Data Co.	All patents for 47 countries for past six weeks
INSPEC	IEEE Services Center	Electronics, physics, computers, electrical patents
Metadex	American Society for Metals	Metallurgical patents
Paperchem	Institute of Paper Chemistry	Pulp and paper technology patents
Patlaw	Bureau of National Affairs	United States federal and state court decisions pertaining to patents and trademarks
Surface Coating Abstracts	Paint Research Association	Patents for all aspects of surface coatings
Telegen	EIC	Genetic engineering and biotechnical patents

Data Base	Publisher	Description
Water Resources Abstracts	United States Department of the Interior	Patents for conservation, engineering, and water control
Weldasearch	The Welding Institute	Patents (mostly British) for plastics and metal welding
World Aluminum Abstracts	American Society for Metals	Aluminum patents

THE VALUE OF BUSINESS SCHOOL CASES

Business school cases are an often-overlooked source of company information. In five to thirty pages, on the average, business-school cases examine a company's management, operations, marketing strategies, business failures, and successes. A researcher can find answers to many of the following questions in a typical business school case:

What is the industry structure?

Who are the chief industry players?

What are the company's income and current assets?

Who reports to whom in the organization?

How does the company market its products?

How has the company dealt with past managment or business problems?

Although any particular case could be years out of date, it could provide your research with a starting point. For example: A case may present an old organization chart that does not represent the current management structure. Yet it is a beginning. It offers the researcher a means to ask those experts he or she interviews how and where the organization has changed since this case first appeared.

Business school cases also tend to offer a good deal of general industry data, including overall sales and competitor position in the market.

One caveat—Even though you may find a case that directly answers a question you may have about a corporation, beware! Many companies agree to submit to a university researcher's questions only after it is agreed that the actual case, when it does appear, will disguise many of the names and the financials discussed. So although the case's overall thrust remains accurate, it may obscure many of the details.

Another drawback to be aware of: You may find that the information contained in a case is too dated to use.

Some case studies are only available to business school students, and are restricted to certain classes. However, you can buy hundreds of cases over the counter. Prices range from $2 to $20.

The Harvard Business School is the greatest promotor of the case study method and has one of the largest collections of case studies. Abstracts and indexes are available in a softbound catalog. To order a Harvard case study or a catalogue, call or write:

Intercollegiate Case Clearing House
Morgan Hall
Harvard Business School
Soldiers Field Road
Boston, MA 02163
617–495–6117

REGIONAL MAGAZINES FOR REGIONAL INTELLIGENCE

Earlier in the book, I mentioned the regional factor as important in uncovering details on a company. This means that to uncover information about a company, go to local sources of information. For example, go to a local newspaper or magazine.

In the past, it has been difficult not only to locate particular magazines, but once found it has been hard to find the issue with the article you're looking for. Since July of 1983, Area Business Databank has attempted to fill in this gap. It has placed over 80 regional business magazines on microfiche and indexed them by region, as well as by subject. The ABD service issues new fiche and an updated index each month.

To find out more about this unique service, write or call:

Area Business Databank
P.O. Box 829
1018 S. Fourth Street
Louisville, KY 40201
502–589–9666

MANAGEMENT BIOGRAPHIES IN PRINT

Many times you simply cannot find a packaged biography on the manager or executive you are examining. Yet so much has been written about so many people that you can bet on occasion you will find that special biography in a directory.

Below is a list of some biographical directories you might find handy:

Bio-Base: A Master Index to Biographies in 500 Biographical Dictionaries (Gale Research Company). This directory contains an estimated 4 million citations of biographical directories and dictionaries. Each entry contains the person's name, the date of birth or death, and the publication in which the biography appears.

Biographical Dictionaries and Related Works (Gale Research Company). A guide or listing to other biographical reference books.

Biography Almanac (Gale Research Company). A listing of over 20,000 biographies.

Blue Book: Leaders of the English-Speaking World (Gale Research Company). A book that offers approximately 15,000 capsule biographies of leaders in business, government, the arts, and science. Countries covered include the United States, Canada, Britain, Ireland, Australia, and New Zealand.

International Who's Who of the Arab World (International Who's Who of the Arab World). Lists approximately 3500 leading Arabs.

Leaders In Electronics (McGraw-Hill). A key text for researching prominent individuals in the electronics industry. There are over 5000 biographies.

Leading German Industrialists/Leitende Männer der Wirtschaft (Verlag Hoppestedt). This text lists over 43,000 Germans who are involved in German business or in the economy in general.

Marquis Who's Who (Marquis Who's Who). Probably thought of as the seminal biographical work in the field. It may not have been the first biographical reference book (or books), but it is thought of first. Among the Who's Who books Marquis offers are *Who's Who in America*, *Who's Who in the East*, *Who's Who in the West*, *Who's Who in the Southwest*, and *Who's Who in Finance and Industry*. These reference books contain approximately 300,000 capsule biographies in all. In addition, Marquis offers a *Directory of Medical Specialists*.

New York Times Biographical Service (Microfilming Corporation of America). This is a service, not a single reference work. This subsidiary company of the New York Times photocopies and indexes biographies that have appeared in the Times. Supplements are sent to subscribers on a monthly basis.

Standard & Poor's Directory of Corporations (McGraw-Hill). In volume 3 of its three-volume work, S & P offers brief biographies of the senior executives mentioned in its corporate listing.

Textile World's Leaders in the Textile Industry (McGraw-Hill). A highly specialized directory, it lists approximately 1500 prominent individuals in the textile business.

Trustees of Wealth (Taft Corporation). Ordinarily thought of as a fund-raiser's biographical reference tool, it actually is much more if you will think for a moment who these biographies are about. They cover approximately 7800 foundation officers in the United States. These trustees are often directors and senior executives with major U.S. corporations. In effect, then, this directory becomes an invaluable tool for researching the corporate executive. Each entry lists office address, business affiliations, title, year of birth, employment history, and educational background.

Who's Who (A & C Black). Very much a British biographical index and reference book, but also lists individuals throughout the world. It includes over 28,000 individuals.

STATE INDUSTRY DIRECTORIES: FOCUSING IN ON YOUR MARKET

National company directories, such as *Standard & Poor's* or *Dun & Bradstreet's Million Dollar Directory*, will take you a long way towards finding information on national firms, but they will fall short on local, smaller companies. Here state directories come to the rescue.

These directories are published by either the state government or by private publishers. A typical entry in a state industry directory appears very similar to an entry in the *D & B Million Dollar* or the *Standard & Poor's Corporate Directory*. It contains company name and address, telephone number, product or service, estimated sales, number of employees, and names of senior officers.

One of the largest publishers of state industry directories is Harris Publishing Company. Their directories range from $15 to over $100. They offer a directory for almost every one of the 50 states. To order a directory from Harris, write or call:

Harris Publishing Company
2057-2 Aurora Road
Twinsburg, OH 44087
800–321–9136

To find out if a state government offers an industry directory, contact its Secretary of State's office or Office of Corporations (see the section on state filings in Chapter 3).

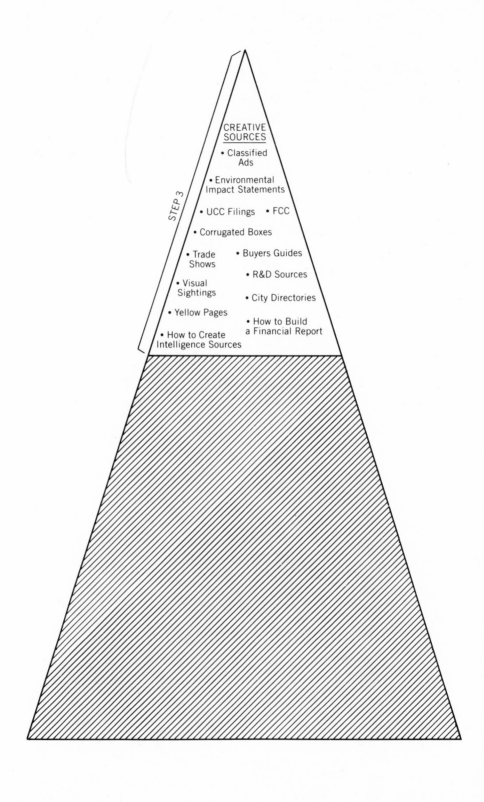

STEP 3

CREATIVE
SOURCES

• Classified
  Ads

• Environmental
  Impact Statements

• UCC Filings   • FCC

• Corrugated Boxes

• Trade   • Buyers Guides
  Shows
               • R&D Sources
• Visual
  Sightings   • City Directories

• Yellow Pages
               • How to Build
• How to Create a Financial Report
Intelligence Sources

PART 3

CREATIVE SOURCES AND TECHNIQUES

This might be considered the "fun" section. It discusses sources that my clients and colleagues have found the most exciting and thought-provoking. Imagine! Corrugated boxes as a source of production data!

Use this section as a beginning. For as you will see, there is virtually no limit to the number and types of creative sources you will find in your future intelligence-gathering experiences. The sources discussed here only represent the tip of the intelligence iceberg. In reality, there are too many for any one book to list, because there are too many possible intelligence-gathering situations that arise, each requiring a different creative source or technique.

That is why I have chosen to begin this section with advice on how you can locate your own creative sources. Review this section well—read it a second and a third time. Use it to spark new intelligence-gathering ideas. For if you can locate your own creative sources, you will likely succeed in your intelligence-gathering assignments.

CHAPTER 10

CREATING CREATIVE SOURCES

HOW TO CREATE YOUR OWN CREATIVE INTELLIGENCE SOURCES

This book lists thousands of sources, yet no book can hope to list all the available sources. Each industry has its own pet research gems, sometimes unique to one industry. What I would like to do in this chapter is take you through the "creative sourcing" process—that is, help you identify creative sources in your industry, when the ones suggested in this book do not work or are not appropriate.

But before you can understand the process, let me show you the sources other industries have used successfully in tracking down bits of corporate intelligence. The following chart lists various creative techniques or sources and the industries in which they are used.

Industry	Technique	What Is Learned
Consulting	Staying outside a plant and watching the personnel enter and leave	Number of employees
Petroleum	Counting the number of links being sunk down a well shaft	Depth of the well

Industry	Technique	What Is Learned
Packaging	Observing the shipping truck: Is it single or double axled?	Single axle indicates a lighter load, such as corrugated paper; double axle indicates a heavier load, such as plastic packaging
Consumer electronics	Snoop and scoop (See "Trade Shows: Open Season on Competitors" in Chapter 14)	Understanding of the marketing strategy and new products being offered
Retailing	Counting the number of stores listed in the Yellow Pages	Competitor's market share or at least store locations

WHAT YOU NEED TO LOCATE CREATIVE SOURCES

The executives who first told me about the above techniques and sources did not go through great philosophical discussions to identify these sources. They simply came across them through their experiences and the experiences of their colleagues.

What do you need to identify creative sources that work in your industry or with the company you are investigating? By following the steps listed below, you will be able to identify formerly unknown, unrevealed sources:

1. *Understand exactly what you are looking for.* This may sound like an insipid or even ridiculous statement. Yet unless you can pinpoint your research goals, you will be unable to identify the necessary sources.

For example: When looking for "marketing strategy," are you really looking for the number of stores the company will open within the next five years, or are you trying to determine their intended pricing structure? By defining the question, you save yourself wasted research time and begin zeroing in on sources that directly address the question.

The consultant in the chart above, for instance, did not want to merely know the plant size. He actually wanted to know the number of employees. That was the question he successfully addressed.

2. *Determine the number of answers you want.* Each answer will likely require a different source. To find out a company's number of employees and the compensation it pays its sales force requires two different sources. They are two very different intelligence problems. The number of employees you may solve with a simple plant sighting, counting the people walking in and out. Determining compensation level may require your interviewing industry executive search firms, unions, or a competitor's compensation officer.

3. *Find a proxy.* This is a key point to understand. Once you have defined your questions and know the answers you are looking for, you have to ask yourself "Is there another source that will give me the same or similar information?"

Finding a proxy is one of the most important ideas in this entire book. This rule tells the researcher to remain loose and open to all possible sources. Don't put on those research blinders and think, for example, that only a newspaper article will have your answer and that if there is no article available you should give up. Quite the contrary!

Let's look at some examples of research proxies:

Intelligence Needed	Basic Source	Creative Proxy
Company assets	Balance sheet (not available because it is a privately held company)	UCC filing
Volume shipped	Bills of lading (not publicly available)	Using corrugated boxes to find size and number shipped

WHAT IS THE BEST WAY TO FIND A CREATIVE SOURCE?

Speak to those people who work directly in the area you are investigating. For instance, if we wanted to know how to find the volume shipped, we would go first to our company's shipping department and ask them: "If you had to find our competitor's shipping volume and you did not have their bills of lading, what other sources would you use?"

Two important ideas to note here are:

1. *These individuals are almost never market researchers.* In fact they are anybody but researchers. Your creative sources by definition are new and unusual. These are sources the researchers themselves must find. But they are not necessarily sources the researchers are directly acquainted with.

2. *The best people to approach for ideas for creative sources are the people who deal with the day-to-day operation of the business—from the ground level.* That means shippers, production people, product managers, salespersons, service technicians, programmers. These folks don't do research, but they do understand how their company operates.

A clever shipper would tell you about the corrugated boxes as a source. Another might suggest that you estimate the number of products per truckload and find a way to estimate the number of trucks that leave the plant per month. You can check on the number of trucks by simply counting them from a distance, or by speaking to the truck leasing company that the competitor uses. The leasing firm might also give you an idea of how often the competitor uses the firm's trucks.

But let's say you are new to an industry. You are investigating a company that is outside your area of expertise. In order to locate those creative sources, you will have to find key individuals who might know a good number of sources or alternate sources. Below I have listed examples of individuals who might supply you with ideas for excellent creative proxies for several industries.

Industry	Individuals Who May Know Sources
Banking	Product managers
	Tellers
Software	Buyers
	Programmers
Chemicals	Production managers
	Salespeople
	Shippers
Insurance	Brokers
	Salespeople
Packaged foods	Food brokers
	Packagers

In order to get the person to think of a creative source for you, never ask the entire question. Rather, ask your question in parts. The entire question could create a mental block. For example, instead of asking a shipper "What is Company X's sales volume?" ask:

Do you know how much of the product Company X fits in one truckload?

Do you know how many trucks Company X ships out in one week?

Are its sales seasonal? If so, when does Company X ship more and when does it ship less? Is it currently in a slow or a busy season?

What you have just done is taken your major question (Company X's sales) and broken it down into its components:

Products sold = (products/truckload) × (number of truckloads)

The last question given above takes into account anomalies in sales and seasonal fluctuations.

Note—Reality will often dictate that one shipper may not be able to answer all of your questions. You may have to go to a number of shippers, or other industry sources, to derive your estimate of Company X's sales.

CHAPTER 11

BUILDING A FINANCIAL STATEMENT

HOW TO ESTIMATE A FINANCIAL STATEMENT

Financial statements are the bugaboos of intelligence-gathering. They are difficult to derive. Unless your competitor literally hands the statement over to you, you can never be totally sure the financials you have assembled are correct.

This section will help you make the best out of a difficult situation. You have already seen how and where you can purchase state and SEC filings. Never overlook these financials sources (remember your homework). But what happens when public filings are not available, when no one ever required that this privately held corporation file a statement in the first place? Or even a stickier problem, what if you have to derive the financials of a company that is a subsidiary of a publicly held corporation? Yes, you will find the parent company's financials, but most of the time not those of its subsidiaries.

There are three major sources used to derive company financials in cases where they are not revealed in public filings or news articles. They are (1) credit reports, (2) financial ratios, and (3) expert interviews (sources of production costs).

In truth, you should use all three of these sources in conjunction with

WAR STORY 10

A Shattering Piece of Information

Hunting for a glass manufacturer's estimated sales figures, we made sure to do our homework first: we ordered a credit report on the company.

At first glance, we had our answer. The report stated that the company reported $15 million in sales each year. Yet when we read a little further into the report, we discovered that the company had switched from being just an import office for a foreign manufacturer to building its own plant.

After making a few inquiries we discovered that the company was actually generating sales on the order of $30 million, or twice what the credit report stated. We also learned that the reason for this jump in revenue was the new plant itself, and that one year ago, before the plant was built, the company's sales were actually $15 million.

What we saw was a credit report that was updated to the extent that it reported the new plant. Unfortunately, the other half of the report was not changed to match this new information

one another. Each alone is weak and needs corroboration. Together these sources will either corroborate or disprove each other. In the end, though, you will be able to make a stronger case for the final income statement or balance sheet you eventually draft.

CREDIT REPORTS

Credit reports are the lazy way to garner information on the competition. As the expression goes: You get what you pay for. If a credit report costs you $20 or $30, that is exactly the amount of intelligence you will be getting—$20 or $30 worth. Yet, it is a source you should turn to first.

Credit reporting agencies are either independent services, such as Dun & Bradstreet, or are in some way affiliated with a trade group, such as the Lumbermen's Credit Association. The depth and quality may differ markedly between one credit agency and another. One credit report may offer extensive financial information, and another may present no more than a vague and broadly defined rating code.

To order a credit report, you may only need to phone the credit agency of your choice and order the report. In other instances, as with D & B, customers must pay in advance for their estimated usage.

At their best, credit reports offer the following to the researcher in search of corporate intelligence:

Basic information—name, address, standard industrial classification, age of firm, and parent–subsidiary relationship.

Financials—usually this means sales or net worth figures. Where public filings are available, these reports may cite their financial data.

General purpose of business.

Reports of financial difficulty or court cases outstanding.

Payment record.

But take note. Most credit reports are designed for purchasing agents, not for researchers. That is, they concentrate on payment record, not on the choice marketing or plant data you need.

When ordering a report, here are some drawbacks to be aware of:

Credit reports concentrate on payment record and debt, not on income or operating expenses.

These services often cover a broad range of companies. They become a jack-of-all-trades, lacking a specialty or insight into any one field. This mass production system may cause the particular service to overlook potentially valuable data.

Their broad selection of companies may cause them to omit vital details.

Little investigation is carried out by their researchers, aside from a review of the available public filings (SEC, state, UCC).

Because of agency update cycles, the credit agency may miss the latest income statement issued by a company. The result: The latest available company financials may not be reflected in the credit report until one year later.

These reports contain little background information on the company's principals and their corporate affiliations.

Credit reports are not designed to supply marketing, planning, production, or sales information, except for the most general data.

Instead of admitting there is no information, reports will often substitute pat phrases such as "trend up" or "premises neat and clean." This is noninformation or nonintelligence.

These services have little to offer on small, privately held companies.

On the following pages, we identify and offer a brief description of many of the more popular—and some of the more obscure—credit services. The services in this section were chosen because of their nationwide coverage. There may be other, local services that serve one region or town. We did not include these smaller services in this section. To find the credit agencies in your area, just flip to your Yellow Pages under the heading "Credit Reporting Agencies."

Dun & Bradstreet

99 Church Street
New York, NY 10007
212–285–7000

BACKGROUND.   Offices based around the world. Millions of company reports on file. Report information gathered through on-site visits and telephone and mail inquiries. Updates approximately once a year, unless specially requested. Details sometimes spotty and disjointed.

MAJOR PURPOSE.   While business Information Reports are used primarily as credit tools, they are also widely used for marketing, purchasing, insurance underwriting, and other purposes.

REPORT CATEGORIES.

Duns Number.
Summary.
Payments.
Finance.
Banking.
History.
Operation.
Special events.
Public filings.

Lumbermen's Credit Association

55 East Jackson Boulevard.
Chicago, IL 60604
312–427–0733

BACKGROUND. A credit agency specializing in reporting on the lumber and woodworking industries. Its major credit product, the Red Book, contains credit ratings on lumber operators, retail dealers, wholesalers, distributors, remanufacturing consumers, woodworking shops, furniture factories, cabinet shops, and others who buy lumber, dimension, veneer, or plywood for manufacturing purposes.

MAJOR PURPOSE. Credit reference guide for the lumber industry.

REPORT CATEGORIES.

Name, address.
Business classification.
Credit rating (including financial strength, paying habits).

Note—Ratings are extremely general. More details may be obtained from the credit agency.

National Credit Office

1290 Sixth Avenue
New York, NY 10019
212–957–3800

BACKGROUND. A subsidiary of Dun & Bradstreet, NCO reports are similar to D & B's, but more comprehensive. NCO reports on about 25,000 companies in six major manufacturing groups—electronics, apparel, mobile homes, wholesale/retail, chemical, and automotive.

Report information is gathered through telephone inquiries. Analysts specialize by industry (125–150 analysts employed). Updates three times per year. NCO has access to D & B data bank. NCO sponsors 35–40 industry credit groups.

MAJOR PURPOSE. National Credit Office reports are used primarily for credit checks; however, information is available on marketing, purchasing, and other functions.

REPORT CATEGORIES.

Name, address.
Financials, where available.

Bank.

Debts outstanding.

Trends.

Principals.

Fidelifacts

25 Broad Street
New York, NY 10004
212–425–1520

BACKGROUND. Fidelifacts is an investigative credit reporting firm. Reports are issued on a case-by-case basis. Report information is gathered through court records, UCC, mortgages, SEC, and other public records, as well as telephone interviews and literature searches.

MAJOR PURPOSE. Fidelifacts is used primarily to verify personal background of officers and employees of a company.

REPORT CATEGORIES.

Name, address.

Report on public filings.

Verification of reputation.

Paper and Allied Trade Mercantile Agency

225 Broadway
New York, NY 10007
212–964–8600

BACKGROUND. Reports credit and trading information on those companies involved in the paper and printing trades.

MAJOR PURPOSE. Used for references concerning a company's reputation.

REPORT CATEGORIES.

Trade references.

Credit ratings.

Company background.

Trade record.

Bank references.

Available financial information.

Photographic Credit Institute

71 Broadway
New York, NY 10006
212–482–8383

BACKGROUND.   General corporate reports on companies requesting information on retail stores selling camera and photographic equipment.

MAJOR PURPOSE.   The Institute does not rate the retailer's credit record. Information submitted is based on the specific questions placed by the requestor. Reports are submitted by geographical area.

When a request on a particular retailer is made, the Institute will send out a questionnaire to all members of the Institute asking them about the retailer. The returns are then assembled in aggregate form and presented as a tabulation to the requestor. The response time is two to three months from the time of request to receipt of report.

REPORT CATEGORIES.

Payment information.

Financials on new companies.

DBA (doing-business-as) filings.

Address, telephone number.

Ownership.

Bank information.

Produce Reporter Company

315 W. Wesley Street
Wheaton, IL 60187

BACKGROUND.   Credit listings for suppliers and wholesalers in the fruit and vegetable trade.

MAJOR PURPOSE.   Credit information for those in the trade, concerning their wholesalers and suppliers.

REPORT CATEGORIES.

Basic financials.
Trading conditions.

Sporting Goods Clearing House

323 S. Franklin Street
Chicago, IL 60606
312–427–8699

BACKGROUND.   Established to determine credit and reliability of sports clubs and pros as consumers of sporting goods.

MAJOR PURPOSE.   The Clearing House assembles the reports for manufacturers and retailers, who in turn sell to sports clubs and sports pros (primarily in the golf and tennis lines). The report information is gleaned from the subjects themselves.

REPORT CATEGORIES.

Antecedent history.
Employment history.
Payment record.
Other pertinent financial data.
Reports of delinquent payment.

TRW Business Credit Services

505 City Parkway West, Suite 100
Orange, CA 92668
714–937–2670

BACKGROUND.   Available through TRW's timesharing system, this data base is smaller than Dun & Bradstreet's and offers basic financial information to TRW Business Credit Services subscribers.

Major purpose.   To serve as a credit report. It is most useful to potential vendors and customers.

Report categories.

Account status, including last sale date recorded, payment terms, high credit, account balance, and status of payment.

Affiliated bank.

Product line description.

Sales.

Market share estimate.

Employment.

Parent name.

Ownership status (publicly or privately held).

FINANCIAL RATIOS

Bankers use this tool every day. They apply industry financial ratios to companies seeking loans from their bank to see if, for example, a company's debt picture is above average. A banker may also want to look at a firm's current-asset-to-current-liability ratio (also known as "current ratio").

These ratios tell the banker whether or not Company X is a good risk for a loan, both from a short and long-term perspective. You can use this same tool to help piece together a target company's balance sheet or income statement. How can you employ a financial ratio to derive a firm's fiscal picture? Here is an example:

The Murf and Turf grass-seeding company has assets totaling approximately $100,000.

You need to find out its total liabilities.

You also happen to find in an industry guide that the standard current assets/current liabilities ratio for this industry is 2:1 (where total assets are two times the total liabilities).

Using the formula of $2.0 =$ current assets/current liabilities, you plug in the one value you know, which is the current assets figure, and simple algebra will tell you that the total current liabilities amount to $50,000 (that is, of course, assuming that the ratio you were given was correct in the first place).

Theoretically, all you might need are three of Murf and Turf's financial figures (let's say current assets, gross revenue, and cost of goods sold) to derive the entire income statement and balance sheet.

Later in this section we list books that contain lists of financial ratios for various industries and company sizes. But we are also aware that these ratios can be a dangerously misleading tool. The big question you must always ask before using a set of ratios is: Does this set of ratios accurately portray my target company's true financial picture?

Drawbacks

Industry groups—banks and trade associations included—will compile financial averages for those in the industry to compare their company to others in the industry. Usually there are two major problems inherent in the use of such ratios:

1. *The ratios don't represent your target company's industry.*   Murf and Turf is a grass-seeding and lawn-care company. Yet the only ratios you can find describe agriculture and farming. Agriculture is the larger and more general industry heading. Should its ratios happen to match with your target company's ratios, it would be purely coincidental. Lesson—Make sure that the ratios you use belong to your industry.

2. *The ratios reflect companies that are much larger or much smaller than your target company.*   Murf and Turf may be ten times larger than its nearest competitor. But the ratios you are using are based on a group of companies far smaller than Murf and Turf. The proportions between the smaller and larger companies will not match—and again, if they do, it would be coincidental. Lesson—Make sure the companies you use have the same asset size as your target company's.

Table 11.1 shows an example of Dun & Bradstreet's Key Business Ratios. The center, bold line within each business group represents the average ratio for that group.

The Ratio Test

We took seven manufacturers of office computing and accounting machines with known financials. (These companies were all publicly traded and filed

TABLE 11.1   Dun and Bradstreets Key Business Ratios for Manufacturing. (Source: Selected Key Business Ratios in 125 Lines of Business, D&B. Reprinted with permission.)

MANUFACTURING

Line of Business (and number of concerns reporting)	Quick Ratio (Times)	Current Ratio (Times)	Current liabilities to net worth (Percent)	Current liabilities to inventory (Percent)	Total liabilities to net worth (Percent)	Fixed assets to net worth (Percent)	Collection period (Days)	Net sales to inventory (Times)	Total assets to net sales (Percent)	Net sales to net working capital (Times)	Accounts payable to net sales (Percent)	Return on net sales (Percent)	Return on total assets (Percent)	Return on net worth (Percent)
2011-2017 Meat Products (113)	2.1	4.2	20.4	89.2	33.3	31.9	12.7	44.2	14.0	31.0	0.9	2.9	11.6	25.7
	1.3	2.2	47.0	144.8	71.8	57.9	17.8	29.0	19.2	15.3	1.8	1.5	6.5	13.9
	0.8	1.6	118.0	221.5	177.2	82.6	24.8	16.3	28.9	11.0	3.2	0.6	2.4	4.8
2021-2026 Dairy Products (125)	1.2	2.0	52.0	133.7	64.3	43.7	18.9	55.0	18.6	41.3	3.7	2.8	9.5	23.1
	1.0	1.4	84.6	228.8	114.7	68.2	26.4	26.9	23.1	19.1	5.6	1.2	5.2	11.1
	0.7	1.2	149.4	434.2	205.0	92.4	32.8	13.9	33.2	12.5	7.7	0.5	1.1	3.1
2051-2052 Bakery Products (113)	2.0	3.3	16.9	116.4	24.1	58.9	17.0	41.5	27.3	32.5	2.5	5.5	12.7	21.8
	1.1	1.9	36.2	216.8	49.1	85.6	24.4	29.8	37.0	15.0	4.3	2.4	6.9	13.8
	0.8	1.3	66.1	362.6	112.0	133.5	31.7	17.4	48.2	7.1	6.2	1.2	2.7	6.7
2082-2087 Beverages (140)	1.5	3.3	20.3	61.8	41.4	16.7	20.1	33.4	17.6		2.9	7.3	14.6	27.3
	0.9	2.0	38.7	118.1	68.2	72.1	24.9	13.2	44.8	9.6	4.8	4.1	8.3	15.6
	0.5	1.3	70.4	188.1	136.7	100.7	37.2	5.1	68.1	5.2	7.4	1.8	3.6	8.5
2321-2329 Men's & Boy's Apparel (114)	1.6	3.5	39.9	63.5	43.4	5.5	23.3	10.8	27.8	8.3	3.3	5.5	10.2	23.3
	1.0	2.4	80.9	99.8	97.2	11.8	43.8	6.3	42.1	5.2	6.4	3.0	5.1	11.4
	0.6	1.7	146.2	144.5	180.9	35.6	66.0	4.2	56.1	3.7	10.1	1.6	2.4	6.2
2331-2339 Women's, Misses' & Juniors' Outerwear (107)	1.5	2.7	35.4	112.0	59.7	3.3	23.7	16.4	25.1	14.8	4.3	3.2	10.4	31.4
	1.0	1.7	104.3	159.0	131.6	7.7	43.0	10.7	32.5	9.4	7.4	2.0	6.2	16.3
	0.7	1.4	207.3	237.6	235.9	18.6	62.6	7.3	43.5	5.6	10.5	0.5	1.2	3.8
2421 Sawmills & Planing Mills, General (128)	2.1	4.7	11.9	58.3	22.9	31.7	14.2	13.2	40.3	12.8	1.6	6.4	10.6	17.9
	0.9	2.4	30.2	94.9	63.2	67.9	20.4	8.0	57.9	6.4	2.6	4.3	7.1	10.7
	0.3	1.3	84.6	173.2	150.0	108.9	29.5	5.0	84.2	3.4	4.8	1.6	3.3	6.2
2511-2519 Household Furniture (116)	2.0	3.9	27.6	55.6	31.3	19.7	18.2	13.2	29.0	10.9	2.5	6.1	13.5	25.9
	1.1	2.5	46.9	83.6	71.3	35.9	34.1	9.4	42.2	6.9	3.7	3.0	7.0	13.3
	0.7	1.8	97.2	130.2	148.4	70.3	47.4	5.2	51.8	4.2	6.5	0.9	2.6	4.2
2651-2655 Paperboard Containers & Boxes (115)	2.1	3.3	28.1	81.1	39.6	32.6	30.2	21.9	31.5	14.0	3.1	5.0	9.7	18.7
	1.3	2.1	56.3	146.8	99.6	58.3	41.5	13.1	43.8	8.8	4.8	3.4	7.0	12.5
	0.9	1.5	110.0	248.0	197.4	107.7	46.3	7.6	55.8	4.4	7.6	0.9	2.6	4.6
2731-2732 Books (101)	1.9	4.2	20.4	57.1	30.0	5.6	32.1	14.1	45.0	6.8	2.6	12.5	14.8	20.7
	1.2	2.7	42.2	98.0	69.4	20.1	48.5	7.3	62.7	3.7	6.0	6.7	9.3	13.5
	0.7	1.8	90.0	167.8	150.5	45.4	81.3	3.6	97.7	2.4	10.6	2.8	5.4	7.6
2812-2819 Industrial Inorganic Chemicals (132)	1.5	3.0	28.8	95.0	40.2	37.6	34.3	16.4	37.4	9.7	5.4	8.0	9.1	17.4
	1.1	2.1	52.2	141.9	84.1	64.9	49.2	10.1	56.6	6.9	8.1	3.8	6.1	12.8
	0.6	1.5	93.7	266.3	152.9	101.4	66.0	6.4	75.2	4.8	12.2	1.8	3.3	5.8
2821-2824 Plastics, Synth. Rubber, Resins, Man-Made Fibers, Expt. Glass (102)	1.9	3.4	28.7	94.1	32.1	29.4	42.6	12.7	34.1	10.7	3.5	8.3	14.1	23.2
	1.3	2.2	47.7	141.3	77.0	63.3	52.2	9.7	49.0	6.5	6.7	4.6	9.1	16.4
	0.8	1.4	117.4	209.8	173.1	102.2	63.0	7.0	68.8	3.8	9.7	2.3	4.6	10.8
2851 Paints, Varnishes, Lacquers, Enamels & Allied Products (109)	2.2	4.1	25.9	56.2	34.7	18.4	29.2	10.0	32.3	7.8	3.4	5.8	12.4	23.3
	1.4	2.8	45.6	84.9	63.2	34.1	36.5	8.0	40.7	5.5	5.3	3.4	8.7	12.4
	1.0	2.0	68.7	115.2	121.5	65.4	45.2	5.8	50.0	3.9	7.9	2.0	5.4	7.9
2873-2879 Agricultural Chemicals (95)	1.9	3.3	34.9	86.7	40.9	18.7	24.0	15.7	34.1	13.1	2.5	5.3	12.6	23.9
	1.0	1.9	58.5	142.3	83.5	40.1	45.0	9.9	46.7	7.4	6.6	3.3	7.8	15.8
	0.6	1.4	111.9	233.1	175.9	87.1	64.9	5.9	61.7	4.3	10.1	1.5	3.4	7.8
2911-2999 Petroleum Refining & Related Industries (120)	1.4	2.6	35.3	130.3	46.4	29.5	28.4	31.4	31.7	28.5	3.4	9.3	11.1	24.7
	0.9	1.5	63.4	210.9	99.7	69.9	38.3	15.0	47.0	12.3	7.3	4.8	7.7	19.4
	0.6	1.2	115.0	391.8	177.0	134.0	58.4	9.2	74.7	4.8	12.9	1.9	4.3	12.1
3142-3149 Footwear, Except Rubber (119)	1.9	3.6	32.2	58.9	42.3	13.0	42.7	8.3	35.7	7.7	3.9	6.1	12.3	25.7
	1.2	2.6	60.0	85.8	73.6	30.0	54.0	5.7	44.9	4.4	5.5	3.9	7.6	14.5
	0.8	1.8	112.7	128.9	141.8	40.2	66.7	4.3	55.7	3.3	8.5	1.5	4.0	8.0
3271 Concrete Block & Brick (138)	1.9	4.0	18.1	74.6	29.9	33.9	29.2	15.8	46.1	9.5	3.8	6.4	9.5	16.4
	1.1	2.3	43.1	114.4	65.5	66.0	38.3	8.8	57.1	5.0	5.2	3.8	6.2	9.4
	0.7	1.6	83.0	242.7	148.0	106.6	50.3	5.5	79.3	3.4	7.9	1.3	1.6	4.0
3312-3317 Blast Furnaces, Steel Works, & Rolling & Finishing Mills (92)	1.3	3.0	33.2	78.5	52.2	51.5	36.2	13.5	38.2	10.7	4.4	5.9	8.9	17.8
	1.0	2.1	52.9	104.4	120.5	75.9	46.3	7.5	58.8	5.7	6.4	4.0	6.5	13.6
	0.7	1.6	111.1	171.7	192.0	115.7	53.8	4.7	74.1	4.2	9.0	2.4	4.1	7.3
3421-3429 Cutlery, Hand Tools & General Hardware (116)	2.2	4.9	17.2	43.6	27.0	14.1	33.9	8.8	42.4	6.3	2.2	7.9	16.0	26.2
	1.2	3.4	33.9	71.9	53.8	35.9	42.7	5.9	59.1	4.2	4.3	5.0	9.5	18.4
	0.9	1.9	65.6	130.7	111.4	58.4	54.0	4.4	73.8	2.8	6.8	3.3	5.4	9.5
3441-3449 Fabricated Structural Metal Products (104)	2.1	3.5	24.8	72.8	32.6	22.4	31.7	15.1	35.1	11.2	2.5	7.3	14.3	33.2
	1.1	2.0	59.9	136.8	73.5	37.3	43.8	9.3	45.1	6.6	5.6	5.3	11.1	21.6
	0.8	1.5	124.7	215.8	152.5	78.9	56.5	5.9	57.2	4.4	9.5	3.1	7.3	14.4
3462-3469 Metal Forgings & Stampings (119)	2.1	3.7	20.9	74.2	33.1	37.6	30.2	14.4	43.0	12.2	2.1	7.6	13.1	21.0
	1.1	2.2	38.6	129.7	56.7	51.3	40.5	10.1	50.1	6.7	4.4	4.1	6.7	12.1
	0.8	1.5	78.9	205.5	127.7	98.3	48.3	7.2	65.6	4.2	8.1	2.0	4.1	6.7
3531-3537 Construction, Mining, & Materials Handling Mach. & Equipment (102)	1.6	3.3	34.4	61.8	42.3	14.6	33.9	10.9	36.3	7.4	3.1	7.3	15.0	34.4
	1.1	2.3	53.7	94.3	76.2	30.9	46.3	6.8	51.6	5.1	4.9	5.5	10.6	19.8
	0.6	1.6	96.7	163.8	121.9	54.0	69.6	4.5	66.7	3.2	8.0	3.8	6.2	13.8
3541-3549 Metalworking Machinery & Equipment (107)	2.3	4.0	18.9	88.8	22.8	28.1	36.1	61.2	39.8	8.4	1.6	12.7	16.2	32.7
	1.3	2.3	43.2	174.3	58.1	57.4	47.4	15.6	56.7	5.6	3.1	6.5	10.7	18.1
	0.9	1.6	84.4	636.4	129.6	75.5	62.4	6.1	71.0	3.8	7.5	3.4	7.1	10.8

—Ratio not computed. Balance sheet items necessary for computation are not normally present in this line of business.
( ) Indicates loss.

annual reports with the SEC.) Our goal was to see if companies with known financials had ratios that matched those given by a book containing ratios for this industry.

Results: Our test group differed considerably from the so-called industry average. For example, our group posted an average of 3.3 for the current ratio. The average ratio presented by the book was 2.1.

The net assets/net worth figure was even worse. The book offered 36.5 percent and our group averaged 60.8 percent.

Next we break out the average ratios given by the financial ratio chart versus the line reading "test results:"

	Quick Ratio	Current Ratio	Net Assets/ Net Worth (%)	Return on Equity (%)
Textbook average	1.0	2.1	36.5	17.4
Test group average	1.8	3.3	60.8	10.0
(Ratios for test group companies listed immediately below)				
Standard Register	2.4	3.3	53.1	15.1
Analog Devices	1.8	4.3	106.0	6.5
Digital Equipment	2.3	4.2	30.0	13.0
Technitrol	2.1	3.5	23.6	11.0
Safeguard Scientific	1.6	2.3	63.0	1.0
Lundy Electronics	1.7	3.3	57.0	8.4
National Semiconductor	0.8	1.8	93.0	15.7

The Ratio Rule

Test the ratios you want to use before you apply them! If you can, conduct a test similar to the one described above. Find a group of companies that seems similar in size and industry grouping to your target company and run their financials against the ratios. If the results are close, then you know you most likely have a set of usable ratios. If not, find a new table of ratios or do not use this technique. (Many times your target company is so unique that it will not fit into any industry grouping.)

WAR STORY 11

Ballparking a Number

Our researchers have frequently encountered this situation: We are given an assignment to estimate a company's income statement. All we have to start out with is the company's credit report and a few press clippings.

In one case the company happened to have been a manufacturer of small household hardware supplies. The credit report gave an overall sales figure of $25 million. The credit report did not, however, offer any other financial information.

The researcher identified a set of financial ratios that the company would fit into. She plugged the $25-million-dollar figure into the sales related ratios, and derived such items as assets, expenses, and so on. Yet the researcher could not rely on an extrapolated set of numbers—all of which were based on one speculative sales figure.

By speaking to a plant manager at a competing firm, she discovered that her long-term assets figure was too high, and lowered it accordingly. When she interviewed the public utilities, she received more accurate numbers for the company's power consumption. By speaking to a local union, she found out that the salary figure should be raised (the figure she derived from the ratios was more representative of a nonunion shop).

At the end of the battery of interviews, the researcher was able to assemble a fairly accurate financial picture of the company. But to do this she used the financial ratios as a springboard for discussion, as a way to prompt the experts to offer their best guesses on the corporation's income and expenses.

Where to Find Your Ratios

Speak to the trade association that represents your target company's industry. Go to your local banker. He or she will have textbooks that contain hundreds of industry ratios. The section "Sources of Business Ratios," later in this chapter, lists some of the more basic sources.

FINDING FINANCIALS: GO TO THE EXPERTS

In the previous section we explained the pros and cons of financial ratios. As you were reading through it, you might have caught yourself saying, "He talks about plugging two or three values into the ratios and coming out with a financial statement. But what I need to know is, how did he come up with those two or three numbers in the first place?"

A good question. We have already mentioned, in earlier chapters, that you can get some financial data from various publications and financial filings. Another source of company financials are the experts, and they are many. These experts are not necessarily accountants or nuclear physicists. They are individuals who are close to the company or the community in which the company is located.

For now, though, let's just take an ordinary income statement and examine the line items within it. What we have done is take each line item and ask ourselves: Who would be the best source for this kind of information? Who would know, for example, about a company's labor costs? Based on our experience, we then listed the most likely sources as found below in the right-hand column.

Statement Categories	Likely Sources
Sales	Commercial credit agencies
	Competitor's sales force
	Independent representatives
	Distributors
	Competitors
Cost of goods sold	Product stripdown engineers
Raw materials	(e.g. Underwriters Laboratories)
	Department of Commerce
	Suppliers, distributors
Direct labor	Bureau of Labor Statistics
Indirect labor	Industry directories
	Union
	State filings
Supplies	Banks
	Local suppliers
	Industry studies
	Industry directories
Heat, light, and power	State power commission
	Utilities

Statement Categories	Likely Sources
Repairs	Industry analysts
	Unions
	Competitors, regional
Property taxes	Commercial realtors
	Assessor
	Town records
Maintenance	Unions
	Trade associations
	Competitors
	Contractors
Insurance	Local insurers
	State rate commissions
Rent	Commercial realtors
	Assessor
Loans	Banks
R&D	Trade reporters
	Trade associations
	Directors of R&D
Advertising	Advertisers
	Advertising account executives
	Advertising dept. of newspapers

Modifying the Ratios Through Interviews

No ratio will be the perfect equation of a target company's balance sheet or income statement. You will need to adjust the numbers you arrive at.

Interviewing the experts will tell you if your numbers are way out of line or right on the money. Interviewing is an excellent means of adjusting the inventory numbers you may have derived (although, in the same industry, one company's inventory may be totally different from its competitor's).

TABLE 11.2   Steps in Uncovering Financial Data Using Ratios

	Step 1	Step 2	Step 3	Step 4
	known data	industry ratios	financial data derived through ratios	final result data adjusted based on interviews
Current assets	$100,000			$100,000
Current ratio		2:1		5:3
Current liabilities	—		$50,000	$60,000

Table 11.2 carries the Murf and Turf example from earlier in the chapter through to adjusted ratios.

SOURCES OF BUSINESS RATIOS

The following pamphlets and books list financial and operating ratios for a wide variety of industries, both service and manufacturing. In certain instances, industry trade associations compiled the statistics; in other cases, the data may have been gleaned from banks, government agencies, or credit services.

A tip—When you are looking for ratios on a particular industry that you don't spot in the list below, or in the Robert Morris Associates bibliography cited, just call the major trade association for that industry. Chances are that they have already compiled and collected financial data from member companies. Although the financials themselves might be proprietary, the ratios derived from those figures are available to the public.

General (including manufacturing)

Key Business Ratios in 800 Lines.   Dun & Bradstreet.

Cost of Doing Business—Corporations.   Dun & Bradstreet.

Annual Statement Studies.   Robert Morris Associates.

Department stores

Financial and Operating Results of Department and Specialty Stores.   National Retail Merchants Association.

Discount stores

Discount Merchandisers/Discount Industry. Annual, May issue, Charter Publishing Company.

Drug stores

The Lilly Digest. Eli Lilly and Company.

Food stores

Operating Results of Food Chains. Cornell University.

Restaurants

Restaurant Industry Operations Report. Laventhol and Horwath.

Banks

Bank Operating Statistics. Federal Deposit Insurance Corporation.

Finance companies

Analysis of Year End Composite Ratios of Installment Sales Finance and Small Loan Companies. Journal of Commercial Bank Lending.

Bibliography

Sources of Composite Financial Data—A Bibliography. Robert Morris Associates.

CHAPTER 12

LET YOUR FINGERS
DO THE STALKING

Using Yellow Pages and City Directories

The Yellow Pages and city directories are two very potent corporate intelligence-gathering tools. Each can reveal a company's neighbors, the size of the market, and background information.

They are very different, yet in many ways very much alike. The following chart will illustrate these similarities and differences.

Features	Yellow Pages	City directory
Cost	$6 to $10 (on average)	$25 to $400
Contents	Company names, addresses, telephone numbers, and advertisements.	Company and individual names, addresses, and telephone numbers, as well as biographical background on business owners and residents.
Indexing	Lists companies by product or service category only. There is no alphabetical or telephone listing.	Lists companies and private residences by street, alphabetically by name, and numerically by owner's telephone number.

Features	Yellow Pages	City directory
Number of volumes	One volume for each metropolitan area. One volume may include many cities. For example, the Greater Boston Yellow Pages contains listings for dozens of towns.	Usually, each city directory contains only one city per directory, and does not include adjacent towns in its listing.
Availability	There is a listing for almost every city in the United States.	City directories are usually published only for the larger cities in the United States. There are thousands of Yellow Pages; there are hundreds of city directories available.

THE YELLOW PAGES

A Yellow Pages directory is probably one of the most effective and least expensive intelligence-gathering tools you can buy for your corporate library. Before a corporate library begins considering any other reference texts, it should make sure it has a selection of Yellow Pages to cover every geographical area in which its company operates.

How can you use this potent intelligence tool?

To locate the number of competitors in a particular market.   By just flipping to the Discount Stores, you can locate all K-Marts or Zayres outlets in that trading area.

To define a realistic trading area.   If you are based on the East Coast and are asked to research a company in the Midwest, how are you to know what a realistic trading area is for that target company? The greater metropolitan Yellow Pages for your target's city will provide a map for that trading area. Figure 12.1 shows an example for the Greater Boston area.

To locate suppliers and distributors.   Let's say you had to locate suppliers for a glass company. You already know that in the glass industry certain suppliers are situated near the manufacturing plant. These suppliers may include sand, coal, and scrap. Here again, the Yellow Pages will provide you with a comprehensive list of these suppliers—some of whom most likely deal with the target company.

WAR STORY 12

Meating Your Match

A client had once given us the assignment of uncovering a competitor's customer base and expansion plans. The target company was in the meat-packing industry. We pulled out the Yellow Pages for the target's metropolitan area and turned to the Meat Packing section, where we located over a dozen competitors. We then started calling each company on the list.

The owner of the sixth company we called said he was a former employee of the target company and broke away to start a packing operation of his own.

He was more than happy to tell us who the target's customers were, and gave us details about a new plant the target had just built to increase chicken production.

To retrieve marketing and product line information.   Take a close look at your typical Yellow Pages display advertisement. It is a highly informative document, almost resembling a miniature D & B credit report. It may list, aside from the company's name and address, its product line, the year it was established, and the marketing message and image it wishes to project to its customers.

To determine industry size.   Just run your finger down the column for any one category and you will have a good idea of industry size (that is, the number of companies and competitors in the market).

To understand industry terminology and check your search.   Whenever you begin searching an industry for competitors, suppliers, or any related companies, you want to make sure you have not left out any categories. Unknown to many users, most Yellow Pages now have a fairly thorough cross-index in the back of each volume. This insures that you do not overlook a crucial category or industry heading.

For example, you may want a complete list of department stores in the area, so you look under the category of Department Stores in the Yellow Pages. But once you check the index in the back of the YP, you discover that you should also be looking under Discount Stores to make your list truly complete.

These classifications can be sorted by geographical area, Standard Industrial Classification (SIC), company size, and a number of other ways.

While not recommended as a complete substitute for the paper edition, the Electronic Yellow Pages is an excellent supplement to your regularly used Yellow Pages collection.

WHEN YOU USE YOUR YELLOW PAGES, IT'S A SNAP!

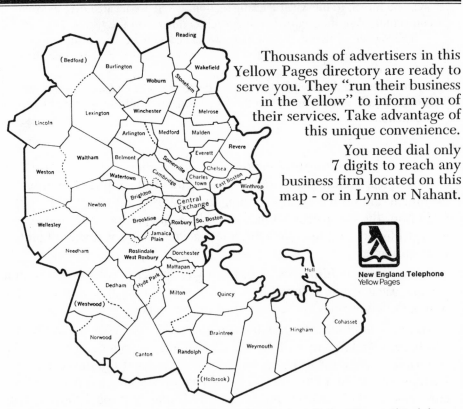

Thousands of advertisers in this Yellow Pages directory are ready to serve you. They "run their business in the Yellow" to inform you of their services. Take advantage of this unique convenience.

You need dial only 7 digits to reach any business firm located on this map - or in Lynn or Nahant.

New England Telephone
Yellow Pages

Figure 12.1. Map of area covered by Greater Boston Area Yellow Pages. This defines an actual—not artificial—trading area.

How to Order the Yellow Pages

Open your local Yellow Pages, and there on the first few pages will be the address and phone number of your local telephone business office. Call to find out the specific order requirements. You may discover, for instance, that if your toll calls to the metropolitan area you are interested in exceed a certain dollar volume, you may be able to receive that Yellow Pages edition at no charge. Otherwise, each edition may cost you about $7.

The Difference Between the Business-to-Business and Consumer Yellow Pages

The Business-to-Business Yellow Pages may cover a larger trading area— 50 miles instead of 35 miles, for instance. But it will also eliminate any of the consumer listings, such as retail stores or dry cleaners. Conversely, the Consumer Yellow Pages will eliminate strictly industrial categories. Your best bet, if your area still prints it, is the general metropolitan area Yellow Pages, which includes both the Consumer and the Business-to Business editions. The general metropolitan Yellow Pages is becoming a rare commodity as the various telephone companies begin to further divide their market segments, catering to each group with a specialized edition.

Yellow Pages in Other Forms

Electronic Yellow Pages.   One enterprising company saw the need for a national Yellow Pages in electronic form. Market Data Retrieval assembled the first edition of its Electronic Yellow Pages in 1982, and has been constantly adding new classifications ever since.

Yellow Pages on Microfiche.   The Bell & Howell corporation has placed over 1500 White and Yellow Pages directories on microfiche. If you become a serious Yellow Pages user, you will soon discover that these tomes take up a lot of space. In such cases a few little plastic sheets become far more palatable than paper Yellow Pages, which occupy a great deal of square footage. Bell & Howell also produces microfiche for European and Canadian directories. For price and availability of the fiche, contact Bell & Howell at 800–321–9881.

SLEUTHING YOUR COMPETITION WITH CITY DIRECTORIES

Woodward and Bernstein used a city directory (also known as a criss-cross directory) to help crack the Watergate case. Detectives and just plain savvy researchers have employed these invaluable reference tools for a variety of reasons.

The telephone book listed the private security consulting agency run by McCord. There was no answer. They checked the local "criss-cross" directories which list phone numbers by street addresses. There was no answer at either McCord's home or his business. The address of McCord Associates, 414 Hungerford Drive, Rockville, Maryland, is a large office building, and the cross-reference directory for Rockville lists the tenants. The reporters divided the names and began calling them at home. One attorney recalled that a teenage girl who had worked part-time for him the previous summer knew McCord, or perhaps it was the girl's father who knew him. The attorney could only remember the girl's last name—Westall or something like that. They contacted five persons with similar last names before Woodward finally reached Harlan A. Westrell, who said he knew McCord. (Carl Bernstein and Bob Woodward, *All the President's Men*, Warner Books, 1975, p. 21).

Although not as current as a Yellow Pages might be, city directories can do things Yellow Pages were never designed for. For instance, let's say you wanted to find out about a company and needed to interview some neighboring companies or residents within blocks of the establishment. The city directory will have a section that lists the neighboring buildings and their occupants, street by street.

Should you need to track down a company by its telephone number, most city directories list a town's residents by their phone numbers.

Information Data Search has found that a city directory can quickly give a researcher an idea of a town's layout and the target company's location. In other words, is the target in a commercial or a residential section of town? Who are some of the target company's neighbors? Is there a stationery store nearby that may deal with the target company and its employees on a daily basis? Those in and around the target company may very well be able to tell the researcher if, for example, the target has begun hiring more employees, or laying them off.

One caveat with regard to city directories: They tend to be somewhat dated. Many times you will find phone numbers and addresses have been changed. But for the most part, when dealing with corporations you find that addresses and phone numbers do not change quite so fast. And even directories that are years old still have a good deal of usable information.

City directories vary widely in price, based on the size of the city or town and the individual publisher. They may cost as little as $25 or as much as $400. Write the publisher for the price and ordering information.

There are a number of well-known city directory publishers. They cover both large and small cities and towns. Below is a list of some of the more popular publishers, many of whom have been around for decades.

Bresser's Cross-Index Directory
Company
684 West Baltimore Street
Detroit, MI 48202
313–874–0570

City Publishing Company
118 South Eighth Street
Independence, KS 67301
316–331–2650

Cole Publications
901 Bond Street
Lincoln, NE 68521
402–475–4591

Criss-Cross Numerical Directory
P.O. Box 75579
Oklahoma City, OK 73147
405–943–4491

Dickman Directories
6145 Columbus Pike
Delaware, OH 43015
614–548–6130

Haines and Company
8050 Freedom Avenue, NW
North Canton, OH 44720
216–494–9111

Hill-Donnelly Corporation
2602 South MacGill Avenue
P.O. Box 14417
Tampa, FL 33690

Marc Publishing Company
707 Bethlehem Pike
Philadelphia, PA 19118
215–836–4147

Metropolitan Cross-Reference
Directory
2 Ripley Avenue
Toronto, M6S 3N9
Ontario, Canada
416–763–5515

National Telephone Directory
Corporation
1050 Galloping Hill Road
Union, NJ 07083
201–687–7880

R. L. Polk & Company
2001 Elm Hill Pike
P.O. Box 1340
Nashville, TN 37202
615–889–3350

Stewart Directories
304 West Chesapeake Avenue
Baltimore, MD 21204
301–823–4780

Woodard Directory Company
8609 Cheltenham Court
Louisville, KY 40222
502–425–1054

Data You Can Extract from the Directories Themselves

Even before you venture outside the directory, the book itself contains a wealth of data about your target. In certain instances you will find a company's officers as well as corporate size indicated in the book.

To give you a better idea of what information is covered and how this information differs from section to section, a sample of a typical directory's contents follows:

ALPHABETICAL DIRECTORY
WHITE PAGES

(h) HOUSEHOLDER   (r) RESIDENT OR ROOMER

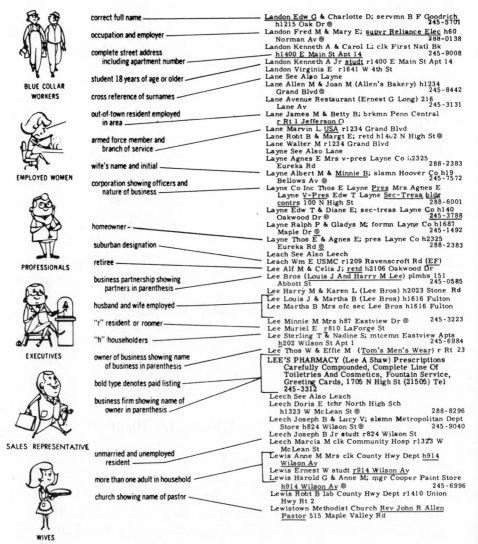

correct full name —— Landon Edw G & Charlotte D; servmn B F Goodrich
h1215 Oak Dr ⊚   245-5701

occupation and employer —— Landon Fred M & Mary E; supvr Reliance Elec h60
Norman Av ⊚   288-0138

complete street address
including apartment number —— Landon Kenneth A & Carol L; clk First Natl Bk
h1400 E Main St Apt 14   245-9008

Landon Kenneth A Jr studt r1400 E Main St Apt 14
Landon Virginia E r1641 W 4th St

student 18 years of age or older —— Lane See Also Layne

cross reference of surnames —— Lane Allen M & Joan M (Allen's Bakery) h1234
Grand Blvd ⊚   245-8442

Lane Avenue Restaurant (Ernest G Long) 216
Lane Av   245-3131

out-of-town resident employed
in area —— Lane James M & Betty B; brkmn Penn Central
r Rt 1 Jefferson ◯

Lane Marvin L USA r1234 Grand Blvd
armed force member and
branch of service —— Lane Robt B & Margt E; retd h14ʋ2 N High St ⊚
Lane Walter M r1234 Grand Blvd

Lane See Also Lane

wife's name and initial —— Layne Agnes E Mrs v-pres Layne Co h2325
Eureka Rd   288-2383

Layne Albert M & Minnie B; slsmn Hoover Co h19
Bellows Av ⊚   245-7572

corporation showing officers and
nature of business —— Layne Co Inc Thos E Layne Pres Mrs Agnes E
Layne V-Pres Edw T Layne Sec-Treas bldg
contrs 100 N High St   288-6001

Layne Edw T & Diane E; sec-treas Layne Co h140
Oakwood Dr ⊚   245-3788

homeowner —— Layne Ralph P & Gladys M; formn Layne Co h1687
Maple Dr ⊚   245-1492

suburban designation —— Layne Thos E & Agnes E; pres Layne Co h2325
Eureka Rd ⊚   288-2383

Leach See Also Leech

retiree —— Leach Wm E USMC r1209 Ravenscroft Rd (EF)

Lee Alf M & Celia J; retd h2106 Oakwood Dr

business partnership showing
partners in parenthesis —— Lee Bros (Louis J And Harry M Lee) plmbs 151
Abbott St   245-0585

Lee Harry M & Karen L (Lee Bros) h2023 Stone Rd

husband and wife employed —— Lee Louis J & Martha B (Lee Bros) h1616 Fulton
Lee Martha B Mrs ofc sec Lee Bros h1616 Fulton

"r" resident or roomer —— Lee Minnie M Mrs h87 Eastview Dr ⊚   245-3223

Lee Muriel E r810 LaForge St

"h" householders —— Lee Sterling T & Nadine S; mtcemn Eastview Apts
h202 Wilson St Apt 1   245-6984

Lee Thos W & Effie M (Tom's Men's Wear) r Rt 23

owner of business showing name
of business in parenthesis —— **LEE'S PHARMACY (Lee A Shaw) Prescriptions
Carefully Compounded, Complete Line Of
Toiletries And Cosmetics, Fountain Service,**
bold type denotes paid listing —— **Greeting Cards, 1705 N High St (21505) Tel
245-3312**

business firm showing name of
owner in parenthesis —— Leech See Also Leach
Leech Doris E tchr North High Sch
h1323 W McLean St ⊚   288-8296

Leech Joseph B & Lucy V; slsmn Metropolitan Dept
Store h824 Wilson St ⊚   245-9040

Leech Joseph B Jr studt r824 Wilson St

Leech Marcia M clk Community Hosp r1323 W
McLean St

unmarried and unemployed
resident —— Lewis Anne M Mrs clk County Hwy Dept h914
Wilson Av

Lewis Ernest W studt r914 Wilson Av

more than one adult in household —— Lewis Harold G & Anne M; mgr Cooper Paint Store
h914 Wilson Av ⊚   245-6996

Lewis Robt B lab County Hwy Dept r1410 Union
Hwy Rt 2

church showing name of pastor —— Lewistown Methodist Church Rev John R Allen
Pastor 515 Maple Valley Rd

Figure 12.2.   Extract from alphabetical section of R. L. Polk City Directory. (Published with permission of R. L. Polk & Co.)

STREET DIRECTORY
GREEN PAGES

◎ HOMEOWNER SYMBOL   ★ NEW NEIGHBOR SYMBOL

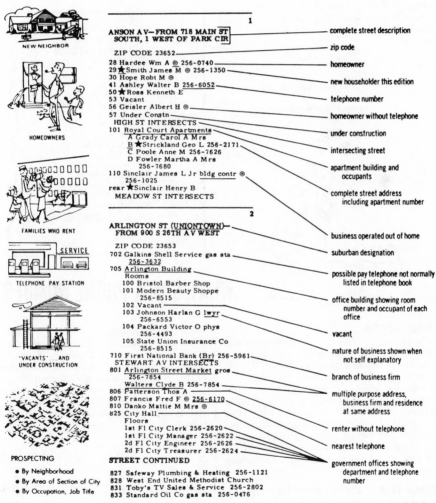

Figure 12.3.   Extract from street directory section of R. L. Polk City Directory. (Published with permission of R. L. Polk & Co.)

NUMERICAL TELEPHONE DIRECTORY
BLUE PAGES

This Directory takes the "mystery" out of blind numbers. It lists telephone numbers in numercial sequence, making it easy to "decode" blind phone numbers in classified ads—especially valuable for real estate agencies, used car dealers, etc.

dial code

numbers in sequence

name of telephone subscriber

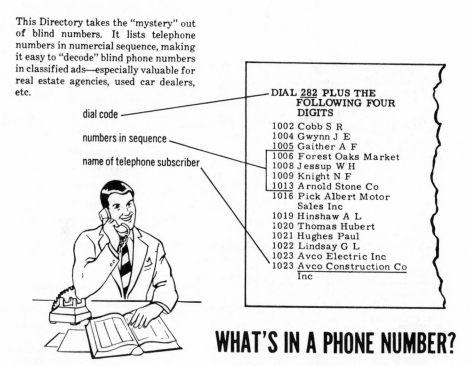

DIAL 282 PLUS THE FOLLOWING FOUR DIGITS

1002 Cobb S R
1004 Gwynn J E
1005 Gaither A F
1006 Forest Oaks Market
1008 Jessup W H
1009 Knight N F
1013 Arnold Stone Co
1016 Pick Albert Motor Sales Inc
1019 Hinshaw A L
1020 Thomas Hubert
1021 Hughes Paul
1022 Lindsay G L
1023 Avco Electric Inc
1023 Avco Construction Co Inc

WHAT'S IN A PHONE NUMBER?

ABOUT THE FIRM:
Who called me? When your call back message gives a telephone number only—or includes a common surname such as Jones, Smith, Brown, etc.—this Numerical Telephone Directory will assist in determining correct firm name. Make use of both Alphabetical and Street Guide information to establish names of officers, owners or partners, products and services, and correct address. Properly identify firm and caller and have needed records, file or correspondence on hand before returning call.

ABOUT THE INDIVIDUAL:
Who called me? When only a telephone number is known, this Numerical Telephone Directory will assist in determining the name of the subscriber—with this information combined with other sections of your City Directory you may quickly establish such information as wife's name, place of employment, job title, home address, business address and telephone number.

Figure 12.4. Extract from Reverse Telephone Section of R. L. Polk City Directory (Boston). (Published with permission of R. L. Polk & Co.)

352

1. The alphabetical section will typically contain in each listing the occupant's name and address, his or her occupation, age, surname cross-reference, spouse's name, corporation's officers, corporation's products, distinction between corporation and partnership, and business owner's name. An example is given in Figure 12.2.

2. Aside from name and address, the street listing section lists everything you will find in the alphabetical section, but this time offers the information on a street-by-street basis.

3. The telephone section lists a town's occupants by their telephone numbers. No other information is contained about the occupants. For more details, you will have to turn to the alphabetical section in the front of the book. A telephone section example is shown in Figure 12.4.

CHAPTER 13

EYEBALLING YOUR COMPETITOR

How to Use Visual Sightings

Remember those cowboy and Indian films of the 1940s and 1950s? Remember how many times those films would depict an old Indian brave giving sagacious advice to a young buck that would go something like this: "Do not worry, my son, the answer can be found in the clouds in the sky, the leaves on the trees. Do not worry, we will triumph. The answer is in the clouds, my son."

Translated into modern industry terms, visual sightings can provide the astute researcher with a new tool for monitoring a competitor's activities.

A visual sighting means researching your competitor by counting the number of parking spaces or noting the size and shape of a plant. These simple observations can tell you if a company has been hiring more workers lately, or laying some off; it may hint at the type of machinery that you can find inside, thereby revealing some element of the production process.

You do not use a visual sighting alone to estimate a competitor's strengths or weaknesses. This technique or creative source should be used in conjunction with intelligence you may have gleaned from a variety of other sources. After all, eyeballing a competitor can only give you a superficial reading, not a firm conclusion.

WAR STORY 13

That Sinking Feeling

Oil and gas companies regularly use visual sightings to confirm information they may have received about a competitor. One senior executive told me that when he was in his early 20s and new on the job, every so often his boss would send him out to a competitor's drilling rig. There he would stand outside a chain-link fence and look in on the competitor's drilling operations.

As he recounted the story, he said that with the aid of a pair of binoculars, he counted each pipe link that would be sunk into the shaft. Since he already knew the length of each piece of pipe and link that went into the shaft, he simply multiplied the number of links times the length of each and derived the depth of the well. In the oil and gas business, the depth of a well in part determines how much that oil and gas cost to produce.

In other words, this single sighting yielded a competitor's cost of production.

The petroleum industry is not the only industry where visual sightings prove a useful research tool. An astute researcher can learn a good deal by looking at a manufacturing or nonmanufacturing facility.

A number of highly competitive industries will use visual sightings on a regular basis to assess competitors. Often, these industries may find a visual sighting one of the few intelligence sources they can use.

There are many ways of using a visual sighting to gather competitor intelligence. Here are a few more examples.

Plant watching. A high-powered management consulting firm has been known to hire business school students to simply stand outside a plant with binoculars and a hand counter. A count is taken of all the people exiting and entering the plant throughout the week, day and night. By the end of the week, a tally can be made of the total number of employees per shift.

Space assessment. Count the number of parking spaces to roughly estimate the number of employees in a plant. You can be pretty sure that if there are only 30 spaces outside a property, the competitor cannot claim 300 employees at that site.

Employee/square footage ratios used by city planners or construction firms can assist in computing the actual number of employees. These ratios will tell you, for example, on the average how many passengers ride in a car in an urban versus suburban area; or they can be used to assess how many employees there are if a plant or office covers a certain number of square feet.

Truck shipments. By spotting the trucks that come and go, you can learn the number and size of shipments entering and leaving a company. How is this the case? Chances are the competitor does not own its own truck fleet and probably leases trucks. By identifying the trucking company, you can then call its traffic department to find out some shipping details, such as how much is loaded into a typical truck or how frequently pickups or deliveries are made.

BOX CAR INTELLIGENCE

Next time you need to check a competitor's plant shipments, take a closer look at the loading docks. Appearances may be deceiving.

A marketing executive told Information Data Search that he determined one company's ruse by examining its box cars. Whenever he drove past the plant, he jotted down the identifying numbers painted on the box cars' sides (each car has a unique set of numbers).

Over time he realized that he was recording the same numbers, and concluded that it had been months since a new car had slid up to the loading dock. In effect, the cars were a front, positioned to mislead the casual observer into believing that this plant constantly had new box car arrivals and departures.

Remember—Look carefully at box cars before making plant shipment assumptions. Those identifying numbers may contain revealing information!

PLANT AND SITE INSPECTION CHECKLIST

Any time a company adds on to its existing plant by building new shipping docks, adding warehouse space, painting additional lines in the parking lot, or bringing in a new electrical transmission line, it is telling the outside world something about its internal activities.

You can observe these changes either from the ground or from the air (aerial photographs are discussed later in the chapter). The checklist in Table 13.1 examines the three basic visual sighting points that you would want to focus on when observing an industrial plant, scanning for bits and pieces of corporate intelligence. These three major observation points are plot, building, and transportation.

This list should teach you that there is a definite relationship among these three units and the company's operations. In some cases, you as the

TABLE 13.1. Checklist for Plant and Site Inspection

Site characteristic	Discovery
Plot	
Number of buildings	If separate buildings, the process is likely to be noisy or dirty
	Separate buildings may imply that certain buildings are not part of production process
Building coverage (percent to acreage)*	Warehouses are often greater than 50 percent of plot
	Offices or light manufacturing account for approximately 30 percent of the total site acreage
Level of maintenance	Appearance of surrounding grounds is indicative of plant maintenance
Utilities	Types of power lines
	Water and energy usage
Zoning regulations	Where there is more compliance with city codes, buildings are usually more adaptable
Buildings	
Shape	Adaptable design, frequent changes in product design, improvements in process, rearranging of layout
Number of stories	If single story, product likely to be large, heavy, relatively inexpensive
	Fewer stories usually more adaptable
Height	Taller building implies taller product and equipment
Number of loading facilities	More loading facilities result in higher adaptability
Level of maintenance	Better maintained outside means better maintained inside
	Better maintained, potentially lower costs, higher productivity
Number of employees/ square foot of plant	Fewer employees/square foot implies more capital-intensive plant (except warehouses)
Transportation	
Number of parking spaces, cars	More parking spaces mean more employees. Relationship depends on where the plant is located (near public transportation, residential area, etc.)

TABLE 13.1. *(Continued)*

Site characteristic	Discovery
Where parking is located	One side of building used means high employee density
Entrances for trucks	If separate from employee entrances, implies stricter security
Rail facilities	If available and in use, implies heavy products, certain commodities (coal, etc.)
	Grade and turning radius are determined by weight of freight
Access to highway	Easier access, higher shipping volume

*These assumptions apply mainly to suburban or rural industrial parks, not to city office space or factories.

intelligence-gatherer may not fully understand the meaning of your sighting discoveries. The discoveries may be too technical. Yet you would be surprised that once you bring the data to your company's engineers, they will be able to translate these seemingly meaningless observations into important pieces of competitor intelligence. Frequently the building's height or the appearance of a silo may tip off an engineer to a new production process or change.

This checklist breaks down each of the three major plant characteristics (plot, building, transportation) into each of its parts. When analyzing a plot, for example, you would look at the number of buildings on the site, the total amount of land that the building or buildings occupy on that plot, the maintenance level, the type of utilities, and how the building and land are zoned by the town.

The list includes observations or discoveries about each site characteristic. Some of these discoveries may sound very common-sensical—and they are. Nevertheless, each discovery, no matter how simple, may lead to a vital piece of information. The number of stories in a plant, for instance, may tell the observer something about the type of machinery used in the plant (e.g., light rather than heavy). The number of cars parked can tell you about the number of employees at the facility.

Two charts are also given to show the relationship of various characteristics to plant function. Table 13.2 shows the relationship between the height of a ceiling and the equipment height. Table 13.3 indicates that there is a very direct relationship between the number of cars parked and the number

TABLE 13.2.   Generally Recommended Ceiling Heights

Type of Production	Without Overhead Installations*	With Overhead Installations+
Small-product assembly on benches, offices	9–14 feet	10–18 feet
Large-product assembly on floor or floor fixtures	Maximum height of product + 75%	Maximum height of product + 125%
Small-product forming	Height of machinery + 100%	Height of machinery + 150%
Large-product forming	Height of machinery + 125%	Height of machinery + 125%

*Other than lighting and sprinkler.

+Air ducts, units heaters, conveyors, etc.

Source: Joseph DeChiara and John Hancock Callender, *Time-Saver Standards for Building Types*, 2nd ed. (New York: McGraw-Hill, 1980), p. 1022. Reprinted with permission.

of employees (the chart also shows how this ratio changes when you go from an urban to a suburban setting).

DETERMINING AN INDUSTRY'S DENSITY

We are not talking about an industry's IQ level, but rather about the employee density (or number of employees per acre) that each industry ex-

TABLE 13.3.   Hypothetical Relationship of Parking Area Requirements to Location

Location	Number of Employees at Peak Shift Overlap	Percent as Drivers or Passengers	Number of Autos To Be Parked*	Approximate Site (square feet)	Area (acres)
Urban	1600	60	740	222	5.0
Suburban	1600	80	990	297	6.8
Rural	1600	95	1180	354	8.0

*Assuming car occupancy of 1.3 persons per car.

Source: Institute of Traffic Engineers, *Parking Facilities for Industrial Plants* (1969). Reproduced with permission of the Institute of Transportation Engineers, 525 School Street, SW, Suite 410, Washington, D.C. 20024.

periences. A Department of Commerce study done in the early 1960s compared acreage and plant size to the number of employees in a plant (Table 13.4). You can draw similar—but telling—observations from some of the figures listed. An electrical switch manufacturer has only six employees per acre, while a brassiere manufacturer has 147 per acre. These figures might imply that the smaller the product and the less automated the production process, the denser the employee count. Where the process is highly automated, there are far fewer employees per acre.

TABLE 13.4.   Characteristics of Modern Industrial Plants

Plant Product	Site (acres)	Plant Size (square feet)	Land/Building Ratio		Employees per acre	Square Feet of Building per Employee
Consumer tape recorders	13	92,000	5	to 1	30	239
Beer	152	347,000	26	to 1	2	1280
Brassieres	1	35,000	0.2	to 1	417	87
Carpet sweepers	42	200,000	9	to 1	11	444
Corrugated shipping containers	40	76,800	22	to 1	3	925
Instant whipped potatoes	4.6	83,569	1.4	to 1	22	836
Stapling and wire stitching	84	530,000	6	to 1	9	688
Automatic pinsetter machines (bowling)	16	225,080	2	to 1	31	434
Blouses and sportswear	25	133,000	7	to 1	50	106
Relays and stepping switches	77	40,000	83	to 1	7	77
Electrical switches and circuit breakers	97	315,000	12	to 1	6	573
Play guns and rifles	27	300,000	3	to 1	26	428
Mobile homes	37	110,000	14	to 1	6	505
Dictating and recording machines	5	13,500	15	to 1	11	241
Commercial and consumer furniture	25	46,000	1.4	to 1	N/A	N/A

TABLE 13.4. (*Continued*)

Plant Product	Site (acres)	Plant Size (square feet)	Land/Building Ratio		Employees per acre	Square Feet of Building per Employee
Pencils, toys, and stationery products	38	310,000	5	to 1	17	473
Flower and vegetable seeds	25	254,000	3	to 1	11	941
Corrugated shipping containers	1.3	45,000	0.03	to 1	19	2200
Air and hydraulic power cylinders	95	220,000	18	to 1	4	613
Brushes, mops, and brooms	84	360,000	9	to 1	10	419
Passenger tires	160	575,000	8	to 1	2	2798
Flush hollow and solid core doors	5	31,500	6	to 1	8	787
Polyester resins and film	340	89,727	164	to 1	0.26	997
Organic polymers	143	69,000	88	to 1	0.8	680
Electromechanical and electronic components	14	36,000	16	to 1	11	222
Rifle bullets	40	12,880	134	to 1	0.4	805
Papermaker's felts	104	208,000	21	to 1	2	816
Potato flakes and potato slices	47	25,000	81	to 1	2	227
Portland cement	119	110,000	51	to 1	0.8	110
Clocks, watches, and timepieces	30	102,000	12	to 1	16	210
Components for electronic data and business machines	220	72,000	149	to 1	2	160
Flexible packaging wraps and cellophane bags	6	40,000	5	to 1	12	548
Wire products, mattress and furniture springs	13	15,000	36	to 1	2	600
Dissolving wood pulp	70	650,000	4	to 1	7	1340

TABLE 13.4. *(Continued)*

Plant Product	Site (acres)	Plant Size (square feet)	Land/Building Ratio		Employees per acre	Square Feet of Building per Employee
Agricultural research	600	165,000	157	to 1	0.4	734
Envelopes	3.4	75,000	0.9	to 1	40	557
Liquid infant formula	16	80,000	8	to 1	2	3200
Champagne, wine, and brandy	17	125,000	5	to 1	6	1136
Lawn sprinklers and garden hardware	15.5	110,000	5	to 1	19	367
Automotive wheels and exhaust systems	35	85,000	17	to 1	4	680
Zinc diecastings, plastic moldings, and machined castings	20	55,000	22	to 1	4	733
Glass containers for foods, drugs, beverages, and chemicals	85	720,000	5	to 1	9	774
Blown glass specialties	10	44,200	9	to 1	9	502
Plate glass	600	1,165,823	22	to 1	1	1743
Plastic jugs and braziers	13	120,00	7	to 1	11	857
Sea water periclase and basic refractories	404	165,000	106	to 1	0.6	711
Toothpastes and shampoos	69	169,000	17	to 1	4	635
Suntan lotions	2	29,000	1.2	to 1	48	464
Portable typewriters	82	198,734	11	to 1	13	285
Medical and industrial precision instruments	23	137,000	6	to 1	39	152
Bolts, nuts, and screws	78	530,000	6	to 1	10	707

TABLE 13.4. *(Continued)*

Plant Product	Site (acres)	Plant Size (square feet)	Land/Building Ratio		Employees per acre	Square Feet of Building per Employee
Paint, varnish, and lacquer	25	270,000	4	to 1	11	993
Electric motor and welding controls	48	175,000	11	to 1	9	389
Ballbearings	18	33,500	22	to 1	9	209
Pharmaceutical specialties	31	85,000	15	to 1	10	283
Pharmaceuticals	5.5	88,000	3	to 1	36	440
Uranium concentrate, sulfuric acid	260	63,000	179	to 1	0.4	624
Computer components, assemblies, and coils	11	77,000	5	to 1	47	150
Commercial air conditioning and heating products	58	72,000	34	to 1	2	579
Plywood	67	153,000	18	to 1	4	635
Filters and filter separators	16	77,000	8	to 1	12	385
Crossbar switching equipment for communications systems	252	1,600,000	7	to 1	13	488
Locks and hardware	23	142,900	6	to 1	29	212

Source: *Characteristics of 63 Modern Industrial Plants,* U.S. Department of Commerce, Economic Development Administration.

THE PLOT THICKENS: LEARNING THROUGH MAPPING

Somewhere in our deep, dark grade-school past, we all learned to read a map. This fundamental skill can prove to be an extremely valuable asset in identifying patterns in corporate activity.

By mapping a company's sales offices, distribution, or warehousing locations you can uncover or anticipate a company opening or be able to better study its marketing strategy.

Here is an example. Figure 13.1 is a map on which we have marked a company's sales offices that we uncovered through interviews with competitors and suppliers in the industry. Looking closely at the map, can you discover a pattern? Also, do you have questions about this pattern?

This is what we learned:

1. The company has concentrated its sales offices in the Northeast and Southwest.

2. The following states all have two sales offices each: New York, New Jersey, Connecticut, New Hampshire, Vermont, Maine, Rhode Island, Texas, Arizona, Utah, and Colorado.

3. The following states all have one sales office: New Mexico, Oklahoma, Massachusetts, and Pennsylvania.

It appears that the target company wants to establish two sales offices per state. Then why do New Mexico, Oklahoma, Massachusetts, and Pennsylvania have only one sales office each? Is it possible that these states also have two sales offices and that this information just never came through in the interviews conducted?

Yes, that is exactly the case. Upon further investigation, we discovered that New Mexico, Massachusetts, and Pennsylvania all have two sales offices. Oklahoma does only have one.

Mapping can be a creative technique that lets you know visually where gaps exist in your research and in the information you collected.

AERIAL PHOTOGRAPHY: GETTING AN OVERVIEW OF THE COMPETITION

Aerial photography has proven invaluable in military intelligence-gathering. There is no reason why it cannot prove equally useful in industrial intelligence.

The federal government, the military, and local and state governments often conduct photographic surveys of regions in the United States for purposes of mapping terrain or charting how a waterway or highway system has changed over the years.

In rapidly changing states, such as Texas, there is frequent photographic mapping done. Recent computerized filing and indexing of these photographs make it relatively easy to request them.

Because the U.S. Geological Survey has combined the photographic files of many different state, federal, and private groups into one master index, you may actually have a number of different snapshots of a manufacturing

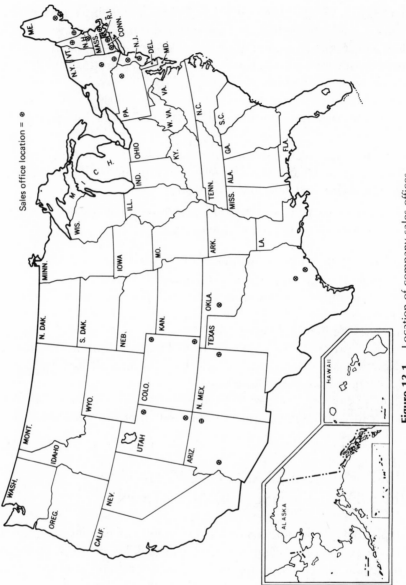

Sales office location = ⊕

Figure 13.1. Location of company sales offices.

366

CHAPTER 14

ADDITIONAL CREATIVE SOURCES THAT WILL PAY OFF

When I talk about creative sources, I mean those sources that may not ordinarily be used for intelligence-gathering but which may very well serve to answer the specific questions you may have on your competitor's activities or plans. A glance at the sources and techniques described here will tell you that their origins are from many sectors, including universities ("R&D: The University Connection"), government ("Locating Foreign Suppliers through the FCC"), and trade groups ("Chambers of Commerce: A Ubiquitous Intelligence-Gatherer").

In addition, I have included a number of techniques and intelligence-gathering tips for specific industries that would only apply to those industries ("A Prescription for Pharmaceutical Research," "A Trusted Banking Source").

R&D: THE UNIVERSITY CONNECTION

Aside from company financials or plant capacity, locating "inside information" about a competitor's research and development activities can be one of the most difficult intelligence tasks. Yet there are ways you, the corporate sleuth, can gain entry into the R&D labyrinth.

The University Liaison Office

Through a liaison office, you can locate the university scientist who may be involved in the R&D work you need to know about. Many high-technology universities, such as the Massachusetts Institute of Technology, have corporate liaison offices. These offices act as go-betweens and coordinators between the university research department and corporate R&D activities.

A liaison office serves an administrative function, making sure that no university researcher falls into a conflict of interest situation. Also, such offices encourage corporations to grant universities funds to carry out R&D research under corporate sponsorship.

Many universities do not have liaison offices. In such instances, you should head straight for the public relations office. It should be able to steer you to the researcher you need to contact.

The Company-University

Often when you spot a major corporation located in a small town, you will likely find a university nearby.

Much like the company town, there are also company-universities. These are educational institutions located in and around major corporations—and in many ways dominated by these corporations. After all, when a company supplies a good portion of the student body and funding to a university, the university develops a dependency and, in many instances, a mutually rewarding relationship.

One way this relationship shows up is through a university's research facilities. Corporations frequently enter into joint ventures with nearby universities.

Many times all you have to do is pull out the Yellow Pages for the town where the company is located and contact the list of universities in that town. Of course, this sleuthing is not always that simple. And in many instances, a company may offer grants to universities quite a distance away from its plant. If you strike out after contacting all of the local institutions, try the next tip.

Tips in Technical Literature

By conducting a simple literature search, you can find most of the experts in a field. These experts in turn can either give you direct information on a particular company's R&D activities, or they can direct you to the people that are involved in other universities or research institutions.

The key to conducting this type of search is to understand that the articles you turn up will probably be severely out-of-date, at least by fast-moving corporate standards. This means you will find articles that are older than six months—often years old.

Your aim is not to examine the articles. In fact, you do not even have to read much farther than the abstracts. Your best bet is to contact the researchers listed in the bibliographic references. These experts—not the articles—will be up to date on the R&D occurring in the corporate world.

There are many technical data bases cited in Chapter 7 that list the scientist, the institution, and the area of expertise. Data bases such as Compendex, Medline, and CA Search are some of the key technical data bases we use to locate experts in a particular field. When we wanted to find an expert in femoral catheters, for instance, all we had to do was enter the Medline (National Library of Medicine) data base. We found an appropriate article's title, the author (or researcher), and the institution he was affiliated with.

Newsletters—Tap into the R&D Pipeline

When the university route fails you, there is still another way to tap into the vast scientific rumor mill that exists. Industry newsletters cater to research scientists and venture capitalists. Some are nothing more than high-tech gossip sheets; others are detailed scientific journals.

Calling the editors of a newsletter that represents your R&D area can provide you with numerous industry contacts that may eventually lead you to your target company.

Note, however, that editors protect their contacts and are not likely to give out names wholesale. If you want a name, you will have to offer something in return. You should expect to offer the editor a new piece of industry gossip or a new name to contact. Remember, acquiring a piece of intelligence is just like any business transaction—you must give something to receive something.

There are an endless number of R&D newsletters. A list of some popular ones in a variety of fields follows.

Bioengineering News
Box 290
Willits, CA 95490
415–777–4572

Genetic Engineering Letter
Environews
1097 National Press Building
Washington, DC 20045
202–347–3868

Biotech Scanner
International Techniquest
P.O. Box 10006
Minneapolis, MN 55440

McGraw-Hill's Biotechnology
Newswatch
McGraw-Hill Publications
1221 Avenue of the Americas
New York, NY 10020
212–997–4343

Fiber Optics Weekly News Service
Information Gatekeepers
167 Corey Road, No. 111
Brookline, MA 02146
617–239–2022

New From Japan
Prestwick Publications
19 Airport Road
Scotia, NY 12302
518–399;–6985

Other R&D Sources

Other than the above, there are a number of directories and publications that regularly list leading research centers and research contracts (government, nonprofit, and corporate). Some of the leading sources are:

Industrial Research Laboratories of the United States (R. R. Bowker). A directory of industrial and corporate R&D facilities. The listings cover an estimated 10,000 facilities and present information on the personnel and the specialties of each facility.

Research Centers Directory (Gale Research Company). A well-indexed directory, listing university and nonprofit research institutions throughout the United States.

Research and Development Contracts Monthly (Government Data Publications). A federal government magazine that lists the latest contracts and who the awardees are. The announcements also appear in an annual directory published by the same department.

TELEXING FOR INTELLIGENCE

Many countries have established foreign trade offices that will supply traders with company information on a per-inquiry basis. Some foreign trade offices have extensive files or data bases on manufacturing plants within their borders, to the point where they can supply you with plant capacity, sales, and number of employees.

If you do not know where to telex for this information, you should contact one of the following two sources, which will steer you to the right office.

WAR STORY 14

Plant Capacity by Telex

For one assignment, we had to find the plant capacity, address, and number of employees in a Taiwanese company's manufacturing plant. This company was a sole-source supplier to our client's competitor. If we could determine the capacity, we could better gauge the competitor's potential. We sent a telex to the number given to us by the Taiwanese Consulate. The following is a disguised version of the report, as we received it over the telex. The entire telex cost $13; the inquiry itself was free.

Far East, Inc.
124 Main Street
Taiwan

Number of employees: 52
Product line: Electronic burglar alarms
Capacity: 10,000 units per month

President: Mr. Yamoto

International Division
United States Chamber of Commerce
1615 H Street, NW
Washington, DC 20062
202–659–6111

They maintain lists of foreign trade missions and chambers of commerce.

Foreign consulates based in the United States are the second source. See the list of consulates in Chapter 8. When calling the consulate or embassy, ask for the information officer. If the consulate does not have the information or contact names, it can tell you where to call, write, or telex.

UNIFORM COMMERCIAL CODES

Ever wonder how some service company discovered that you just bought a photocopier or a new computer and would like to sell you parts or supplies for the new equipment?

If you took out a commercial loan to purchase the equipment, most banks

---

WAR STORY 15

Wood It Not Be for the UCC

When researching a wood stove manufacturer, the researcher was trying to locate one of the manufacturer's equipment suppliers. Sure enough, listed at the bottom of a Dun & Bradstreet credit report was a list of UCC filings. One of these UCC listings indicated that the wood stove company had purchased a furnace for the plant.

When we called the furnace supplier, he indicated that his was the major piece of casting equipment in the plant. He was able to offer us capacity and production information specifically relating to that one wood stove manufacturer.

---

would file a Uniform Commercial Code (UCC) form that states what it is you bought and often for how much. The bank is then required to file a copy of the form with the secretary of state's office in the state capital.

All a researcher need do to discover what company took out a loan for which piece of equipment is to go down to the state house office and review the latest UCC filings.

UCCs are a prime source of reviewing a company's latest addition to plant assets. This is the source used by Dun & Bradstreet, as well as by other credit and investigative agencies, to help uncover plant assets.

The form itself may vary from state to state. To find out how a particular state files its UCCs, write or call the UCC Filings Office for the state in question.

The UCC may appear in a number of forms, which record the type of loan and its limitations. These forms are:

Original financing statement.

Continuation of original financing statement.

Amendment to financing statement.

Partial release of collateral.

Assignment of financing statement.

Subordination.

A sample of one type of UCC form (used in the Commonwealth of Massachusetts) is reproduced in Figure 14.1.

For quick retrieval of UCC filings on annual state corporate forms, I recommend you call the UCC Network. This company can provide a UCC

Uniform Commercial Code — FINANCING STATEMENT — Form UCC-1

IMPORTANT — Read instructions on back before filling out form

This FINANCING STATEMENT is presented to a filing officer for filing pursuant to the Uniform Commercial Code.

4. ☐ Filed for record in the real estate records.	5. ☐ Debtor is a Transmitting Utility.	6. No. of Additional Sheets Presented:
1. Debtor(s) (Last Name First) and address(es)	2. Secured Party(ies) and address(es)	3. For Filing Officer (Date, Time, Number, and Filing Office)
The Company, Inc. 50 Main Street Cambridge, MA 02138	First Bank 150 Broadway Boston, MA 02110	

7. This financing statement covers the following types (or items) of property:

Ten (10) high-speed video display terminals, one (1) Central Processing Unit, Data General 100 with 512 KB memory, two (2) high -speed controllers, two (2) hard disk drives, one (1) high-speed laser printer, one (1) data base management package of software.

Purchase# A1325d   Purchase Date 10/8/84

Filed With Boston City Clerk

☒ Products of Collateral are also covered.

Whichever is Applicable (See Instruction Number 9)	The Company, Inc. By: /s/ John Smith, Partner Signature(s) of Debtor (Or Assignor)	First Bank By: /s/ Officer, Asst.VP Signature(s) of Secured Party (Or Assignee)

Filing Officer Copy — Alphabetical
STANDARD FORM — UNIFORM COMMERCIAL CODE — FORM UCC-1   Rev. Jan. 1980   *Forms may be purchased from Hobbs & Warren, Inc., Boston, Mass. 02101*

Figure 14.1. Uniform Commercial Code form (for Massachusetts).

from any state in a matter of days. The service is quick and inexpensive. The phone number in Sacramento, California is (916) 929–4311.

INDUSTRIAL DEVELOPMENT: THE BOND THAT EYES

More often than not, government filings are next to useless for finding timely and detailed competitor information. One of the few exceptions is the industrial development bond.

Anytime a company requires government funding to finance its operations, it immediately opens itself up to scrutiny. Once the company decides it wants state funding, it must file forms with the state agency that administers the funding, usually the state development authority located in the state's capitol. In contrast to the ordinarily skimpy commercial credit reports, the financial information revealed in a state funding application can be most enlightening.

In a recent case, Information Data Search was asked to trace a rumor in the furniture industry. The rumor concerned a small company buying out the product line of a much larger concern—a company ten times its size. The question before us: How could a David-like company manage to swing the deal, buying out a Goliath of a plant? One way might be through state financing.

Information Data Search had contacted the state capital to find out if the company filed for financial assistance with the state. We found the seven-page document that not only verified the rumor, but also told us the magnitude of the loan and provided background on the smaller, more obscure of the two companies. Among the pieces of intelligence the application supplied were:

Date company was established

Number of employees, by specialty

Listing of owners (with birthdates, titles, and percent ownership)

Lawyer's name

Principal bank

Information on expected construction

Value of plant and equipment

Salary of senior officers

To locate corporate financial assistance applications, follow these steps:

1. Call the state capital.
2. Ask for the Industrial Development Authority.
3. Pose your question to the administrator or librarian. This person will know the file or docket number, and will either send you a copy of the application or tell you where you can find a copy.

TRADE SHOWS: OPEN SEASON ON COMPETITORS

Trade shows are vital sources of competitor information. Ironically, as hard as a competitor will try to mask its marketing strategies during the course

---

WAR STORY 16

The Japanese Snoop and Scoop

The Japanese have long been aggressive in their pursuit of trade show data. Japanese companies will swoop down upon industrial trade shows, cameras in hand. They will then proceed to scoop every piece of literature into their satchels, as well as photograph every booth. Once they return to their offices they then pore over their finds, picking through the material to discover new products and marketing strategies.

---

of a year, it will try just as hard to reveal as much as possible about a new product while attending a trade show.

Trade shows are notorious for talkative salespeople, piles of literature, and lots of real-life products to see, examine, and try out. It is also the best place to gather a quick and fairly accurate idea of the market, its dynamism, growth prospects, and trends.

What Can You Learn from a Trade Show?

An awful lot. Here are a few suggestions and thoughts you may want to keep in mind when visiting your next trade show:

Identify new products.

Determine if your competitor has shifted strategies.

Have there been price point changes?

Has some company emerged as a major influence in the market?

Has an old product suddenly sprouted new product features?

What will a company's upcoming promotional activities look like?

Learn the latest industry rumor.

Identify industry leaders.

Examine a competitor's product line strengths and weaknesses.

Trade Show Directories

You will see from the following list of trade show directories that different publishers track the numbers and types of trade shows differently. This section will not discuss the various advantages or disadvantages of each directory; it simply lists them. Because the criteria for these volumes change often enough, I recommend that you write the publisher directly for details of the directory's contents.

Directory of Expositions Audited by Exposition Audit (Division of Business Publications Audit of Circulation). This text monitors 100 expositions and trade shows in the United States. Each entry covers the show's name, date, and location. Also mentioned are the show's past attendance, number of exhibitors, and the current show's manager.

Directory of United States Trade Shows, Expositions, and Conventions (United States Travel Service, Department of Commerce). Arranged by industry, this text discusses over 500 shows of interest to business abroad. Each entry mentions the show's title, dates, and locations for the coming two years. It will also tell you whom to contact for further information about the show.

Exhibits Schedule: Annual Directory of Trade and Industrial Shows (Bill Communications). Organized by industry, this volume also has cross-indexes that list the shows by date and location. Entries include the show's name, address, name of the show manager, number of booths, dates, locations, expected attendance, and number of times the show is expected to be held over the course of the year.

National Trade Show Exhibitors Association—Exhibit Industry Guide (National Trade Show Exhibitors Association).

Trade Show Fact Book (Sanford Organization). Somewhat more detailed than the other texts in this section, this directory—in addition to giving the show's date, name, location, and manager's name—also describes the products exhibited, their cost, and contract provisions. The book is indexed by date and industry.

Tradeshow/Convention Guide (Budd Publications). A large book, listing over 14,000 conventions and trade shows worldwide. It is indexed alphabetically by location and by event name. Each entry contains the show sponsor or manager, principal executive to contact, dates, attendance figures, number and size of booths, and suppliers.

Trade and Professional Exhibits Directory (Gale Research Company).

Studying a trade show directory is a good first step in competitive market analysis. A typical trade show directory contains information on the market itself as well as details on individual companies. It can reveal the names of hundreds of experts who are not only equipped to talk about the field but more than willing to offer their opinions about the competition—good or bad.

WAR STORY 17

The Directory as a Referral List

We have used the Winter 1983 Las Vegas Consumer Electronics Show Directory countless times. Before the directory, we had searched for valuable names by milking trade articles for expert sources. But some of these experts were no longer in the industry or were not interested in talking.

The names in the directory were mostly salespeople or marketing executives for their respective companies. Almost all were friendly to us and some granted lengthy interviews. In addition, we discovered that this industry—like many— has an active Old Boy network. If an executive whose name we located in the directory could not help us, he or she usually had someone else in mind who could.

Take the recent (Winter 1983) Las Vegas Consumer Electronics Show Directory, for example. It contains the following valuable lists:

Hundreds of consumer electronics companies. Each entry contains the product names, the key executives you would want to interview after the show is over, and the major sales office.

Ten of the industry's key trade associations.

Eighty-six publishers, responsible for over 160 magazines and newsletters. One publisher, *High Fidelity Magazine*, sent over two dozen people to the show to glean industry data and company information.

Over a dozen service firms, including credit and financial services, computer timesharing companies, buying groups. Buying groups, for instance, may know about import trends and manufacturers' costs.

By employing the directory index, one can locate companies by product line. Next, one can turn to the alphabetical listing to find a more detailed listing of each company: its management reps, titles and phone numbers, and which divisions are represented.

BUYER'S GUIDES

Are you looking for a list of purchasing agents in an industry? Or trying to find a group of companies that purchase a certain brand of oil supply equipment? Do you need a comprehensive list of manufacturers of a certain type of electronic component?

Buy a buyer's guide. These guides are compiled with the industrial reader in mind. Let's say you come up short in your initial attempt to locate experts on a company you are investigating. These buyer's guides will offer names of competitors, suppliers, distributors, and so on.

Leafing through a buyer's guide is the next step you should be taking after you have listed your assignment's objectives and retrieved your articles. These buyer's guides may supply you with the first real expert names to call.

When asked to define a buyer's guide, most people think of a trade magazine's special issue that they have seen at one time or another. Listed in the back of the magazine are names of companies that are in some way important to the magazine (advertisers) or to the industry (suppliers, manufacturers, distributors). Almost every trade magazine will have one special issue during the year that serves as a buyer's guide. You can either purchase these buyer's guides separately from the publisher, or as part of a subscription. One recommendation: Many times the buyer's guide will cost as much as the entire magazine's subscription price. Most of the time if you subscribe you will get the buyer's guide for free. So if you feel you will use the magazine extensively in any case, subscribe.

The Granddaddy of Buyer's Guides: Thomas Register

Here you have a 16-volume, hardbound set of books the width of the Encyclopaedia Britannica. It contains lists of companies from literally thousands of industries. Although not as comprehensive as a telephone directory, the Thomas Register is frequently called the bible of buyer's guides.

Not only does it list a vast number of companies, but it also indexes these names by industry group. Another feature is the brand or trade name directory in the book's Yellow Pages. Here you will find a company's brand name listed in alphabetical order—a real time-saver when you have the brand name but do not know which company manufactured the product. Finally, the Register's company advertising and catalog summaries will give the researcher a good idea of that company's product line and marketing strategy. Besides the company name, these display ads will announce the product line and to whom the company wants to pitch its products.

Sweet's Directory is another general buyer's guide, much like the Thomas Register. If you cannot locate a Thomas, then Sweet would be a good substitute.

A directory such as Thomas, or any buyer's guide for that matter, offers an important fringe benefit: it educates the researcher. By using industry nomenclature, these guides quickly make the reader aware of industry jargon and also, by using industry terminology, make very clear which firms are suppliers and which are distributors. When you do not know an industry, one list of companies looks the same as another. A buyer's guide quickly makes the necessary distinctions.

Trade Association Membership Lists: Buyer's Guides of Another Sort

When you cannot find a buyer's guide that represents the industry you are interested in, or the Thomas Register does not fit the bill, then a trade association might have a membership list that will meet your need.

Often these lists are free or are sold at a nominal charge. Sometimes, associations do have restrictions regarding whom they can sell to.

The best source for locating the association that best suits your project requirements is Gale Publishing Company's Encyclopedia of Associations. A three-volume reference work, it contains names of literally thousands of organizations. All associations in the Encyclopedia are indexed by title, city, state, and subject.

HELP-WANTED ADS AS AN INTELLIGENCE SOURCE

Help-wanted ads and the newspapers that publish them are invaluable sources of competitor information.

Aside from the company itself, there are three major sources of information about company employment: state employment offices, local classifieds and display advertisements, and the staff of the classified advertising departments in local newspapers. Properly utilized, the last two are particularly valuable sources of competitor information.

1. *State employment offices.* They are frequently given a contract by a local company to seek out people to fill a specified number of slots. One example: A large conglomerate had just opened a new plant in a relatively small town. The local state employment office was given the exclusive contract to fill all production positions. Because of its unique position, it knew the plant's expected employment capacity, its start-up plans, and breakdown of the types of individuals the company was looking for.

WAR STORY 18

A Source of Backwoods Intelligence

We were given a fairly difficult assignment of determining exactly how many blue- and white-collar employees a tobacco plant was going to employ over the next six months and expectations for employment for the next five years. The plant was located in a small Southern town, with one newspaper and no other major company dominating the town.

Here was the problem: The plant was not yet open. It was a very small portion of a multinational conglomerate. Public filings were of no use.

The fact that it was a small town and that there was only one newspaper, we discovered, worked to our advantage. We called the local newspaper. But instead of asking for the editor, we requested the classified ads department. The woman there told us that she was aware of the new plant and knew it was hiring. She also told us that the newspaper was not carrying any help-wanted advertising for the plant (at which time our hopes fell).

Then she told us a bit of good news: The local state employment office had the contract to hire for the plant. We then called the state office, as she suggested, and the manager there told us all the current as well as projected hiring figures for the plant. Had we wanted to, we could have gone down to the office and actually reviewed the job descriptions that were posted.

2. *Newspaper classified advertising departments.* In cities where there may be only one major newspaper, the classified advertising department often will be aware of the current hiring picture for a large local company, or can tell you who might be responsible for hiring. The classified's sales staff can steer you to the more active personnel agencies in town who are likely sources of information on competitor hiring practices.

3. *Help-wanted or display advertising.* These ads are a company's way of selling itself to prospective employees. In part the advertisements are a come-on, giving the reader more fluff than substance. But the advertisements can also disclose if a competitor is shifting direction or expanding a division or product group.

These classifieds tips suggest that the business analyst can track competitor movement in specific regions in great detail and at minimum expense through the help-wanted advertising pages. Where else would a researcher be able to discover intelligence on hiring trends and disclosures on plant value or marketing strategy?

Help-Wanted Advertisements: An Exercise

Let's look at a typical display ad placed by an employer in a Sunday newspaper. In this case, the employer is McDonnell Douglas. This one advertisement (see Figure 14.2) revealed more information than you will find in a press release or other trade news.

In practice, that is what a classified advertisement is: a press release. The McDonnell Douglas help-wanted ad reveals the following:

1. *Plant assets.* "Our commitment began with a new sixty-five million dollar Microelectronics Center now being built. . . ."
2. *Projected product line.* " . . . to produce custom designed electronics circuits and radiation detectors for use by our other divisions. . . ."
3. *Type of employee.* The ad lists only technical people, those with electrical engineering degrees or the like. More important, it also lists their specialties—a significant piece of information. For example: "Detector Testing Engineer: A BS/MS. EE. Minimum of two years experience in in-process and final testing of HgCdTe photovoltaic detectors and focal plane arrays is needed. Automated test experience desirable."

How to Use Classified Ads Effectively

Now that you know what classified or display help-wanted advertising can do for you, how do you manage to use these ads in a way that will reveal competitor activity?

1. Locate the competitor's plants or service locations you want to watch.
2. Through the Ayer's guide to newspapers and magazines (a source discussed later in the book), find the newspapers located within a 50-mile radius of the towns where the plants are situated.
3. Either subscribe to all the newspapers or hire a news clipping service to clip all the ads pertaining to your competitor.

This technique works best when you are able to monitor the classified ads over a period of time. One-shot attempts at locating an intelligence-packed ad will often yield poor results.

By monitoring your competitor's ads over a period of time, you will be able to spot hiring trends, details on product shifts, and changes in marketing strategy.

DETECTOR SPECIALISTS
MAKE A COMMITMENT WITH US

McDonnell Douglas, a recognized leader in the Aerospace Industry, has made a commitment to excellence in the field of Microelectronics, and we're looking for the best Microelectronics and Detector Specialists to help us.

Our commitment began with a new sixty five million dollar Microelectronics Center now being built to produce custom-designed electronics circuits and radiation detectors for use by our other divisions and in military applications.

This has created many excellent opportunities for Scientists and Engineers in the field of Silicon Technology, Mercury Cadmium Telluride Photovoltaic Detectors, Focal Plane Arrays, Hybrid Design and Development.

If you're looking to be the best in your field, we're looking for the best people we can find for the following openings:

MANAGER, DETECTOR DEVELOPMENT
A PHD in EE or Physics as well as a minimum of five years infrared detector experience is desired. Should have supervisory skills, a background in semiconductor device development, and customer related experience.

**MANAGER, FOCAL PLANE
ARRAY DEVELOPMENT**
A PHD in EE or Physics with five or more years experience in semiconductor device development. Should have supervisory experience, be familiar with automatic focal plane testing, and customer related experience.

DETECTOR FABRICATION ENGINEERS
A BS/MS, EE or Physics. Minimum two years experience in HgCdTe device processing, including one or more of the following: photolithography, implantation, suface passivation and metallization.

DETECTOR TESTING ENGINEER
A BS/MS, EE. Minimum of two years experience in in-process and final testing of HgCdTe photovoltaic detectors and focal plane arrays is needed. Automated test experience desirable.

SEMICONDUCTOR DEVICE SPECIALIST
A PHD (or equivalent) in EE or Physics with a minimum of three years experience in design, modeling and simulation of electronic devices in narrow gap materials.

So if you're ready to work with the best, send your resume to:

Manager, Professional Employment
McDonnell Douglas Corporation
P.O. Box 516 • Department 62-06
St. Louis, Missouri 63166

MCDONNELL DOUGLAS
MICROELECTRONICS CENTER

An Equal Opportunity Employer • U.S. Citizenship Required

Figure 14.2. Display advertisement example.

SHOPPING FOR INTELLIGENCE AT THE MALL

Every shopping mall has a real estate developer associated with it, as well as a manager or managing office. Both of these groups can tell you a good deal about a mall's tenants.

When interviewing a mall's manager, we have been able to uncover a target company's square footage costs, current square footage, expansion plans, and lease arrangements.

Locating mall management offices is easy. Just find the phone number of the mall you are interested in by flipping through your Yellow Pages or White Pages. The listing's number usually belongs to the mall's management office or real estate developer.

LOCATING FOREIGN SUPPLIERS THROUGH THE FCC

FCC Telephone Equipment List

A telephone equipment manufacturer must register its products with the FCC. Aside from registering the product, the FCC also—researchers be alert—publishes a quiet little list that discloses who all the manufacturers are.

What makes this list doubly powerful is its completeness. Not only will it identify the U.S. assembler or marketer of the equipment, but it will also go one step further by identifying the original manufacturer or manufacturers.

Who actually files? Manufacturers, refurbishers of telephone and telephone equipment, private labelers, and assemblers of equipment. The type of equipment that must be registered includes:

Specialty telephone adaptors.

Alarm dialing systems.

Answering machines.

Conferencing bridges, phone patches.

Call distributors.

Call diverters.

Repertory dialers.

Data modems.

Data terminals.

WAR STORY 19

Telecommunications Equipment

A manufacturer who had been in the telephone equipment business for the past five years had recently spotted two new competitors in his line of products. Because of the frenzied growth of this newly deregulated market, the manufacturer was not able to make the right connections to determine who these two competitors were buying their products from.

The manufacturer only knew that they were importing the equipment from Taiwan and South Korea. And he only knew that because he turned the equipment on its side and read the label "Made in Taiwan."

Now he needed to know more. He had already tried to contact his independent reps for information as to their source of supply. He had also contacted the companies he imported from to see if they knew who might be producing the equipment. No luck. There are hundreds of electronics manufacturers, small and large, in the Far East. He was searching for a microchip in a haystack.

Our experience with the telecommunications industry told us to turn first to the Federal Communications Commission. The FCC's Telephone Equipment List gave us our answer, including the name, address, and piece of equipment produced by the foreign supplier.

Facsimile equipment.

Multifunction ancillary equipment.

Monitoring equipment (e.g. alarm line monitors).

Multifunction telephones.

Music-on-hold.

Conversation recorders (these are pieces of equipment that inject a beep tone over the line to inform both parties that the conversation is being recorded).

Stand-alone telephone ringers, chimes, bells, ring relays, ring detectors, and visual indicators.

Traffic recorders.

Nondialing speakerphones.

Telephones.

Unprotected telephone terminal equipment (e.g., two-line telephone systems with an intercom).

Partially protected telephone terminal equipment.

Test equipment.

Toll restrictors.

Adjunct components used with two-line telephones.

Wireless telephones.

Devices using switchboard/headset plugs and jacks.

Limited use terminal devices.

Special purpose terminal equipment.

A typical entry will have information in the following categories:

1. Name of applicant.
2. Code for applicant (an ID number).
3. Code for manufacturer of equipment.
4. File number for this entry.
5. Code for equipment category.
6. Code for network address signaling.
7. File number for tracking entry through registration. Once registration is complete, then the file number is dropped.
8. Description of the equipment.
9. Description of the type of jack necessary.

Any time a manufacturer changes its supplier or modifies the equipment in any way, it must file with the FCC. The form it uses is number 731, as shown in Figure 14.3.

Ordering the Registration List

The forms are kept on file with the FCC at the address given below. You can also receive quarterly lists of the most recent registrants on microfiche from the FCC office below or from the National Technical Information Service. The list is free. At this time, the FCC does not have a mailing list. You would, therefore, have to reorder the list each quarter. To order, write or call:

Federal Communications Commission
Room 304
1200 19th Street, NW
Washington, DC 20554
202–634–1833 or 202–634–1835.

<table>
<tr><td colspan="2">FCC FORM
731</td><td colspan="2" align="center">FEDERAL COMMUNICATIONS COMMISSION
Washington, DC 20554

APPLICATION FOR EQUIPMENT AUTHORIZATION</td><td>Approved by OMB
3060-0057
Expires 3/31/85</td></tr>
</table>

1.(a) Grantee Code assigned by FCC ☐☐☐	(b) Manufacturer Code assigned by FCC ☐☐☐	**FOR FCC STAFF USE**

2.(a) Applicant's FULL business name

(b) Applicant's COMPLETE address
(Number, street,
city, state,
ZIP code)

(c) Name and title of person at above address to receive grant (SEE INSTRUCTIONS)

3.(a) Instead of applicant, FCC is authorized to mail original grant to
(Firm name,
number, street,
city, state,
ZIP code)

File No.: EQU

Application dated

Data entered _____ by

Examiner _____

(b) Name and title of person at above address to receive grant

4.(a) FULL name of equipment manufacturer, if different from Item 2(a) above

Reviewer(s)

(b) Address of equipment manufacturer, if different from Item 2(b) above
(Number, street,
city, state,
ZIP code)

Equipment Code:

Print_____authorization(s)

Microfiched_____ by_____
date

---

5. Has a request for confidentiality been filed for any portion(s) of the data contained in this application pursuant to Section 0.459 of the Commission's rules, or has a waiver of any sections of the Commission's rules been filed? YES ☐ NO ☐

6. Kind of equipment authorization requested (Check ONE box only) ☐ Certification ☐ Type Acceptance ☐ Type Approval ☐ Notification (See Instructions)

7.(a) Kind of equipment | **(b)** Equipment will be operated under FCC Rules Part(s)

8. Application is for (Check ONE box only)

☐ 1 Original Equipment	☐ 2 Change in identification of presently authorized equipment	☐ 3 Change in manufacturer of presently authorized equipment	☐ 4 Modification of presently authorized equipment
List FCC ID in Item 9(a) and trade name, if any in Item 9(b).	List FCC ID in Item 9(a) and trade name, if any in Item 9(b). Complete Items 10(a), (c), (d), and (e).	List FCC ID in Item 9(a) and trade name, if any in Item 9(b). Complete Items 10(b), (c), (d), and (e).	List FCC ID in Item 9(a) and trade name, if any in Item 9(b). Give date of original grant _____ If no FCC ID assigned, complete Items 11(a)-11(d).

9.(a) FCC ID (grantee and manufacturer codes listed in Item 1(a) and 1(b), plus number assigned by applicant. SEE INSTRUCTIONS ☐☐☐☐☐☐☐☐☐☐☐

(b) Trade Name(s), if any (maximum of 30 characters each - see instructions)

10.(a) Name of present grantee, if different from Item 2(a) above | **(b)** Name of present manufacturer, if different from Item 4(a) above

(c) FCC ID, if assigned/Model or Type No., and Trade name, if any | **(d)** FCC Type Approval No., if assigned   **(e)** Date of original grant

11.(a) Complete ONLY if no FCC ID assigned to equipment to be modified (Model or type No.) | **(b)** Trade Name, if any

(c) FCC Type Approval No., if assigned | **(d)** Date of original grant

12.(a) Is the equipment, or section(s) thereof, subject to more than one equipment authorization? ☐ Yes ☐ No If yes, complete Item 12(b), and 12(c), 12(d), or 12(e), as appropriate.

(b) Additional equipment authorization(s) required for equipment ☐ Certification ☐ Type Acceptance ☐ Type Approval

(c) FCC ID listed on simultaneously filed RCVR or RCVR section application	**(d)** FCC ID listed on simultaneously filed XMTR or XMTR section application	**(e)** FCC ID listed on other simultaneously filed application
FOR FCC STAFF USE ONLY		**FOR FCC STAFF USE ONLY**

All previous editions of this form are obsolete.

FCC Form 731 - Page 1
April 1982

Figure 14.3.   FCC Form 731.

13. EQUIPMENT SPECIFICATIONS	
(a) Frequency range (list all frequency bands covered in equipment)	(b) Rated RF Power output (if variable, give range)
(c) Power output to final RF amplifier (If applicable)	(d) Rated frequency tolerance
(e) Emission designator(s)	(f) Power supply (Check appropriate box(es)) ☐ AC ☐ Battery ☐ Other (specify)_____

14. Total number of exhibits submitted with application _____ Attach list of exhibits

15.(a) Technical information contact (Firm name, number, street, city, state, ZIP code)				(b) Nontechnical information contact, if different from Item 15(a) (Firm name, number, street, city, state, ZIP code)			
(c) Name and title of person at above address				(d) Name and title of person at above address			
(e) Telephone Information (USA ONLY)	Area code	Number	Extension	(f) Telephone Information (USA ONLY)	Area code	Number	Extension

16. APPLICANT CERTIFICATION

I certify that I am authorized to sign for the applicant and that all the statements in this application and in the exhibits attached hereto are true and correct to the best of my knowledge and belief. If I am an agent authorized to complete, and sign this application on behalf of the applicant, a copy of such authorization, signed by the applicant, is attached hereto.

I further certify that, if the applicant is not the actual manufacturer of the equipment listed herein, appropriate arrangements have been made with the manufacturer to assure that production units of this equipment bearing the name and FCC IDENTIFIER listed in this application will continue to comply with the Commission's requirements.

Applicant's full business name ▶ _____
(Must agree with name in Item 2(a))

▲ Written signature of authorized signer   ▲ Typed / printed name of authorized signer

▲ Title of authorized signer   ▲ Date (Month, Day, Year)

WILLFUL FALSE STATEMENTS MADE ON THIS APPLICATION ARE PUNISHABLE BY FINE AND IMPRISONMENT, U.S. CODE, TITLE 18, SECTION 1001.

FCC Form 731 - Page 2
April 1982

Figure 14.3. *(Continued)*

In addition to the information contained on Form 731, the registrant is required to file almost any other item relating to the equipment, including equipment test procedures and diagrams and photographs of the equipment and schematics.

FCC Radio Equipment List

This list is similar to the telephone equipment list, but covers only radio equipment. To order the list, contact the FCC at the above address. The list costs $40.

Frequency Master List

The FCC also publishes a Frequency Master List. It is a master list of radio frequencies and whom they are assigned to. Each entry contains company name and address, transmission locations, power, and tower height. Registrants include private radio services, public radio telephone operators, television broadcasters, amateur radio operators, personal radio services, and shippers. This listing is available on microfiche (no. 416) for $208.

OUR EFFLUENT SOCIETY: ENVIRONMENTAL IMPACT STATEMENTS, A BACK-DOOR APPROACH TO COMPANY INTELLIGENCE

Speak to experienced researchers in the chemical and pharmaceutical industries and they will tell you how valuable environmental impact statements are. As the title implies, companies that are planning to build plants or change production processes that might in some way affect the environment must file with a local—and possibly a federal—agency.

These are just some of the questions an environmental impact statement can answer:

1. What is the projected plant size?
2. What type of process will they be using?
3. Approximately how many people will they employ (which you can learn through the number of parking spaces reported)?
4. What will the project cost the company?
5. How many production sites will they be creating?

Experienced industry researchers will also tell you that the state or local environmental filings are more frequently filed and are often more detailed than the federal forms.

Some states require more than just one filing per project. For instance, in Massachusetts a company first has to file an Environmental Notification Form (ENF) before filing an impact statement. This notification is placed on public record with the state environmental agency. The notification will then allow state authorities to determine whether or not further examination of the project is required.

Throughout this chapter, I will use the Massachusetts system as an example of state requirements and the type of corporate information that these forms may reveal. Understand, though, that Massachusetts may be somewhat typical but may not include all categories or rules that other states have. Yet I believe that even a brief glance at the Massachusetts reporting requirements will make you aware of just how extensive—and how revealing—these impact or notification statements are.

To show you just how a company must file and what kind of information it must reveal, let's first look at a portion of the instructions for the Massachusetts Environmental Notification Form (ENF) shown in Figure 14.4. The form is intended to provide the Secretary of Environmental Affairs and the general public with relatively early notification that projects are being planned which may or may not have significant impacts on the environment. The purpose of the ENF is to identify general types of impacts from a project as best one can without having to perform final design or detailed analysis. The ENF is intended to identify those projects that may have significant impact potential, and if so, to identify which types of impacts are significant and which are not. Through this process, the scope of any further environmental studies can be limited simply to those issues of concern, and the project proponent need not investigate those factors that are not at issue.

The process to be followed is fairly straightforward. The project proponent should fill out the ENF as accurately and completely as possible, given the preliminary state of project development. Then there will be a public review process and a determination by the Secretary whether or not an Environmental Impact Report (EIR) will be required, and if so, what topics should be covered. The Secretary will use information submitted by the project proponent in Section I-D., "Scoping," as the initial basis for determining the scope of an EIR and which alternative should be studied.

The ENF itself is not meant to be a comprehensive environmental analysis of the project. In most cases, a best professional estimate based on available data, practice, and information will suffice. More detailed information on specific items may be requested during the review of the ENF

ENVIRONMENTAL   NOTIFICATION   FORM

I.   SUMMARY

A. Project Identification
1. Project Name_____

2. Project Proponent_____
      Address _____

B. Project Description: (City/Town(s)_____
1. Location within city/town or street address_____

2. Est. Commencement Date:_____Est. Completion Date:_____
     Approx. Cost $_____   Current Status of Project Design: _____% Complete

C. Narrative Summary of Project
    Describe project and give a description of the general project boundaries and the present use of the project
    area. (If necessary, use back of this page to complete summary).

Copies of this may be obtained from:
Name:_____Firm/Agency:_____
Address:_____ Phone No._____

1979   THIS IS AN IMPORTANT NOTICE. COMMENT PERIOD IS LIMITED.
        For Information, call (617) 727-5830

Figure 14.4.   Environmental Notification Form (Massachusetts).

Use This Page to Complete Narrative, if necessary.

This project is one which is categorically included and therefore automatically requires preparation of an Environmental Impact Report: YES_____ NO_____

D. Scoping (Complete Sections II and III first, before completing this section.)

1. Check those areas which would be important to examine in the event that an EIR is required for this project. This information is important so that significant areas of concern can be identified as early as possible, in order to expedite analysis and review.

	Construc- tion Impacts	Long Term Impacts		Construc- tion Impacts	Long Term Impacts
Open Space & Recreation	_____	_____	Mineral Resources	_____	_____
Historical.	_____	_____	Energy Use	_____	_____
Archaeological	_____	_____	Water Supply & Use.	_____	_____
Fisheries & Wildlife	_____	_____	Water Pollution	_____	_____
Vegetation, Trees	_____	_____	Air Pollution.	_____	_____
Other Biological Systems	_____	_____	Noise	_____	_____
Inland Wetlands.	_____	_____	Traffic.	_____	_____
Coastal Wetlands or Beaches	_____	_____	Solid Waste	_____	_____
Flood Hazard Areas	_____	_____	Aesthetics	_____	_____
Chemicals, Hazardous Substances,			Wind and Shadow	_____	_____
High Risk Operations.	_____	_____	Growth Impacts.	_____	_____
Geologically Unstable Areas	_____	_____	Community/Housing and the Built		
Agricultural Land	_____	_____	Environment.	_____	_____
Other (Specify)_____			. . . .	_____	_____

2. List the alternatives which you would consider to be feasible in the event an EIR is required.

Figure 14.4. *(Continued)*

E. Has this project been filed with EOEA before?   Yes _____   No _____
   If Yes, EOEA No. _____   EOEA Action? _____

F. Does this project fall under the jurisdiction of NEPA?   Yes _____   No _____
   If Yes, which Federal Agency? _____   NEPA Status? _____

G. List the State or Federal agencies from which permits will be sought:

   Agency Name   **Type of Permit**

H. Will an Order of Conditions be required under the provisions of the Wetlands Protection Act (Chap. 131, Section 40)?
   Yes _____   No _____
   DEQE File No., if applicable: _____

I. List the agencies from which the proponent will seek financial assistance for this project:

   Agency Name   **Funding Amount**

II.   PROJECT DESCRIPTION

A. Include an original 8½ x11 inch or larger section of the most recent U.S.G.S. 1:24,000 scale topographic map with the project area location and boundaries clearly shown. Include multiple maps if necessary for large projects. Include other maps, diagrams or aerial photos if the project cannot be clearly shown at U.S.G.S. scale. If available, attach a plan sketch of the proposed project.

B. State total area of project: _____
   Estimate the number of acres (to the nearest 1/10 acre) directly affected that are currently:

   1. Developed .... ____ acres   4. Floodplain .... ____ acres
   2. Open Space/Woodlands/Recreation ____ acres   5. Coastal Area .... ____ acres
   3. Wetlands .... ____ acres   6. Productive Resources
                                                           Agriculture .... ____ acres
                                                           Forestry .... ____ acres
                                                           Mineral Products .... ____ acres

C. Provide the following dimensions, if applicable:

   Length in miles _____   Number of Housing Units _____   Number of Stories _____

	Existing	Immediate Increase Due to Project
Number of Parking Spaces	_____	_____
Vehicle Trips to Project Site (average daily traffic)	_____	_____
Estimated Vehicle Trips past project site	_____	_____

D. If the proposed project will require any permit for access to local or state highways, please attach a sketch showing the location of the proposed driveway(s) in relation to the highway and to the general development plan; identifying all local and state highways abutting the development site; and indicating the number of lanes, pavement width, median strips and adjacent driveways on each abutting highway; and indicating the distance to the nearest intersection.

Figure 14.4.   *(Continued)*

III. ASSESSMENT OF POTENTIAL ADVERSE ENVIRONMENTAL IMPACTS

Instructions: Consider direct and indirect adverse impacts, including those arising from general construction and operations. For every answer explain why significant adverse impact is considered likely or unlikely to result.

Also, state the *source* of information or other basis for the answers supplied. If the source of the information, in part or in full, is not listed in the ENF, the preparing officer will be assumed to be the source of the information. Such environmental information should be acquired at least in part by field inspection.

A. Open Space and Recreation
1. Might the project affect the condition, use or access to any open space and/or recreation area?
   Yes _____ No _____

   Explanation and Source:

B. Historic Resources
1. Might any site or structure of historic significance be affected by the project? Yes _____ No _____

   Explanation and Source:

2. Might any archaeological site be affected by the project? Yes _____ No _____

   Explanation and Source:

C. Ecological Effects
1. Might the project significantly affect fisheries or wildlife, especially any rare or endangered species?
   Yes _____ No _____

   Explanation and Source:

Figure 14.4 *(Continued)*

2. ght the project significantly affect vegetation, especially any rare or endangered species of plant?
Yes _____ No _____
(Estimate approximate number of mature trees to be removed: _____)

Explanation and Source:

3. Might the project alter or affect flood hazard areas, inland or coastal wetlands (e.g., estuaries, marshes, sand dunes and beaches, ponds, streams, rivers, fish runs, or shellfish beds)?   Yes _____   No _____

Explanation and Source:

4. Might the project affect shoreline erosion or accretion at the project site, downstream or in nearby coastal areas?   Yes _____   No _____

Explanation and Source:

5. Might the project involve other geologically unstable areas?   Yes _____   No _____

Explanation and Source:

D. Hazardous Substances

1. Might the project involve the use, transportation, storage, release, or disposal of potentially hazardous substances?
Yes _____   No _____

Explanation and Source:

Figure 14.4.   *(Continued)*

E. Resource Conservation and Use
  1. Might the project affect or eliminate land suitable for agricultural or forestry production?
     Yes _____ No _____
     (Describe any present agricultural land use and farm units affected.)

     Explanation and Source:

  2. Might the project directly affect the potential use or extraction of mineral or energy resources (e.g., oil, coal, sand & gravel, ores)? Yes _____ No _____

     Explanation and Source:

  3. Might the operation of the project result in any increased consumption of energy? Yes _____ No _____

     Explanation and Source:
     (If applicable, describe plans for conserving energy resources.)

F. Water Quality and Quantity
  1. Might the project result in significant changes in drainage patterns? Yes _____ No _____

     Explanation and Source:

  2. Might the project result in the introduction of pollutants into any of the following:
     (a) Marine Waters .... Yes _____ No _____
     (b) Surface Fresh Water Body .... Yes _____ No _____
     (c) Ground Water .... Yes _____ No _____

     Explain types and quantities of pollutants.

Figure 14.4. *(Continued)*

3. Will the project generate sanitary sewage?   Yes _____   No _____
   If Yes, Quantity: _____ gallons per day
   Disposal by: (a) Onsite septic systems . . . . Yes _____   No _____
   　　　　　　 (b) Public sewerage systems . . . . Yes _____   No _____
   　　　　　　 (c) Other means (describe) _____

4. Might the project result in an increase in paved or impervious surface over an aquifer recognized as an important present or future source of water supply?   Yes _____   No _____

   Explanation and Source:

5. Is the project in the watershed of any surface water body used as a drinking water supply?
   Yes _____   No _____
   Are there any public or private drinking water wells within a 1/2-mile radius of the proposed project?
   Yes _____   No _____

   Explanation and Source:

6. Might the operation of the project result in any increased consumption of water?   Yes _____   No _____

   Approximate consumption _____ gallons per day. Likely water source(s) _____

   Explanation and Source:

7. Does the project involve any dredging?   Yes _____   No _____
   If Yes, indicate:
   　　Quantity of material to be dredged _____
   　　Quality of material to be dredged _____
   　　Proposed method of dredging _____
   　　Proposed disposal sites _____
   　　Proposed season of year for dredging _____

   Explanation and Source:

Figure 14.4.   *(Continued)*

398

G. Air Quality
   1. Might the project affect the air quality in the project area or the immediately adjacent area?
      Yes _____ No _____
      Describe type and source of any pollution emission from the project site. _____

   2. Are there any sensitive receptors (e.g., hospitals, schools, residential areas) which would be affected by any
      pollution emissions caused by the project, including construction dust? Yes _____ No _____

      Explanation and Source:

   3. Will access to the project area be primarily by automobile? Yes _____ No _____
      Describe any special provisions now planned for pedestrian access, carpooling, buses and other mass transit.

H. Noise
   1. Might the project result in the generation of noise? Yes _____ No _____

      Explanation and Source:
      (Include any source of noise during construction or operation, e.g., engine exhaust, pile driving, traffic.)

   2. Are there any sensitive receptors (e.g., hospitals, schools, residential areas) which would be affected by any
      noise caused by the project? Yes _____ No _____

      Explanation and Source:

Figure 14.4. *(Continued)*

I. Solid Waste
  1. Might the project generate solid waste?   Yes _____   No _____

     Explanation and Source:
     (Estimate types and approximate amounts of waste materials generated, e.g., industrial, domestic, hospital, sewage sludge, construction debris from demolished structures.)

J. Aesthetics
  1. Might the project cause a change in the visual character of the project area or its environs?
     Yes _____   No _____

     Explanation and Source:

  2. Are there any proposed structures which might be considered incompatible with existing adjacent structures in the vicinity in terms of size, physical proportion and scale, or significant differences in land use?
     Yes _____   No _____

     Explanation and Source:

  3. Might the project impair visual access to waterfront or other scenic areas?   Yes _____   No _____
     Explanation and Source:

K. Wind and Shadow
  1. Might the project cause wind and shadow impacts on adjacent properties?   Yes _____   No _____
     Explanation and Source:

Figure 14.4.   *(Continued)*

IV. CONSISTENCY WITH PRESENT PLANNING

    A. Describe any known conflicts or inconsistencies with current federal, state and local land use, transportation, open space, recreation and environmental plans and policies. Consult with local or regional planning authorities where appropriate.

V. FINDINGS AND CERTIFICATION

    A. The notice of intent to file this form has been/will be published in the following newspaper(s):

       (Name) _____ (Date) _____

               _____   _____

               _____   _____

    B. This form has been circulated to all agencies and persons as required by Appendix B.

            _____   _____
                 Date   Signature of Responsible Officer
                                  or Project Proponent

                              _____
                              Name (print or type)

                              Address _____

                              Telephone Number _____

            _____   _____
                 Date   Signature of person preparing
                                  ENF (if different from above)

                              _____
                              Name (print or type)

                              Address _____

                              Telephone Number _____

Figure 14.4. *(Continued)*

401

to help in performing a satisfactory environmental evaluation. The degree of accuracy will vary from project to project.

The sequence of procedures that proponents are advised to follow is:

1. Begin preparation of the ENF at a relatively early state of project development.
2. Determine likely state permits and financial assistance.
3. Consult with affected agencies and assemble information useful in completing the ENF and finding out whether the project may be exempt from the MEPA (Massachusetts Environmental Protection Agency) process.
4. Publish the intent to submit an ENF in a newspaper of local circulation in each community affected by the proposed project or in a newspaper of regional or statewide circulation if an affected community is not served by a local publication. The notice should be published no more than 30 days before submitting the ENF.
5. Complete the ENF and submit it, with original USGS (U.S. Geological Survey) or other map.

What Can You Learn from a Notification Form?

To see it is to believe it. There is a wealth of plant information in one of these statements. To offer a sample, here are a number of the categories the state environmental board requires of companies filing for notification:

Project name.

Project address.

Project's commencement date.

Cost of project.

Description of project.

Short- and long-term impacts (the environmental categories, such as inland wetlands, air pollution, and noise).

Listing of equivalent federal environmental filings also required.

Requests for financial assistance and the agencies from which aid will be requested.

Total acreage likely to be affected by the project.

Description of the building or processing plant.

Number of parking spaces.

Estimated traffic to and from the site.

Accompanying drawings of plant and access roads.

Explanation of the pollutants produced.

Estimated daily water consumption.

Detailed description of type and nature of air and noise pollution generated.

To order a filing, you can call or write your state capitol's environmental office, or the office of water or air pollution.

CORRUGATED BOXES: A SOURCE OF PRODUCTION DATA

"Just let me find the competitor's box supplier and I can find the number of units that the competitor is shipping at any particular season." These are the words of a Canadian packaging manufacturer who understands that over 95 percent of all products manufactured today ultimately wind up being placed in corrugated boxes of some type. His suggestion is to simply locate the box supplier and through it identify the number of boxes shipped.

Sounds like a simple solution, right? In truth, it is—but execution of this research technique requires additional insight into the box manufacturing industry.

1. *Lesson one.*   Not all box manufacturers are alike. Some are better sources than others.

Box manufacturers fall into two categories: the conglomerate box producer and the independent box supplier. The conglomerate producer is also a major paper manufacturer and has hundreds of other product lines besides corrugated boxes. The independent supplier buys prepared corrugated paper from a conglomerate paper manufacturer, then cuts, bends, and glues it together to form a box.

The conglomerate is not likely to know or care much about a particular client's seasonal box needs—especially those of a small purchaser of boxes. These conglomerates must maintain expensive corrugation machinery. Because of this additional overhead, salespeople are only interested in selling bulk orders. They are neither interested in, nor do they watch for, small orders. They also do not monitor seasonal usage on the part of clients.

The independents, on the other hand, do not generally own these ex-

---

WAR STORY 20

Know Thy Brothel

After hearing how corrugated boxes could be used to trace a company's shipments or sales, one executive who attended an Information Data Search intelligence-gathering seminar came up with this anecdote that closely resembles the case of the corrugated box.

He said that the IRS had been trying to uncover a particular brothel's yearly sales, without success. Internal Revenue agents apparently did not want to plant themselves outside the house of ill repute, counting the number of customers parading in and out. Too time consuming.

They chose another, creative intelligence-gathering technique. They asked themselves: What does every brothel need. . . aside from talent? Why, the answer was simple—towels, of course. The agents managed to locate the company supplying the towels to the institution in question. By learning the number of towels used by the brothel, the IRS then estimated sales for this tax evader.

So, you see, corrugated boxes are only one source of production data. But the lesson that the corrugated box teaches is universal: Locate a company's source of supply and you will likely determine that company's sales.

---

pensive corrugation machines. They can, therefore, offer services to the special needs of smaller clients or special orders. These independents know when their clients need boxes and how many. They can often gauge seasonal demands, because such orders are part of their business.

2. *Lesson two.*   One easy way to locate the competitor's box manufacturer is simply to examine the box itself. The supplier will make sure to place its imprint on one of the outside walls of the box. An example is given in Figure 14.5.

3. *Lesson three.*   Most companies will use more than one box supplier. The researcher will then have to locate a competitor's entire list of box suppliers in order to track all shipment data.

The following are names of some of the box industry's leading directories and trade groups. Both can be used to trace a company's immediate box supplier. Remember, because of shipping costs involved in a low-cost item such as cardboard boxes, a competitor's suppliers will likely be located in the same region.

PO#0625-004

11¼X8¾X4

**COMPLIES WITH SPEC.
PPP-B-636I**

Figure 14.5.   Corrugated box supplier imprint.

Lockwood's Directory of Paper and Allied Trades Vance Publishing Corporation 133 E. 58th Street New York, NY 10022	Association of Independent Corrugator Converters 312–328–6556
	Containerization Institute 212–697–3120
Paper, Film & Foil Converter— Annual Directory and Buyer's Guide Maclean-Hunter Publishing Corporation 300 W. Adams Street Chicago, IL 60606	Fibre Box Association 312–697–3120
	National Paper Box Association 609–429–7377
Source of Supply/Buyers' Guide Advertisers & Publishers Service 300 North Prospect Avenue Park Ridge, IL 60068	Pacific Coast Paper Box Manufacturers' Association 213–724–4955

COMMERCIAL BANKING AND THE WITHDRAWAL OF INFORMATION

Banking, like any other industry, has its distributors, wholesalers, and end-users or consumers. Once the researcher can identify these different industry groups, the actual intelligence-gathering can begin.

WAR STORY 21

The Hard Data on Banking Software

This was a case of a rapidly moving end of the corporate banking industry. Software companies and commercial banks themselves were working feverishly to produce computerized cash-management products for corporate clients.

The client wanted to know which banks or software companies were going to come out with a new software package and what the features and pricing might be on those packages.

In other commercial banking assignments we could go directly to the targetted end-user—the large corporation—to get our answers. The corporation's treasurer would likely know a good deal about the prospective product and may have shopped around, looking at other products. In other words, the treasurer, ordinarily, would have made an excellent contact.

That wasn't the case here. In this instance, the product was too new. And, because it was so new, we could not easily—and quickly— identify the likely corporate end-users.

So we took that proverbial step back to get a sense of perspective on the industry. Here is what we learned:

1. *Corporate end-user.* There were potentially thousands of corporations that might use these new cash-management products. It would be futile to try to locate them under the existing time constraints.

2. *Software producer (bank or independent software company).* True, there are relatively few of these companies. But ask yourself, what is the chance that they are going to spill the beans to you, the interviewer? The chances are slim. So while this is the easiest industry group to define (the manufacturers), it is the most difficult to interview.

3. *Licensee bank.* This is the middleman or distributor we were looking for. A licensee bank purchases or pays royalties to the producer bank or software company for using its software. The licensee bank, in turn, sells the product to its corporate banking clients. The licensee bank had no reason to hold back the information and may have felt little loyalty to the software firm or producing bank. Also, since there were few of these licensee banks, we were able to quickly spot the licensees who used a particular product.

By interviewing the licensee banks we were able to construct an accurate picture of the various products, along with features and pricing information.

WAR STORY 22

In Pensions Do We Trust

Many large corporations have their pension fund investments managed by an outside commercial bank or independent pension fund consulting firm. Our client, though, wanted to know what particular features interested a competitor's clients and what features the client offered were worth building on in future marketing efforts.

After paging through the *Money Market Directory*, we located the competitor's customers. Next, we designed a questionnaire and polled these corporate customers. As long as we kept the questionnaire short, respondents were certainly willing to talk.

Also, finding the right person to speak to was fairly easy, since the person most responsible for working with the pension fund was likely located in the company treasurer's or controller's office.

Let's take another look at the above example and see how commercial banking may in many ways compare to a typical manufacturing industry.

Industry	Manufacturer	Distributor	End-user
Lumber	Sawmill	Lumber outlet	Builder
Banking software	Software producer	Licensee bank	Corporation

As mentioned in the section "Know Thy Industry Before Thy Target Company" in Chapter 2, by understanding how your target industry is structured you have a far better chance of locating information on your target company. Banking, like lumber, has a set industry structure. The structures themselves may be different, but studying each separately reveals distinct patterns. By following these patterns, you will uncover your intelligence.

A Trusted Banking Source

Pension and trust banking have become a highly dynamic and fiercely competitive industry in the past decade. Fortunately for the corporate researcher there is a source that has come to the rescue: the *Money Market Directory* (Money Market Directories, P.O. Box 1608, Charlottesville, VA 22902, 800–446–2810).

Whenever you are doing competitor research, you run into a number of basic questions:

1. Who is the supplier?
2. Who are the customers or end-users?
3. How much are the customers buying from the suppliers?

In effect, these are the very questions the *Money Market Directory* answers for the researcher. The *Money Market Directory* contains the names of the independent pension fund managers, their corporate clients, and the size of the accounts managed. This is one of the few sources in any industry that actually supply a competitor's customers.

STOCKHOLDERS' MEETINGS

There is no better way to get first-hand information on a publicly held company than to become a stockholder and attend stockholders' meetings. These meetings discuss the latest company products, key personnel changes, company financials, and stockholders' questions.

It is probably the last item that will serve you best. First, buy a share of stock. This is your admission ticket to the meeting—and all future meetings. Next, keep your ears open for crucial questions being asked. Sometimes the smallest but most vocal stockholders can ask the sharpest and most confounding questions. Management may sidestep the vital issues; but then again, it may not.

By attending these meetings you are getting the corporate information a day ahead of its appearing in the press. Also, when you are a shareholder in a small over-the-counter company, you will be privy to meetings that may never reach the press.

UNDERSTANDING THE SOFTWARE INDUSTRY

A software company is a far more elusive target than a large manufacturing concern, bank, or insurance company. The reasons for this are:

WAR STORY 23

The Growth of a Company

A client that was about to release a major software product needed to know how another company with a similar product was managing to grow so successfully. The client needed to find out something about the competitor's organization structure.

The first and most obvious source was the competitor's software manual. It listed all the authors. After a check of some computer clubs and local consulting firms, we managed to get further biographical background on some of the authors as well as some key executives within the firm.

The national trade press had given a lot of coverage to this type of software and had included a number of in-depth interviews with the target company's executives.

The result: We were able to construct a company organization chart and growth plans.

A software company may operate out of a garage. Once the owner buys the microcomputer, let's say, he or she does not have to contact anyone until the product is finished or ready for market.

There are still no official, proven, or established distribution channels in the software industry.

A software company does not depend on a flowing river for its power or for disposing of waste, unlike a manufacturing plant.

The major resource of a software company is people, not machinery.

As a rule, no one software company dominates an entire market. There are exceptions, of course. For quite a while VisiCorp (producers of VisiCalc) had the spreadsheet market sewed up, until Multiplan and the Lotus 1-2-3 packages came along, in addition to dozens of other versions of the electronic spreadsheet. Therefore, there is no concentration of market.

Here are some tips we have used successfully to uncover detailed intelligence on software companies:

1. *The end-user/computer clubs.* Software companies, especially the newer ones, have to convince the computer elite that their product is superior

and well worth the investment. We have used computer clubs to find current clients or companies where the product is being test-marketed.

To find the computer club in your area, contact a local college. Ask for its computer science department. Someone there will know where and when the local club branch will meet and when your particular piece of software will be discussed.

These end-users can tell the interviewer the product's features, its pricing, and its pluses and minuses.

2. *The press.* Just before a product is about to be released, software companies and their ad agencies love to innundate the trade press with press releases and photographs of the product and its packaging. Unlike other industries, the computer (and especially the microcomputer) industry has hundreds of magazines and newsletters. Many magazines are not content with just reprinting press releases. Instead, they will conduct lengthy interviews with the firm's principals. To locate a particular interview, you can turn to any number of indexes, some computerized (naturally!) and others in text form.

3. *The software manual.* The manual itself contains the authors' names and details on the product's purpose and features. Rarely does a company in any other industry offer the end-user such a detailed view of its product.

4. *Local computer stores.* Retail stores located near the software supplier probably know the creators of the software and some details about the company's organization and future product releases.

5. *Trade shows.* Like any other thriving industry, the software industry has latched onto the trade show as a means to display its product and gain visibility. Events calendars of upcoming trade shows are published in magazines such as *Byte* and *Computerworld*. Your local computer club will also keep you posted.

A PRESCRIPTION FOR PHARMACEUTICAL RESEARCH

The pharmaceutical industry prides itself on its secrecy and its ability to market and make lots of money on commodity-type products. In reality, though, the pharmaceutical industry is not as secretive as it would like to

---

WAR STORY 24

A Drug's Future Shipments

The future is probably the hardest piece of intelligence to locate—since it hasn't happened yet.

One client had requested that we pinpoint a competitor's intended shipping plans for a new product that was months or even a year away from introduction. Specifically, the client wanted to know which plant was supplying the product and what the initial shipments would look like.

First, we consulted the FDA. They would only say what was already public knowledge. They could tell us that the drug was under review. The FDA would not tell us about the company's advertising plans (although they could release papers on the target company's advertising for other products already released). The FDA could not legally release information prior to the approval date.

Next, we consulted a number of other sources for names of experts to contact. Among the sources we referred to were the *Physicians' Desk Reference*, the *Wall Street Transcript*, the *Directory of Contract Packagers*, and the *National Wholesale Druggists' Association Membership Directory*.

After spending a number of days on the telephone talking with wholesalers, potential suppliers, competing companies, and Wall Street analysts, we managed to compile an accurate picture of the company and its shipping plans. Specifically, we identified the plant that was going to ship the raw material, we identified the competitor's plant that was going to package the product, and we received estimates of expected shipments as well as the product pricing.

---

believe. Like any industry, its activities leave traces. This section will help you find those traces.

Before I go directly into some of the sources mentioned, let's take a look at the pharmaceutical industry to see why it is not a closed shop. I stated earlier that information is exchanged along with money. In other words, virtually every business transaction results in information being passed along about the parties involved. The pharmaceutical industry is no exception to this rule. Let's see what happens to a drug company when it begins to manufacture and market a product—whom they speak to and come in contact with outside the company.

Advertising agencies. Sometimes companies will have their own in-house agencies. But in most cases they will contract with outside agencies. Many times these agencies will proudly announce their new client in the local and national advertising trade press, such as *Advertising Age.*

Contract packagers. Drug companies will often have outside companies do their packaging for them. Packagers will know well in advance if a new product may enter the market. They are the ones who produce the labels and bottles. They are also important sources of marketing shifts. That is, they will often know if a drug company is changing its marketing stance by seeing the change in its packaging.

Wall Street analysts. These folks may admittedly not know much about a company's detailed manufacturing operations, but they will understand the marketing signals a company is sending out to its investors. We have used these analysts to confirm shipping and pricing information about a new product.

FDA (Food and Drug Administration). This federal authority regulates the drug industry and has on file applications for new products and historical filings on past products and product approvals.

Retailers. Buyers for major drugstore chains are more likely to know about a manufacturer's marketing and pricing plans than would a small single-store pharmacy. A manufacturer's salesperson may have approached the buyer weeks or months before a pricing or marketing change was announced to the public and the press.

Aside from these major sources, there are always the knowledgeable marketing and production executives within each pharmaceutical house who must keep up on the industry and have heard or have verified for themselves the rumors about a particular product. Whether or not they legally can or are willing to release this information is another matter. The issue of friendliness may be a problem. Also, there may be strict FDA and antitrust guidelines that could prevent them from speaking to anyone outside their own company.

Throughout this section I have referred to a number of sources that will help you uncover the experts who can tell you about a drug and a competitor's activities regarding the drug. Here is a description of those sources.

FDA (Food and Drug Administration). This federal agency has on hand information on a company's investigations, packaging, and labeling. These records are kept on file and are available by visiting or calling the Freedom of Information Office or Dockets Management room located at 5600 Fishers Lane, Rockville, MD 20857. Telephone numbers are 301–443–6310 for

the Freedom of Information Office, and 301–443–1753 for labeling and hearing records photocopying.

Physicians' Desk Reference/PDR (Medican Economics Company). This is the bible of the drug industry. It is equivalent to a Thomas Register for pharmaceuticals, only far more detailed. Its sections include:

Manufacturer's index—name, address, and product lines.

Product category index—products listed by general category, with a cross-reference to the product's manufacturer.

Generic and chemical name index—a listing of products by their generic and chemical name.

Product identification section—drug products are displayed in color and size in this separate section.

Product information section—the largest section in terms of pages lists over 2500 pharmaceuticals, with a description of their characteristics, usage, administration, warnings, and generic or chemical names.

Other sections—diagnostic product information, poison control centers, guide to management of drug overdose.

We have used this source to identify a parent company's subsidiary operations and to understand other details about a particular drug. The PDR is written in clear English. We have found that it uses technical jargon only when it has to; otherwise, the PDR imparts a good deal of information about the drug industry in a direct fashion. What's amazing is the price. You can find this excellent reference tool at most major bookstores for under $30.

Directory of Contract Packagers (The Packaging Institute). This directory lists over 200 packagers nationwide. It indexes them by the industry they serve (for example, food, pharmaceuticals, chemical specialties, consumer goods, military, and shipping). A typical entry lists the manufacturer's services, equipment used, status of quality and control testing, shipping and receiving licensing, and type of warehousing.

National Wholesale Druggists' Association Membership Directory (National Druggists' Association). Wholesalers may be one step removed from the retailing end of the drug industry, but they are also a step closer to the manufacturing operations and may be an excellent source of rumored information. They may also help place certain hunches you have in perspective, to tell you how accurate your shipping and pricing information might be.

FINDING MANAGEMENT OUT: GETTING INFORMATION ABOUT A COMPANY'S OFFICERS

Here are two statements:

1. Management background can be one of the most difficult segments of corporate information to uncover.
2. Management background is fairly easy to locate.

These statements seem to contradict each other. It is the second statement that holds true for the researcher who knows where to look. Aside from the standard Who's Who directories that list prominent officials and national leaders, there is a wealth of additional information about those in the business community.

Where else can you turn to uncover an individual's background?

Town Newspaper and Home Town Releases. You have seen the press announcements—for example, "Mr. Smith has been promoted to Vice President of Marketing." These announcements are usually accompanied by a photograph. Whenever a corporation announces a major employee promotion, it sends out what is called a hometown release. This press release is geared to the executive's local town paper. Without knowing that any news item was ever published, you can often call a local newspaper and ask the editor when and if a news release had ever appeared about Mr. Smith. More frequently than you would expect, the paper will have published an announcement and can send you a clipping. These clippings can contain the executive's new title, experience with the company, and possibly some mention of the person's family.

Newspaper morgues. Larger city newspapers will have established newspaper clipping files, or morgues as they are called. Here, papers have stored tens of thousands of news articles. Even if you cannot find the person you are looking for mentioned in a morgue article, you may find the name of a relative who can provide a lead to your prospect.

Family businesses are prime candidates for the morgue. These concerns are usually civic-minded and have received a good deal of press over the years.

Since most morgues are designed for use by in-house news staff only, you may have to receive permission to use the files.

Town halls. The municipal town hall will have on file real estate records that report the value of an individual's house. Voter registry will have

information on a person's age. Most of this information is available to you with just a telephone call.

Universities.   Universities are proud of their graduates and make it their business to publicize their alumni stars. You can find alumni information in a number of university sources:

Yearbooks.   Every alumni relations office or university public relations office has a historical collection of yearbooks that can provide name, address, and other biographical information.

Biographies.   Many universities have compiled extensive biographies on their graduates—especially the wealthier or more prominent graduates. Again, you can probably find these bios in either the alumni relations or public relations office.

Faculty.   Should you be able to find out what school or division your subject attended while at the university, you may possibly locate a faculty member who knows him or her and can provide some background on the former student.

POWER COMPANIES: AN UNDERUTILIZED SOURCE

Here is another intelligence gem. Public utilities are probably the best single source for locating the number of homes in a state or region that are using a particular appliance. Most market penetration studies are national in scope. Utilities allow the researcher to examine usage on a local level. The researcher can then use this data to determine a company's market share on a local level.

For years, utilities have collected information on their customers to determine power consumption and usage.

Power companies need to know what appliances are being plugged in and how many of them there are out there. The data they collect is publicly available. In most instances, utilities conduct these surveys yearly, but there is no prescribed pattern. In addition, the information collected will vary widely from utility to utility. This makes the data difficult to compile for a national study, but it can provide crucial information for a company needing to know exactly how many products (a dishwasher, for example) are being used in a geographic area.

How do utilities collect their information? In many cases they take a sample of their user population and conduct face-to-face interviews.

WAR STORY 25

How Many Dishwashers in North Carolina?

We had to locate the number of dishwashers operating in North Carolina.

After reviewing all of the merchandise and trade magazines, we were only able to come up with national sales figures on the number of dishwashers sold. We could not find state-by-state or regional data.

After contacting the Duke Power Company in North Carolina, we soon had our answer.

A Southern electric utility company had recently completed an appliance survey. The object of the study was to learn the penetration, or number of households, that use various electrical appliances. The survey covered only residential customers; not commercial or industrial users.

The result: The study identified the percent of homes that used each category of appliance.

To find out where and when a utility has completed a consumer study, contact its public relations or public information department.

CUSTOMS HOUSE BROKERS: IMPORTING COMPANY INFORMATION

Middlemen abound in everyday business transactions. A customs broker is one of these go-betweens. And anytime you have a middleman involved in the purchase or sale of a product, you have another intelligence source, another possible conduit of information about a competitor.

What are customs brokers and how do they work? You will find them listed in the Yellow Pages in any major port city or any city with an international airport. Companies hire brokers to check their goods in once they arrive at their U.S. destination. By federal law, companies must have a broker represent them for any shipment worth $250 or more.

Once the brokers have paid the import duties (which they have 10 days to do once the merchandise arrives in port), they then notify the receiving company's traffic manager, who will arrange for pickup.

There is no easy way to identify any one customs broker with a particular company. Brokers are known to keep their customer list secret. The brokerage business is highly competitive and brokers are often out of their

---

WAR STORY 26

Napkins and the Number of Employees

The client needed to know the plant size and number of employees that worked at a napkin manufacturing plant located in California. The credit report offered nothing more than name, address, and credit rating.

The town assessor's office could not help us in this case. For some reason, its records were ten years out of date (the last date of their tax assessment).

By calling up the Chamber of Commerce in the town, we managed to determine the number of employees working in the plant and the plant's total employment capacity.

---

offices, running to solicit clients. Their offices frequently are at the airport or dock area.

Once you have located the right broker, though, you have found an expert on import trends for a particular product. The broker may also know quite a bit about an individual company's latest product line long before the details reach the trade press or the merchants.

Aside from the Yellow Pages, you can locate brokers through their national association, the National Customs Brokers Forwarders Association of America. The address is:

NCBFAA
One World Trade Center, Suite 1109
New York, NY 10048
212–432–0050

CHAMBERS OF COMMERCE: UBIQUITOUS INTELLIGENCE-GATHERERS

You can look at a Chamber of Commerce in two ways:

1. It is merely a booster organization for local businesses.
2. It is a superb research organization that possesses a good deal of information on local businesses. The information is often unpublished (remember that public information does not always mean published information), but is cataloged by the Chamber.

It is the latter viewpoint that makes a C of C a terrific regional intelligence source. Not only does a Chamber often have the name of the company you are looking for on file, but it may also have the name of the owners and other details, such as the number of employees, as well as the company's reputation, history, and participation in civic activities.

Chambers range in size from a desk-drawer operation to a large business with an enormous staff. There is a Chamber of Commerce in just about every business community in the United States. To give you an idea of just how many that means, there are approximately 100 in Alabama, 200 in New York State, and 50 in West Virginia.

You can find Chambers of Commerce any number of different ways, the Yellow Pages being just one means to locate them. The best directory I have found to locate not only domestic Chambers of Commerce but also foreign Chambers and Consulates is *Johnson's World Wide Chamber of Commerce Directory*. This superb 300-plus page book offers:

American Chambers of Commerce in foreign countries.

Canadian Chambers of Commerce.

Foreign Chambers of Commerce throughout the world.

Foreign Embassies and Consulates in the United States.

U.S. Consulates, Embassies, and Foreign Service posts throughout the world.

Foreign Consular offices in the United States.

You can order the directory by writing:

Johnson Publishing Company
P.O. Box 455
Eighth and Van Buren
Loveland, CO 80537

ACQUIRING ACQUISITION INTELLIGENCE

One of the most difficult pieces of information to track down is that of the merger or acquisition. Unless you are talking about two publicly held companies merging, you will find little information. In many states, privately held corporations are not required to file extensive statements detailing a recent merger. If a company is not publicly traded, the SEC cannot demand that the company file reports. So the question remains, how do you go about tracking down intelligence on a competitor that may have recently acquired another corporation?

Unlike stock and bond trading, there is no one source that tracks this type of corporate activity. Yet there are sources you can turn to for information.

A 1982 study entitled *The Acquisition Search: How Major Corporations Locate and Assess Acquisition Candidates* (Information Data Search, Cambridge, MA), discovered that:

Those experienced in the merger and acquisition business rely on news articles and indexes only half of the time.

The best source for the latest acquisition news is the Old Boy network— that group of executives who are in touch with the industry and actively take an interest in its corporate changes.

Investment bankers are an excellent means to tap into this Old Boy network. Investment banking houses have established files, profiling which companies are acquirable and, conversely, which companies other companies like to acquire. In other words, the investment banking community has profiled the major acquiring companies and their targets.

Don't misunderstand their knowledge or importance, though. They are financial gadflies, deal makers. By their own admission, they know a little about a lot of companies. They are not technocrats who know about a machine's inner workings; their job is to keep their financial fingers on the pulse of the corporate community.

Some of the best sources of your industry's merger and acquisition news may be right in your own company. Almost one half of those responding to the survey claimed that they prefer to call up a company contact to get the low-down on a company's status.

Based on the survey's findings and interviews with acquisition executives, here are the best recommendations to find details on an acquisition:

1. First review the literature and the news articles. Many times you will find that the acquisition you heard about was already cited in an article. The directories below specialize in catching this type of news.

2. Through your company's bank, your company's financial officers, or your stockbroker, locate a helpful investment banker. If this banker doesn't know much about your industry, you can bet he or she will know a colleague who does.

3. Contact your company's controller, treasurer, or financial vice-president.

Merger and Acquisition News Sources and Directories

Announcements of Mergers and Acquisitions (The Conference Board). The Conference Board is known as the watchdog of the business community. This publication lists, on a monthly basis, recent mergers and acquisitions.

Capital Adjustments (Prentice-Hall). A looseleaf series of books that track, among other subjects, worthless securities.

Capital Changes Reports (Commerce Clearing House). A five-volume work that offers the financial history of a company. A typical report will trace a company's stock splits, dividends, exchange of securities, and—what is important to this section—mergers and consolidations.

Directory of Obsolete Securities (Financial Stock Guide Services). A wonderful book for the researcher in search of a lost company. This hardcover book, in a very concise way, will tell the reader at a glance if a company has changed its name, merged, was acquired, was dissolved, liquidated, reorganized, went bankrupt, or in some other way changed its corporate status.

F&S Index of Corporate Change (Predicasts). Predicasts has taken its voluminous bibliographic data base (containing millions of articles) and once again has spun off an extremely useful reference work. This work is divided into three sections: (1) an alphabetical index of companies, (2) companies listed by their SIC or Standard Industrial Classification, and (3) a section that lists all the name changes. Although this index may not cover every merger and acquisition that has occurred, if the announcement went public you can be fairly sure that this text has picked it up. This index is also available on an on-line data base.

Mergers and Acquisitions: The Journal of Corporate Venture (Mergers & Acquisitions). A quarterly periodical that, besides publishing statistics on recent merger and acquisition activity, also presents a roster of the latest reported mergers and acquisitions.

Moody's Investor's Manuals (Moody's Investment Service). Moody's blue index, found in its investment manuals, will also index the latest corporate name changes, or mergers.

New data base for mergers and acquisitions. Securities Data Company, New York City, offers a data base entitled "Mergers and Acquisitions." As the name implies it monitors recent and pending mergers and acquisitions. Not only does each record offer the names of the participants, but it also states the amount of cash or securities offered. Data bases are listed in Chapter 7.

PART 4

ADDRESSES AND PHONE NUMBERS OF PUBLISHERS AND SOURCES

CHAPTER 15

ADDRESSES AND PHONE NUMBERS OF PUBLISHERS AND SOURCES

ABC Leisure Magazines
825 Seventh Avenue
New York, NY 10019
212–265–8360

ABC Voor Handel En Industrie C.V.
Postbus 190
2000 AD Haarlem
The Netherlands
023–32–39–40

Actualidad Economica
Reloletos, 1
Madrid–I
Spain
276–12–05–06–07–08

Advertising Age
20–22 Bedford Row
London WC1R 4EB
England

Advertising and Media Consultants
6th Floor Thaniya Building
62 Silom Road
P.O. Box 12-1060
Bangkok
Thailand
233–8126–8

Aerospace Industries Association of
America
1725 DeSales Street, NW
Washington, DC 20036
202–347–2315

Affars Varlden
Box 5617
Stockholm 114 86
Sweden

Agricultural & Industrial Life
1400 Augusto S.
Francesco
San Andreas Subdivision
P.O. Box 3062
Manila
Philippines
59–40–92

Air Cargo
1819 Bay Ridge Avenue
Annapolis, MD 21403
30l–261–1121

Air Force Association
1750 Pennsylvania Avenue, NW
Washington, DC 20006
202–637–3300

Air Freight Motor Carriers Conference
1616 P Street, NW
Washington, DC 20036
202–797–5363

All-Americas Publishers Service
222 West Adams Street
Chicago, IL 60606
312–782–5194

American Academy of Environmental
Engineers
P.O. Box 1278
Rockville, MD 20850
301–762–7797

American Advertising Federation
1225 Connecticut Avenue, NW
Washington, DC 20036
202–659–1800

American Apparel Manufacturers
Association
1611 North Kent Street, Suite 800
Arlington, VA 22209
703–524–1864

American Association of Advertising
Agencies
666 Third Avenue, 13th Floor
New York, NY 10017
212–682–2500

American Banker
525 West 42nd Street
New York, NY 10036
212–563–1900

American Bankers Association
1120 Connecticut Avenue, NW
Washington, DC 20036
202–467–4000

American Bureau of Metal Statistics
420 Lexington Avenue
New York, NY 10017
212–867–9450

American Chamber of Commerce in
Argentina
Avda. Pte. Roque Saenz Pena/567—
Sixth Floor
Buenos Aires 1352
Argentina
33–5591–5592

American Chamber of Commerce in
Australia
50 Pitt Street, Third Floor
New South Wales 2000
Australia
241–1907

American Chamber of Commerce in
Belgium
Avenue des Arts 50, BTE5
Brussels 1040
Belgium
513–67–70

American Chamber of Commerce for
Brazil
Praca P10 X, Fifth Floor
Rio de Janeiro
Brazil
222–1983

American Chamber of Commerce in
France
21 Avenue George V
Paris 75008
France
1–723–80–26

American Chamber of Commerce in
Ireland
20 College Green
Dublin 2
Ireland

American Chamber of Commerce in
Italy
12, Via Agnello
Milano 20121
Italy
02–807955/6 or 877935/6

American Chamber of Commerce of
Mexico
Lucerna 78/Col. Juárez
Del. Cuahtémoc 06600
Mexico
566–08–66

American Chamber of Commerce
U.K.
75 Brook Street
London W1Y 2EB
England
01–493–0381

American Chemical Society
1155 16th Street, NW
Washington, DC 20036
202–872–4600

American Council of Life Insurance
1850 K Street, NW
Washington, DC 20006
202–862–4000

American Dental Association
211 East Chicago Avenue
Chicago, IL 60611
312–440–2500

American Dental Trade
Association
1140 Connecticut Avenue, NW
Washington, DC 20036
202–659–1630

American Electronics Association
2680 Hanover Street
Palo Alto, CA 94304
415–857–9300

American Embassy
Mc-Dan Merdeka Selatan 5
Jakarta
Indonesia

American Health Care Association
1200 15th Street, NW
Washington, DC 20005
202–833–2050

American Hellenic Chamber of
Commerce
17 Valaoritou Street
Athens 134
Greece

American Hospital Association
840 North Lake Shore Drive
Chicago, IL 60611
312–280–6000

American Hotel and Motel Association
888 Seventh Avenue
New York, NY 10019
212–265–4506

American Institute of Aeronautics and
Astronautics
1290 Avenue of the Americas
New York, NY 10017
212–581–4300

American Institute of Certified Public
Accountants
1211 Avenue of the Americas
New York, NY 10036
212–575–6200

American Iron and Steel Institute
1000 16th Street, NW
Washington, DC 20036
202–452–7100

American Machine Tool Distributors
Association
4720 Montgomery Lane
Washington, DC 20014
301–654–1200

American Meat Institute
P.O. Box 3556
Washington, DC 20007
703–841–2400

American Newspaper Publishers
Association
11600 Sunrise Valley Drive
Reston, VA 22091
703–620–9500

American Paper Institute
260 Madison Avenue
New York, NY 10016
212–340–0600

American Petroleum Institute
2101 L Street, NW
Washington, DC 20037
202–457–7000

American Petroleum Institute/
Abstracting & Indexing
156 William Street
New York, NY 10038
212–587–9660

American Public Power Association
2301 M St. N.W.
Washington, DC 20037
202–775–8300

American Savings and Loan League
1435 G Street, NW, Suite 1019
Washington, DC 20005
202–628–5624

American Society for Hospital
Purchasing & Materials
American Hospital Association
840 North Lake Shore Drive
Chicago, IL 60611
312–280–6137

American Society for Metals
Metals Park, OH 44073
216–338–5151

American Surgical Trade Association
111 East Wacker Drive
Chicago, IL 60601
312–644–6610

American Textile Manufacturers
Institute
1101 Connecticut Avenue, NW, Suite
300
Washington, DC 20036
202–862–0500

American Warehousemen's Asociation
1165 N. Clark Street
Chicago, IL 60610
312–787–3377

Amman Chamber of Industry
P.O. Box 1800
Amman
Jordan
21142

Apparel Industry Magazine
6226 Vineland Avenue
North Hollywood, CA 91606
213–766–5291

Arab Petroleum Research Center
7 Avenue Ingres
Paris 75016
France

Arnold Bernhard and Company
711 Third Avenue
New York, NY 10017
212–687–3965

Arthur D. Little
Acorn Park
Cambridge, MA 02140
617–864–5770

Asian Finance Publications
Suite 9B, Hyde Centre
223 Gloucester Road
Hong Kong
5–724221

Associated Equipment Distributors
615 West 22nd Street
Oak Brook, IL 60521
312–654–0650

Association for Computing Machinery
11 West 42nd Street, Third Floor
New York, NY 10036
212–869–7440

Association of Consulting
Management Engineers
230 Park Avenue
New York, NY 10169
212–697–9693

Association of Data Processing Services
1300 North 17th Street
Arlington, VA 22209
703–522–5055

Association of Home Appliance
Manufacturers
20 North Wacker Drive
Chicago IL 60606
312–984–5800

Association of Iron and Steel
Engineers
Three Gateway Center, Suite 2350
Pittsburgh, PA 15222
412–281–6323

Association of Steel Distributors
3974 Lansdale Road
Cleveland, OH 44118
216–291–1000

Automotive Information Council
28333 Telegraph Road
Southfield, MI 48034
313–358–0290

Automotive Market Research Council
Sheller Globe Corporation
Box 962
Toldeo, OH 43697
419–255–8840

Automotive Service Industry
Association
444 North Michigan Avenue
Chicago, IL 60611
312–836–1300

Bank Administration Institute
60 Gould Center
2550 Golf Road
Rolling Meadows, IL 60008
312–228–6200

Bankers Monthly
601 Skokie Boulevard
Northbrook, IL 60062
312–498–2580

Bank News
912 Baltimore
Kansas City, MO 64105
816–421–7941

Banque International à Luxembourg
Boulevard Royal 2
Boite Postale 2205
Luxembourg

Barque & Company/"Barque
Chambers"
87 Barque Square
Shahreh-E-Liaquat Ali Khan
Post Box 201
Lahore
Pakistan
64140

Belenos Publications
50 Fitzwilliam Square
Dublin 2
Ireland
764587/760869

Belgium Foreign Trade Office
World Trade Center
Boulevard Emile Jacqmain 162
Brussels B-1000
Belgium
02–219–44–50

Bell & Howell
Micro Photo Division
Old Mansfield Road
Wooster, OH 44691
800–321–9881 or 216–264–6666

Bennet, Coleman & Co.
P.O. Box 213
Bombay
India

A.M. Best Company
Ambest Road
Oldwick, NJ 08858
201–439–2200

Beverage Marketing Corporation
2670 Commercial Avenue
Mingo Junction, OH 43938
614–598–4133

BHRA Fluid Engineering
Cranfield
Bedford MK43 CAJ
England
0234–750422

Billboard Publications
9000 Sunset Boulevard
Los Angeles, CA 90069
213–273–7040

Billboard Publications
1515 Broadway
New York, NY 10036
212–764–7300

Bill Communications
633 Third Avenue
New York, NY 10017
212–986–4800

BIOSIS (BioSciences Information
Service)
2100 Arch Street
Philadelphia, PA 19103
800–523–4806 or 215–587–4800

BI UK
Banda House
Cambridge Grove
London WG OLN
England
01–741–4661

A & C Black, Publishers
35 Bedford Row
London WC1R 4JH
England

Bobit Publishing
2500 Artesia Boulevard
Redondo Beach, CA 90278
213–376–8788

R.R. Bowker Company
1180 Avenue of the Americas
New York, NY 10036
212–764–5100

R.R. Bowker Company
Customer Service Department
P.O. Box 1807
Ann Arbor, MI 48107
313–761–4700

Bradford's Directory of Marketing
Research Agencies
Box 276
Fairfax, VA 22030
703–631–1500

Broadcasting Publications
1735 DeSales Street, NW
Washington, DC 20036
212–638–1022

Budd Publications, Inc.
P.O. Box 7
New York, NY 10004
516–671–6300

Bulkey Dunton and Company
285 Madison Avenue
New York, NY 10017
212–689–6400

Bureau of Mineral Resources, Geology
and Geophysics
Australian Government Publishing
Service
Publishing Branch
P.O. Box 84
Canberra ACT 2600
Australia
61–62–95–4411

Business Communications Company
P.O. Box 2070 C
Stamford, CT 06906
203–325–2208

Business Guides
425 Park Avenue
New York, NY 10022
212–371–9400

Business Intercommunications
CPO Box 587
Toyko 100-91
Japan
03–408–8065

Business International Asia/Pacific
1111–1119 Mount Parker House
City Plaza
Taikoo Shing
P.O. Box 385
Hong Kong
5–670–491

Business International Corporation
One Dag Hammarskjold Plaza
New York, NY 10017
212–750–6300

Business Journals
22 South Smith Street
Norwalk, CT 06855
203–853–6015

Business/Professional Advertising
Association (BPAA)
205 East 42nd Street
New York, NY 10017
212–661–0222

Business Publishers
Blair Station, P.O. Box 1067
Silver Spring, MD 20910
301–587–6300

Cahners Publishing Company
1350 East Touhy Avenue
Cahners Plaza
P.O. Box 5080
DesPlaines, IL 60018
312–635–8800

Cahners Publishing Company
221 Columbus Avenue
Boston, MA 02116
617–536–7780

California Business News
6420 Wilshire Boulevard
Los Angeles, CA 90048
213–653–9340

Cambridge Scientific Abstracts
5161 River Road
Bethesda, MD 20816
800–638–8076 or 301–951–1400

Canadian Manufacturers' Association
One Yonge Street
Toronto, Ontario M5E 1J9
Canada
416–363–7261

Capital International
3, Place des Bergues
Geneva 1201
Switzerland
022–32–01–30

C.B.D. Research
154 High Street
Beckenham Kent BR3 1EA
England
01–650–7745

CB Media
70 The Esplanade, 2nd Floor
Toronto, Ontario M5E 1R2
Canada
416–364–4266

Central Statistical Board of the USSR
Finansy I Statika Publishers
Moscow
USSR

Central Statistical Organisation
Department of Statistics
Ministry of Planning
Government of India
Parliament Street
New Delhi 110001
India

Century Communications
5520 West Touhy, Suite G
Skokie, IL 60077
312–676–4060

Chamber of Commerce and Industry
Aiwan-E-Tijarat Road
P.O. Box No. 4158
Karachi 2
Pakistan

Chamber of Commerce of the
Republic of Cuba
Calle 21 No. 701/Apartado 307
La Habana
Cuba

Charleson Publications
124 East 40th Street
New York, NY 10016
212–953–0940

Charles H. Kline and Company
330 Passaic Avenue, Department 39
Fairfield, NJ 07006
201–227–6262

Charter Publishing Company
215 Lexington Avenue
New York, NY 10016
212–340–7500

Chemical Abstracts Service
P.O. Box 3012
Columbus, OH 43210
800–848–6533 or 614–421–3600

Chemical Manufacturers Association
2501 M Street, NW
Washington, DC 20037

Chilton Book Company
201 King of Prussia Road
Radnor, PA 19809
215–687–8200

China Phone Book Company
GPO 11581
Hong Kong

China Productivity Center
201-26 Tun Hwa N Road, 11th Floor
P.O.Box 769
Taipei
Taiwan, The Republic of China
02–773–2200

China's Foreign Trade
Fu Xing Men Wai Street
Beijing
China

Civitan International
Box 2102
Birmingham, AL 35201
205–591–8910

CMN Associates
4465 El Carro Lane
P.O. Box 126
Capinteria, CA 93013
805–684–7659

Colombo Broker's Association
The Colombo Apothecaries Company
125, Glennie Street
Colombo 2
India

Columbia Books
777 14th Street, NW, Suite 1336
Washington, DC 20005
202–737–3777

Commerce Clearing House
4025 West Peterson Avenue
Chicago, IL 60646
312–583–8500

Commerce Publications Ltd.
Manek Mahal, 90
Veer Nariman Road
Bombay 400 020
India
253–505, 253–562, or 253–392

Commercial Counselor to the French
Embassy
40 West 57th Street
New York, NY 10019

Communication Channels
6285 Barfield Road
Atlanta, GA 30328
404–256–9800

Communication Channels
185 Madison Avenue
New York, NY 10016
212–889–1850

COMP-U-CARD of America
777 Summer Street
Stamford, CT 06901
800–243–9000 or 203–324–9261

Computer and Communications
Industry Association
1500 Wilson Boulevard, Suite 512
Arlington, VA 22209
703–524–1360

Computer Directions Advisors
11501 Georgia Avenue
Silver Springs, MD 20902
301–565–9544

Confedeacao Nacional da Industria
Servico de Relacoes Publicas
Nilo Pesanha 50
Porto Alegre 6 2512/13
Rio de Janiero
Brazil
244–6658

The Conference Board
845 Third Avenue
New York, NY 10022
212–759–0900

The Conference Board of Canada
25 McArthur Road
Ottawa, Ontario K1L 6R3
Canada
613–746–1261

Conference of State Bank Supervisors
1015 18th Street
Washington, DC 20036
202–296–2840

Control Data
Technology and Information Service
8100 34 Avenue S
Minneapolis, MN 55440
800–328–1921 or 612–853–3575

Copenhagen Handelsbank
2, Holmens Kanal
DK-1091 Copenhagen K
Denmark
45–1–12–86–00

Cooper Industry Service Bureau
P.O. Box 22100
Kitwe
Zambia

Cornell University
School of Hotel Administration
Statler Hall
Ithaca, NY 14853
607–256–5093

Corporacion de Fomento de la
Produccion
One World Trade Center, Suite 5151
New York, NY 10048

Corporate Intelligence
P.O. Box 16129
St. Paul, MN 55116
612–699–7310

Corriere Mercantile
Via Varese 2
Genoa 16122
Italy

CPS Communications
P.O. Box 3011
Boca Raton, FL 33431
305–368–9301

Crain Automotive Group
965 East Jefferson Avenue
Detroit, MI 48207
313–567–9520

Crain Communications
740 North Rush Street
Chicago, IL 60611
312–649–5200

C.C. Crow Publications
834 Saint Clair, SW
Portland, OR 97205
503–222–9576

Crown
HMSO P.O. Box 569
London SE1
England
01–928–6977

Current Publications
504 Enterprise Building
238 Queens Road Central
G.P.O. Box 9848
Hong Kong

CW Communications
375 Cochituate Road
Framingham, MA 01701
617–879–0700

Dana Chase Publications
York Street at Park Avenue
Elmhurst, IL 60126
312–834–5280

Dana Chase Publications
1000 Jorie Boulevard, CS 5030
Oak Brook, IL 60521
312–789–3484

Data Courier, Inc.
620 South Fifth Avenue
Louisville, KY 40202
800–626–2823

Data Resources
1750 K Street, NW, Suite 1060
Washington, DC 20006
202–862–3760

Datastream International
Monmouth House 58
64 City Road
London EC1Y 2AL
England
01–250–3000

David N. Skillings
700 First Federal Savings Building
Duluth, MN 55802
218–722–2310

Davies Publishing Company
136 Shore Drive
Hinsdale, IL 60521
312–325–2930

Davison Publishing Company
175 Rock Road
Glen Rock, NJ 07452
201–455–3135

Dealers Digest Publishing Company
150 Broadway
New York, NY 10038
212–227–1200

Decisions Publications
342 Madison Avenue
New York, NY 10017
212–953–1888

De Financieele Koerier
Postbus 3906
Amsterdam 1001 AS
The Netherlands
31–20–585–2207

De Letzeburger Merrur
Luxembourg Chamber of Commerce
Rue Alcide De Gasperi 7
Luxembourg-Kirchberg
352–43–58–53

Dempa Publications
11-15 Higashi Gotanda 1-Chome
Shinagawa-Ku Tokyo 141
Japan
03–445–6111

Department of the Treasury
Internal Revenue Service
111 Constitution Avenue, NW
Washington, DC 20224
202–566–5000

Derwent Publications
Rochdale House
128 Theobalds Road
London WC1X 8RP
England
01–242–5823

Disclosure
5161 River Road
Bethesda, MD 20816
800–638–8076

Discount Merchandiser
641 Lexington Avenue
New York, NY 10022
212–872–8430

Distilled Spirits Council of the U.S.
1300 Pennsylvania Building
Washington, DC 20004
202–628–3544

Dow Jones Books
P.O. Box 300
Princeton, NJ 08540
609–452–1511

Dow Jones & Company
Dow Jones News/Retrieval
22 Cortland Street
New York, NY 10007
212–285–5225

Dow Jones & Co.
Morning Post Building
Tong Chong Street
Hong Kong

Dun & Bradstreet
International Marketing Services
One World Trade Center, Suite 9069
New York, NY 10048
212–938–8495

Dun & Bradstreet
Marketing Services Division
99 Church Street
New York, NY 10007
212–285–7829

Dun & Bradstreet
National Credit Office Division
1290 Avenue of the Americas
New York, NY 10019
212–957–2468

Dun & Bradstreet
6–8 Bonhill Street
London EC2A 4BU
England
01–628–3691

Dun & Bradstreet Canada
Marketing Services
365 Bloor Street East, 15th Floor
Toronto, Ontario M4W 3L4
Canada

Dun & Bradstreet (Australia)
GPO Box 4256
Melbourne, Victoria 3001
Australia
03–699–2500

Dun & Bradstreet (Israel)
105 Hahashmonaim Street
Tel Aviv
Israel

Dun's Marketing Services
3 Century Drive
Parsippany, NJ 07054
201–455–0900

Dr. Dvorkovitz & Associates
P.O. Box 1748
Ormond Beach, FL 32074
904–677–7703

Ebel-Doctorow Publications
1115 Chrifton
Clifton, NJ 07015
201–779–1600

Economic Information Systems
310 Madison Avenue
New York, NY 10017
212–697–6080

Economic Salon
60 East 42nd Street
New York, NY 10165
212–986–1588

Economikos Tachydromos
Christou Lada 3
Athens
Greece

The Economist Intelligence Unit
Spencer House
27 St. James Place
London SW1A 1NT
England

ECRI Shared Service
5200 Butler Pike
Plymouth Meeting, PA 19462
215–825–6700

Editor and Publisher
575 Lexington Avenue
New York, NY 10022
212–752–7050

Editora de Guias
2 Rua Desembargador Viriato
20000 Rio de Janiero GB
Brazil

Edward E. Judge and Sons
79 Bond Street
Westminster, MD 21157
301–876–2052

Edward N. Haynes, Publisher
4229 Birch Street
Newport Beach, CA 92660
714–540–8470

EIC/Intelligence
48 West 38th Street
New York, NY 10018
212–944–8500

Ekonomska Politica (Special Edition)
Trg Marksa i Enge/sa 7
P.O. Box 629
11000 Belgrade, Yugoslavia
334–531

Electronic Industries Association
2001 I Street, NW
Washington, DC 20006
202–457–4900

Eli Lilly and Company
307 East McCarty Street
Indianapolis, IN 46285
317–261–6010

Emergency Care Research Institute
5200 Butler Pike
Plymouth Meeting, PA 19462
215–825–6000

Empresa Publica dos Jornais Noticaxs
e Capital
Rua Rodriques Faria 103
Lisbon 3
Portugal

Engineering Information
345 East 47th Street
New York, NY 10017
800–221–1044 or 212–644–7635

Ernest H. Abernethy Publishing
Company
75 Third Street, NW
Atlanta, GA 30308
404–881–6442

Espansione
20090 Segrate
Milano
Italy
02–75421

Etas Kompass Periodici Tecnici Spa
Via Mantegna 6
Milano 20154
Italy
02–347051, 312041, or 313241

Euromoney Publications
Nestor House, Playhouse Yard
London EC4V 5EX
England
01–236–3288

Europa Publications
18 Bedford Square
London WC1B 3JN
England

European Free Trade Association
9–11 Rue de Varembe
CH-1211 Geneva 20
Switzerland
022–34–90–00

Excerpta Medica
3131 Princeton Pike
Lawrenceville, NJ 08648
609–896–9450

Export Council of Norway
825 Third Avenue
New York, NY 10022
212–421–9210

Fairchild Publications
7 East 12th Street
New York, NY 10003
212–741–4000

John Fairfax & Sons
Jones Street, Broadway
Box 506, GOP
Sydney 2001
Australia

Far Eastern Economic Review Ltd.
Centre Point
181–185 Gloucester Road
GPO Box 160
Hong Kong
5–724217

Federal Deposit Insurance Corporation
550 17th Street, NW
Washington, DC 20429
202–389–4221

Federal Reserve System Board of
Governors
Constitution Avenue and 20th Street,
NW
Washington, DC 20551
202–452–2407

Financial Mail
171 Main Street
Box 9959
Johannesburg 2000
South Africa
710–9111

Financial Post Investment Databank
481 University Avenue
Toronto, Ontario M5W 1A7
Canada
416–596–5693

Financial Publishing Company
9 Dedalou Street
Aghia Paraskevi
Attikis
Greece

Financial Times Business Information
Bracken House
10 Cannon Street
London EC4P 4BY
England
01–248–8000

Financial Times of Canada
920 Yonge Street
Toronto, Ontario M4W 3L5
Canada
416–922–1133

Finanz und Wirtschaft
Backenstraase 7
Zurich CH-8004
Switzerland

FIND/SVP
500 Fifth Avenue
New York, NY 10110
212–354–2424

Finnish Foreign Trade Association
POB Arkadiankatu 4–6B
SF-00101 Helsinki 10
Finland

Finnish Journal of Business
Economics
Runenberyinkativ 22–24
00100 Helsinki 10
Finland

Finsbury Data Services
68/74 Carter Lane
London EC4V 5EA
England
01–248–9828

Fintel
102–108 Clerkenwell Road
London EC1M 5SA
England
01–251–9321

Firestone
1200 Firestone Parkway
Akron, OH 44301
216–379–7000

Flesch Financial Publications
Van Der Stel Building
58 Burg Street
P.O. Box 3473
Capetown 8000
South Africa
43–6625

Folio Magazine Publishing
Corporation
P.O. Box 697
125 Elm Street
New Canaan, CT 06840
203–972–0761

Forbes
60 Fifth Avenue
New York, NY 10011
212–620–2200

Foreign Investment Review Agency
Box 2800 Station "D"
Ottawa, Ontario K1P 6A5
Canada

A/S Forlaget Kompas-Danmark
Lyngby Hovedgade 4
DK 2800 Lyngby
Denmark
02–88–60–00

Freed-Crown Publishing Company
6931 Van Nuys Boulevard
Van Nuys, CA 91405
213–997–0644

French Company Handbook
1 Rue Bourdaluve
Paris 75009
France
285–1316

Frost and Sullivan
106 Fulton Street
New York, NY 10036
212–233–1080

FTLL Publications
105, Unitovers/Chundrigar Road
Karachi
Pakistan
21272

Gale Research Company
1109 Book Tower
Detroit, MI 48226
313–961–2242

Gas Appliance Manufacturers
Association
1901 North Fort Myer Drive
Arlington, VA 22209
703–525–9565

Gebouw Metropol
Weesperstraat 85
Postbus 216
Amsterdam 1000 AE
The Netherlands

Gemeinschaftsverlag
Postfach 110509
Spreestrasse 9
D-6111 Darmstadt
West Germany

General Aviation Manufacturers
Association
Suite 517
1025 Connecticut Avenue, NW
Washington, DC 20036
202–296–6540

Geophysical Directory
2200 Welch Avenue
Houston, TX 77019
713–529–8789

German American Chamber of
Commerce
666 Fifth Avenue
New York, NY 10103
212–974–8830

Global Marketing Services
19562 Ventura Boulevard
Tarzana, CA 91356

Gorman Publishing Company
O'Hare Plaza, 5725 East River Road
Chicago, IL 60631
312–693–3200

Government Development Bank for
Puerto Rico
P.O. Box 42001
San Juan, PR 00940

Graduate Management Program
The American University
Business Administration Department
School of Commerce
Cairo
Egypt

Graham & Trotman
Bond Street House
14 Clifford Street
London W1X 1RD
England
01–493–6351

Gralla Publications
1515 Broadway
New York, NY 10036
212–869–1300

Graphic Arts Technical Foundation
4615 Forbes Avenue
Pittsburgh, PA 15213
412–621–6941

Grey House Publishing
360 Park Avenue South
New York, NY 10010
212–684–6485

Griffin Publishing Company
555 Columbian Street
South Weymouth, MA 02190
617–335–0913

GTE Information Systems
East Park Drive
Mount Laurel, NJ 08054
609–235–7300

Guardian Communications
Albany House
Hurst Street
Birmingham B54BD
England
021–622–4011/2

Gulf Publishing Company
P.O. Box 2608
Houston, TX 77001
713–529–4301

Harcourt Brace Jovanovich
757 Third Avenue
New York, NY 10017
212–888–4444

Harfax Database Publishing
54 Church Street
Cambridge, MA 02138
617–492–0670

Harris Publishing Company
2057-2 East Aurora Road
Twinsburg, OH 44087
216–425–9143

S.A. Hasnat for Associated Book
Promoters
9/2A, Ekbalpur Lane
Calcutta 700 023
India

Haymarket Publishing
76 Dean Street
London W1A 1BU
England
01–977–8787

Health Industry Manufacturers
Association
1030 15th Street, NW, Suite 1100
Washington, DC 20005
202–452–8240

Health Insurance Institute
1850 K Street, NW
Washington, DC 20006
202–862–4276

Hiaring Company
1800 Lincoln Avenue
San Rafael, CA 94901
415–453–9700

Hirsch Organization
6 Deer Trail
Old Tappan, NJ 07675
201–664–3400

Hitchcock Publishing Company
Hitchcock Building
Wheaton, IL 60187
312–665–1000

Holmes McDougall
Ravenseft House
302–304 St. Vincent Street
Glasgow G2 5NL
Scotland
041–221–7000

Horizon House
610 Washington Street
Dedham, MA 02026
617–326–8220

ICAP Hellas
54 A Vasilissis Sophias Avenue
Athens 612
Greece

Imprint Editions
420 South Howes
Fort Collins, CO 80521
303–482–5574

IMS International
800 Third Avenue
New York, NY 10022
212–371–2310

Incentive Manufacturers
Representatives Association
7912 Ardleigh Street
Philadelphia, PA 19118
215–242–4144

Inc. Publishing Company
30 Commercial Wharf
Boston, MA 02110
617–227–4700

Independent Bankers Association of
America
1625 Massachusetts Avenue, NW,
Suite 202
Washington, DC 20036
202–332–8980

Independent Newspapers
90 Middle Abbey Street
Dublin 1
Ireland

India Narayan Tadon/Sanjay
Composers and Printers
Green Park Extn
New Delhi 110016
India

Industriens og Eksportens Hus
Drammensveien 40
Postboks 2435-Solli-
Oslo 2
Norway
02–56–43–90

Industry of Free China
Council for Economic Planning and
Development
118 Hwat Ning Street
Taipei
Taiwan, The Republic of China

Industry Publications
200 Commerce Road
Cedar Grove, NJ 07009
201–239–5800

Info Globe
The Globe and Mail
444 Front Street West
Toronto, Ontario M5U 2S9
Canada
416–598–5250

Information Access Corporation
404 Sixth Avenue
Menlo Park, CA 94025
800–227–8431

Information Resources Press
1700 North Moore Street, Suite 700
Arlington, Virginia 22209
703–558–8270

INSPEC/IEEE Service Center
445 Hoes Lane
Piscataway, NJ 08854
201–981–0060

Institute of Business Administration
University of Dacca
Barnamichhil
U2A/Kazi Abdur Rovf Rd.
Dacca 1
Bangladesh
25–44–94

Institute of Export Development/Board
of Investments
Investment Building
Buendia Avenue Extension
Makati, Metro Manila
Philippines

Institute of Food Technologists
221 North LaSalle Street
Chicago, IL 60601
312–782–8424

Institute of Management Consultants
19 West 44th Street
New York, NY 10036
212–921–2885

Institute of Paper Chemistry
P.O. Box 1039
Appleton, WI 54912
414–734–2195, ext. 241

Institute for Scientific Information
University City Science Center
3501 Market Street
Philadelphia, PA 19104
800–523–1850 or 215–386–0100

Institutional Investor Systems
488 Madison Avenue
New York, NY 10022
212–832–8888

Instituto Latino Americano del Ferro y
el Acero
Dario Urzua 1994
Casilla 16065
Santiago 9
Chile

Institut Za Spoljnu Trgovinu
Beograd Mose Pijade 8/III
Yugoslavia
339–041/299

Insurance Information Institute
100 N. Interregional, Suite 3200
Austin, TX 78701
512–476–7025

Insurance Services Offices
160 Water Street
New York, NY 10038
212–487–5000

International Advertising Association
475 Fifth Avenue
New York, NY 10017
212–684–1583

International Association of
Refrigerated Warehouses
7315 Wisconsin Avenue
Washington, DC 20014
301–652–5674

International Coffee Organization
22 Berners Street
London W1P 4DO
England

International Commercial Bank of
China
100 Chi-Lin Road
Taipei 104
Taiwan, Republic of China
02–563–3156

International Data Corporation
214 Third Avenue
Waltham, MA 02154
617–890–3700

International Institute of Synthetic
Rubber Producers
2077 South Gessner Road, Suite 133
Houston, TX 77063
713–783–7511

International Rubber Study Group
Brettenham House
5–6 Lancaster Place
London WC2E 7ET
England
01144–0183668112

International Who's Who of the Arab
World
Two South Audley Street
London W1Y 5DO
England

Intervals
86 Ave. Louis Casai
Ch-1216 Cointrin
Geneva
Switzerland
01141–022–980505

Investment Research Group of EBIC
Avenue Louise 61
Brussels
Belgium
538–62–40

IPA Information System
4630 Montgomery Avenue
Bethesda, MD 20814
301–657–3000

IPC Industrial Press
Dorset House
Stamford Street
London SE1 9LU
England
011440–261–8000

Irish Business/Irish Financial
Publications
10 Vesey Place
Dun Laughaire
Dublin
Ireland

Irish Management Institute
Sandyford Road
Dublin 14
Ireland
01–983911

Irish Press
O'Connell Street
Dublin 1
Ireland

Irish Times
31 Westmorland Street
Dublin 2
Ireland

Iron and Steel Society of AIME
410 Commonwealth Drive
Warrendale, PA 15086
412–776–1535

Irving-Cloud Publishing Company
7300 North Cicero Avenue
Lincolnwood, IL 60646
312–588–7300

Israel Overseas Publications
P.O. Box 11587
Tel Aviv 11587
Israel

Japan External Trade Organization
Publications Department
2–5 Toranomon 2-Chome
Minato-Ku Tokyo 105
Japan

Japan Press
12-8 Kita Anyama 2-Chome
C.P.O. Box 6
Minato-Ku Tokyo 107
Japan
03–242–5374

Japan Spinners Association
Mengyo Kaikan Building/8
Bingo-Machi 3-Chome
Higashi-Ku
Osaka
Japan
06–231–8431

Jetro International Communication
Department
2-5, Toranomon 2-Chome
Minato-Ku Tokyo 105
Japan
03–582–5511

Jobson Publishing Corporation
352 Park Avenue, South
New York, NY 10010
212–685–4848

Jordan and Sons
Jordan House
47 Brunswick Place
London N1 6EE
England
01–253–3030

Journal de Geneve
Rue Du General-Dufour 5–7
Geneva CH-1204
Switzerland

Journal of Commerce
110 Wall Street
New York, NY 10005
212–425–1616

Kansallis-Osake-Pankki
Box 10
SF-00101 Helsinki 10
Finland

Keller Publishing Corporation
150 Great Neck Road
Great Neck, NY 11021
516–829–9210

Kelley's Directories
Windsor Court
East Grinstead House
East Grinstead
West Sussex RH19 1XB
England
0342–26972

Kennedy and Kennedy
Templeton Road
Fitzwilliam, NH 03447
603–585–2200

Kollek and Sons
3 Mapu Street
Tel Aviv 63577
Israel
03–244–157

Kompass Belgium
Molierelaan 256 1060
Brussels
Belgium
345–1983

Kompass Deutschland
Wilhelm Strasse 1
Verlag P.O. Box 964
D-7800, Freiburg
West Germany

Kompass España
Avda. del General Peron, 26
Madrid 20
Spain
455–97–53

Kompass Nederland
Spoorstraat 62
7261 Ag Ruurlo
The Netherlands
05735–23–33

Kompass-Norge
Lokkeveien 87
N-4000 Stavanger
Norway
04–53–45–80

Kompass Publishers
Windsor Court
East Grinstead
West Sussex RH191XD
England
0342–26972

Kompass Schweiz Verlag/Editions
Kompass Suisse
Zurich-Gockhaussen
In Grosswiesen 14
Postfach 8044
Zurich
Switzerland
0041–1–821–25–55

Komp Information Services
811 Fountain Avenue
Louisville, KY 40222
502–426–7754

Kothari and Sons
Confederation of Asian Chambers of
Commerce and Industry
Madras 600 034
India

Kraks Legat
17, Nytorv
DK-1450 Copenhagen
Denmark
45–1–12–03–08

Kurt Salmon Associates
350 Fifth Avenue
New York, NY 10118
212–564–3690

Laventhol and Horwath
1845 Walnut Street
Philadelphia, PA 19103

Leading National Advertisers
515 Madison Avenue
New York, NY 10022
212–888–1940

Lebhar-Friedman
425 Park Avenue
New York, NY 10022
212–371–9400

Le Courrier de Commerce
1 Rue Phillipe II
Luxembourg-Ville
Luxembourg

A.F. Lewis & Company
79 Madison Avenue
New York, NY 10016
212–679–0770

Life Insurance Marketing and
Research Association
Box 208
Hartford, CT 06141
203–677–0033

J.B. Lippincott Company
10 East 53rd Street
New York, NY 10022
212–593–7213

Local and Short Haul Carriers
Conference
1616 P Street, NW
Washington, DC 20036
202–797–5414

Lockwood Trade Journal Company
551 Fifth Avenue
New York, NY 10176
212–661–5980

L'Expansion
67, Avenue de Wagram
Paris 75842
France
763–12–11

McCarron Bird
594 Lowsdale Street
Melbourne, Victoria 3000
Australia

MacDonald's & Jane's Publishers
Paulton House
8 Shepherdess Walk
London N1 7ZW
England

McFadden Business Publications
6364 Warren Drive
Norcross, GA 30093
404–448–1011

McGraw-Hill Book Company
1221 Avenue of the Americas
New York, NY 10020
212–997–1221

McGraw-Hill Information Systems
F.W. Dodge Division
1220 Avenue of the Americas
New York, NY 10020
212–997–1212

McKnight Medical Communications
550 Frontage Road
Northfield, IL 60093
312–446–1622

Machinery and Allied Products
Institute
1200 18th Street, NW
Washington, DC 20036
202–331–8430

MacLean Hunter
481 University Avenue
Toronto, Ontario M5W 1A7
Canada
416–596–5000

MacLean Hunter Publishing
Corporation
300 West Adams Street
Chicago, IL 60606
312–726–2802

Macmillan Publishers
Journals Division
c/o Globe Book Services
Canada Road, Byfleet
Surret KT14 7JL
England

MacNair-Dorland Company
101 West 31st Street
New York, NY 10001
212–279–4455

Macro Communications
150 East 58th Street
New York, NY 10022
212–826–4360

Magazines for Industry
777 Third Avenue
New York, NY 10017
212–838–7778

Magazines for Industry
70 Lexham Gardens
London W8
England
0114401–828–6107

Magazines Limited
P.O. Box 261
Carlton House
69 Great Queen Street
London WC2B 5BZ
England
01–404–4333

Malaysian International Chamber of
Commerce and Industry
Wisma Damansara, Eighth Floor
Jalan Semantan
P.O. Box 192
Kuala Lumpur
Malaysia

Management Contents
P.O. Box 3014
Northbrook, IL 60062
800–323–5354

Market Data Retrieval
Ketchum Place
Westport, CT 06880
800–243–5583 or 203–226–8941

Marketing Research Associates
221 North La Salle Street
Chicago, IL 60601
312–346–1600

Market Research Society of Australia
Conv-Organ Research Services Pty.
P.O. Box 3
South Oakleigh, Victoria 3167
Australia
03–579–0181

Marquis Who's Who, Inc.
200 East Ohio Street
Chicago, IL 60611
312–787–2008

Meat Industry Supply and Equipment
Association
1919 Pennsylvania Avenue, NW
Washington, DC 20006
202–872–1990

Media General Financial Services
301 East Grace Street
Richmond, VA 23261
804–649–6587

Medical Economics Company
680 Kinderkamack Road
Oradell, NJ 07649
201–262–3030

Medical Marketing & Media
CPS Communications
265 Post Road, West
Westport, CT 06880
203–438–9301

Metal Bulletin Books
Park House/Park Terrace
Worcester Park, Surrey KT4 7HY
England

Microcomputer Information Services
2464 El Camino Real, Suite 247
Santa Clara, CA 95051
408–984–1097

Microfilming Corporation of America
1620 Hawkins Avenue
Sanford, NC 27330

Middle East Economic Digest
21 John Street
London WC1N 2BP
England
01–404–5513

Miller Freeman Publications
500 Howard Street
San Francisco, CA 94105
415–397– 1881

Ministerio De Economia y Hacienda
Paseo de la Castellana, 162
Planta 16 Madrid 16
Spain
419–16–18

Moody's Investors Services
99 Church Street
New York, NY 10007
212–553–0300

Morgan Grampian
2 Park Avenue
New York, NY 10016
212–340–9700

Mortgage Bankers Association of
America
1725 K. Street, NW, Suite 1402
Washington, DC 20005
202–785–8333

Motor Vehicle Manufacturers
Association of the U.S.
300 New Center Building
Detroit, MI 48202
313–872–4311

National Association of Chain Drug
Stores
P.O. Box 1417-D49
Alexandria, VA 22314
703–549–3001

National Association of Chemical
Distributors
1406 Third National Building
Dayton, OH 45402
513–223–8486

National Association of Photographic
Manufacturers
600 Mamaroneck Avenue
Harrison, NY 10528
914–698–7603

National Association of Plastics
Distributors
Glison Road
Jaffrey, NH 03452
603–532–7457

National Association of Printers and
Lithographers
780 Palisade Avenue
Teaneck, NJ 07666
201–342–0700

National Association of Printing Ink
Manufacturers
550 Mamaroneck Avenue
Harrison, NY 10528
914–698–1004

National Association of Retail Grocers
of the U.S.
1825 Samuel Morris Drive
Reston, VA 22090
703–437–5300

National Automatic Merchandising
Association
Seven S. Dearborn Street
Chicago, IL 60603
312–346–0370

National Cable Television Association
1724 Massachusetts Avenue, NW
Washington, DC 20036
202–775–3550

National Consumer Finance
Association
1101 14th Street, NW
Washington, DC 20036
202–289–0400

National Council for US China Trade
1050 17th Street, NW, Suite 350
Washington, DC 20036
202–429–0340

National Credit Office
1290 Avenue of the Americas
New York, NY 10019
212–957–3800

National Electrical Manufacturers
Association
2101 L Street, NW, Suite 300
Washington, DC 20037
202–457–8400

National Forest Products Association
1619 Massachusetts Avenue, NW
Washington, DC 20036
202–797–5800

National Hardwood Lumber
Association
P.O. Box 34518
Memphis, TN 38104
901–377–1818

National Library of
Medicine/MEDLARS
8600 Rockville Pike
Bethesda, MD 20209
800–638–8480 or 301–496–6193

National Live Stock and Meat Board
444 North Michigan Avenue
Chicago, IL 60611
312–467–5520

National Lumber and Building
Material Dealers Association
40 Ivy Street, SE
Washington, DC 20003
202–547–2230

National Machine Tool Builders'
Association
7901 Westpark Drive
McLean, VA 22102
703–893–2900

National Mail Monitor
1321 U.S. 19 South,
Clearwater, FL 33516
813–531–5893

National News Service
4 Water Street
Arlington, MA 02147
617–643–7900

National Printing Equipment and
Supply Association
6849 Old Dominion Drive, Suite 200
McLean, VA 22101
703–734–8285

National Printing Ink Research
Institute
Sinclair Laboratory No. 7
Lehigh University
Bethlehem, PA 18015
215–861–3000

National Quotation Bureau
116 Nassau Street
New York, NY 10038
212–349–1800

National Register Publishing Company
5201 Old Orchard Road
Skokie, IL 60077
312–470–3100

National Research Bureau, Inc.
424 North Third Street
Burlington, IA 52601
800–553–2345

National Retail Merchants Association
100 West 31st Street
New York, NY 10001
212–244–8780

National Soft Drink Association
1101 16th Street, NW
Washington, DC 20036
202–463–6732

National Technical Information
Service
5285 Port Royal Road
Springfield, VA 22161
703–487–4807

National Telephone Cooperative
Association
2626 Pennsylvania Avenue, NW
Washington, DC 20037
202–342–8220

National Underwriter Company
420 East 4th Street
Cincinnati, OH 45202
513–721–2140

National Wholesale Druggists'
Association
105 Oronoco Street
Scarsdale, NY 10853
914–723–3571

Netherlands Chamber of Commerce
in the U.S.
One Rockefeller Plaza
New York, NY 10020
212–265–6460

Newman Books
48 Poland Street
London W1V 4PP
England
01144–01–4390335

Newsletter Clearing House
44 West Market Street
Rhinebeck, NY 12572
914–876–2001

NewsNet
945 Haverford Road
Bryn Mawr, PA 19010
800–345–1301 or 215–527–8030

Newsprint Information Committee
633 Third Avenue
New York, NY 10017
212–697–5600

News Publishers
Norwich Union House
Mama Ngina Street
P.O. Box 30339
Nairobi
Kenya
25502

New Jersey Business and Industry
Association
50 Park Place
Newark, NJ 07102
201–623–8359

New York Times Company
229 West 43rd Street
New York, NY 10036
212–556–1234

New York Times Information Service
1719 A Route 10
Parsippany, NJ 07054
201–539–5850

Nihon Keizai Shimbun
9-5 Otemachi 1-Chome
Chiyoda-Ku Toyko 100
Japan

Nigerian Institute of Management
7, Alhaji Murtala Animashaun
Close/Off Adelabu Street
Surulere
P.O. Box 2557
Lagos
Nigeria

Non-Ferrous Founders' Society
455 State Street, Suite 100
Des Plaines, IL 60016
312–299–0950

North American Publishing Company
401 North Broad Street
Philadelphia, PA 19108
215–574–9600

North American Telephone
Association
511 Second Street, NE
Washington, DC 20002
202–547–4450

Northern Miner Press
7 Labatt Avenue
Toronto, Ontario M5A 3P2
Canada
403–266–6360

Nuclear Exchange Corporation
3000 Sand Hill Road
Menlo Park, CA 94025
415–854–1510

A/S Okononisk Literature
Harry Fetts Y 2–4
Oslo 6
Norway

Orgao da Confederacao Nacional do
Comercio
Av. General Justo 307/6
Rio de Janeiro
Brazil
240–7170

The Oriental Economist
1-4 Hongoku-Cho Nihonbashi
Chuo-Ku Toyko 103
Japan
03–270–4111

Oxbridge Communications
40 East 34th Street
New York, NY 10016
212–689–8524

Paine Webber Mitchell Hutchins
One Battery Park Plaza
New York, NY 10004
212–623–4500

Paper Distribution Council
111 Great Neck Road
Great Neck, NY 11021
516–829–3070

Paper Industry Management
Association
2400 East Oakton Street
Arlington Heights, IL 60005
312–956–0250

Penn Well Publishing Company
P.O. Box 1260
1421 South Sheridan Road
Tulsa, OK 74101
918–835–3161

Pensions and Investments
740 North Rush Street
Chicago, IL 60611
312–649–5280

Penton/IPC
1111 Chester Avenue
Cleveland, OH 44114
216–696–7000

Pequot Publishing
P.O. Box 494
Southport, CT 06490
203–259–1812

Petroleum Equipment Institute
P.O. Box 2380
Tulsa, OK 74101
918–743–9941

Petroleum Information Corporation
4100 Dry Creek Road
Littleton, CO 80122
303–740–7100

Pharmaceutical Manufacturers
Association
1155 15th Street, NW
Washington, DC 20005
202–463–2000

Pharmaceutical Technology
320 North A Street
P.O. Box 50
Springfield, OR 97477
503–726–1200

Phelon, Sheldon and Marsar
32 Union Square
New York, NY 10003
212–473–2590

Philadelphia Newspapers
400 North Broad Street
Philadelphia, PA 19101
215–854–2000

Photographic Manufacturers and
Distributors Association
866 United Nations Plaza, Suite 436
New York, NY 10017
212–688–3520

Pit and Quarry Publications
105 West Adams Street
Chicago, IL 60603
312–726–7151

Predicasts
200 University Circle Research Center
11001 Cedar Avenue
Cleveland, OH 44106
800–321–6388

Premium Merchandising Club of
New York
1605 Vauxhall Road
Union, NJ 07083
201–687–3090

Prestige Publications Company
P.O. Box 416
Yaba Lagos State
Nigeria

Printing Industries of America
1730 North Lynn Street
Arlington, VA 22209
703–841–8100

Privredni Pfregled
Marsala Birjuzova 3–5
Belgrade
Yugoslavia

Proexpo/Export Promotion Fund
Banco de la Republica
Centro de Comercio International
Calle 28, No. 13A–15
Bogota, D.E.
Colombia
269–0777

Progressive Grocer
708 Third Avenue
New York, NY 10017
212–490–1000

Promotion Marketing Association of
America
420 Lexington Avenue
New York, NY 10170
212–867–3990

PTD Publishing Services
4th Floor Field North
23 DeBeer Street
Box 31753
Braamfontein 2017
South Africa
39–6181

PTN Publishing Corporation
101 Crossways Park West
Woodbury, NY 11797
516–496–8000

Publications Economiques pour
l'Étranger
4, Galerie Ravenstein
Brussels 1
Belgium
02–13–41–10

Publications International
Bunduxwala Building No. 4/I.I.
Chundrigar
Karachi
Pakistan

Pulp and Paper Machinery
Manufacturers Association
1707 H Street, NW
Washington, DC 20006
202–298–6344

Putnam Publishing Corporation
430 North Michigan Avenue
Chicago, IL 60612
312–644–2020

Rand McNally and Company
10 East 53rd Street
New York, NY 10022
212–751–6300

Review Publishing Company
P.O. Box 60
Oreland, PA 19075
215–887–6312

Roach Tilley Grice & Company
351 Collins Street
Melbourne, Victoria 3000
Australia
62–7521

Robert Freeman Publishing Company
1713 Central Street
Evanston, IL 60201
312–328–4111

Robert Morris Associates
1432 PNB Building
Philadelphia, PA 19107
215–563–0267

Robert Morris Associates
Credit Division
Philadelphia National Bank Building
Philadelphia, PA 19107
215–665–2874

Rubber Manufacturers Association
1901 Pennsylvania Avenue, NW
Washington, DC 20006
202–828–7700

Salesman's Guide
1140 Broadway
New York, NY 10001
212–684–2985

T. K. Sanderson Organization
200 E. 25th Street
Baltimore, MD 21218
301–235–3383

Scan-Report
Stadvestve; 49
Kobenhaun 2600 Glostrup
Denmark
02–63–02–22

Schnell Publishing Company
100 Church Street
New York, NY 10007
212–732–9820

Science Books International
Statler Office Building
20 Park Plaza
Boston, MA 02116

Securities Data Corporation
62 Williams Street, Sixth Floor
New York, NY 10005
212–668–0940

Seibt-Verlag
24 Bavariaring
D-8000 München 2
West Germany

T. K. Seshadri
Indian Merchants' Chamber Building
76 Veer Nariman Road
Bombay 400 020
India

Simmons-Boardman Publishing
Company
1809 Capital Avenue
Omaha, NE 68102
402–346–4300

Simmons Market Research Bureau
219 East 42nd Street
New York, NY 10017
212–867–1414

Smith Barney Harris Upham and
Company
1345 Avenue of the Americas
New York, NY 10019
212–399–6000

Société Nouvelle d'Éditions
Industrielles
22, Avenue F.D. Roosevelt
Paris 75008
France
1–359–37–59

Society of Automotive Engineers
400 Commonwealth Drive
Warrendale, PA
412–776–4841

Society of Soft Drink Technologists
1101 16th Street, NW
Washington, DC 20036
202–833–2450

Society of the Plastics Industry
Statistical Department
355 Lexington Avenue
New York, NY 10017
212–573–9400

Sopec
O'Connell 5
Madrid 9
Spain

Southam Business Publications
1450 Don Mills Road
Don Mills, Ontario M3B 2X7
Canada
416–445–6641

Southern Business Publishing
Company
1621 Snow Avenue
Tampa, FL 33606
813–251–1080

Specialized Agricultural Publications
3000 Highwoods Boulevard
Box 95075
Raleigh, NC 27625
919–872–5040

Specialty Advertising Association
International
1404 Walnut Hill Lane
Irving, TX 75062
214–258–0404

SRI International
Marketing Services Group
333 Ravenswood Avenue
Menlo Park, CA 94025
415–326–5200

Standard & Poor's Compustat Services
7400 South Alton Court
Englewood, CO 80112
303–771–6510

Standard & Poor's Corporation
25 Broadway
New York, NY 10004
212–248–2525

Standard Rate and Data Service
5201 Old Orchard Road
Skokie, IL 60076
312–966–8500

State-Owned Companies Advisory
Board
Valtionyhtioiden Toimisto
Aleksanterinkatu 10
Helsinki 17
Finland

Steindorsprent HF
Armula 5
P.O. 495
Reykjavik
Iceland

St. Gall Institute of Banking Studies
Bodanstrasse 6
CH-9000 St. Gall
Switzerland

Surgical Business
2009 Morris Avenue
Union City, NJ 07083
201–687–8282

Swedish Industrial Publications
Box 5501
Stockholm S-11485
Sweden

Swedish Trade Council
Box 5513
Stockholm S-11485
Sweden
46–8–783–8500

Swiss-American Chamber of
Commerce
Talacker 41
Zurich 8001
Switzerland

Sydney Stock Exchange
Research Department
20 Bond Street, 20th Floor
Sydney, New South Wales 2000
Australia

Taft Corporation
5125 MacArthur Boulevard, NW
Washington, DC 20016
202–966–7086

Technical Publishing Company
666 Fifth Avenue
New York, NY 10019
212–489–2200

Technomic Publishing Company
265 Post Road West
Westport, CT 06880
203–266–1151

Telephony Publishing Corporation
55 East Jackson Boulevard
Chicago, IL 60604
312–922–2435

Television Digest
1826 Jefferson Place, NW
Washington, DC 20036
202–872–9200

Textile Designers Guild
30 East 20th Street
New York, NY 10003
212–777–7353

Textile Distributors Association
1040 Avenue of the Americas
New York, NY 10018
212–398–0600

Textile Economics Bureau
101 Eisenhower Parkway
Roseland, NJ 07068
201–228–1107

Textile Information Users Council
P.O. Box 7793
Greensboro, NC 27407

Textile Research Institute
P.O. Box 625
Princeton, NJ 08540
609–924–3150

Thai Investment Publications
Company
4th Floor Pansak Building
138/1/Petchaburi Road Phyathai
Bangkok 4
Thailand
282–8166–75

Theta Technology Corporation
462 Ridge Road
Wethersfield, CT 06109
203–563–9400

Thomas Publishing Company
One Penn Plaza
New York, NY 10001
212–695–0500

Thomas Skinner Directories
Windsor Court
East Grinstead Ho.
East Grinstead
West Sussex RH1G 1XE
England
011440342–26972

Thomson Publications
P.O. Box 1683
Salisbury
Zimbabwe
706054

Thrift Publishers
200 Park Avenue
New York, NY 10017
212–973–4727

Ticon Industrier
Postboks 191
Nedre Storgt, 45
Drammen 3001
Norway
03–83–85–80

Time
Time/Life Building
Rockefeller Center
New York, NY 10020
212–841–4800

Times Books
16 Golden Square
London W1R 4BN
England

The Times of India Press
7 Bahadurshah Zafar Marg
New Delhi 110 002
India

Titsch Publishing
2500 Curtis Street, Suite 200
Denver,CO 80205
303–573–1433

Traffic Service Corporation
1435 G Street, NW, Suite 815
Washington, DC 20005
202–783–7325

Turkish Trade Directory and Telex
Index
Peykhane Caddesi 14/Daire I,
Cemberlitas
Istanbul
Turkey

Twin Coast Newspapers
110 Wall Street
New York, NY 10005
212–425–7000

Udonkim & McOliver, Publishers
50 Lawanson Street
Survlere, Lagos
Nigeria

Underwriter Printing and Publishing
Company
50 East Palisade Avenue
Englewood, NJ 07631
201–569–8808

Union Bank of Switzerland
Bahnofstrasse 45
Zurich CH-8021
Switzerland
01–234–11–11

United Business Service Company
210 Newbury Street
Boston, MA 02116
617–267–8855

United Chambers of Commerce of
Malaysia
Chinese Assembly Hall/Jalan Birch
Kuala Lumpur
Malaysia
87337

United Marine Publishing
38 Commercial Wharf
Boston, MA 02110
617–227–4700

United Nations Economic
Commission for Latin America
Distribution Unit, Documents &
Publications Service
Cepal Casilla 179-D/Santiago
Chile

United States League of Savings
Associations
111 East Wacker Drive
Chicago, IL 60601
312–644–3100

United States Library of Congress
10 First Street, SE
Washington, DC 20541
202–287–6100

University of Lagos Press
University of Lagos
Lagos
Nigeria

University Microfilms International
300 North Zeeb Road
Ann Arbor, MI 48106
800–521–0600, ext. 351

University of New South Wales
P.O. Box 1
Kensington, New Australia 2033
Australia

University of Toronto Press
University of Toronto
Toronto, Ontario M5S 1A6
Canada
416–364–2543

University of Toronto Press
Order Department
33 East Tupper Street
Buffalo, NY 14203
416–978–2052

University of Tulsa
Information Services Division
1133 North Lewis Avenue
Tulsa, OK 74110
918–592–6000, ext. 295

USSR Ministry of Foreign Trade
11, Minskaya Street
Moscow 121108
USSR
145–68–94

U.S. Civil Aeronautics Board
1825 Connecticut Avenue
Washington, DC 20428
202–673–5313

U.S. Department of Commerce
Industry and Trade Administration
Washington, DC 20230
202–277–3608

U.S. Directory Service
121 Southeast First Street
P.O. Box 011565
Miami, FL 33101
305–371–8881

U.S. Federal Communications
Commission
1919 M Street, NW
Washington, DC 20554
202–655–4000

U.S. Federal Deposit Insurance
Corporation
Information Office
550 Seventeenth Street, NW
Washington, DC 20429
202–389–4221

U.S. Federal Home Loan Bank Board
320 First Street, NW
Washington, DC 20552
202–337–6000

U.S. Government Printing Office
North Capital and H Street, NW
Washington, DC 20401
202–275–2051

U.S. Independent Telephone
Association
1802 K Street, NW, Suite 201
Washington, DC 20006
202–872–1200

Vance Publishing Corporation
133 East 58th Street
New York, NY 10022
212–755–4000

Van Oss' Effectenbock De Bussy
Deizersgracht 810
Amsterdam
The Netherlands

Vending Times
211 East 43rd Street
New York, NY 10017
212–697–3868

Venezuelan-American Chamber of
Commerce and Industry
Centro Plaza Torre A, 15th Floor
Av. Francisco de Miranda
Urbanizcion los Palos Grandes
P.O. Box 5181
Caracas 1010-A
Venezuela
283–8355

Verlag Hoppenstedt
9 Havelstrasse
D-6100 Darmstadt 1
West Germany
Telex 419258

Verlag Ruegger
Kirchgasse 23
Diessenhofen CH-8253
West Germany

Volkskas Limited
Pretoria
South Africa

V/O Vneshtorgreklama
Korp. 21 31 Ul Kahouka
Moscow 113461
USSR
121–41–90

Walker's Manual
14032 Lake Street Suite 101
Garden Grove, CA 92643
714–636–2952

Ward Publications
P.O. Box 380
Petaluma, CA 94952
707–762–0737

Ward's Communications
23 West Adams Street
Detroit, MI 48226
313–962–4433

Weisenberger Services
Warren Gorham & Lamont
210 South Street
Boston, MA 02111
617–423–2020

Western Wood Products Association
Yeon Building
Portland, OR 97204
503–244–3930

Wezata Forlag
P.O. Box 5057
S-402 22 Goteborg
Sweden

John Wiley & Sons
Electronic Publishing Division
605 Third Avenue
New York, NY 10158
212–850–6331

The Witcom Group
El Caribe Building, 15th Floor
San Juan, PR 00901
809–725–8075

Yankee Inc
Main St.
Dublin, NH 03444
603–563–8111

Year/News Front
130 West 42nd Street
New York, NY 10036
212–354–0350

Yugoslav Chamber of Economy
Council for Economic Relations
Abroad
1100 Beograd
Icnez Mihailova 10
Yugoslavia

Ziff-Davis Publishing Company
One Park Avenue, Room 1011
New York, NY 10016
212–725–3500

A Snapshot:

How Companies Are Currently Collecting Competitor Intelligence

A study that Information Data Search conducted in 1983 sought to determine exactly how companies were gathering information on the competition—and how well they were or were not doing.

We wanted to know what sources they used, whom they spoke to for information, and what technology they employed in the intelligence-gathering process. The report is presented in the following pages for you to read. I think you will find many similarities to the way you are currently collecting information on your competitors.

INTRODUCTION

The following report analyzes corporate intelligence systems through the responses of 13 market research or planning executives in industries from telecommunications to insurance. Each executive received a 19-page, highly detailed questionnaire. While their responses may not be statistically significant, they do provide insight into the daily workings of intelligence machinery within a corporation. Percentages, therefore, are offered only as an indicator, not as a definitive guide.

In most corporations, intelligence-gathering is at best a spotty system. Divisions are sometimes answerable only to themselves. Each subgroup in an organization tends to develop its own information channels and conduits. What are the links, if any, that may tie one division to another when collecting information on an industry? How is data transmitted through the organization?

Other questions arise concerning executives' immediate intelligence needs. Are the executives receiving the industry data they require? If not, where are they often missing intelligence on competitors? Do they find it most difficult to locate sales, production, or marketing information?

Aside from measuring the effects the organization may have on the intelligence flow, the survey also examines how executives actually go about researching their prospects. Do they rely on internal or external data bases to supply them with the necessary intelligence?

Respondents were also asked what they do with the information once they receive it. They were asked to describe the importance of the report or memo.

Finally, executives were asked to offer a wish list of organization and intelligence changes they would like to see within their organization—assuming no budget limit.

AMONG THE SURVEY'S KEY FINDINGS

1.   Most executives, independent of any industry, went to the same sources to look for competitor data.

2.   Product line income, marketing strategy, and production costs were the most sought-after competitor data.

3.   Executives seemed least interested in knowing about a competitor's human resources or management policies.

4.   Respondents also thought that although financials were crucial to any analysis, they were not necessarily the most important pieces of information.

5.   Most companies with foreign sales offices found these field units slow in responding to a request for information.

6.   Only one-third of the respondents had an in-house data base they maintained on their competition or on the industry.

7.   When respondents deemed an in-house memo or report as unim-

portant or insignificant, they tended to file it in a manual file drawer, usually in their personal files. So-called "important" documents received far greater attention.

MANAGEMENT INFORMATION SYSTEMS

1. Thirty-one percent of the respondents' companies currently have an *automated competitor data base* to monitor the competition and the industry.

2. Those companies that do have data bases find them most useful when looking for:

Quick analysis of financial trends.

Summary of marketing and manufacturing activities.

Market share by line or activity.

Trends.

3. All respondents with data base facilities felt that their capabilities were 100 percent better than those supplied by an outside source.

4. Those with in-house competitor data bases offered the following remarks in response to these questions:

a. "Under what circumstances do you find your in-house competitor data base most useful?"

Quick analysis of financial trends.

Summary of marketing and manufacturing activities.

Ground laying for acquisition study.

Establishing product development priority.

Long-term company marketing strategies.

b. "If you had the opportunity to change the data base's format or content, what changes would you make and why?"

Add historical and strategic development data.

Add information on company management policies.

Update more frequently.

Update more consistently.

c. "Do you generally find your internal data base superior to a comparable data base produced by an independent supplier?" Some of those who said yes offered the following explanations:

Independent suppliers generally don't have time or incentive to analyze, interpret, or reformulate easily available public data—they usually sell information, not intelligence.

No one commercial vendor has the information available in the same format to meet our needs.

CORPORATE COMMUNICATION OF INTELLIGENCE

1.   Almost one-half of the respondents have and use some form of a business library (either corporate, divisional, or departmental).

2.   When sending or receiving communications between departments, almost all of those participating consider the telephone their number one tool. The memo falls just under the telephone as the favorite means of communicating to someone within the company. Third in line is the meeting. Almost two-thirds of the same respondents prefer going to meetings to receive information about their company or their industry.

INTELLIGENCE VALUE OF CORPORATE DEPARTMENTS

Of all executives interviewed, 82 percent stated that most competitor information came from within their own organization. The most useful information came from the following departments:

Marketing	67%
Sales force	56%
Corporate planning	56%
Senior management	23%

Note: You will notice that in many of the categories, the responses will total greater than 100%. The reason for this discrepancy is that many of the respondents chose to offer more than one answer per question. For example, with regard to the above category, 67% of the respondents said that the Marketing department offered the most useful competitor information, yet, 56% of this same group also said that the sales force provided equally useful information. In a number of instances the same respondent claimed that the Marketing department and the sales force were equally useful.

TRACKING COMPETITORS

Tracking competitors accurately is difficult for the following reasons:

Intelligence sources hard to locate	54%
Existing intelligence sources inaccurate	38%
Highly dynamic market	38%
Industry poorly defined	23%

DATA BASES FOR HIRE

1. Respondents said they used Dun & Bradstreet, EIS, DRI, or Compustat more than any other externally produced data base.

2. Statistics are the respondents' major interest when selecting a data base. Otherwise, the group would choose a data base for its financial or demographic value (where applicable).

3. Over one-half of the group has office terminals. Only one-fifth will rely exclusively on the corporate library to search their data bases.

4. The major weakness of any data base, according to many respondents, is its lack of timeliness. An off-the-cuff estimate by respondents states that data bases are often at least three months behind the current period.

INTELLIGENCE PROFILE

1. Almost two-thirds (64%) of the executives interviewed state that their companies have individuals specifically assigned to collect intelligence on their competition (see Figure A.1.). Positions most cited were Marketing Research and Research Analyst.

2. Based on the respondent's department, divisions, and company size, the ratio of research personnel to total employees is approximately three researchers for every 200 employees.

INTELLIGENCE PROBLEM AREAS

1. Respondents described their greatest intelligence problem areas. "Extremely difficult" were:

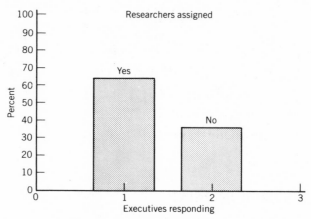

Figure A.1.   Companies with intelligence researchers employed.

Net income (by product line)	69%
Marketing strategy (by product)	62%
Production costs	62%
Sales (by product line)	54%

2.   Although financial intelligence proved to be the most elusive, respondents mentioned certain nonfinancial intelligence areas as "somewhat difficult" to send information on:

Competitor strength and weakness	92%
Sales force	77%
Advertising strategies	69%
International activities	69%

RESEARCH STEPS

1.   When asked the question "How would you dig up information on a privately held company?" the most frequent steps mentioned were:

Dun & Bradstreet credit report	38%
10-K or annual report	23%
Contact company	15%

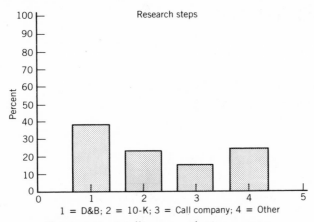

Figure A.2.   Intelligence-gathering sources.

Figure A.2 shows these preferences graphically.

2.   Overall, most of the executives surveyed follow the same research approach: They often start with secondary or already-published materials; they then progress toward primary research, which includes calling competitors and interviewing experts in the field.

INTELLIGENCE PROFILE

When asked which departments the respondents supply information to, these were some of their answers:

Strategic business units.

Other functional areas and subsidiaries.

Planning staff.

Rates and tariffs.

Public services.

Research and development.

Advertising.

Finance.

Customer service.

RANKING INTELLIGENCE

When ranking competitor intelligence data, 75 percent of the respondents believed that *marketing strategy and tactics* were the most important area. At the same time, 77 percent ranked *human resource and management policies* to be the least important (see Figure A.3).

ANNUAL REPORT DATA

1. When reviewing annual report data, 54 percent of the executives believed the company's financials were *crucial but not necessarily the most important item in the annual report*; 54 percent thought gross sales to be the most important line item, followed by:

Cost of goods sold	31%
Gross margin	23%
Operating expense	23%
Net earnings	23%

2. Balance sheet/income statement ratios of interest to the participants were:

Return on equity	31%
Net earnings/sales	31%

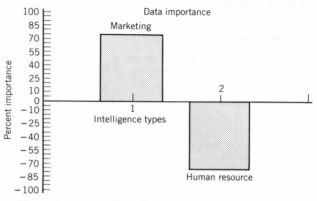

Figure A.3. Ranking of competitor intelligence data.

Inventory turnover	23%
P/E ratio	23%

3. According to the respondents, the most revealing information found in a company's annual report or 10-K statement is in the market analysis and income statement—each mentioned 30 percent of the time.

INTERNATIONAL ACTIVITIES

1. Of the respondents who said their companies are involved in international markets, less than half their companies' marketing and planning efforts were directed in this area.

2. Those markets most often mentioned:

Europe	38%
Japan	23%
South America	23%
Far East	15%

Eighty percent of the companies with foreign affiliations have branch offices in those countries.

Three-quarters of the executives (76 percent) dealing with foreign markets stated that their foreign field offices were often slow in responding to their intelligence requests.

3. When company resources fail to deliver, 56 percent of the respondents will contract with outside services to locate and retrieve foreign competitive data.

GOVERNMENT SOURCES

1. Government sources of information are used by 77 percent of the respondents, with 70 percent listing U.S. census statistics as a major source.

2. Seventy-eight percent of all participants believe that government data, when located, does not go into enough depth to suit their needs.

USEFUL SECONDARY SOURCES

1.   The secondary sources used most frequently by the respondents are listed here and summarized graphically in Figure A.4.

Dun & Bradstreet	23%
Standard & Poor's	15%
10-K report	9%
Annual reports	9%

2.   Respondents' regular business reading consists of:

Wall Street Journal	77%
Business Week	38%
Harvard Business Review	15%
Forbes	15%
Fortune	23%

3.   Other information gathered by staff and others in the form of articles and clippings was received by 73 percent of the respondents. Staff members gathered the information 88 percent of the time.

USING INTELLIGENCE

1.   After review by the respondents, less important competitor intelligence information is placed in a manual file 85 percent of the time. Thirty-

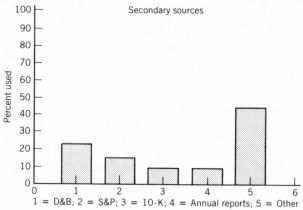

Figure A.4.   Secondary intelligence-gathering sources.

one percent of the time respondents felt this information called for review by superiors.

2.   When respondents received major intelligence reports on their competitors, 62 percent of those polled regularly wrote an office memo to superiors; 46 percent most often chose instead to meet with superiors or subordinates.

3.   In some instances, major reports on competitor intelligence have changed the decision of the respondents in the following areas:

New pricing	38%
Product line	23%
Corporate strategy	15%

PRODUCTS AND TECHNOLOGIES

1.   Eighty-five percent of the respondents said that information on *new products* concerned them the most, while 31 percent believe news on *existing products* is at least as important as new product data.

2.   News on competitors' products reaches executives from sources both *inside* and *outside* their companies. One-half stated that product information generally came from inside their organization, while the other half stated that outside sources were the major supplier of news on a competitor's products.

PERSONAL CONTACTS

1.   Respondents claimed that they received their most valuable competitor intelligence through trade shows.(Respondents were asked to choose among telephone conversations, internal company meetings, and trade shows.) Trade shows were selected by 36 percent as their first choice. Company meetings were chosen by 27 percent and telephone conversations were chosen by 15 percent.

2.   The group also claimed that well over 50 percent of their telephone calls made during the week are general purpose business calls. Calls seeking competitor information usually amount to less than 10 percent of their calls, and often less than 5 percent.

CONCLUSION

The marketing and planning executives who participated in this survey were somewhat aware of the intelligence sources available to them outside of their organization.

They could quickly compile a basic list of research sources, but often could not go beyond the commonly known reference books and credit agencies.

Their roster of experts was also limited. Time after time, they called on the same group of experts, rarely appearing to go outside their established network of contacts.

On the corporate level, organizations have made few strides toward constructing an internal intelligence network. Lack of cooperation and unity of purpose further compounds the organization's ability to convey intelligence internally. Much internally collected competitor information is slipping through the cracks, not reaching the executive who needs it. In the case of companies with foreign sales offices, these offices rarely respond to the intelligence needs of the parent company.

On a more positive note, corporations are becoming more aware of the plethora of data bases that they can tap into. Sometimes, though, the same companies rely too heavily on these tools to supply data.

INDEX